The Children of Neglect

The Children of Neglect
WHEN NO ONE CARES

MARGARET G. SMITH
ROWENA FONG

Brunner-Routledge
New York and Hove

Published in 2004 by
Brunner-Routledge
29 West 35th Street
New York, NY 10001
www.brunner-routledge.com

Published in Great Britain by
Brunner-Routledge
27 Church Road
Hove, East Sussex
BN3 2FA
www.brunner-routledge.co.uk

Brunner-Routledge is an imprint of the Taylor & Francis Group.
Printed in the United States of America on acid-free paper.

Cover design by Pearl Chang.
Cover Photo © Corbis.

10 9 8 7 6 5 4 3 2 1

Library of Congress Cataloging-in-Publication Data

Smith, Margaret G., 1942-
    The children of neglect : when no one cares / Margaret G. Smith, Rowena Fong.
        p. cm.
    Includes bibliographical references and index.
    ISBN 1-58391-024-7 — ISBN 0-415-94658-1 (pbk.)
    1. Child abuse—United States. 2. Child welfare—United States. 3. Children with social disabilities—United States. I. Fong, Rowena. II. Title.

    HV6626.52.S63 2003
    362.76'0973—dc21
                                                                                2003012663

This book is dedicated to our children:
Amanda, Michael, and Charles
Naomi and Daniel

Contents

About the Authors

Margaret G. Smith is a social worker in private practice in Seattle, Washington. A graduate of the University of Hawai'i (Ph.D.), Portland State University (M.S.W), and the University of Arizona (B.A.), she has been a child welfare social worker and child advocate for over thirty years. She has taught at the University Hawai'i at Manoa, Honolulu Community College, Leeward Community College, and Brigham Young University, Hawai'i campus. Her field of practice, writing, research, and teaching focus on children and families including child welfare, child advocacy, children and high-conflict divorce, child neglect, and family preservation.

She has been active in professional and community service; and was instrumental in developing the Volunteer Guardian ad Litem, the Custody Guardian ad Litem, and Friends of Foster Kids programs in Hawai'i. She has served on various community and professional boards and committees including Parents and Children Together, Inc.; Child and Parent Advocates Section of the Hawai'i Bar Association; National Association of Social Workers, where she served as board president; and Friends of the Children's Advocacy Center.

Rowena Fong is a Professor at the University of Texas at Austin. A graduate of Harvard University (Ed.D.), University of California at Berkeley (M.S.W.), and Wellesley College (B.A.), she has taught at the University of Hawai'i at Manoa (1990–2002), Ohio State University (1989–1990), Bethel College (1981–1988), and Nankai University in Tianjin, China (1988–1989), where she did her dissertation research on China's Only Child Policy.

She is the editor and coeditor of three books, *Culturally Competent Practice with Immigrant and Refugee Children and Families* (published by Guilford Press, 2004); *Culturally Competent Social Work Practice: Skills, Interventions, and Evaluations* (written with Dr. Sharlene Furuto at Brigham Young University and published by Allyn & Bacon, 2001), and *Multisystem Skills and*

Interventions in School Social Work Practice (coauthored with Edith Freeman, Cynthia Franklin, Gary Shaffer, and Elizabeth Timberlake and published by NASW Press in 1998).

Her areas of teaching, writing, and research are concentrated on children and families, specifically in adoptions and child welfare, immigrant children and families, Chinese children and families, and culturally competent practice. She has taught classes on social work practice with children and families, child welfare, family preservation, children of divorce, and human behavior and the social environment. She has published widely, and has done teaching, consultation, and training in the United States and in the People's Republic of China on foster care, adoptions, parenting skills, child development, social work curriculum development, sociology of the family, and sociology of education.

She is serving on the Commission on Practice of the Council on Social Work Education and is Consulting Editor to *Social Work, Journal of Social Work Education* and *Journal of Ethnic and Cultural Diversity in Social Work*. She has been involved with Casey Family Programs, serving in the capacity of Chair of the National Diversity Advisory Committee and member of the Honolulu and Austin Divisions' Community Resource Councils. Previous to her academic career, she was a preschool teacher, a clinical social worker at a residential treatment program for adolescent boys, and the founder and director of a Chinese bilingual, bicultural preschool in San Francisco.

Preface

This book examines child neglect in families and its relevance to research, policy, and practice in the field of services to children and their families. The authors chose to explore this subject because child neglect is an overlooked area of child welfare practice. Families neglect their children almost twice as frequently as they abuse their children. The most recent figures indicated that 879,000 children were victims of abuse and neglect in the year 2000. Of these 62.8% were neglected, 19.3% were physically abused, and 10.1% were sexually abused (USDSSH, 2002). The consequences of neglect to children are at least as serious as the consequences of abuse. In 2000, 1,200 children died of abuse and/or neglect. These fatalities were most often (34.9%) the result of neglect only. When including children who died as a result of abuse and neglect, 57.1% (approximately 685) of child fatalities due to maltreatment involved child neglect, as compared to 50% that involved abuse (i.e., abuse only [27.8%] and abuse and neglect [22.2%]) (USDHHS, 2002).

Nevertheless, the focus of those working in the field of child maltreatment has been on abuse, to the neglect of neglected children and their families. It is the intention of the authors to present a comprehensive view of the current state of the art regarding child neglect issues and to offer a rationale for directing focus to this overlooked and/or disregarded aspect of family relationships. It is time to refocus on these families, both to assist in healing these families and, given the relationship between neglect and poverty, as a vehicle for implementing structural changes that will benefit all families. The authors present and critically analyze major definitional, theoretical, policy, and treatment issues associated with the children of neglect. Research and cultural issues associated with definition, theory, policy, and treatment are incorporated in chapters discussing those subjects. Separate chapters regarding the relationship between child neglect and culture, substance abuse, and poverty are also included, as is a final chapter detailing conclusions and future directions.

Chapter One

❧

The Children of Neglect
AN OVERVIEW OF THE ISSUES

INTRODUCTION

Child neglect is an overlooked area of child welfare practice. The consequences of neglect to children are at least as serious as the consequences of abuse. Nevertheless, the focus of those working in the field of child maltreatment has been on abuse, to the neglect of neglected children and their families. The strong association between neglect and poverty and the lack of societal will to address issues associated with poverty create difficulties in terms of effective policy and practice in regard to families who neglect their children. It is as if "no one cares," neither the parents of neglected children, nor the society in which they live. It is time to refocus on the issues of child neglect in families, both to assist in healing these families and as a vehicle for implementing structural changes that will benefit all families. This book will examine research, social policy, and practice with respect to neglectful families. It presents and critically analyzes major definitional, theoretical, policy, and treatment issues associated with families who neglect their children. Research, policy, and practice implications associated with these issues are included. Separate chapters regarding the relationship between neglectful families and culture, substance abuse, and poverty are also included; as is a final chapter stating conclusions and future directions.

ISSUES ASSOCIATED WITH CHILD NEGLECT

When one addresses the problem of families who neglect their children, two issues are immediately apparent. The first concerns its epidemic proportions in terms both of numbers and severity, including fatal consequences to children. The second is the lack of attention paid to the problem in terms of neglect-specific research, policy, and intervention. Thus, two primary issues related to the problem of child neglect are (a) its epidemiology, including incidence, prevalence, and consequences to children; and (b) the child welfare field's focus on child abuse, not child neglect.

Epidemiology

Fatal child neglect. Children are seriously injured and die at the hands of their parents or caretakers at least as frequently from neglect as from abuse (DiLeonardi, 1993; Erickson & Egeland, 2002; Margolin, 1990; United States Department of Health and Human Services ([USDHHS], 1999b, 2002; Wolock & Horowitz, 1984). Most child deaths resulting from identifiable events involve some type of neglect (Block, 2002). The following statistics reveal just how deadly child neglect can be.

- In 1983 the American Humane Association (AHA) reported that of all the children who died from maltreatment in 1981, 56% died as the result of neglect.
- In 1986 the percentages for fatalities indicated that 44.3% involved neglect, while 62% involved abuse (AHA, 1988).
- Lung and Daro, as cited in Bonner, Crow, and Logue (1999), estimated that between 1993 and 1995, 37% of the children who died as the result of maltreatment died of neglect. An additional 15% died of a combination of abuse and neglect, indicating that 52% of the deaths during that time period involved child neglect.
- In 1994, 42% of the fatalities were due to neglect (Erickson & Egeland, 2002).
- Over one child per 1,000 children in the United States, or a total of 977 children, died as a result of maltreatment in 1995 (Petit & Curtis, 1997). Of these deaths, 50% were due to neglect and 22% were due to physical abuse.
- Petit et al. (1999) reported that in 1996, 478 infants (children under twelve months old) died as a result of abuse and/or neglect. The total number of children who died as a result of maltreatment that year was 930, of which 47% involved neglect and 21% involved physical abuse.

- In 1998, the Child Welfare League of America (CWLA, 2002a) found that 421 children died of physical abuse and 406 deaths involved neglect. The total deaths from child maltreatment for that year were 1,039.
- The USDHHS (1999b) reported that child maltreatment deaths are most often associated with child neglect, as opposed to child abuse. The rate for that year was 38.2% for neglect only.
- In 2000, 1,200 children died of abuse or neglect. Again, these deaths were most often (34.9%) the result of neglect only. When including children who died as a result of abuse and neglect, 57.1% (approximately 685) of children's deaths due to maltreatment involved child neglect as compared to 50% that involved abuse (i.e., abuse only [27.8%] and abuse and neglect [22.2%]) (USDHHS, 2002).

To put these numbers in perspective, during 1996 fifty-five law enforcement officers and twenty-one military personnel were killed in the line of duty (Petit et al., 1999).

This long list of statistics is included to substantiate the conclusion that child neglect is consistently (over time and various methods of data collection) at least as fatal as child abuse, and is usually more so. This information is, for the most part, not considered or, worse, ignored when researchers, policymakers, practitioners, or the public in general focus on child maltreatment issues.

Child neglect. In terms of overall reports of child maltreatment, not just fatalities, neglect is the most prevalent type of child maltreatment. A study of the effects of the Child Abuse Prevention and Treatment Act of 1974 indicated that the majority of reports made as a result of this legislation have been reports of child neglect (Stein, 1984). Studies have shown that the ratio of neglect to abuse reports ranges from 3:1 to 10:1 (Wolock & Horowitz, 1984).

- In 1986 the American Association for Protecting Children found a 2.5:1 ratio of neglect to abuse for the year 1984.
- More recently, Rose and Meezan (1993) reported that child neglect constituted 55% of all reported child maltreatment.
- Sedlak and Broadhurst (1996) in The Third National Incidence Study of Child Abuse and Neglect (NIS-3) reported that of the 2.8 million children substantiated as endangered or harmed due to maltreatment in 1993, 70% suffered from neglect and 43% from abuse.
- In 1995, 47% of substantiated reports were for neglect and 22% were for physical abuse (Petit & Curtis, 1997).
- Smith (1998) found similar results (47.1% neglect to 23.1% abuse) in a study of Child Protective Services (CPS) in Hawai'i.

- In 1998, Emery and Laumann-Billings reported that 54% of child maltreatment cases were child neglect.
- The CWLA (2002b) reported that neglect comprised 42%, physical abuse 17%, and sexual abuse 9% of substantiated/indicated cases of child maltreatment for the year 1999. The total number of substantiated cases of child maltreatment for that year was reported to be 991,355.
- Again for 1999, the USDSSH (1999b) reported that 826,000 children were maltreated—58.4% were neglected, 21.3% were abused and 11.3% were sexually abused.
- A total of 879,000 children were victims of abuse and neglect in the year 2000. Of these 62.8% were neglected, 19.3% were physically abused, and 10.1% were sexually abused (USDSSH, 2002).

Once more a list of statistics, which is evidence that, in spite of discrepancies in data collection and methodologies (which could account for dissimilar results), the approximate 2:1 ratio of neglected to abused children persists over time.

Child neglect and poverty. Presented here is a brief overview of this complex issue. A more complete and comprehensive portrayal is given in Chapter Ten. In regard to socioeconomic status (SES), child maltreatment is correlated with low-income families. Looking at SES, a Canadian study of cases referred to Ontario's Children's Aid Society (CAS), which is the Canadian equivalent of Child Protective Services (CPS), found that 50% of those whose income was known were supported by social assistance, as compared to 23% of the total population in Ontario (Trocme, McPhee, & Tam, 1995).

There appears to be an inverse relationship between a family's economic status and child maltreatment in the family; and the poorer the family, the harsher the outcomes for the children. When considering the various types of child maltreatment, the relationship with poverty is stronger for child neglect than it is for child abuse. It is clear that child neglect is unquestionably linked with poverty (Emery & Laumann-Billings, 1998; Erickson & Egeland, 2002; Pelton, 1994; Sedlak & Broadhurst, 1996; Thomlison, 1997).

In support of this conclusion, Pelton (1994) and Thomlison (1997) reported that in 1986 the risk of neglect in families whose income was less than $15,000 per year was nine times greater than in families whose income was more than $15,000. The NIS-3 (Sedlak & Broadhurst, 1996) found this rate had grown significantly over the next seven years. In 1993 families who earned less than $15,000 per year were 44 more times likely to neglect their children than similar families who earned greater than $30,000 per year.

Sedlak and Broadhurst (1996), Petit and Curtis (1997), and Petit et al. (1999) reported similar ratios of neglect to family income.

- For families whose income was less than $15,000, 27.2 children per 1,000 in the population were harmed as the result of child neglect.

The figures for families whose incomes exceeded $15,000 were significantly lower.

- Children were harmed due to neglect at a rate of 11.3/1,000 for families whose income was between $15,000 and $30,000.
- For families whose income was above $30,000 the ratio was 0.6/1,000.

Using an endangerment standard (i.e., the number of children endangered or harmed by child neglect) the NIS-3 (Sedlak & Broadhurst, 1996) found the ratios and discrepancies to be even greater:

- 72.3/1,000 for the lowest income group and
- 1.6/1,000 for those with incomes over $30,000.

These figures were significantly higher than for physical or sexual abuse. Thus, the relationship between poverty and neglect is clear. However, as minorities are overrepresented in the welfare, as well as the child welfare, system, the relationship between child neglect and culture is not so clear.

Child neglect and culture. Generally, when analyzing statistics to determine the incidence of child maltreatment related to culture, as opposed to SES, culture and social class overlap and are difficult to separate (e.g., is neglect in a family associated with poverty and/or with ethnicity?). Minorities tend to be overrepresented in both the CPS case loads and the lower SES groups, making it difficult to pull out the effects of race from the effects of class on child maltreatment (Korbin & Spilsbury, 1999). In addition, ethnicity usually operationalizes as Whites, Blacks, and others (Garbarino & Ebata, 1983), which does not yield useful information regarding differences among various other cultural groups.

Some incidence studies have been done in regard to the Native-American community with the following results.

- Fischler (1985) indicated that the neglect to abuse ratio for off-reservation Native Americans in 1978 was 2.5:1.
- For Native Americans living on a reservation it was 6:1 for Navajos and 2:1 for Cheyenne River tribes.

• In Canada, 47% of First Nations Peoples families referred to CAS were referred for child neglect as compared to 26% of White families, indicating a higher incidence of neglect among the First Nations Peoples in Canada (Trocme et al., 1995).

In the United States minorities, as well as low-income families, were consistently overrepresented in the studies reported by Garbarino and Ebata (1983). These results could be attributed to the facts, as mentioned above, that most studies use only White, Black, and sometimes Hispanic subcultures; and minorities are consistently overrepresented in low-income categories.

When Spearly and Lauderdale (1983) took income out of the equation, they found increases in child neglect rates among the Black population as opposed to White and Hispanic.

• In this study Whites had a maltreatment rate of 12.3 reports per 1,000 White families and
• Blacks had 23.3 per 1,000 Black families.
• Hispanics were in the middle with 18.2 reports per 1,000 Hispanic families.

This study indicates there may be an association of ethnicity, as well as class, with child neglect. However, most studies found no differences in child maltreatment rates among the various ethnic groups studied (Nelson, Landsman, Cross, Tyler, & Twohig, 1994; Paget, Philp, & Abramczyk, 1993; Pelton, 1994; Sedlak & Broadhurst, 1996). An in-depth look at the relationship between neglectful families and culture is presented in Chapter Eight.

One problem that is made abundantly clear as one looks at the statistics concerning the prevalence of child neglect, and the association of neglect with economic status and race, is the need for better definitions and methodologies in collecting child incidence data regarding child maltreatment in general, and child neglect in particular. Most of the data regarding child neglect are estimates at best. Zuravin (1999) reported findings that indicated underestimation of the prevalence and severity of child maltreatment, including neglect. We really do not know with any degree of certainty how many children are neglected each year; nor, indeed, how many are neglected to death (Block, 2002; Bonner et al., 1999; Federal Interagency Forum on Child and Family Statistics, 1998). However, the best information that we do have indicates that children are neglected more frequently than they are abused; and severe damage, including death, is a consequence of neglect just as often as child abuse.

Effects of child neglect. "In the past, the consequences of child neglect were not considered to be as severe as the consequences of other forms of maltreatment . . . Indeed, neglect in early stages of life may lead to severe, chronic and irreversible damage" (Perry, Colwell, & Schick, 2002, p. 193). Empirical research has shown substantial negative effects of child neglect on children over and above fatalities. Thornberry, Ireland, and Smith (2001) reported that neglect experienced in childhood has a more negative impact on early adolescent outcomes than physical abuse. Trocme et al. (1995) found the effects of neglect were primarily psychological or emotional. The findings of Ney, Fung, and Wickett (1994) indicated that the most severe psychological conflicts resulted from being neglected as opposed to being abused. Neglected children also experience more problems with academic achievement and discipline in school than their nonneglected peers (Kendall-Tackett & Eckenrode, 1996). In addition, neglected children suffer more physical health problems including malnutrition, failure to thrive, handicaps and impaired visual and motor skills (Fischler, 1985; Helfer, 1987a; Martin & Walters, 1982; Nelson, Saunders, & Landsman, 1990; Polansky, Chalmers, Williams, & Buttonwieser, 1981; Polansky, DeSaix, & Sharlin, 1972; Sweet & Resick, 1979; Tower, 1993; Zuravin & Greif, 1989). Erickson and Egeland (2002) arrived at the conclusion that "the impact of neglect on children's development was at least as damaging as other more overt types of abuse" (p. 12).

Neglect, when combined with other forms of maltreatment, increases a child's vulnerability even more; for example, when neglect precedes abuse, the effect of neglect is significantly increased (Ney et al., 1994). Neglect when combined with abuse has a stronger effect than abuse alone on the number of disciplinary referrals and grade repetitions for school-aged children, especially for children in the middle grades (Kendall-Tackett & Eckenrode, 1996). Watters, White, Parry, Caplan, and Bates (1986) found that the most serious injuries to children, more serious than abuse alone, occurred in families where abuse and neglect coexisted. These studies indicate that both the most serious physical and psychological harm to children occur in the presence of child neglect.

Jonson-Reid, Drake, Chung, and Way (in press) and Marshall and English (1999) found that neglect was the most likely reason for recidivism in families reported to CPS on more than one occasion. Neglect was the most common reason for second complaints, regardless of the type of the initial report (Jonson-Reid et al., in press). In addition, the USDHHS (2002) reported that neglected children were 27% more likely to experience recurrence of maltreatment than were physically abused children. Given previous research indicating the presence of more severe outcomes for children when neglect is involved, these findings suggest that more children are at higher risk than is commonly believed. When this information is combined with the statistics regarding fatalities, it is clear that neglect has an effect that is at least as devastating as abuse on more children than is generally known. A more comprehensive review of the specific effects of neglect is presented in Chapter Three.

Lack of Focus on Neglect

As the demographic statistics and empirical research regarding the effects of neglect on children indicate, neglect is more prevalent than abuse and can result in more serious physical and psychological injury to children. In addition, neglect is just as lethal as abuse. Rather than focusing on abuse, it has been suggested that all cases referred to CPS, regardless of maltreatment type, be screened for neglect (Jonson-Reid et al., in press).

In spite of these data, society seems to be more tolerant of neglect as evidenced by the focus of research, policy, and practice regarding maltreatment of children on abusive, not neglectful, families (Garbarino & Collins, 1999; Kadushin, 1978; Margolin, 1990; Roscoe, 1990; Wolock & Horowitz, 1984). Perry et al. (2002) agreed when they stated, "neglect, possibly the most detrimental form of child maltreatment, receives less attention from government and media than do physical and sexual abuse" (p. 196). Marshall and English (1999) indicated that complaints to CPS alleging neglect are less likely to be accepted, investigated, or substantiated. Given the dates of these citations (1978–2002), the "neglect of neglect" (Wolock & Horowitz, 1984) appears to be as chronic as child neglect itself. Indeed, it would appear that in fact, in general, "no one cares."

Wolock and Horowitz (1984) suggested four reasons for the greater amount of attention given to child abuse. First is the publication by Kempe, Silverman, Steele, Droegemueller, and Silver in 1962 of "The Battered Child Syndrome," which initially defined child maltreatment in terms of child abuse. Second is the strong link between neglect and poverty combined with society giving low priority to resolving poverty issues. Lindsey (1994) went so far as calling child abuse a "red herring" that diverts attention and resources from the larger issues of poverty and child neglect. Another reason for the focus on abuse is the perception that child abuse is more "newsworthy" (i.e., dramatic) than child neglect and, therefore, receives more publicity. A fourth reason is society's preoccupation with violence, of which child abuse is one manifestation and neglect is not.

Kadushin (1978) also cited the battered-child syndrome, linkages with poverty, and the dramatic nature of child abuse as causes for the focus on abuse as opposed to neglect. In addition, he proposed three additional causes: (a) the rise of the children's rights movement in the mid-1960s; (b) strong support for child abuse legislation and a lack of vested interests supporting child neglect legislation; and (c) the need, in 1969, for the newly created Office of Child Development (OCD) to have something on which to focus. Eventually, the OCD decided to foster the issue of child abuse as their raison d'être, thus turning attention away from child neglect. More recently, Perry (2002a, 2002b) suggested that, although neglect may be the most destructive of all types of child maltreatment, it remains understudied for three reasons: (a) neglect is less apparent than abuse (i.e., bruises and broken bones are easier to see); (b) neglect is a continuum, a time-dependent process (i.e., measures of neglect change owing to the shifting developmental needs of children), and (c) it is difficult to find adequate populations where consistent neglectful experiences have been documented.

This emphasis on the issue of child abuse and de-emphasis on neglect may have led to an unexamined belief among practitioners that neglect is not as severe a form of maltreatment as abuse, a belief that is unfounded based on the forgoing statistics. Ards and Harrell (1993) found that CPS personnel were "less likely to be aware of children who were physically or emotionally neglected than children who were physically or emotionally abused" (p. 339). Garbarino and Collins (1999) suggested that this may be the result of a "professional prejudice" that assumes that interventions for child abuse are more sophisticated than interventions for child neglect. While there is consensus, given the incidence and prevalence numbers, regarding the magnitude of the problem of families who neglect their children, there appears to be an assumption that neglect is less serious than abuse (Yuan & Struckman-Johnson, 1991). As indicated above, given statistics regarding child fatalities due to neglect and findings regarding the effects of neglect on children, it is difficult to understand the basis for this assumption. Child neglect is clearly more prevalent than, and perhaps even graver than, child abuse. Erickson and Egeland (2002) suggested that neglect might be the core issue underlying all child maltreatment.

This lack of focus on neglect has resulted in a failure to systematically study the underlying causes, conditions, and consequences of neglect as a distinct form of child maltreatment. As an example, a review of 489 articles in five volumes of *Child Abuse and Neglect* revealed only 25 articles regarding child neglect (Zuravin, 1999). Since less is known about child neglect, already stretched resources are aimed at resolving issues of abuse. This may be one reason why interventions with neglecting families are less effective than interventions with abusive families. In fact, contrary to previously mentioned professional assumptions, treating families who neglect may require a greater degree of sophistication than treating families who abuse. It may be simpler to remediate acts of commission than "acts" of omission.

As a result of this lack of focus, recognition of neglect has lagged far behind recognition of abuse (Erickson & Egeland, 2002). Lindsey (1994) asserted that child abuse and child neglect are two qualitatively different issues and their merging into the single category of child maltreatment is a fundamental problem for decision making in this field. Only in the last ten years has a body of literature conceptualizing neglect as a distinct form of child maltreatment, which needs to be studied empirically, begun to emerge. However,

> the extant literature on child neglect is characterized by fragmented efforts on the part of theorists and researchers to establish definitional parameters and to understand the etiological and outcome variables associated with inadequate childrearing practices. It is a literature plagued by conceptual and operational difficulties, rising in part from the complexity of the issues related to childrearing and the relatively recent recognition that the parental behaviors comprising neglect are substantively different from those resulting in abuse. (Paget et al., 1993, p. 122)

The findings of this chapter support Crittenden's (1999) assertion that neglect is the most serious and least understood type of child maltreatment. The following chapter addresses problems with establishing definitional parameters. Etiological and outcome models will be discussed in Chapters Three and Four.

Chapter Two

∞

What Is Child Neglect?

DEFINITIONAL ISSUES

There is a lack of agreement among experts in the field of child maltreatment regarding the definition of child neglect. This lack has resulted in the failure to develop a reliable, useful definition of the problem; which has limited research efforts and the accumulation of knowledge regarding families who neglect their children (Dubowitz, Black, Starr, & Zuravin, 1993; Dubowitz, Klockner, Starr, & Black, 1998; Hutchison, 1990; Leiter, Myers, & Zingraff, 1994; Paget et al., 1993; Rose & Meezan, 1993; Socolar, Runyan, & Amaya-Jackson, 1995; Wolock & Horowitz, 1984). This lack of knowledge has, in turn, been a barrier to social service agencies in developing an effective response to the problem (Nelson et al., 1990). The absence of a clear definition provides inadequate direction for family courts in deciding cases of neglect, insufficient guidance for social workers in providing effective interventions, and lack of consistency in empirical studies regarding this issue (Alter, 1985).

Looking at the specific definitions of the various types and subtypes of neglect (over thirty in some classifications systems) is beyond the scope of this book. However, this chapter will present issues surrounding defining child neglect and the purposes for which these definitions are used. In addition to conceptual and utilization issues, questions of precision and inclusiveness, family autonomy, parental intentions and risk of harm, chronicity, community values, culture, and religion, all of which pose problems with framing a consistent definition of neglect, will be addressed.

What all definition proposals regarding child neglect seem to have in common is the concept that one or more of a child's basic needs (e.g., food, shelter, and clothing; safety; love, and affection; health care; education;

11

and/or socialization) are not being met and as a result the child suffers harm or is at risk of harm. For purposes of this book, when speaking about child neglect, the authors are employing such a definition.

DEFINING CHILD NEGLECT

A review of the child maltreatment literature indicates that child neglect has been defined, in general terms, in three different ways: (a) as parenting deficits; (b) as community deficits; or (c) as child deficits (i.e., the effects of neglect on children or child outcomes associated with neglect).

Parenting Deficits

Young (1964) and Burgess and Conger (1978) defined neglect as a lack of appropriate parenting behavior on the part of the child's caretaker. Wolock and Horowitz (1984) defined neglect as "the failure of the child's parent or caretaker, who has the material resources to do so, to provide minimally adequate care in the areas of health, nutrition, shelter, education, supervision, affection or attention, and protection" (p. 531). The Ohio Revised Code defined as neglected a child "who has been abandoned, illegally placed for adoption, or lacks proper parental care because of the faults or habits of parents, guardians, or custodians" (Johnson, 1993, p. 606). Neglect in these families is an omission or failure to act, a deprivation of necessities. What these definitions have in common is the concept that parents, usually mothers, demonstrate a failure to provide adequate physical health care, nutrition, and/or age-appropriate supervision for their children; or they may fail to meet the child's educational, mental health, and/or relationship needs. These failures place the child in harm's way. From the medical/psychological perspective these parents have personal and/or interpersonal characteristics that result in the neglect of their children. From a social service point of view, there is some identifiable behavior on the part of the parent that places the child at risk (Valentine, Acuff, Freeman, & Andreas, 1984). The assumption is that providing these essentials for children will lead to their optimal growth and development, and that the lack of provision will lead to an opposite effect. Biologically speaking, neglect "is the absence of critical organizing experiences at key times during development" (Perry, 2002a, p. 88). The implication is that the child's caregiver is responsible for providing these "critical organizing experiences" for the child and fails to do so. As Swift (1995a) points out, the problem is defined as the child's mother. Child neglect is a personal, not a community, problem (i.e., child neglect is failed motherhood).

In order to clarify the definition of neglect based on parenting deficits, typologies of behaviors have been developed. Zuravin, as reported by Nelson et al. (1990), has suggested a list of fourteen subtypes that includes "refusal to provide health care, delay in providing health care, refusal to provide mental health care, delay in providing mental health care, supervisory neglect, custody refusal, custody-related neglect, abandonment/desertion, failure to provide a permanent home, personal hygiene neglect, housing hazards, housing sanitation, nutritional neglect and educational neglect" (p. 28). Paget et al. (1993) reported that Hegar and Yungman have cited three subtypes of neglect: (a) physical, (b) developmental, and (c) emotional, which includes nonorganic failure to thrive (NOFTT). Cantwell and Rosenberg (1990) added prenatal and neonatal neglect to the lists of typologies. These types of neglect would include those acts on the part of parents that would endanger the fetus or newborn child (e.g., substance abuse while pregnant, lack of prenatal care, and denial of the pregnancy). In all, Cantwell and Rosenberg (1990) specified six types of neglect with over thirty subtypes. NIS-3 (Sedlak & Broadhurst, 1996) indicated three types (physical, educational, and emotional neglect) with seventeen subtypes. What all subtypes of neglect have in common is the concept that children are or could be harmed by their parents' failure to provide appropriate care.

It is clear that defining neglect is not a simple matter, and this definition, based on parental failure to provide adequate care for their children, is inadequate from several points of view. It fails to clearly determine what neglectful behavior is to be considered problematic by the legal and social service communities: that is, parental behavior, or lack thereof, that requires coercive intervention to protect the child. Neglectful behavior is a continuum that produces benign to devastating results. Where is the line to be drawn that differentiates benign neglect from neglect that requires state intervention? For example, a parent is washing dishes and her toddler inserts a fork in an unprotected electrical outlet. The child suffers burns necessitating a trip to the hospital. The hospital reports the family to CPS for child neglect. The question is—is an injury befalling a child as the result of parental inattention to be considered as evidence of a family that neglects its children? Where is the line between neglect and accident? In this particular instance the child protective agency made one home visit to assess the situation and closed the case as unfounded. It was an isolated incident, the parent took appropriate action to provide medical care for the child, and the parent placed child protectors on the electrical outlets. This example introduces the concept of chronicity (i.e., a pattern of inadequate care) in respect to child neglect, a concept that will be discussed later in this chapter.

What if the child in question had wandered outside, fallen in the family pool, and drowned? Would this justify state intervention? Do the consequences to the child determine whether or not neglect has taken place? Would it make a difference if this child was an only child, or if there were young siblings? Neglect as determined by the consequences to the child and the question of siblings will also be considered later in the chapter.

Are parents who withhold medical treatment from an adolescent, at the adolescent's request, guilty of neglecting their child? In such a case, where the parents respected their sixteen-year-old son's wishes not to have chemotherapy, the parents were charged with neglect. What about the case where parents refuse medical treatment on religious grounds? In some jurisdictions they would be guilty of neglect, in others they would not. In these examples caregiver motivation comes into play and becomes a possible consideration in the development of a definition of child neglect (Hutchison, 1990). Caregiver motivation/intention, too, will be discussed subsequently.

There is, too, the question about families who clearly are not providing adequately for their children, for example, chronic substance abusers, yet their children seem to evidence no ill effects. Paget et al. (1993) indicated that the 1988 National Incidence and Prevalence of Child Abuse and Neglect study (NIS-2) commissioned by the U.S. Department of Health and Human Services included child endangerment in its definition of child neglect. However, are those families neglecting their apparently resilient children when no apparent harm has been done? Is "endangerment" an appropriate standard to use in determining child neglect? "Central to the issue of whether parental behaviors should be included in definitions of child maltreatment is the question whether causal relationships between those behaviors and negative consequences to the child can be established" (Valentine et al., 1984, p. 501). Thus, it may be that even though the child-caring behavior on the part of the parent does not meet minimal standards, if the children remain unharmed (i.e., were "only" at risk of harm, or endangered), the parents may be exempted from definitions of neglect.

The child neglect literature indicates that there is no clear connection between parental behaviors and outcomes for children; that is, there is no evidence to link a specific parental behavior, or lack of behavior, to a specific child outcome (Hutchison, 1990; Knutson, 1995). The assumption that the failure to provide what is believed will lead to a child's optimal growth and development will produce negative effects for the child has not been empirically demonstrated (Rose & Meezan, 1993). "Few guidelines have been derived from studies that show statistically that a given practice in childcare results in specific damage to the child in later life" (Polansky & Williams, 1978, p. 397). Yet, child endangerment continues to be a part of many state statutes, including Hawai'i's (Child Protective Act, 1993).

Another issue is one of magnitude of behavior. Child care is a continuum of behaviors (Dubowitz et al., 1993) over time. When devising a definition of neglect, one must be cognizant of where on this continuum one places minimal standards of parenting behavior (Hutchison, 1990) for what age child. Lack of supervision is defined differently for one-year-olds than for adolescents. As Alter (1985) indicated, "neglect itself is a relative state" (p. 100).

In summary, the parental deficits definition of neglect indicates that the parent fails to provide the child with basic needs. The categorization of these basic needs comprise the many types and subtypes of neglect delineated above. This definition appears to include the assumption that the failure to provide for the child places the child in harm's way. Problems with this definition include questions regarding parent motivation or intention, outcomes for children, causal relationships between parental behavior and outcomes for children, and setting minimum standards for adequate child rearing. An additional problem with the parental-deficits definition of child neglect is that social conditions affect parents' ability to provide for their children (Dubowitz et al., 1993). Thus the community in which the family lives may be neglectful.

Community Deficits

As early as 1967, Kadushin introduced the concept of community neglect when he wrote,

> The community itself is guilty of neglect when it fails to provide adequate housing, adequate levels of public assistance, adequate schooling, adequate health services, or adequate recreational services, or when it allows job discrimination and makes no effort to control an open display of vice, narcotic traffic, and other illegal activity. (p. 216)

Wolock and Horowitz (1984), Nelson et al. (1990), and Hamburg (as reported in Erickson and Egeland, 2002) agreed that under these conditions communities, not families, are neglectful. The communities fail to meet the physical, social, and emotional needs of families. Korbin and Spilsbury (1999) argued, "poverty is, in itself, a form of societal neglect" (p. 83). A Canadian study found it difficult to establish a statistical distinction between families living in poverty conditions and those referred to the CAS for child neglect (Trocme et al., 1995).

Spearly and Lauderdale (1983) reported results that support this definition of neglect. They found that the economic strength of a community is a significant predictor in determining which communities are at high-risk for child maltreatment. "Maltreatment is not a function of poverty, *per se*, but depends upon the availability, adequacy, and use made of a family's supportive resources in the community" (p. 103). This definition relieves the family of the onus of being neglectful and focuses on communities as being the perpetrator of harm. Thus, parents who live in conditions of poverty may be exempted from the definition of neglect, as they are not in control of their circumstances (Johnson, 1993). There are problems with this definition as well.

Arguments for an uncaring society as the source of neglect raise several issues. If it is society that neglects families and not families who neglect children, then what about families, living in environments similar to those in which neglecting families reside, who do not neglect their children? Is there some characteristic of families living in these circumstances who do not neglect their children that is different from the families who do? These differences may then be accounted for by the parental deficit definition presented earlier. Similarly, this definition does not account for those families who do neglect their children who do not live in deprived environments. It has been suggested that parents' ability to provide for their children must be taken into account in deciding the parameters of child neglect (Rose & Meezan, 1993). Yet, exclusion of community conditions, especially poverty, from a definition of neglect may prevent services from reaching families who are most in need (Rycraft, 1990).

In summary, the community deficits definition of child neglect suggests that society neglects its children when it does not provide families with the means to adequately meet their children's basic needs. Problems with this definition arise in terms of families living in impoverished circumstances who do not neglect their children; and families who are more affluent who do. Questions regarding service provision also need to be considered. Issues regarding the scope of a definition for child neglect are discussed below.

Child Deficits/Outcomes

A third cluster of authors defines neglectful families as those that produce negative outcomes for their children (Polansky et al., 1972; Rose & Meezan, 1993; Valentine et al., 1984). Whether the source of the neglect is parental behavior or inadequate societal supports, children from neglectful environments experience developmental, neurological, emotional, and behavioral disturbances that prevent healthy growth and development (DiLeonardi, 1993; Landsman, Nelson, Allen, & Tyler, 1992; Perry, 2002b; Perry & Pollard, 1997; Sweet & Resick, 1979). "It is the first work to explicitly state that harm to a child, not characteristics of the abusers or the act of mistreatment, should serve as the determining factor in defining child abuse and neglect" (Valentine et al., 1984, p. 501). There must be some demonstrable harm to the child. Neglect is defined, therefore, in terms of characteristics of the children; for example, neglected children may be more hostile, aggressive, destructive, sad, depressed, and/or lonely than children raised in nonneglecting homes (Nelson & Landsman, 1992; Polansky, Ammons, & Gaudin, 1985). This definition focuses on the manifestations of harm done to children (i.e., child deficits or the effects of neglect, not parental or societal deficits).

This third category of definition focuses more on the harm or risk of harm to children from being neglected than on parental or community deficits. As a result, it is the most troublesome of all the definitions. In the first place, it is tautological to define child neglect in terms of the outcomes to children of child neglect. Furthermore, children suffering other forms of maltreatment (e.g., child abuse and sexual abuse) also exhibit some of the symptoms of children who have been neglected. In addition, children who have not been maltreated manifest these symptoms for other reasons, for example, bereavement. Thus, this definition fails to differentiate among families who neglect their children, families who maltreat their children in nonneglecting ways, and families who do not maltreat their children.

Erickson and Egeland (2002) suggested that looking only at effects ignores other types of neglect. To include only the outcomes of neglect or harm to the child in a definition of neglect excludes the concepts regarding parenting behaviors that are inadequate or inadequate community support, thus eliminating a means of preventing harm. Finally, there is the issue of the magnitude of harm. The question is how serious must the harm be to be defined as child neglect (Hutchison, 1990).

In summary, this definition of child neglect indicates that neglected children demonstrate outcomes that suggest that they have been harmed in some way, or are in situations that place them at risk for such outcomes. This definition suggests that children who do not have negative outcomes do not live in neglectful families. Problems with this definition include the logical issue of defining neglect by observing the results of neglect; the possibility that asymptomatic children have indeed been harmed, the evidence for which has not yet surfaced; the lack of differentiation of symptoms of neglect from causes other than neglect; and the lack of ability to prevent neglect owing to a focus on outcomes, not antecedents.

Issues, in addition to those indicated above, surface when attempting to frame a useful definition of child neglect. These issues, along with issues raised previously, are discussed in the following section.

ISSUES WITH DEFINING CHILD NEGLECT

While the various definitions contribute to a conceptualization of families who neglect their children, it can be seen that none are complete in determining what the necessary and sufficient conditions in this domain are. Definitions are further determined by the purposes for which they are used by policymakers, researchers, family courts, and health care/social service providers (Dubowitz et al., 1998; Hutchison, 1990; Socolar et al., 1995). In addition, questions are raised regarding the precision and inclusiveness of the definition, family autonomy, parental intentions and risk of harm, chronicity, community values, culture, and religion.

Purpose of Definitions

Social planners, researchers, legal professionals, medical personnel, and social workers use definitions of child neglect in various contexts and for various purposes (Dubowitz et al., 1993; Erickson & Egeland, 2002; Socolar et al., 1995). This further complicates the issue of deriving a single, consistent definition.

Definitions of child neglect used by social planners would include the cost of child maltreatment. They would be used to make determinations regarding resource allocations. Research definitions affect theory building regarding the etiology of neglect, which can guide the development of preventive social policies and remedial interventions. Swift (1995a) reported that child neglect is a legal concept, whereby the state enforces the parents' responsibility to take care of their children. Legal definitions, therefore, include issues of "family autonomy, cultural diversity, state encroachment on the private sector, and ensuring due process of the law to parents" (Valentine et al., 1984, p. 499); and guide judicial decisions regarding such issues as (a) when the state can intervene with families, (b) the role of practitioners and the court in identifying and working with neglectful families, and (c) the termination of parental rights.

In the medical field "maltreatment is seen in terms of results: demonstrable harm to the child that is linked with parental behaviors" (Valentine et al., 1984, p. 503). The purpose of the definition is to aid in diagnosis and treatment. Definitions, from a social service perspective, take an ecological approach that includes preventive and rehabilitation functions, a social control function, and environmental issues. Social, legal, and policy definitions are used by social workers to make decisions regarding identification of neglecting families, to inform clients regarding which behaviors are unacceptable and need remediation, and to plan service interventions.

Precision

Precision is another problem in defining neglect. Stein (1984) indicated two elements that need to be defined: (a) what conditions need to be regulated and (b) what existing conditions should be defined as child neglect. As one moves into conditions that are less well defined, for example, emotional neglect, a lack of precision increases the likelihood that unwarranted interventions into family life may take place. However, from a legal point of view, vagueness would allow for enough flexibility in findings to take into account community and cultural values (Giovannoni & Becerra, 1979; Rose & Meezan, 1993; Valentine et al., 1984). Nonetheless, vagueness, also, would allow for arbitrary application of the law and could interfere with the parents' right to due process (Giovannoni & Becerra, 1979; Valentine et al., 1984).

Inclusiveness

Like vagueness, a broad definition of child neglect would allow for more flexibility in the judicial and CPS systems' responses to neglectful families. Hutchison (1990) indicated that a broad definition of neglect, which would include community neglect, might require structural changes in social policy, as a more inclusive definition focuses on improving the quality of life for children. Broadening the definition of neglect to include the issue of poverty could result in improved services for families struggling with survival. "What is required is a major redefinition of the problem as our failure to meet the physical, social and emotional needs of a large proportion of our children" (Wolock & Horowitz, 1984, p. 538). However, from a legal point of view, a definition that is too inclusive might sanction parents for conditions over which they have no control (i.e., they may be sanctioned for what is appropriately community neglect). In this instance, Feldman, Monastersky, and Feldman (1993) caution against confusing a lack of resources with neglect. A definition that is too broad, also, might result in the unnecessary placement of a child outside of the home, which could be damaging to the child as well as to the family. States that include neglect related to poverty issues in their definitions have higher reporting and substantiation rates than states that do not include poverty-related issues (Rycraft, 1990). Higher reporting and substantiation rates impact CPS caseloads and, subsequently, service delivery. Thus, a more inclusive definition may overwhelm the CPS infrastructure. On the other hand, Dubowitz et al. (1993) pointed out that "broader definitions may appear to absolve parents of all responsibility as the focus is shifted onto environmental conditions" (p. 17); and many broad definitions are criticized for vagueness.

Instead of the structural changes advocated by the proponents of a broad definition, a narrower definition would focus on changes within the family. A narrow definition reduces the possibility of practitioner or judicial bias; protects the parents' right to due process; and clarifies what cases should be reported to CPS and what should be acted on by the CPS system, including the police. It does this by being explicit about what constitutes child neglect and implicit regarding parental responsibility (Dubowitz et al, 1993; Hutchison, 1990; Rycraft, 1990). Such a definition is designed to protect children from serious harm, not necessarily all harm (Hutchison, 1990). A less inclusive definition, also, may decrease the number of reports coming into CPS agencies. However, a too narrow definition could effectively deny services to families in need. Stein (1984) argued for a narrowing of the definition of neglect in order to establish the parents' unwillingness to provide for their child. This implies the use of intent to harm as a criterion for determining neglect, an issue that is discussed later in this chapter. In addition to the above issues, Swift (1995a) suggested that the inclusiveness of a definition of child neglect involves the standard of care (good or minimal) and the level of intervention (least intrusive, standardized, or flexible) to be utilized, as well as the issues of incorporating community norms, focusing on parents or on children, and defining neglect as a personal or community problem.

Another issue that relates to the breadth of a definition of neglect is whether or not to include endangerment or risk of harm (English, 1998). Again, inclusion of endangerment would increase CPS caseloads, further strap scarce resources, and might unnecessarily involve families in the child welfare system. However, narrowly defining children as neglected as those who actually have been harmed might result in the failure to provide services to prevent future harm, as well as failure to protect those children who are only apparently unharmed (i.e., the harm has not yet surfaced as distinct symptoms).

Family Autonomy

The passage of legislation to mandate reporting and intervention in cases of child maltreatment, in order to protect children, undermines long-held values of privacy and family autonomy (Stein, 1984). This essentially involves questions of parents' rights versus children's rights (i.e., where to draw the line between a family's autonomy and right to privacy, and a child's right to be protected from harm) (Newberger & Bourne, 1978; Swift, 1995a; Valentine et al., 1984). Giovannoni and Becerra (1979) indicated that this debate has led child maltreatment proceedings away from a therapeutic emphasis to a more legalistic point of view calling for a narrower, more precise definition of child maltreatment. Also, a lack of consistency in definition from jurisdiction to jurisdiction results in differences among jurisdictions as to what constitutes child neglect (Alter, 1985). As a result, some jurisdictions may be more inclusive/intrusive than others, a situation that creates inequities in the child welfare system as a whole.

Parental Intention and Risk of Harm

To include only parental behavior (including their intentions) in the definition of child neglect excludes the concept of whether or not the child has been harmed by that behavior (Socolar et al., 1995; Valentine et al., 1984). Also, some parental practices may be harmful to children; however, the parent is not aware of the possible consequences of the behavior. Therefore, the parent does not intend to harm the child. Is this parent guilty of child neglect? Parental ignorance regarding appropriate child care and lack of resources to provide care, both, raise the issue of intention in the meaning of neglect. In addition, some children seem not to be harmed by parent behavior that is judged to be deficient. Endangerment, again, is at issue. Valentine et al. (1984) concluded that both elements appear to be associated with a definition of child maltreatment—the child must have been harmed and the parent must have intended to harm the child. Endangerment would not be included in such a definition. Ohio state law indicates that there must be "a motive of negligence or intent" (Johnson, 1993, p. 606). Thus, parents who are disabled may be exempted from neglect definitions.

Young (1964) concluded that neglect was defined as the parent's inability to care for a child, however unintentional. Thus, one of the earliest definitions of neglect indicates that parental intention to harm does not have to be present for neglect to take place. Dubowitz et al. (1993) asserted that the risk of harm, in addition to harm, needs to be included in a definition of child neglect; however, they did not find it useful to include intentionality. The AHA (2002) indicated that a child might be neglected whether or not the parent intended to do so. Stein (1984) suggested that intention to harm is related to child abuse, while the concern about substandard child care practices that result in unsafe conditions for a child is the focus of neglect cases. Margolin (1990), also, made this distinction; that is, the definition of child abuse includes the intention to harm, while the definition of child neglect does not.

Alter (1990) reported that CPS workers were more likely to substantiate a report of child neglect if they believed that the neglect was willful on the part of the parent. However, Nelson et al. (1990) contended that definitions that focus on the parents' failure to act eliminate the need to find intent. As Erickson and Egeland (2002) pointed out, whether the parent intentionally neglects a child or not, the child is still living in unsafe conditions and deserves adequate care and protection. Thus, the debate continues.

Chronicity

This issue revolves around the question of whether or not to include the factor of chronicity in a definition of neglect; that is, single incidents that might result in the death of a child, as well as a long-term pattern of inadequate care (Hutchison, 1990). Leaving a child unattended, even for a short period of time, which results in a child's death, may be a tragic accident or a single event of neglect. It may also be an indicator of a pattern of neglect. In addition, determining whether this event is the result of neglect or an accident may not be as important as determining whether other children in the home are at risk (Feldman et al., 1993).

Margolin (1990) found that the majority of deaths resulting from neglect resulted from the caretaker not being present at a critical moment, not from chronic neglect. The child's age was also a critical factor, with very young children being at greatest risk. Another factor was family size, with larger families being at greater risk. However, these same factors (i.e., children's ages [younger] and family size [larger]) have been found to be associated with chronically neglecting families as compared to families with more acute, if not fatal, incidents of neglect (Nelson et al., 1990), further confusing this definitional issue. Dubowitz et al. (1993) attempted to resolve this issue by focusing on the needs of the child and taking into account both the frequency of the neglect and the severity of risk.

Community Values

As early as 1964, Meier found that definitions of neglect were strongly influenced by community norms. Giovannoni and Becerra (1979) and Swift (1995a) took the position that child maltreatment is socially constructed. Polansky, Ammons, and Weathersby (1983) indicated that it is community values that determine at what point CPS reporting and intervention is appropriate. Thus, this body of research indicates that the community to some extent defines what child neglect is and when CPS will intervene. As Swift (1995a) indicated, "Although there are specific and local differences of law, precedent, and organizational size and structure that lead to some variation in emphasis and procedure, the work processes through which cases of child neglect (and other kinds of cases as well) must pass are attuned to larger social processes" (p. 63).

A study of class differences in the perception of child neglect conducted by Polansky and Williams (1978) found no differences when comparing the perceptions of social workers with that of working-class mothers. "Despite the differences in education and socioeconomic status among these mothers, they were extremely homogeneous in their evaluations of the basic elements in childcare" (p. 400).

Valentine et al. (1984) contended that neglect is defined in terms of minimal expectations of the community for parenting behavior; and society has difficulty in determining what minimum expectations are. However, Craft and Staudt (1991), Giovannoni and Becerra (1979), Polansky et al. (1983), and Rosco (1990) found that there does seem to be a general consensus about what constitutes minimally adequate child care.

In 1979 Giovannoni and Becerra compared the perceptions of child maltreatment of various professionals (lawyers, pediatricians, social workers, and police) and various lay members of the general community defined by ethnicity (White, Black, and Hispanic), thus incorporating culture as well as class. Their findings were similar to those of Polansky and Williams (1978). Overall there was "a high level of agreement among some lay subpopulations, and between professional and lay ones" (Giovannoni & Becerra, 1979, p. 207) especially in the area of determining the seriousness of different types of child maltreatment. All agreed on what were the most and least serious examples. This agreement "indicates a very high potential for consensus with respect to the social definitions of mistreatment" (Giovannoni & Becerra, 1979, p. 208). In a 1990 study, Rosco found that adolescents consistently rank-ordered neglectful parental behaviors as had community and professional comparison groups. Their responses indicated that, like comparison groups, they were more tolerant of neglect than abuse. However, they rated all categories of abuse and neglect more severely than adults.

Nevertheless, contrary to the findings of Polansky et al. (1983), Craft and Staudt (1991) found that community values do not seem to have an influence on what is actually accepted as a case for CPS intervention (i.e., substantiated as a case of child neglect). Therefore, the working definition of child neglect, the definition acted on, for the legal and social work professions may not reflect community values, even though there is agreement about what is minimally acceptable parenting.

Culture and Religion

Parents may be exempted from a charge of medical neglect on religious grounds; thus, a definition of neglect may include exceptions for religious beliefs (Johnson, 1993). In regard to culture, although research in the area of how various cultures view child-rearing practices has not been extensive, it is apparent that the definition of neglect is at least partly culturally determined. Therefore, the legal definition of child neglect, which determines when to intervene with a family, will probably be biased in the direction of the dominant culture (Gray & Cosgrove, 1985).

When including the aspect of culture in defining what inadequate parenting means, one must take into consideration the meaning of a particular behavior within that culture (the *emic* perspective) and a minimal standard of care across cultures (the *etic* perspective). Thus, "definitional issues must be structured into a coherent framework so that child abuse and neglect can be appropriately identified within and across cultural contexts" (Korbin, 1987, p. 25) in order to avoid inappropriate interventions. However, one must be cautious not to ascribe all child caring differences to cultural practices, thus denying that child maltreatment exists in other cultures (White & Cornely, 1981).

Studies indicate that Native-American communities view child maltreatment as a political issue. It is a belief of Native Americans that non-Natives, unfamiliar with Native customs, have removed children from their families on the basis of an erroneous determination of child neglect (Fischler, 1985). Gray and Cosgrove (1985) explored accepted (*emic*) practices of various ethnic groups (Mexican Americans, Samoan Americans, Vietnamese Americans, Filipino Americans, Japanese Americans, and the Blackfeet Indians) that might be at odds with the dominant culture. Two areas of cultural difference in child rearing emerged from this study: (a) the amount of responsibility given to children by various cultural groups and (b) the ways cultures handle dominance and submission issues between parent and child.

Korbin (1987) pointed out that some initiation rites of various cultures appear to be forms of child maltreatment, yet, within the meaning of that culture, are not. Thus, legitimate differences in child rearing practices among various cultures may be constructed as being neglectful by the dominant culture. However, cultural practices that seriously threaten a child's development or survival are not exempt from child neglect under the rubric of being culturally responsive.

Studies have indicated that there is some agreement among various ethnic groups regarding what constitutes minimally adequate child-caring practices. Giovannoni and Becerra (1979) found that Blacks and Hispanics, while in agreement with Whites regarding what constitutes child maltreatment, generally rated various elements of maltreatment as more serious than Whites. When accounting for class, this difference still remained, indicating that cultural differences in perceptions of child maltreatment are not the same as social class differences.

In a similar project, focusing on child neglect, Rose (1990) studied the differences in perception of the seriousness of examples of child neglect among Black mothers, White mothers, Hispanic mothers, child welfare workers, and child welfare investigators. She found that the mothers groups agreed on the seriousness of the dimensions of neglect and when there was disagreement, the White mothers tended to describe the items as less serious than the Black or Hispanic mothers. All of the professionals found all of the incidents less serious than the lay participants, both as a whole and when matched for ethnicity. The only exception was that Hispanic workers rated only some of the components of neglect as less serious than

Hispanic mothers. In terms of the rank ordering from most serious to least serious, all groups were in agreement. This study supported the earlier findings of Giovannoni and Becerra (1979) that the various ethnic groups under study are in agreement in terms of what are the most and least serious types of child maltreatment, that minorities tend to rate components of maltreatment as more serious than Whites, and that social class and ethnicity may be considered as distinct concepts (i.e., each accounts for some difference in definitions of child maltreatment), and thus do not entirely overlap with regard to attitudes regarding child neglect.

When Chinese, Whites, and Hispanics, living in the United States, were asked to rate twelve vignettes in terms of severity of abuse or neglect from none to very serious, Hispanics, again, selected higher severity ratings than did Whites (Hong & Hong, 1991). The Chinese, however, had lower ratings than both groups. The rank order of severity between Whites and Hispanics did not differ, supporting previous studies. However, there were differences between the White/Hispanic group and the Chinese. The groups were also asked what kind of response was warranted to each of the case situations, ranging from none to CPS referral. Again the White/Hispanic group differed from the Chinese in that, overall, they selected more invasive interventions than did the Chinese. The Chinese were more likely than both groups to recommend that no action be taken.

All three groups, however, agreed on the severity of mistreatment in terms of physical neglect, for example, "when parents plainly ignore their children's physical conditions and signs of physical problems. The responses to these vignettes suggest that it is possible to have intergroup consensus on what constitutes child mistreatment" (Hong & Hong, 1991, pp. 472–472).

In a study of the interaction of geography (urban or rural), class (working or middle), and ethnicity (Black or White) with perceptions regarding standards of child care Polansky et al. (1983) found that there "was evidence of substantial commonality of standards among the various subcultures sampled" (p. 343). They concluded, "it appears there is such as thing as an American standard of minimal childcare that is commonly held and that may be invoked in the definition of child neglect for legal and social work purposes" (p. 345). In a similar study, Dubowitz et al. (1998) compared the views on children's needs of White and African-American mothers from lower and middle classes living in urban or rural settings and professionals in the child welfare field. Outcomes were similar also, as it was reported that "it appears that there is general agreement in the community about adequate care of children across racial, class, and geographic groups . . . the level of agreement suggests a general consensus in what the community regards to be the adequate care of children and a definition of neglect" (Dubowitz et al., 1998, pp. 241–242).

Gaudin and Polansky (1986) found virtually no racial differences in terms of neighbors distancing themselves from deviant (i.e., neglectful) neighbors. This indicates agreement across cultures, at the community level, of responses to community members perceived as neglectful of their children. (See Chapter Eight for a more thorough discussion of child neglect and culture.) Given the above-cited studies, there appears to be some ground for establishing a culturally and community-informed standard of minimally adequate child care. We may not be able to reach a consensus regarding a definition of child neglect, but we know it when we see it.

In summary, definitional issues regarding child neglect include (a) determining a minimum standard of adequate child rearing that takes into account community, cultural, and religious values; (b) chronicity of the neglectful behaviors and family size; (c) harmful consequences to the child, if any; (d) parental motivation/intention and risk of harm (i.e., the endangerment standard); (e) establishing causal links between neglectful behavior and outcomes for children; (f) the relationship between family behaviors and community deficits; (g) the logical problem of defining neglect by observing the results of neglect; (h) the lack of differentiation of symptoms of neglect from causes other than neglect; (i) the lack of ability to prevent neglect owing to a focus on outcomes, not antecedents; (j) the purpose of the definition; (k) the precision and inclusiveness of the definition (i.e., its scope); and (l) family autonomy versus the responsibility of the state to protect children.

IMPLICATIONS OF DEFINITIONAL ISSUES

The foregoing issues surrounding the definition of child neglect have significant implications for research, policy, and practice involving families who neglect their children. Some of these implications are as follows.

Implications for Research

Most empirical studies in the field of child maltreatment focus on child abuse. This may be due in part to the fact that neglect is an abstract concept; whether neglect has taken place may be relative to the situation (Alter, 1985) and abuse may be easier to define. Those studies that have included neglected children as a variable have design difficulties consisting of problems with sampling (Paget et al., 1993) and control group selection, owing in part to the lack of clarity regarding definitions. The lack of consistency of definition across studies prevents the comparison of research findings and inhibits the drawing of conclusions regarding the effects of neglect on children (Giovannoni & Becerra, 1979; Hutchison, 1990; Paget et al., 1993). Research definitions are informal (Swift, 1995a); and researchers generally define neglect in one of two ways: (a) they use the operational definitions of the agencies whose cases are in the research sample or (b) an operational definition is designed by the researchers (Giovannoni & Becerra, 1979; Hutchison, 1990; Leiter et al., 1994; Paget et al., 1993). Neither of these two methods ensures consistency of definitions across studies and limits the generalizability of results. In addition, problems arise involving (a) the naming of important factors that are missing; (b) the use of descriptive material to illustrate, not precisely define, neglect; and (c) the focus on chronic neglect (Swift, 1995a).

The focus on abuse and the lack of clear definitions regarding neglect has resulted in few systematic studies with a focus on neglect (Wolock & Horowitz, 1984; Zuravin, 1999). The insufficiency of research specific to neglect hampers efforts on the policy and program levels to develop effective interventions in the treatment of families who neglect their children (Nelson et al., 1990).

Implications for Policy

Lack of definition impedes development of public policy regarding neglect of children separate from child abuse (Nelson et al., 1990). A broad definition implies an institutional approach to policy formation, while a more narrow definition implies a residual, remedial approach. Wolock and Horowitz (1984) suggested that a redefining of neglect to include community factors (i.e., neglect as a failure of the community to provide societal and environmental supports) would result in a child care policy that "is the only one likely to curtail significantly the incidence and prevalence of both neglect and abuse" (pp. 536–537). However, "without clear definitions, researchers cannot measure the incidence of maltreatment or determine its individual and societal costs" (Hutchison, 1990, p. 63). Social planners, therefore, do not have the tools to design social policy responsive to the issue, including appropriate resource allocation.

Implications for Practice

The parental deficit and child deficit definitions of child neglect may result in harmful labeling that interferes with successful treatment. Also, this approach of "sick parent/sick child" ignores other factors associated with neglect (i.e., environmental, including poverty) and, thus, limits intervention and prevention efforts. Some researchers contend, "It appears more critical to provide interventions based on assessed family need, regardless of how the problem is labeled, than to delay services in an attempt to define precisely the problem itself" (Valentine et al., 1984, p. 506).

The definition of neglect for legal and social service purposes acts as a gatekeeper, determining who receives services and who does not. The lack of a clear definition may mean that families who need services don't receive them, and families who don't need services do receive them, including the unnecessary removal of children from their homes. In addition, lack of definition hampers the development of effective intervention programs (Nelson et al., 1990). It is difficult to resolve a problem when there is unclarity regarding what the parameters of the problem are.

REDEFINING CHILD NEGLECT

The question of defining child neglect is a controversial one involving, among other issues, parents' rights versus children's rights, the extent of the responsibility of the state to intervene in family life, and a residual versus a structural foundation for social policy decisions. The resolution of these issues impacts what can and will be done to provide relief for families who neglect their children. The child neglect literature suggests at least partial solutions to the problems discussed above. While supporting a broad, inclusive definition of neglect, in terms of service delivery and social policy, Hutchison (1990) proposed a narrow definition in terms of grounds for coercive interventions into family life. This two-tiered approach to definition would resolve some issues in regard to the purposes for which the definition is used. A narrow definition could be used for legal purposes and a broad definition could be used for social policy and planning purposes. There still remains, however, the problem of where on the continuum of neglect to set the parameters of these definitions. Social service and medical issues may be partly resolved by this approach; however, research issues appear to be unresolved by this solution to the definition problem.

Polansky et al. (1983), Craft and Staudt (1991), and Dubowitz et al. (1998) found evidence for community agreement as to what is meant by child neglect. They suggested that a consistent definition of neglect could be developed from these elements of agreement. However, this does not resolve the issues of what action should then be taken in terms of coercing families into compliance with agreed-upon child care standards, or the potential for the helping professionals to abuse their power in these matters. Newberger and Bourne (1978) indicated that definition issues will remain unresolved until steps are taken to deal with the potential for the abuse of power by the helping professions.

Alter (1985) included elements of child deficit and community-based definitions to develop another two-tiered strategy. "State law revision could establish serious demonstrable harm as the only criterion justifying state intervention, or state agencies could concretize their abstract standards concerning adequate parental behavior by using behaviorally based screening instruments" (p. 110). This approach would narrow the definition regarding grounds for legal intervention to serious child outcomes and base the grounds for social intervention on common standards of adequate child caring. This strategy would address the issues of abuse of power by using objective measures to determine whether neglect has taken place. However, this method of defining neglect does not ensure that all families needing services will receive them, that is, those families without serious demonstrable harm, who fall below the standard of adequate child caring, who do not seek services on a voluntary basis. Dubowitz et al. (1993) advocated for a conceptual definition of child neglect based on the needs of children rather than on parental behavior: "Child neglect occurs when a basic need of a child is not met, regardless of the cause(s)" (p. 23). This again places the family at risk of inappropriate intervention by the state.

Emery and Laumann-Billings (1998) suggested a way of looking at family functioning in terms of outcomes to the family members. Family maltreatment would involve minimal harm or endangerment and family violence would involve serious trauma, either physical or emotional. The issue of definition of neglect per se does not arise. The level of harm involved would determine the appropriate intervention (i.e., family maltreatment would receive supportive services and family violence would require more adversarial/coercive interventions).

Some jurisdictions, such as Ontario, Canada (Trocme et al., 1995) and Hawai'i, USA (Child Protective Act, 1993), also avoid the definitional issue by not using the term "child neglect" in their statutes regarding child protection. Both Hawai'i's and Ontario's laws focus on evidence of harm or risk of harm to the child in defining the grounds for the state having jurisdiction in a child protection matter.

> The court shall have exclusive original jurisdiction in a child protection proceeding concerning any child who was or is found within the State at the time such facts and circumstances occurred, are discovered, or are reported to the department, which facts and circumstances constitute the basis for the finding that the child is a child whose physical or psychological health or welfare is subject to imminent harm, has been harmed, or is subject to threatened harm by the acts or omissions of the child's family. (Child Protective Act, State of Hawai'i, 1993, p. 582)

In terms of referrals for neglect, Rose and Meezan (1993) pointed out that referrals to child welfare agencies will continue to increase no matter how neglect is defined. In addition to caseload size, Rycraft (1990) suggested that the state's definition of child maltreatment also has a limited impact on the actual provision of services and, therefore, it does not make a substantial difference how the state defines child neglect. For service providers and child welfare practitioners, the important issue is that families who need services get them at a level commensurate with their need. Interventions must be based on assessment of individual families in order to resolve issues specific to the family in question, not delayed until child neglect is clearly defined (Feldman et al., 1993; Valentine et al., 1984). The focus is, therefore, on problem resolution for individual families; and steps necessary to reach this goal, including coercive strategies if appropriate, are related to the needs and resources of a particular family, not based on a definition of neglect or labeling families as neglecting.

This resolution of the definitions issue (i.e., avoiding the issue altogether), while resolving many questions, does not resolve issues regarding a definition of neglect useful for research purposes. In order to be helpful in designing effective interventions for this population, researchers must be able to define the population in such a way as to be consistent across studies to allow for comparability and generalizability. In an effort to resolve this issue, Trocme (1996) developed the Child Neglect Index (CNI), which includes six scales designed to measure the type and severity of neglect. These scales include measures of (a) supervision, (b) physical care (i.e., food/nutrition, and clothing and hygiene), and (c) provision of health care (i.e., physical health care, mental health care, and developmental and educational care). Based on the Ontario law, the CNI defines child neglect in terms of harm or risk of harm to the child. As this index is further tested in empirical inquiry it may offer some assistance in providing for consistency of (a) operational definitions across studies and (b) grounds for CPS intervention across jurisdictions. In this vein, Zuravin (1999) has suggested that (a) multiple data sources be used to obtain information on neglect, (b) maltreatment be conceptualized as multidimensional including neglect as one type, (c) neglect be conceptualized as multidimensional, and (d) researchers adopt those classification and operational schemes with the best psychometric properties.

As indicated in the beginning of this chapter, this text conceptualizes child neglect as a failure to meet children's basic needs that places them in harm's way. Whether this failure rests in the hands of their parents, the environments in which they live, or a combination of both, children are at risk and the focus is the child. Children deserve to have their needs met and to be protected from harm. We know what children need to grow and thrive. In addition, there is evidence that there is a community standard of minimally acceptable child-rearing practice. Failure to provide for children's needs at minimum levels calls for intervention to remediate this failure. Ideally the level of intervention would be commensurate with the child's particular unmet need (i.e., type of neglect) and the degree or severity of risk or actual harm. Interventions ranging from the availability of voluntary and/or preventive family support services to more coercive/intrusive remedial interventions to protect children from serious harm could be available to families. Thus a definition of child neglect would include the implication of a continuum of developmentally appropriate care to meet children's needs; the lack of which would require a continuum of responses appropriate to the type of neglect involved, the age of the child, and the level of harm/risk of harm.

As the debates in the literature continue, the issues regarding the definition of families who neglect their children are becoming clearer. Using the child as a starting point, the definition of neglect may be further refined out of this process, with results that will be useful for the purposes of the social policy, medical, legal, child welfare, and social science professions.

Chapter Three

What Causes Child Neglect?
THEORETICAL ISSUES

In the previous chapter definitional issues surrounding child neglect that influence the accumulation of research data, policy formation, and program and intervention development were discussed. Questions regarding what causes families to neglect their children also have an effect on research, policy, and practice. In this chapter proposed causes of child neglect will be explored, including various causal models that have been suggested.

THEORETICAL MODELS ASSOCIATED WITH CHILD NEGLECT

The complex nature of the concept of child neglect does not lend itself to simple theoretical explanation. There is no "theory" of child neglect or even, for that matter, of child maltreatment in general. In the conclusion to their study regarding child maltreatment, Martin and Walters (1982) were speaking of child abuse; however, the same can be said about the current state of the literature in regard to child neglect.

> The theorizing that characterizes the literature in child abuse is heterogeneous in nature. There is no parsimonious set of principles, no model, no paradigm, which provides a basis for integrating all of the findings, which have been mentioned. Although theorizing concerning the determinants of child abuse exists, considerable effort is yet to be undertaken to provide order to the findings. (p. 275)

The etiology (i.e., causal factors) and consequences (i.e., outcomes for children) of child neglect in families are as disparate as the definitions. In addition, theoretical frameworks that have been proposed are not discrete entities. They overlap in terms of concepts, constructs, and hypotheses. The literature suggests various ways of classifying theories relating to the issue.

1. Sweet and Resick (1979) categorized theoretical formulations as psychodynamic, social learning, social psychological, and sociological.
2. Biller and Solomon (1986) suggested (a) the psychiatric or medical model, (b) the social systems model, (c) the sociocultural model, (d) the social-situational model, and (e) the transactional model.
3. Hutchison (1990) described three theoretical perspectives: (a) medical-psychological; (b) sociological, including labeling theory, sociocultural perspectives, and sociosituational approaches; and (c) interactionist.
4. In their reviews Ammerman (1990) and Paget et al. (1993) classify as traditional those theoretical models that focus on parental psychopathology, stress due to social-cultural and social-situational issues, and characteristics of parents, children, and situations; and as integrative those models that are ecological, transactional, and transitional. They also cite social learning theory and attachment theory as contributing to conceptual models for understanding child neglect.

For the purposes of this text, the classifications of causal models regarding child neglect have been developed out of the definitions of neglect presented earlier. Rather than delineating what is or is not child neglect, as the definitions attempted to do, these models seek to explain why child neglect occurs and what are the outcomes for children. If the cause(s) and consequences of child neglect can be determined, theoretically at least, interventions can be designed to prevent or remediate these conditions, thereby halting or preventing the neglect of children by their families. Defining child neglect contributes to decisions regarding the necessity to intervene in a family situation; and identifying factors that contribute to the causes and consequences of child neglect can direct the development of those interventions.

In terms of the previous definitions of neglect, models regarding the causes, conditions, and consequences of child neglect may be classified as those that indicate neglect is caused by (a) parental deficiencies (psychological development and social learning theory), (b) deficiencies in the social-cultural-situational environment in which families live (social ecology theory), and (c) the interaction between factors associated with family members and factors associated with the environments in which families live (ecological and transactional theory); and (d) results in harm to children; that is, child deficits (child development, attachment, and neurobiological development theory). This last model attempts to explain the sequelae of child neglect (i.e., what are the causal links between child neglect and its consequences?). The four proposed models, related models, and their theoretical foundations and associated intervention strategies are illustrated in Table 1. This chapter will discuss these models in terms of their conceptualization. Chapter Four will then evaluate the models in terms of their quality and utility in the development of theory regarding child neglect, and explore their implications for research, policy, and practice.

PARENTAL DEFICIENCIES MODEL

Related to the parenting deficits definition of child neglect, this theoretical framework postulates that child neglect in families is caused/explained by parental or familial characteristics, to which the parent responds, that result in inadequate child-caring behaviors of the parents, including faulty parent/child interactions. Martin and Walters (1982) found that "more than any other type of child maltreatment, neglect may be influenced by parental inadequacies" (p. 272). Kelleher, Chaffin, Hollenberg, and Fischer (1994) found "that parental psychopathology, independent of social ecology, is an important determinant of child maltreatment" (p. 1590); and Nelson et al. (1994) found that the personal characteristics of families living in low-income situations had more impact on whether or not children were neglected than did social support. In terms of intervention, this model takes a medical approach; that is, in order to eliminate neglect one identifies (diagnoses) parental deficiencies and treats them.

Research has shown that there are parental and familial characteristics associated with child neglect that are considered to be risk factors in predicting which families are likely to neglect their children; thus, these risk factors may be explanatory in nature. These attributes of parents and families are considered to be the results of physical, personality, and/or behavioral disorders of the parents. These attributes cause them to provide inadequate care for their children; and, in turn, these attributes are the results of (i.e., caused by) the parents' life histories, including being inadequately parented. Helfer (1987a) conceptualized the etiology of neglect as "a complex series of circumstances beginning with early rearing experiences and the way these circumstances affect a parent's learned ability to develop and maintain close personal relationships" (p. 62–63). Thus, it is theorized that there is an intergenerational factor in the etiology of child neglect. The conclusion of Nelson et al. (1994) indicated that many neglectful

TABLE 1
Causes and Outcomes of Child Neglect
Related Models—Theoretical Foundations—Interventions Strategies

Models	Parental Deficiencies	Environmental Deficiencies	Interactions	Effects of Neglect
Basic cause of child neglect and its effects	Familial traits: personal deficits and lack of personal resources	Environmental factors: material deficits and lack of material resources	Interaction between familial traits and environmental factors	Neglectful families/environments harm children
Related models	Medical Psychological Psychoanalytical	Sociological Social ecological Social support/isolation	Stress and coping Resiliency Ecological Interactive Family strengths Social support/isolation	Stress and coping Resiliency Medical
Theoretical foundations	Social learning theory Behavior theory Psychological development theory Neurobiological development theory Information processing theory	Social learning theory Social ecology theory Social psychology theory Behavior theory	Psychological development theory Transaction theory Evolution theory Sociobiology theory Ecology theory	Child development theory Attachment theory Neurobiological development theory
Practice strategies	Medical model: provide treatment based on diagnosis	Environmental model: provide concrete and social supports based on assessment of the family situation	Social work model: provide comprehensive psychological and concrete services based on assessment of the family in situation	Social work model: provide comprehensive psychological and concrete services based on an assessment of the child in situation

parents were victims of deprivation in childhood. These findings are consistent with theory regarding the intergenerational transfer of neglecting behaviors and lend support to this point of view.

The intergenerational concept relates most closely to the parental deficits model as current parental problems (deficiencies), which are associated with their neglecting behavior, are caused by their own inadequate upbringing. This "cycle of neglect" concept results in validating the provision of CPS services to a narrow set of clients, generally poor, with psychological problems—the result of inadequate upbringing—that result in inadequate child rearing. Neglect, through CPS practice, is thus defined as a personal problem (Swift, 1995a).

Parental Characteristics Associated with Child Neglect

Early researchers in the field, who have found a strong relationship between parental characteristics and caliber of child care, support this model of child neglect. These studies focused on parental attributes and parental childhood histories as explanations for child neglect (Belsky, 1993). Young (1964) found neglectful parents were so overwhelmed with their own needs that they were unable to care for their children. They had no direction and were unable to plan toward reaching a goal. They were further characterized as being undereducated, impulsive, confused, emotionally detached, sad, lonely, apathetic, and distrustful. Problems confronting these families included chronic and acute illness, alcoholism, psychosis, mental retardation, criminal behavior, and large numbers of children. Speculating on the causes of parental attributes, Young (1964) presumed them to be the result of their own upbringing.

Echoing Young's (1964) findings, Polansky et al. (1972) indicated that child neglect is caused by "infantile elements in the maternal personality" (p. 8) characterized by apathy, a sense of futility, and impulsive behavior. Neglectful mothers also may be depressed, mentally retarded, and/or psychotic. Again these attributes are considered to be due to the effects of faulty parenting in their own families of origin.

More recent studies have had similar findings. In terms of personal demographics, parents who neglect their children are more likely than comparisons to be female, single, older, younger, and to have fewer years of formal education (Bath & Haapala, 1992; Benedict, Wulff, & White, 1992; DiLeonardi, 1993; Doerner, 1987; Dubowitz & Black, 2002; Egeland & Sroufe, 1981; Gaudin, Polansky, Kilpatrick, & Shilton, 1993; Giovannoni & Billingsley, 1974; Horowitz & Wollock, 1981; Kelleher et al., 1994; Landsman et al., 1992; Margolin, 1990; Nelson & Landsman, 1992; Nelson et al., 1990; Ory & Earp, 1980; Pelton, 1981; Polansky et al., 1981; Polansky, Gaudin, Ammons,

& Davis, 1985; Sedlak & Broadhurst, 1996; Smith, 1998; Trocme et al., 1995; Watters et al., 1986; Weston et al., 1993; Wolock & Horowitz, 1979; Zuravin, 1987; Zuravin & Greif, 1989). An earlier work by Giovannoni and Billingsley (1974) found no relationship between parental education and subsequent child neglect. Thus, conflicting results have been found in terms of maternal age; and one study found no differences for educational level.

Neglecting parents are more likely to feel fearful, confused, restless, apathetic, stressed, hostile, lonely, depressed, helpless, and that nothing is worth doing than nonneglecting parents (Dubowitz & Black, 2002; English, 1998; Erickson & Egeland, 2002; Friedrich, Tyler, & Clark, 1985; Gaudin et al., 1993; Herrenkohl, Herrenkohl, & Egolf, 1983; Horowitz & Wolock, 1981; Landsman et al., 1992; Nelson et al., 1990; Polansky, 1985; Polansky et al., 1981, 1985; Watters et al., 1986; Zuravin, 1991; Zuravin & Greif, 1989). They, therefore, may present a sad, lonely, chaotic picture dominated by helplessness and hopelessness.

Personal traits associated more frequently with neglectful parents include antisocial behavior (including criminal behavior), fanatical beliefs, lack of trust, irresponsibility, emotional numbness, verbal and psychological inaccessibility, and low self-concept and self-esteem (Christensen et al., 1994; Daro, 1988; Dubowitz & Black, 2002; English, 1998; Erickson & Egeland, 2002; Fischler, 1985; Helfer, 1987b; Herrenkohl et al., 1983; Kelleher et al., 1994; Landsman et al., 1992; Polansky et al., 1981; Watters et al., 1986; Zuravin & Greif, 1989). Thus, they may display behavior that is more withdrawn and impulsive than comparison parents.

Studies have shown that neglectful parents are more likely to have serious personal problems than comparison parents. These problems include mental illness; physical illness; lowered intellectual ability; emotional and behavior problems, including issues of dependency, autonomy, and affective disorders; an inability to concentrate or plan for the future, and substance abuse/addiction (Bath & Haapala, 1992; Berry, 1992; Daro, 1988; Dubowitz & Black, 2002; English, 1998; Erickson & Egeland, 2002; Hampton, 1987; Helfer, 1987b; Horowitz & Wolock, 1981; Jones, 1987; Kelleher et al., 1994; Landsman et al., 1992; Martin & Walters, 1982; Murphy et al., 1991; Nelson et al., 1990; Nelson & Landsman, 1992; Pelton, 1981; Watters et al., 1986; Zuravin, 1991; Zuravin & Greif, 1989). As a result of these issues, the neglectful parent may have a great deal of difficulty in working toward goals.

Research indicates that parents who neglect their children are lacking in social, coping, problem-solving, and other life skills (Azar, Robinson, Hekimian, & Twentyman, 1984; Friedrich et al., 1985; Hansen, Pallotta, Tishelman, Conaway, & MacMillan, 1989; Polansky et al., 1981; Zuravin, 1991; Zuravin & Greif, 1989). Therefore, they can manifest a sense of incompetence.

In general, then, the research literature suggests that the neglecting parent presents the following picture. She is female and likely to have had little formal education. She personifies helplessness and hopelessness. Withdrawn and impulsive, this single mother seems incompetent, is more than likely to abuse/be addicted to mind-altering substances, and has trouble working toward reaching any goals. One must keep in mind, however, that this "neglect profile" is based on the limited pool of studies regarding neglectful parents and these findings were not consistent across those studies.

An interesting study of neglect from the child's point of view supports the parental deficiency model. According to children who have been neglected, neglect is caused by parental immaturity, marital problems, and parental alcoholism/drug addiction (Ney, Fung, & Wickett, 1992). Substance abuse/addiction, a consistent predictor of child neglect, will be discussed in detail in Chapter Nine.

Child Characteristics Associated with Child Neglect

Research has suggested that parents tend to neglect children with particular characteristics (i.e., parents respond to these children with inadequate caretaking). Child characteristics that seem to place children at risk for neglect consist of prematurity and low birth weight, which may be associated with disrupted attachment due to extended stays in neonatal intensive care units; handicapping conditions, including developmental delays and physical health problems; normative developmental changes (e.g., adolescence); and mental illness (Bath & Haapala, 1992; Berry, 1992; Doueck, Ishisaka, & Greenaway, 1988; Dubowitz & Black, 2002; Fischler, 1985; Horowitz & Wolock, 1981; Landsman et al., 1992; Martin & Walters, 1982; Nelson, K., 1991; Nelson et al., 1990; Rohner, 1986; Zuravin & Greif, 1989). Adolescents who deny their conditions (e.g., diabetes) and/or are noncompliant with medical recommendations may leave their parents open to charges of neglect. Sedlak and Broadhurst (1996) found that boys were more likely to be emotionally neglected than girls; children older than six years were more likely to be harmed or endangered by emotional neglect than children under six; and children under age eleven years were more likely to be endangered by physical neglect than older children. Perry (2002a, 2002b), Perry et al. (2002), and Perry and Pollard (1997), however, indicated that neglect, including emotional neglect, affects the organization and functioning of the developing brain and thus is most damaging to infants and young children (i.e., children under the age of six years). Contrary to the NIS-III, younger children would be more at risk for harm.

All infants are more vulnerable and to that extent are at higher risk for harm than older children. However, most infants are not neglected; therefore, while infancy may be a risk factor for neglect, it could certainly not be construed as a cause. In addition, Herrenkohl et al. (1983) found no child-related characteristics associated with neglect; and Burgess and Conger (1978) found no differences in the way children interacted with their parents for abuse, neglect, and comparison families. In examining child characteristics/symptoms it is difficult to separate causes of neglect from its consequences. Therefore, it is unclear whether some of these child characteristics are antecedents (reasons for parental neglect) or consequences (the effects of maltreatment). A more complete discussion of this issue will be presented later in this chapter with the causal model regarding the effects of neglect on child development. Ammerman (1990) concluded, "It is widely acknowledged that the contribution of child factors to abuse and neglect is restricted . . . This is especially the case with neglect, in which there is not substantial evidence that children play a role in eliciting inadequate caregiving" (p. 237).

Familial Characteristics Associated with Child Neglect

Several studies have focused on the family attribute of the quality of the parent/child relationship, especially in terms of faulty attachment as a determinant of child neglect. In general, maltreating parents have poor child-rearing skills (Berry, 1992; English, 1998; Hampton, 1987; Nelson, K., 1991). In relation to their children, neglecting parents express more negative attitudes toward them than comparison groups (Aragona & Eyburg, 1981; Burgess & Conger, 1978; English, 1998; Friedrich et al., 1985; Landsman et al., 1992; Nelson et al., 1990; Wolock & Horowitz, 1979). Neglectful mothers tend to initiate fewer interactions with their children, provide less instruction and encouragement, demonstrate less verbal and nonverbal affection, tend to play less with their children than comparison mothers, and provide less stimulation in their home environments (Berry, 1992; Bousha & Twentyman, 1984; DiLalla & Crittenden, 1990; Erickson & Egeland, 2002; Landsman et al., 1992). Neglectful mothers are less positive and more critical and directive than nonneglectful mothers (Aragona & Eyburg, 1981; DiLalla & Crittenden, 1990). Friedrich et al. (1985) found that neglectful mothers relaxed less in stressful situations and found a child's cry more irritating than control mothers. Giovannoni and Billingsley (1974) found neglectful mothers preferred older children and were less emotionally nurturing than nonneglectful mothers.

Research has indicated that neglectful parents lack parenting skills, have more inappropriate expectations of their children, lack knowledge regarding child development and children's needs, and lack empathy and understanding of the complexities of the parent/child relationship (Azar et al., 1984; Daro, 1988; English, 1998; Erickson & Egeland; 2002; Herrenkohl et al., 1983; Nelson et al., 1990; Polansky et al., 1981; Twentyman & Plotkin, 1982). These findings tend to support the proposition that an impaired parent/child relationship and lack of knowledge and skills regarding child rearing play a role in the etiology of neglect.

However, Egeland and Vaughn (1981) found no association between mother/child attachment failure and subsequent neglect; and Twentyman and Plotkin (1982) found no overall differences in expectations of children between neglecting families and comparison families. Wolock and Horowitz (1979) did not find expected differences between neglectful mothers and nonneglectful mothers in terms of child-rearing knowledge, attitudes, and practices. Thus, the research is not conclusive in regard to the role attachment, parental expectations, and child-rearing skills play in the etiology of child neglect.

There are additional familial characteristics that have been found to be associated with child neglect. Studies have shown that families in which neglect takes place are more likely than comparison families to have more children and older children (Berry, 1992; Friedrich et al., 1985; Gaudin et al., 1993; Giovannoni & Billingsley, 1974; Landsman et al., 1992; Margolin, 1990; Martin & Walters, 1982; Nelson et al., 1990; Pelton, 1981; Polansky, Gaudin, et al., 1985; Sedlak & Broadhurst, 1996; Smith, 1998; Wolock & Horowitz, 1979; Zuravin, 1987, 1988, 1991; Zuravin & Greif, 1989). These children were more likely to be unplanned and more likely to be unplanned due to failure to use birth control as opposed to faulty use of birth control (Zuravin, 1987). However, in later studies, Zuravin (1988, 1991) found that, while family size was a factor, unplanned births were not significantly associated with neglect. Bath and Haapala (1992), on the other hand, found no differences in the number of children in the family between comparison groups; and other studies have found that younger children are at high risk for maltreatment (English, 1998; Herrenkohl et al., 1983; Margolin, 1990; Nelson & Landsman, 1992). Again, research has produced conflicting results.

Neglectful families tend to have more children by different fathers (Nelson et al., 1994; Zuravin, 1988). The fathers tend not to be available to their children, either because they are absent or, if they remain in the family, they interact less with their children than comparison fathers (Burgess & Conger, 1978; Nelson et al., 1990; Nelson et al., 1994; Polansky et al., 1981). Families with absent fathers were at higher risk for physical neglect (Polansky, Chalmers, Buttenwieser, & Williams, 1979). This may be due to the fact that there is not another adult in the household to help "pick up the slack" in terms of providing child care. In the absence of fathers, mothers bear the onus of being the "neglectful parent," perhaps because they are the only parent around. Thus a gender bias may exist in the child neglect field, blaming mothers in the absence of fathers. Fathers who abandon their children are certainly no less neglectful than the single mom who is left to bear the burdens of single parenting, yet little attention is paid to absent fathers in the child neglect literature.

Multiple problems significantly differentiate families who neglect their children from comparison families. These families tend not only to have more kinds of concurrent problems, but the problems themselves are more severe than in nonneglecting families. Neglecting families, as opposed to nonneglecting families, tend to have relatively more of the following difficulties.

1. Physical problems consisting of adult mental retardation and adult health issues (Bath & Haapala, 1992; Helfer, 1987b; Horowitz & Wolock, 1981; Martin & Walters, 1982; Nelson et al., 1990; Nelson & Landsman, 1992; Polansky et al., 1981; Watters et al., 1986).

2. Family problems including interpersonal issues; conflicts and partner abuse; changes in household composition, including marital disruption and child placement out of the home; and other types of child maltreatment in addition to neglect (Bath & Haapala, 1992; Berry, 1992; Daro, 1988; Erickson & Egeland, 2002; Friedrich et al., 1985; Giovannoni & Billingsley, 1974; Hampton, 1987; Herrenkohl et al., 1983; Horowitz & Wolock, 1981; Jones, 1987; Jonson-Reid et al., in press; Landsman et al., 1992; Marshall & English, 1999; Nelson et al., 1990; Nelson & Landsman, 1992; Polansky et al., 1983; Wolock & Horowitz, 1979; Zuravin & Greif, 1989).

3. Money management and financial problems and stressful life events (Daro, 1988; Gaudin et al., 1993; Hampton, 1987; Martin & Walters, 1982; Nelson et al., 1990; Wolock & Horowitz, 1979; Zuravin & Greif, 1989).

Notwithstanding this long list of findings, other than being headed by single, undereducated women, DiLeonardi (1993) and Smith (1998) found no clear-cut profile for neglecting families in terms of parent deficits. These findings do underscore, however, *the multiple problems that are encountered by these families and their lack of personal resources to deal with them.*

Parental Childhood History and Its Association with Child Neglect

If the above characteristics create the conditions within which neglect takes place and, therefore, offer at least a partial explanation as to why parents neglect their children, then the ensuing question is what the origins of these characteristics are. One aspect of this causal model for child neglect that attempts to answer this question is that these characteristics are transferred from one generation to the next. Supporting the intergenerational nature of the etiology of child neglect, studies have found that neglectful parents experienced more out-of-home placements as children and more frequently reported childhood histories of maltreatment (including neglect) and family dysfunction than did parents of comparison families (Cantwell & Rosenberg, 1990; Erickson & Egeland, 2002; Helfer, 1987b; Horowitz & Wolock, 1981; Landsman et al., 1992; Nelson et al., 1994; Polansky, Ammons, et al., 1985; Rohner, 1986; Turner & Avison, 1985; Weston et al., 1993; Wolock & Horowitz, 1979).

To explain this intergenerational transfer of inadequate caretaking, concepts of attachment theory, behavior theory, social learning theory, and information-processing theory are incorporated into the model regarding deficiencies in parental behavior. Polansky et al. (1981) speculated that neglect is transferred from mother to daughter "through processes of deprivation leading to detachment, failure to provide stimulation and the child's identification with an inadequate role model" (p. 43). In his review of the literature regarding the etiology of child maltreatment, Belsky (1993) suggested that children learn faulty parenting in childhood through modeling, direct reinforcement and coercion, and inconsistent training. They then express the learned behavior in their adult parenting role. In addition, as hypothesized by attachment theory, children whose needs are not met form an internalized representation of their parents that expresses itself as unresponsiveness to their own children. Neglecting parents carry a pervasive psychological model of emptiness and depression that is reflected as neglect in the parenting of their children (Baumrind, 1994; Belsky, 1993).

Crittenden (1993) looked to information-processing theory, an outgrowth of developmental and cognitive theories, to shed light on the underlying processes by which parents fail to provide necessary care for their children. This theory proposes that the way neglecting parents process information affects (a) the way they perceive their children's needs, (b) the way they interpret their perceptions, (c) the meanings of those perceptions in terms of determining a response to their children's needs, and (d) the way they finally respond to their children's needs.

> Neglectful parents behave differently from other parents in childrearing situations, but also, and more importantly, they experience reality differently, interpret its meaning differently, select different responses from different repertoires of resources and implement those responses under different conditions. (Crittenden, 1993, pp. 29-30)

Their own lack of attachment during childhood, lack of experience with nurturing adults, experiencing of role reversal in childhood, and living in impoverished response environments; which lead to limited problem-solving skills and a tendency to withdraw rather than seek help; are cited by Crittenden (1993) in the etiology of parental processing problems. Thus, information-processing theory validates the intergenerational aspect of neglect.

Another explanation for intergenerational transfer of traits is biological (e.g., genetic or congenital). Although no studies have put forth the theory that child neglect may be genetically linked, the possibility might be considered. Not necessarily in terms of discovering a "neglect" genetic marker; however, when pervasive and consistent characteristics appear to be transferred from generation to generation, and create seemingly intractable problems, it is not unreasonable to suspect a genetic connection. Behavioral geneticists have indeed found genetic factors linked to feelings of depression, anxiety, hostility (Belsky, 1993), mental illness, and substance abuse. These factors are highly correlated with neglecting parents.

The possibility of biological factors such as evolutionary theory (interactional theory) and neurobiological development (child neurodevelopment theory) in the etiology of child neglect in families might offer explanations of neglect that have been overlooked. Evolution theory proposes an explanation of neglect and the lack of resources that is based on survival of the parents' genetic heritage (Belsky, 1993). Neurobiological development provides an explanation of the intergenerational transfer of neglect by suggesting that neglect interrupts children's neurobiological development at critical times in the brain's development that, in all likelihood, will affect their ability to parent their own children (Perry, 2002a, 2002b). Both theories are discussed in detail later in this chapter.

Giovannoni and Billingsley (1974) and Nelson et al. (1990) found no significant differences between neglecting and nonneglecting families in terms of reported problems in parents' families of origin; thus, these two studies did not support theory regarding the intergenerational transmission of neglect. Belsky (1993) concluded that in spite of the significance of findings regarding parental maltreatment history as a risk factor in child neglect, "some, perhaps many, even most parents do not repeat the cycle of maltreatment" (p. 417).

What makes the difference for these parents is an important question, the answer to which could have significant impact on programs designed to prevent child neglect and interventions with children who have been neglected designed to break the intergenerational cycle of maltreatment. In this respect, Erickson and Egeland (2002) reported that there seem to be four major factors that distinguish between mothers with at-risk personal histories who maltreat their children and those who don't. These factors consist of (a) a nurturing adult in childhood who gave them a view of themselves and others that was different than the one derived from their maltreating caretaker(s); (b) a supportive partner at the time of the birth of their child(ren); (c) therapeutic interventions that enabled them to resolve childhood issues, which allowed them to achieve greater emotional stability and maturity; and (d) the integration of their childhood histories into a coherent view of self.

Cultural Differences as They Relate to Parental Deficiencies

In terms of cultural aspects related to child neglect, few studies have focused on cultural differences. The NIS-3 (Sedlack & Broadhurst, 1996) found no differences for race in child maltreatment incidences. Nelson et al. (1994) compared neglectful Native-American and non-Native-American families with nonneglectful comparison groups. Criminal charges, substance abuse, and a history of psychiatric problems distinguished neglecting from nonneglecting families. Non-Native-American neglecting families had parental family histories that included out-of-home placements, deprivation, sexual abuse, and poor education for both mothers and grandmothers. Native-American neglecting families had multiple problems, higher stress, separation or divorce, multiple and/or absent biological fathers, more children, and more children born out of wedlock.

Fischler (1985) and Lujan, DeBruyn, May, and Bird (1989) found alcoholism and parental family histories (e.g., out-of-home placements and child maltreatment) to be associated with Native-American families who neglect their children. Fischler (1985) also found that psychosis, especially related to Native-American mythology, played a role in child maltreatment. In addition, handicapped children were at higher risk for neglect than nonhandicapped children. Fischler (1985) and Lujan et al. (1989) found that most families had more than one type of maltreatment (e.g., neglect and abuse). These studies support the model regarding parental and familial attributes associated with child neglect and the intergenerational transfer of neglectful practices.

Trocme et al. (1995), in Canada, found that First Nations families were more likely to be referred for neglect than White families. Pettigrew (1986), when examining child neglect in rural Punjab, found that, in terms of family characteristics, neglect was related to mother-in-law dominance and interfamilial conflict.

In comparing Black and White families, all of whom were neglectful, Horowitz and Wolock (1981) and Saunders, Nelson, and Landsman (1993) found similar characteristics to other studies, as did Hampton (1987), in comparing maltreating White, Black, and Hispanic families. Differences were mainly in degree. Hampton (1987) found that neglect was the most common form of child maltreatment for Black families and Polansky (1985) found that Black mothers were the loneliest.

In terms of family history, Black mothers were more likely to have been raised in poorer, single-parent households. They were also older and more likely to be single (Horowitz & Wolock, 1981; Saunders et al., 1993). Black and Hispanic mothers had fewer years in school and Black mothers were more likely to be unemployed (Hampton, 1987). White mothers experienced more anxiety and fewer health problems (Saunders et al., 1993). Black families had more children and more children with physical problems. White families had more problems with substance abuse and conflictual relationships, and they were more likely to have been maltreated as children. The nature of their problems was more intrapersonal than for Black families linking White families more clearly to the parental deficiency model of child neglect (Horowitz & Wolock, 1981). Hampton (1987) found that in comparing White, Hispanic, and Black maltreating mothers, Whites and Hispanics were more stressed; and child-rearing and substance abuse problems were more related to Black families. Black families were also more likely to have an absent father than either White or Hispanic families.

Forecasting subsequent findings, Giovannoni and Billingsley (1974) found that neglecting Black and Hispanic mothers tended to be older than adequate mothers. However, they found no differences between groups of White mothers in terms of age.

In terms of characteristics of children, Korbin (1987) indicated that a culture's values determine whether a child is at risk for neglect in that culture. For example, in cultures that undervalue women, girls will be at higher risk for neglect than boys. This was the finding of Pettigrew (1986) in regard to neglect in rural India.

As has been indicated, the research regarding child neglect has not been able to provide a profile of the neglectful parent that is consistent across studies. A composite description of the neglectful parent, based on the preponderance of research, was included in an earlier section of this chapter. The following are some actual case examples of what neglectful families looks like.

> An eighteen-year-old, single, welfare mom, leaves her three-month-old baby alone in the crib while she slips out to the store. The baby's cries result in a referral to CPS.

> An affluent family from a country outside of the United States wants their children to be educated in the American way of life. The parents purchase a home in a large metropolitan city, and place their three children in the home without adult supervision. The oldest child is sixteen. All of the children are enrolled in school. A CPS complaint is made for lack of supervision and possible medical neglect. There is no adult in the home to sign for medical treatment for the children.

A single, SSI-recipient mom, who is developmentally disabled, is referred to CPS for neglect because she is feeding her two-month-old baby chocolate chip cookies. She and her baby share an apartment in public housing. She keeps her home clean and orderly.

A single, methamphetamine-addicted welfare mother of six is referred for physical neglect of her children due to inadequate housing, lack of supervision, medical neglect, and nutritional neglect. The home is dirty, has rats, and is in much need of repair. The children range in age from newborn twins to a fourteen-year-old boy, who provides what supervision his siblings get. Mother tries hard, but she and her boyfriend do not seem to be able to stop using. At times there is domestic violence in the home.

It has been noted that most of the neglectful families being studied live in poverty situations, as is the case with the examples mentioned above. As Abell, Clawson, Washington, Bost, and Vaughn (1996) pointed out, "without a better understanding of the context in which parents must raise their children, it is difficult to determine the relative contributions of psychological distress and environmental adaptation to the values parents hold or to their childrearing behavior" (p. 597). Given the weaknesses of a theory of neglect based solely on parental deficiencies, researchers became interested in looking beyond parenting deficits to social deficits as factors in a causal model of child neglect.

DEFICIENCIES IN THE SOCIAL-CULTURAL-SITUATIONAL ENVIRONMENT MODEL

This theoretical perspective, related to the community deficits definition, implies that deficiencies in social structures and the environment in which families live are the primary causes of child neglect (Baumrind, 1994). Thus, society contributes to child neglect when it fails to provide for families living in disadvantaged situations (Garbarino & Collins, 1999; Korbin & Spilsbury, 1999). This model focuses on factors in the families' environments that are theorized to provide both the necessary and sufficient conditions under which neglect takes place. Based on social psychological theory, this model takes an environmental approach asserting that the situation in which a family lives has an impact on family functioning (Polansky, Ammons, et al., 1985). Findings of Garbarino and Crouter (1978) "strongly support the proposition that child maltreatment (at least as reported) is related to socioeconomic, demographic, and economic variables" (p. 609).

It is hypothesized that many of the parental deficit factors related to the causes of child neglect are the result of social, cultural, and situational

factors, and, hence, are only indirectly related to the etiology of child neglect. These situational factors are ones that are beyond the immediate control of the family and contribute to the neglecting behaviors of parents
(Garbarino & Collins, 1999; Hampton, 1987). Pelton (1978) indicated "there
is good reason to believe that the problems of poverty are causative agents
in parents' abusive and negligent behaviors and in the resultant harm to
children" (p. 614). "These parents' behavior problems are less likely to be
symptoms of unconscious or intrapsychic conflicts than of concrete ante-
cedent environmental conditions, crises, and catastrophes. It is these root
causes that must be addressed" (Pelton, 1978, p. 616).

Supporting this model, Wolock and Horowitz (1979) stated, "The relationship between poverty and social problems is due to a lack of adequate
resources, rather than to a set of characteristics which result both in poverty and in inadequate parenting" (p. 191). According to this model, neglectful families would not be any more likely than normative families to
neglect their children if the environment within which they lived provided
adequate resources. The impoverished environments in which they live
are the result of social and/or political priorities and not a fault in the parent (Helfer, 1987a). Korbin and Spilsbury (1999) contended that

> society has historically conceived neglect as mother's deficient care of
> children and that this conceptualization has served the interests of the
> powerful by . . . deflecting attention from societal causes of neglect (e.g.,
> poverty and marginalization) and, therefore, from the costly societal-
> level solutions of the problem. (p. 83)

Structural and environmental determinants of child neglect include socioeconomic status (SES), social support/isolation, high-risk neighborhoods,
and religious and cultural/ethnic factors, including racial discrimination.

Socioeconomic Status

Poverty is a pervasive and persistent correlate of families who neglect their
children (Berry, 1992; Daro, 1988; Erickson & Egeland, 2002; Jones, 1987;
Knudsen, 1992; Pelton, 1981; Thomlison, 1997). There is a clear inverse
relationship between material affluence and child neglect (Bath & Haapala,
1992; DiLeonardi, 1993; Dubowitz, 1999; Garbarino & Collins, 1999;
Giovannoni & Billingsley, 1974; Hampton, 1987; Horowitz & Wolock 1981;
Kelleher et al., 1994; Landsman et al., 1992; Nelson et al., 1990; Nelson &
Landsman, 1992; Pelton, 1978; Pettigrew, 1986; Sedlack & Broadhurst, 1996;
Trocme et al., 1995; Wolock & Horowitz, 1979; Young, 1964). It has been
suggested that poverty is the strongest single predictor of child neglect,

and factors associated with poverty are more predictive of child neglect than any other form of child maltreatment (Martin & Walters, 1982). Families who neglect their children tend to be the poorest in all studies, even poorer than low-income, welfare-recipient comparison groups (Giovannoni & Billingsley, 1974; Wolock & Horowitz, 1979). Socioeconomic factors are more strongly related to child neglect than to child abuse (Garbarino & Crouter, 1978), indicating a differential between the two forms of child maltreatment. An in-depth look at the relationship between child neglect and poverty is addressed in Chapter Ten.

Other indicators of SES—such as inadequate and unsafe housing; frequent moves due to housing problems; employment problems including unemployment, underemployment, and sporadic employment; and poor, unsupportive, unsafe, transient, and high criminal activity and drug use neighborhoods—have also been linked to the root causes of child neglect (Benedict et al., 1992; Erickson & Egeland, 2002; Giovannoni & Billingsley, 1974; Hampton, 1987; Herrenkohl et al., 1983; Jones, 1987; Kadushin, 1967; Krishman & Morrison, 1995; Landsman et al., 1992; Nelson et al., 1990; Nelson & Landsman, 1992; Pelton, 1994; Watters et al., 1986; Wolock & Horowitz, 1979; Young, 1964). An additional aspect of SES, the low education level of parents in neglecting families, was discussed in an earlier section of this chapter regarding parental deficits.

Pelton (1978, 1981) concluded that the middle class has more leeway to be irresponsible than the lower classes owing to their higher level of affluence; that is, they can spend household money more impulsively without risk of not having food on the table. However, more affluent families do neglect their children, especially in terms of lack of supervision and emotional neglect (Cantwell & Rosenberg, 1990). They may hire a nanny who provides only supervision and food, not emotional connection, the parent having little contact with the child on a day-to-day basis. At times teenagers are left to their own devices while the parents take extended trips. Thus, children from wealthy homes may be neglected in terms of supervision, stimulation, and emotional and disciplinary needs. Research regarding child neglect in the middle and upper classes, however, is negligible.

Social Support/Social Isolation

Related to neighborhoods and communities is the concept of social isolation, which is linked to the etiology of child neglect. Social isolation and its inverse, social support, are hypothesized to have both direct and indirect associations with families who neglect their children. Social support includes both instrumental (concrete) assistance and affective (emotional) support (Polansky, Ammons, et al., 1985). Those aspects of social support/ isolation that are theorized to have a direct causal link to child neglect, focusing more on social isolation, will be considered in this section. The indirect effects of social support will be considered with the interactional model regarding the etiology of child neglect in a later section of this chapter.

As previously has been shown, neglectful families endure multiple problems; and it is hypothesized that the social isolation they experience, therefore, has multiple causes. Thompson (1994) cited (a) limited social competencies, (b) overwhelming life stressors, (c) limited rewards from contact with others, and (d) substance abuse and mental health issues as possible contributors to neglectful families' diminished social networks. The causal link between social isolation and child neglect is provided by behavioral and social learning theory. Parents do not interact with others owing to the lack of a social network. Thus, they do not receive modeling of normative parenting behavior or feedback regarding their own parenting behaviors. As a result, they do not learn appropriate parenting skills and/ or fail to correct faulty parenting (Garbarino, 1981; Salzinger, Kaplan, & Artemyeff, 1983). In this way, risky values and attitudes are exacerbated by social impoverishment. Thomlison (1997) indicated that, poverty aside, the lack of a support system is a key risk factor in the etiology of neglectful families.

In support of this model, maltreating mothers have been found to be more isolated (have smaller social networks) and more insulated (their networks interact less) than nonmaltreating mothers (Daro, 1988; Polansky et al., 1981; Polansky, Ammons, et al., 1985; Polansky, Gaudin, et al., 1985; Salzinger et al., 1983; Young, 1964). Neglectful mothers clearly have deficient social connections (Coohey, 1996); and their social networks consist primarily of family members, not friends, neighbors, or social institutions such as the church (Giovannoni & Billingsley, 1974; Nelson et al., 1990; Polansky, Ammons, et al., 1985; Polansky, Gaudin, et al., 1985; Salzinger et al., 1983; Wolock & Horowitz, 1979; Young, 1964). In addition, they are more isolated from their families than nonneglectful mothers (Zuravin & Greif, 1989); and neglected children report having fewer friends than comparison children (Polansky, Ammons, et al., 1985). Thus, the children, as well as the adults, appear to be more isolated.

Coohey (1996) found that neglect is linked to (a) the structural properties of mothers' support networks, (b) the support as perceived by the mothers, and (c) the actual support received. Neglectful mothers have fewer emotional resources, perceive their participation in support networks as less supportive, and have structurally different types of networks. These characteristics may contribute to the attitudes held by potential sources of support, the neighbors.

Neighbors of neglecting mothers view them as having parenting problems and do not see them as someone to turn to for help. Thus, neglecting mothers are more apt to be perceived as deviant and, indeed, are avoided or distanced by their neighbors (Gaudin & Polansky, 1986; Polansky, Ammons, et al., 1985; Polansky & Gaudin, 1983; Polansky, Gaudin, et al., 1985). Neglecting mothers tend not to participate in reciprocal helping relationships and, thus, are at a disadvantage in establishing support networks (Beeman, 1997; Polansky, Gaudin, et al., 1985).

In terms of family members, neglectful mothers receive fewer total resources from their partners and their own mothers. In addition, they receive fewer total instrumental resources than nonneglecting mothers (Coohey, 1995). Jackson (1998) found that for single, low-income, Black mothers having a member of the older generation in the household (i.e., mother's mother) was a mixed blessing. Having a grandmother in the household lowered stress associated with child-care and financial issues; however, it increased stress due to depression. Lower levels of depression, and thus increased parenting adequacy, were associated with affective support of the child by the nonresident father.

Giovannoni and Billingsley (1974) found no differences between neglecting and adequate mothers in terms of relationships with friends and neighbors. They did find that the frequency and nature of contacts with relatives did differentiate between neglecting and adequate mothers, with inadequate mothers having fewer to no contacts, even if relatives lived close by, thus partly supporting this model.

The findings of Nelson et al. (1990, 1994) do not lend support to social isolation as a cause of child neglect. Neglectful families in these studies were not any more isolated than nonneglecting families; and social support had little direct or indirect impact on neglect. Nelson et al. (1990) found that the most helpful contacts were with siblings. The chronic neglect group tended to live in closer proximity to potential sources of support than did nonneglecting comparison groups, but they did not necessarily have more contact. Contrary to what might be expected in terms of this model, members of the chronic neglect groups followed up with service referrals more frequently than did comparison groups and were more likely to see these services as helpful.

High-Risk Neighborhoods

Neighborhoods themselves may be impoverished and, thus, be at high risk for producing neglectful families. Garbarino (1981) and Young and Gately (1988) concluded that children in neighborhoods that were socially impoverished owing to structural inequities were at risk for child maltreatment.

Garbarino (1981) and Spearly and Lauderdale (1983) found that social and economic factors such as family economic status, working mothers, and single mothers were significant community level predictors of the risk of child neglect. The availability of community resources also affects the adequacy of children's health care (Dubowitz & Black, 2002).

Studies have shown that parents in high-risk neighborhoods take less responsibility for child care; and are less self-sufficient, utilize community resources less, and have fewer reciprocal exchanges with their neighbors than similar parents in low-risk neighborhoods (Garbarino, 1981; Spearly & Lauderdale, 1983). The result is that very needy people are living in areas where there are fewer resources available to meet their needs. Neighborhoods, thus, affect child maltreatment, in part, because the neediness of families living there inhibits sharing. This lack of intimate and confident interaction inhibits nurturance of families and their children (Garbarino, 1981). Supporting this model, Turner and Avison (1985) found that women from impoverished environments have difficulty in providing enriching lives for their children. Therefore, in the case of high-risk neighborhoods, family problems are compounded rather than ameliorated by the environment in which the family lives (Garbarino & Sherman, 1980).

Neglecting mothers see their neighborhoods as being less friendly and supportive than do comparison mothers (Polansky, Gaudin, et al., 1985; Wolock & Horowitz, 1979). However, Polansky, Ammons, et al. (1985) found no differences between neglectful and control mothers and their neighbors in their perceptions of the supportiveness of their neighborhoods; and there were "few variations between the settings in which the neglect and the control families were found" (p. 45). Polansky, Gaudin, et al. (1985) found that neglectful mothers were not living in socially impoverished neighborhoods, even though the neighborhoods were perceived as such by them.

Garbarino and Crouter (1978) found that the rates of child maltreatment in a neighborhood varied in direct relationship to socioeconomic and demographic factors of the neighborhood. Supporting this finding, Steinberg, Catalano, and Dooley (1981) found that as employment opportunities in a community went up, so did the incidence of child neglect. This was attributed to an increase of mothers seeking employment or joining the workforce who were leaving their children at home unattended.

Religion, Culture, and Ethnicity as Environmental Factors

In addition to poverty, Dubowitz (1999) and Dubowitz and Black (2002) asserted that religious and cultural factors affect the quality of children's health care. Families may also refuse or be unwilling to provide adequate care (over and above health care) for children owing to cultural or religious practices and/or beliefs. Land ownership, maternal workload, and a medical presence in the village were related to child neglect in the rural Punjab region of India (Pettigrew, 1986). In the United States Black families were found to be poorer than comparable welfare families (Hampton, 1987; Horowitz & Wolock, 1981; Saunders et al., 1993); and they were more likely to have more environmental difficulties than White families, including unsafe housing, rats in the home, drug- and crime-ridden neighborhoods, unemployment, and racial discrimination (Biller & Solomon, 1986; Hampton, 1987; Horowitz & Wolock, 1981; Saunders et al., 1993). In comparing neglectful and nonneglectful Black, White, and Hispanic families, Giovannoni and Billingsley (1974) found that neglecting Black families have fewer material resources than neglecting White or neglecting Hispanic families. Thus, Black families more clearly can be linked to the social-cultural-situational environmental deficiencies model of child neglect than White families.

Garbarino and Ebata (1983) indicated that acculturation is a key element when looking at the relationship between various ethnic groups and child maltreatment. An ethnic group's risk of child maltreatment is based on its values, child-rearing practices, and biological predispositions. These authors suggest that overall incidence of child maltreatment is a matter of social conditions influenced by basic cultural values regarding children. Gray and Cosgrove (1985) found that Hispanics' poor parenting practices might be cultural adaptations to conditions of poverty. Similar findings were obtained for Vietnamese families, whose neglectful behavior was attributed to their incomplete adjustment to drastic changes in their environment. Thus, children living in situations of rapid socioeconomic and sociocultural change are at increased risk for maltreatment (Korbin, 1987). Cross-cultural studies also validate the position that social supports are a strong deterrent to child abuse and neglect, as these factors seem to operate in many cultures to reduce the incidence of child maltreatment (Korbin, 1987).

INTERACTIONAL MODEL

These models recognize the multidetermined nature of child maltreatment. The ecology of child neglect includes personal characteristics of parent and child, parent/child interaction, their specific life situation, social institutions in the environment, and the culture in which they live (Besharov, 1978). The ability to predict child maltreatment increases as environmental and social factors are added to intrapersonal factors (Wolock & Horowitz, 1979). "Personal, situational and systemic forces can combine to undermine low-income parents' immediate intentions and long-term aspirations, both for themselves and for their children" (Halpern, 1990, p. 14). Individual attributes, cultural values, ignorance, and poverty must be considered together (Knudsen, 1992). The continuation of neglect is related to poverty and impoverished neighborhoods as well as to personal characteristics. Building on Bronfenbrenner (1979), the interactional model focuses on the interaction between familial and environmental factors as the source of child neglect. These factors can act either as potentiators of child neglect or as protectors against neglect (Belsky, 1993; Cicchetti & Lynch, 1993). The parental and environmental deficiencies models, discussed earlier, focus on the risk factors (potentiators) and imply interventions to remediate these factors. In addition to these potentiating factors, interactional models focus on elements (protectors) in the family and the environment that ameliorate or buffer the effects of the potentiating factors, and attempt to answer questions regarding the apparent resiliency of many families and children. Thus, this model focuses not only on factors that are associated with families who neglect their children, but also on factors that operate in similar families who do not neglect their children. When looking for clues to the etiology of child neglect one must look at both potentiating and protective factors and their interactions on all levels of human life (i.e., intrapersonal, interpersonal, community, culture, and society).

Bronfenbrenner (1979) classified these levels as the microsystem, the mesosystem, the exosystem, and the macrosystem, and indicated that in studying these systems, "the principal main effects are likely to be interactions" (p. 38). The findings of Nelson et al. (1990) supported the significance of both demographic/situational factors (i.e., SES) and parenting problems (i.e., mental illness) and their interactions in the etiology of chronic child neglect. Belsky (1993) and Garbarino and Ebata (1983) took this to a new level by including evolutionary theory in the model as interacting with poverty to result in child neglect.

Evolutionary theory is a sociobiological theory that proposes there are biological reproductive (i.e., evolutionary) imperatives in human biological history that serve as explanations for the co-occurrence of child neglect and poverty. Spearly and Lauderdale (1983) found that rates of child neglect were high in low-income communities. As presented previously in this chapter, many studies have found a link between child neglect and poverty. Garbarino and Ebata (1983) and Belsky (1993) suggested there might be a biological factor that has a causal relationship with child neglect.

> The fact that evolutionary theorists highlight the linkage between poverty and maltreatment does not mean that abusing or neglecting offspring is the best way to care for children but, rather, that under impoverished conditions doing so may make, or at one time made, biological sense. When resources are scarce, neglecting some children may enable the

parent to invest more effectively in others—ones who presumably have more reproductive potential . . .—thereby enhancing the parent's (but not the neglected child's) reproductive fitness. (Belsky, 1993, p. 424)

Thus, material deprivation interacts with biological imperatives to result in child neglect.

Supporting the position regarding the importance of interaction effects, Polansky et al. (1979) found that families with an absent father had lower incomes than intact families; and fewer absent fathers in neglectful families contributed child support than in comparison families. Given the significant proportion of single, female-headed households in the neglect population, this finding indicates a possible interaction between social deficits (poverty) and parental and familial characteristics (single mothers/absent fathers) associated with neglect.

In a study that investigated both parental and environmental factors, Gaudin et al. (1993) found that neglectful families were more frequently stressed and isolated than comparison families, and more frequently reported being lonely. This study also found an association, for neglecting families, between loneliness and depression, and loneliness and stressful life events. Chronic loneliness, caused by both personal and social factors, is significantly related to child neglect. A more complete explanatory model of child neglect, therefore, includes both environmental and parental factors, which interact to produce neglectful families. This theory suggests that any model that does not include both elements is insufficient to predict or explain child neglect.

Cicchetti and Lynch (1993) discussed a transactional approach to account for child maltreatment. In this model, "environmental forces, caregiver characteristics, and child characteristics all influence each other and make reciprocal contributions to the events and outcomes of child development" (p. 96). Factors that influence a child's risk of maltreatment are called potentiating (increase risk) and compensatory (decrease risk). Factors also have a temporal nature, and thus can be transient (acute) or enduring (chronic). Maltreatment occurs when potentiating factors (acute or chronic) outweigh compensatory factors (acute or chronic). Intergenerational transfer of child neglect is accomplished by the passing of enduring (chronic) potentiating factors from one generation to the next (Ammerman, 1990). Belsky (1993) proposed a developmental/ecological model that includes three contexts: (a) the developmental-psychological context, which includes parent and child characteristics and the intergenerational transmission of traits; (b) the immediate context, which includes parenting behaviors and parent/child interaction; and (c) the broader context, which includes social support and isolation, and cultural and evolutionary factors.

Stress and Coping

Theory regarding stress and coping suggests an interactional model that explains child neglect in terms of stressors, both within and without the family, that interact with the coping abilities of the parents. These interactions may result in child neglect or may ameliorate a neglectful situation. As has been noted in previous sections of this chapter, stressful situations and high levels of stress are often associated with neglecting families. "Coping and problem solving may be directed at the reduction or elimination of stresses and hardships" (McCubbin, McCubbin, Thompson, & Thompson, 1995, p. 33) and thus may act as protective variables for high-risk families.

Hillson and Kuiper (1994) proposed a stress-and-coping model as a process-oriented explanation of child maltreatment. This model focuses on the role of caregiver stress in child maltreatment and proposes "that knowledge of the caregiver's primary appraisals of stress, secondary appraisals of resources, and dispositional coping strategies may help facilitate a more complete explanation of the onset and maintenance of child maltreatment" (p. 262). Descriptive characteristics summarized in this chapter in the sections regarding parental and environmental deficiencies are all potential stressors. What are important are the caregiver's cognitive appraisal of the situation and resources available, and coping strategies. This model attempts to provide a better explanation of the relationships between risk factors and the incidence of child maltreatment than the more descriptive models presented earlier.

> Functional appraisals and coping strategies will most often result in facilitative interactions between the caregiver and child, and thus not produce maltreatment. Conversely, more dysfunctional appraisals and coping strategies will increase the probability of maltreatment. At moderate levels of dysfunction this maltreatment may take the form of neglect. At more severe levels, physical abuse may be more evident. (Hillson & Kuiper, 1994, p. 771)

Hillson and Kuiper (1994) apparently made the assumption, mentioned in the first chapter, that abuse and neglect are on a continuum of parental behaviors that range from nonmaltreating to abusive, with neglect being a less severe form of child maltreatment than abuse. However, research has shown that not to be the case (Brown, 1984). It is becoming clear that child neglect and abuse are not homogeneous, but are separate concepts with unique etiologies and unique outcomes. As was presented earlier, the consequences of neglect are at least as grave as those of abuse. Neglect would appear *not* to be a more moderate level of dysfunction than abuse. However, Giovannoni and Billingsley (1974) found that low-income neglectful parents were under more stress than adequate parents, and had fewer internal and external resources to cope with it. Thus the hypothesized processes of the stress-and-coping model were validated, if not some of its assumptions.

Benedict et al. (1992) studied the perceived stress and burden of care in maltreating and nonmaltreating families who had children with multiple disabilities. They found that there were no differences in overall perceived stress levels among the groups under study. Also, the extent of the child's disability was inversely related to incidents of maltreatment (i.e., the less disabled children were more likely to be maltreated than the more severely disabled children). This was hypothesized to relate to parental expectations, which might be unrealistically higher for the less disabled child.

McCubbin et al. (1995) applied a family stress-and-coping model in looking at resiliency in ethnic minority families. Called the Resiliency Model, this approach identifies individual, family, and community characteristics and processes that interact and shape minority families' behavior in response to a wide range of stressful situations over time. As an example, when this model was applied to Native Hawai'ian families, family problem-solving communication (i.e., how a family communicates to solve problems) emerged as the critical factor in explaining family dysfunction. The family's fundamental cultural convictions and values (i.e., ethnic schema) and internal strengths and durability (i.e., hardiness) explained differences in family problem-solving communication (McCubbin et al., 1995). Family ethnic schema was also causally related to coherence, which was causally related to hardiness. Therefore, the cultural values of Hawai'ian families are linked to family dysfunction in two ways by their direct and indirect influence on problem-solving communication. Social support is causally linked to both ethnic schema and hardiness. Thus, according to this model, in Native Hawai'ian families child neglect (family dysfunction) could be caused by difficulties in family problem solving communication, which in turn is affected by the degree of the family's hardiness and the strength of their cultural values. The hardiness of the family is affected by family cohesion and social supports. Social supports also affect cultural values, which in turn affect family cohesion. This example illustrates the multidimensional aspects of family dysfunction, which could include child neglect, by looking at various causal pathways that explain its occurrence.

Social Support

As indicated above, isolation is a risk factor for child neglect. In interactional models, social support is hypothesized to be an intervening variable that has buffering/protective effects. It helps to ameliorate the stresses and consequences of social isolation, and reduces the risk of child maltreatment. While not focusing on child maltreatment per se, Cohen and Wills (1985) studied the processes through which social support has a beneficial effect on well-being. They looked at social support both as a protective factor for the negative effects of stress (interactional model) and as having a direct effect on overall well-being (main-effect model). They concluded that social support seems to have both a buffering effect when measured as a personal resource to cope with a stressful situation, and a direct effect when measured as the degree of involvement in the community social network—each effect representing a different process by which social support affects well-being; thus, "social integration and functional support represent different processes through which social resources may influence well-being" (Cohen & Wills, 1985, p. 349).

No studies were found that focused on the direct effect of social support on the general well-being of families at risk for child neglect. However, several studies have focused on social support as a protective (buffering) factor in high-risk families. Polansky, Ammons, et al. (1985) found that the lives of the very poor "may be enriched and, to some extent, buffered by their mutually supportive networks" (p. 47). Turner and Avison (1985) found that while life stress and perceptions of personal control were significant factors in problem parenting, the experience of social support might be the most powerful factor of the three in discriminating between high-risk families who experience problem parenting and those who do not. They concluded that social support plays a dramatic role in assisting parents in building their parenting capacity.

A study by Tymchuk and Andron (1990) of parenting practices of developmentally delayed mothers indicated that those who neglected their children did so more out of a lack of training in appropriate child care and a lack of support in carrying out that training than as a result of their mental handicap. Mothers who received necessary training and support tended not to neglect their children. Also, the maltreating mothers had slightly higher IQs than nonmaltreating mothers. This indicates that there are variables other than reduced intellectual capacity that account for child neglect. The nonneglectful mothers tended to have stronger support networks and used agency resources more frequently. Thus, these factors served as protective factors ameliorating the potentiating factor of the mothers' lesser intellectual ability.

Ory and Earp (1980) studied the interaction of the potentiating factors (a) young motherhood, (b) family social disorganization, and (c) single parenthood with the protective factor, (d) utilization of social services. They found that social disorganization was the only significant potentiating predictor of child maltreatment. The effects of social disorganization were ameliorated by the utilization of agency services. Thus, an inverse relationship existed between child maltreatment and utilization of agency services, even in the presence of social disorganization.

A discussion of theories regarding child neglect would not be complete without taking a look at the outcomes for neglected children. The following section considers the effects of child neglect.

EFFECTS OF NEGLECT ON CHILDREN MODEL

Child neglect is often defined, by the legal system, in terms of harm to children. A body of theory has developed regarding the effects of neglectful behavior on children—effects being evidence of harm. Logically (and legally in some states) if there are no harmful effects from apparently neglectful behavior on the part of parents, the child has not been neglected.

However, the effects of neglect often do not leave visible scars and a child may appear to have been unharmed. Neglect may go undetected and untreated, the victims too young to speak out. Owing to the chronic nature of neglect; children may come to believe that this is the way life is, not realizing that they have been maltreated and are suffering the consequences (Erickson & Egeland, 2002). This reason alone is enough for theorists in the child maltreatment field, as well as the legal community, to be interested in the consequences to children of neglectful behavior. The effect of neglect model speculates that there are specific consequences to children that are the result of neglectful behavior of parents. Child development theory, attachment theory, and, most recently, neurobiological development theory have contributed to research regarding the effects of neglect on children. This chapter will discuss the effects of neglect, including fatalities, from the perspective of each of these theories; and then will explore what happens to adults neglected as children, resilient children, and the effects of poverty on children.

Fatal Child Neglect

In general, the specific effects of child neglect are dependent on the age of the child at the time of maltreatment, the severity and chronicity of the neglect, and the promptness and appropriateness of interventions initiated to remediate the situation (Perry et al., 2002). The most serious consequence of neglect to children is death. Incidence studies have shown that the mortality rate of children due to neglectful behavior of their parents is close to or more than that of physical abuse (AHA, 1983, 1988; DiLeonardi, 1993; Margolin, 1990; USDHHS, 2002; Wolock & Horowitz, 1984). Usually death results when a child is left unattended (Bonner et al., 1999; Margolin, 1990). Death by starvation (Zumwalt & Hirsch, 1987) is another form of fatal neglect, as are smoke inhalation (fires), drowning, medical neglect, and fatal injuries (suffocation, poisoning, etc.) (Bonner et al., 1999). Familial characteristics, similar to those associated with chronic neglect (i.e., more and younger children), may be associated with families of children who die as the result of neglect, especially in the case of death due to starvation (Nelson et al., 1990; Zumwalt & Hirsch, 1987). When children survive parental neglect, outcomes are explained by child development, attachment, and neurobiological development theory.

Child Development Theory

In terms of child neglect, child development theory indicates that faulty parenting results in adverse outcomes for children. An understanding of the effect of neglect requires not only an understanding of the neglectful behavior of the parent, but also an understanding of the developmental needs of children and the nature of the interaction between parents' behavior and children's needs (Crouch & Milner, 1993). In addition, the timing (age of the child at the time of maltreatment), chronicity, and severity of neglect all have a bearing on children's outcomes. Table 2A, based on child development, attachment, and neurobiological theory, summarizes the effects of neglect on children ages 0–54 months in terms of physical, cognitive/behavioral, and social/emotional development.

Children aged 0–3 years. Developmental theory indicates that children's growth and development is sequential with the successful completion of one stage of development dependent upon the successful completion of the previous stage's developmental tasks. Early and sustained maltreatment would be expected to seriously compromise the developing child's capacities to competently resolve current and future developmental challenges (Manly, Kim, Rogosch, & Cicchetti, 2001). Recent studies regarding the neurobiological development of the brain indicated that infants and young children are at highest risk for damaging outcomes due to child neglect (Perry, 2002a, 2002b; Perry et al., 2002; Perry & Pollard, 1997). It is clear that this age group is the most vulnerable and at risk for the most serious damage (Scannapieco & Conneli, 2001). For these reasons this section will discuss outcomes of neglect occurring in the first three years of life, followed by general developmental outcomes for children.

The most striking physical effect of neglect (e.g., isolation, lack of stimulation, disrupted mother/child interaction) in infancy is nonorganic failure to thrive (NOFTT) (Erickson & Egeland, 2002; Perry et al., 2002). Crouch

TABLE 2A
Effects of Neglect on Children from Birth to 54 Months

Age	Physical Development	Cognitive/Behavioral Development	Social/Emotional Development
0–6 months	NOFTT Inadequate weight gain	Not imitating behavior of others Lack of response to others Lack of recognition of others Delayed babbling (precursor to language delays)	Delayed smiling or laughing Lack of affect Does not imitate adult emotions Delayed recognition of self as distinct from others
6–12 months	Inability to organize stimulation into patterns Motor delays (i.e., sitting, crawling, walking)	Unable to find hidden objects Does not mimic adult behavior Lack of goal-oriented, intentional behavior Babbling does not include sounds from family's spoken language Delayed use of preverbal gestures (e.g., pointing) At 9 months, steep decline on infant development scales through 24 months	Indiscriminate socialization (i.e., delayed separation anxiety) Anxious or lack of attachment Caregiver is not seen as a secure base
12–18 months	May have short attention span Possible delayed motor development (i.e., gross and fine motor skills)	Language delays—may not be able to use words	May have difficulty interacting with other children Delayed signs of empathy Difficulty in taking turns

(Continued)

Age	Physical Development	Cognitive/Behavioral Development	Social/Emotional Development
18–24 months	May have difficulty running, jumping, and climbing Continued delays in gross and fine motor skills	Language delays–may not be able to combine words, limited vocabulary Beginning noncompliant behavior	Unable to express self-conscious emotion (e.g., shame, embarrassment) Lack of emotional self-regulation Lacks enthusiasm Is easily frustrated and angry Avoidant and unaffectionate with mother, but is highly dependent on her
24–36 months	May not be able to use a fork or spoon, throw objects, run, and/or hop May be delayed in ability to dress self	Beginning conduct disorder in boys Less developed memory recognition Continued language delays; may be unable to carry on a conversation	May not be able to move beyond more self-centered to more cooperative play More under-socialized Impaired relatedness
42 months	Not reported	Poor impulse control Rigidity Lack of creativity	Greater unhappiness
54 months	Not reported	Continuing poor impulse control General adjustment problems in school Various and serious behavior problems Noncompliant, negativistic, and impulsive behaviors Nervous behaviors	Extreme dependence on teachers Early symptoms of psychopathology

and Milner (1993) described the symptoms of NOFTT as growth delay, poor muscle tone, unhappy facial expressions, persistence of infantile postures, minimal smiling, decreased vocalization, and general unresponsiveness.

Older infants and toddlers (a) exhibit language and intelligence delays; (b) have delayed or faulty development of autonomy and competence; (c) are less likely to feel in control of their environments; and (d) present as withdrawn, isolated, and passive (Bolger & Patterson, 2001; Crouch & Milner, 1993). Attachment issues are also of concern and will be discussed in the section regarding attachment theory. Manly et al. (2001) and Erickson and Egeland (2002) found that long-term neglect in infancy and toddlerhood resulted in greater aggressiveness and lower ego control and ego resilience later in childhood. Apparently children neglected in infancy first respond by being passive and develop acting-out behavior problems as they grow older.

General developmental outcomes. Trocme et al. (1995) found that effects of neglect were primarily psychological or emotional. Rieder and Cicchetti (1989) found that maltreated children differed from nonmaltreated children in the use of impaired mechanisms to organize, interpret, and make use of information. They generally used mechanisms to insulate themselves from incoming stimuli resulting in global and undifferentiated memory of outer information. This is consistent with their findings that maltreated children show little initiative in seeking out new information or in mastering situations.

It is not surprising, therefore, that studies have shown that neglected children have higher rates of (a) child mental illness; (b) school problems, including academic failure and/or truancy; (c) low IQs and/or developmental delays; (d) withdrawn and submissive behaviors; (e) trouble dealing with tasks, making decisions, and problem solving; and (f) lethargy and depression than comparison children (Bath & Haapala, 1992; Buchanan & Oliver, 1980; Cohen, Brown, & Smailes, 2001; DiLeonardi, 1993; Doerner, 1987; Eckenrode, Laird, & Doris, 1993; Egeland, Sroufe, & Erickson, 1983; Erickson & Egeland, 2002; Fischler, 1985; Gaudin, 1999; Helfer, 1987a, 1987b; Horowitz & Wolock, 1981; Kendall-Tackett & Eckenrode, 1996; Lamphear, 1985; Landsman et al., 1992; Nelson et al., 1990; Perry et al., 2002; Polansky et al., 1972, 1981; Prino & Peyrot, 1994; Reidy, Anderegg, Tracy, & Colter, 1980; Reyome, 1993; Schorr, 1988; Sweet & Resick, 1979; Thomlison, 1997; Tower, 1993; Zuravin & Greif, 1989).

Bolger and Patterson (2001) found that child neglect was related to depression, anxiety, and affective disorders in children. Neglected children tended to have higher levels of perceived external control, which may account for these findings (i.e., neglected children lacked the protective factor of feeling in control of their environments). Additional evidence of the cognitive and emotional impairment of neglected children is found in their tendencies to (a) have speech and language disturbances; (b) cling more to their teachers; (c) be more distractible, impulsive, inadequate, and/or immature; (d) have less ego control, flexibility, creativity, self-esteem, trust in others, and/or ability to cope with frustration or delay gratification; and (e) be more passive or have a flatter affect than nonneglected children (DiLeonardi, 1993; Egeland et al., 1983; English, 1998; Helfer, 1987b; Landsman et al., 1992; Ney et al., 1992; Perry et al., 2002; Polansky et al., 1972; Reidy et al., 1980; Tower, 1993). In fact, Egeland et al. (1983) found neglected children "presented the least positive and most negative affect of all groups" (p. 469). In contrast, Kaufman (1991) did not find an association between child neglect and depressive disorders in children.

In terms of physical health, neglected children also suffer more problems including malnutrition, failure to thrive, special needs, impaired visual and motor skills, poor hygiene, and substance abuse (Doerner, 1987; English, 1998; Fischler, 1985; Helfer, 1987a; Law & Conway, 1992; Martin & Walters, 1982; Nelson et al., 1990; Polansky et al., 1972, 1981; Sweet & Resick, 1979; Thomlison, 1997; Tower, 1993; Zuravin & Greif, 1989). The findings of Dean, Malik, Richards, and Stringer (1986) were at variance with other findings in that they discerned no difference in verbal abilities between maltreated and nonmaltreated children.

Neglected children, also, do not do well socially. They suffer more out-of-home placements; poorer peer relationships; more impaired socialization and higher rates of aggressiveness, acting-out/noncompliant behavior, juvenile delinquency, and criminal behavior than their nonneglected peers (Brown, 1984; Dean et al., 1986; Doerner, 1987; English, 1998; Erickson & Egeland, 2002; Fischler, 1985; Helfer, 1987b; Kirby & Fraser, 1997; Landsman et al., 1992; Nelson et al., 1990; Perry et al., 2002; Polansky et al., 1981; Schorr, 1988; Thomlison, 1997; Tower, 1993; Walker, Downey, & Bergman, 1989; Zuravin & Greif, 1989). When they are placed out of home, neglected children tend to stay in custody longer than children placed for delinquency. Thus, out-of-home placements based on parental behavior (neglect) contributed more to length of stay than the child's behavior (delinquency) (Glisson, Baily, & Post, 2000).

Polansky et al. (1972) and Lamphear (1985) found neglected children to be more aggressive; and Reidy (1980) and Reidy et al. (1980) found them to display more behavior problems than nonneglected children. Nonetheless, Leiter et al. (1994) found no differences between maltreating and low-income nonmaltreating families in outcomes for children, except for those families with several substantiated reports, validating the theory that chronic neglect is more damaging; and Gaudin (1999) reported that the evidence for the effect of neglect on socioemotional functioning is equivocal.

Eckenrode et al. (2001) found that neglected children are just as likely to be involved in antisocial and violent behavior as children who have been physically abused. Dean et al. (1986) found both aggressive and withdrawn behaviors in maltreated children. The levels of aggression and withdrawal depended on the child's age—as children grew older their behavior changed from aggressive to withdrawn. Studies mentioned earlier (Erickson & Egeland, 2002; Manly et al., 2001) indicated that withdrawn infants tended to grow into more aggressive young children. The effect of age on behavior could explain these seemingly inconsistent findings regarding how neglected children act, especially if studies involve different-aged children.

In a study exploring the relationship between children's achievement and the quality of their home environment, Baharudin and Luster (1998) found that home environment was positively related to children's achievement scores. Maternal and contextual factors that contributed to the quality of the home environment included (a) mother's age when she had her first child (older), the amount of stimulation she provided in the home (greater), and her intelligence and self-esteem (higher) and (b) family income (greater), presence of a supportive male partner in the home, and number of children (fewer). These findings tend to validate the findings of child neglect studies in that the reverse of these factors is negatively related to children's positive outcomes.

Comorbidity of maltreatment. Stouthamer-Loeber, Loeber, Homish, and Wei (2001), Ney et al. (1992, 1994), and Lujan et al. (1989) indicated that children tend to experience more than one type of maltreatment. Kendall-Tackett and Eckenrode (1996) found that the combination of abuse and neglect increased the number of referrals for disciplinary action, increased the number of grade level repetitions, and lowered grades in math and English for junior high school students. Ney et al. (1992, 1994) found that neglect increased a child's risk of abuse, and, when combined with other forms of maltreatment, increased the child's vulnerability to abuse (i.e., when neglect preceded abuse, the effect of neglect was significantly increased). Watters et al. (1986) found that the most serious injuries to children, more serious than abuse alone, occurred in families where abuse and neglect coexisted.

Jonson-Reid et al. (in press) and Marshall and English (1999) raised the issue of comorbidity of maltreatment subtypes in the context of recidivism and CPS practice. The results of these studies indicate that regardless of the initial complaint to CPS, the likeliest reason for additional referrals was child neglect. Thus, it would appear that most cases referred to CPS involve some type of neglect. One conclusion that could be derived from these studies of the comorbidity of abuse and neglect is that *both the most serious physical and psychological harm to children occurs in the presence of child neglect; and most cases referred to CPS involve some form of child neglect.*

Attachment Theory

Attachment theory hypothesizes that faulty attachment between parent and child causes harmful effects for the child (Bousha & Twentyman, 1984; Dean et al., 1986; DiLalla & Crittendon, 1990; Egeland et al., 1983). It is useful, therefore, in understanding outcomes for children to understand the parent, the child, and their interactions. Parent/child attachment is reciprocal in nature. The attachment can be interrupted or disturbed by characteristics of the child, the parent, and/or the context in which they live. Scannapieco and Conneli (2001) suggested that attachment could be disrupted if the infant does not respond in satisfying ways to the parent's behavior. The child might be fussy, unaffectionate, or mentally or physically impaired. The parent could be insensitive and unresponsive to the baby's cues. Living in overcrowded, violent neighborhoods and/or experiencing domestic violence or maltreatment in the home can also lead to the parent and child not engaging in a relationship. It has been found that emotionally neglected children develop the most serious consequences of all maltreatment groups, including suicide attempts and drug overdoses (Rohner, 1986). In his review of the literature, Rutter (1979) found ample evidence that maternal deprivation exerted a harmful influence on a child's psychological development. However, relationships with others also had an effect. Many children were not damaged by deprivation owing to such protective factors as the child's temperament, a positive experience at school, and supportive extended family members.

Dean et al. (1986) found that maltreated children "held two competing pairs of representational models: one in which children attempt to be kind and helpful towards parents, whereas parents are grudging in their affection and attention to children and the other in which parents are above criticism and children are always to blame" (p. 624). Role reversal, whereby the child takes on the parenting function, is one effect of these representational models (Helfer, 1987b).

Children aged 0–3 years. Generally attachment takes place, if at all, during a child's infancy. As indicated above, this is a time when children are at greatest risk. The following studies have included the effects of child neglect in the form of early faulty attachments with primary caretakers. Erickson and Egeland (2002) reported a high incidence of anxious attachment among neglected children. These children lacked enthusiasm, were easily frustrated, were angry and noncompliant, lacked persistence, and were highly dependent on, and at the same time avoidant of and unaffectionate with, their mothers. There was a steep decline in performance on infant development scales as the children grew older. Manly et al. (2001) found that neglected children are more likely to form representative models that indicate their relationships will not meet their needs; and that they are unlovable. They therefore tend to withdraw and to see relationships as not being self-enhancing. Crouch and Milner (1993) also found insecure patterns of infant/caretaker attachments in neglected children, and higher frequencies of avoidant/resistant attachments. Egeland and Sroufe (1981) found that neglected 12-month-olds tended to have an anxious/resistant type of attachment to their mothers, indicating that they received inconsistent care based more on mother's moods than on baby's needs. By 18 months these infants had become either securely attached, indicating a change in circumstances that resulted in more positive caretaking, or resistant (i.e., insecurely attached), indicating they had given up on expecting adequate caretaking and had withdrawn from the maternal relationship. In many cases the difference seemed to be a result of increased stability in the home and the involvement of supportive family members.

Studies indicated that nonorganic growth deficiencies in children (i.e., nonorganic failure to thrive, psychosocial dwarfism, and growth retardation simulating idiopathic hypopituitarism) are also effects of faulty parent/child relationships, including disturbances in father/infant attachment (Alderette & deGraffenried, 1986; Fischler, 1985; Kempe & Goldbloom, 1987; Money & Needleman, 1980; Ohlsson, 1979; Scannapieco & Conneli, 2001; Sweet & Resick, 1979; Tower, 1993). Further research regarding attachment indicates that neglected children engage in fewer positive social interactions than nonneglected children; and, again, were more avoidant of and had poorer attachments to their mothers (Bousha & Twentyman, 1984; DiLalla & Crittendon, 1990; DiLeonardi, 1993; Egeland et al., 1983). They, also, displayed less verbal and nonverbal instruction and fewer social initiations than did nonmaltreated children (Bousha & Twentyman, 1984). Maltreatment seems to upset the balance between young children's security-promoting operations and effectance-promoting operations (Aber & Allen, 1987).

Children over 3 years of age. Erickson and Egeland (2002) found that victims of emotional neglect in infancy, at age 42 months, demonstrated poor impulse control, rigidity, a lack of creativity, and unhappiness. By 52 months they maintained poor impulse control, were highly dependent on their teachers, and had general adjustment problems in the classroom. Problems persisted throughout elementary school including withdrawn and aggressive behaviors, attention disorders, and an unpopular standing with peers.

In an earlier study, Burgess and Conger (1978) found no differences in the way children interacted with their parents for abused, neglected, and comparison families. These results could indicate the need for further refining of research to more clearly examine the relationship between neglect and outcomes for young children.

Neurobiological Development Theory

Based on work of the Child Trauma Academy in Houston, Texas, neurobiological development theory offers a biological explanation for the perceived outcomes of child neglect that occurs in infancy and early childhood. This theory maintains that developmental problems associated with child neglect (discussed earlier in this section) are caused by abnormalities in the brain (Perry, 2002b). Perry and Pollard (1997) found that children experiencing sensory deprivation early in life had markedly less growth in head circumference than comparison children, indicating brain atrophy. Their brain scans also tended to be abnormal. Behavioral outcomes of severe deprivation included primitive emotional, behavioral, and cognitive functioning that was also consistent with cortical atrophy (Perry, 2002b). Accordingly, it was hypothesized that neglect (i.e., deprivation) in early childhood results in abnormal brain development, which in turn leads to developmental disturbances.

The processes by which this occurs include the following concepts (Perry, 2002a, 2002b).

1. *Nature and nurture.* Children's functioning depends on the expression of their unique constellation of genes; and the expression of their genetic potentials depends on their experiences, whether positive or negative. Experience tells the developing brain which genes to activate and which to deactivate and when.

2. *Sequential development.* The brain develops from simpler to more complex structures. As with child development theory, higher-level organization is dependent on the successful development/completion of the previous level. Depending on when neglect takes place, that and subsequent levels of neurodevelopment will be affected.

3. *Use/activity-dependent neurodevelopment.* Potential genetic expression will not take place unless a gene is activated. Since experience determines which genes will be activated, a child's neurodevelopment and future functioning is dependent on the kinds of experience to which the child is exposed.

4. *Windows of opportunity/windows of vulnerability.* Different areas of the brain will be active (i.e., developing/organizing) at different times. The

areas of the brain that are the most sensitive to the effects of experience (e.g., neglect) are those where the most activity is taking place.

The effects of neglect, therefore, depend on (a) the nature, intensity, pattern, and duration of the neglect and (b) timing—when the neglect takes place (i.e., which areas of the brain are most active at the time). The study of these processes to determine the specific effects of maltreatment is called neuroarcheology (Perry, 2002b). The underlying assumption is that the "earlier and more pervasive the neglect is, the more devastating the developmental problems for the child" (Perry, 2002a, p. 89). Evidence to support this supposition is found in studies related to adoption of emotionally neglected children. Children adopted at an earlier age, who spent less time in a toxic environment, do substantially better than older children; who were adopted later in life and, as a result, had been exposed to more deprivation over time (Perry, 2002b).

Perry, Pollard, Blakely, Baker, and Vigilante (1995) indicated that "the human brain exists in its mature form only as a byproduct of genetic potential and environmental history" (p. 275).

> Although experience may alter the behavior of an adult, experience literally provides the organizing framework for an infant and child. Because the brain is most plastic (receptive to environmental input) in early childhood, the child is most vulnerable to variance of experience during this time . . . atypical neural activity during critical and sensitive periods, then, can result in malorganization and compromised function in brain-mediated functions such as humor, empathy, attachment and affect regulation . . . The child who has been emotionally neglected early in life will exhibit profound attachment problems, which are extremely insensitive to any replacement experiences later, including therapy. (Perry et al., 1995, pp. 276–277)

Neurobiological development theory, then, indicates that patterns of experience that are repetitive and consistent allow children to develop a coherent internal representation of the external environment. However, the neglected child's patterns of experience tend to be chaotic and unpredictable. As a result, the neglected child will develop neural systems and functional abilities that reflect the chaos (Perry, 2002b).

Although related to neurobiological development theory, the effects of substance abuse during pregnancy, one type of child neglect, will be addressed in Chapter Nine. Table 2B, based on the forgoing studies of child development, attachment theory, and neurobiological development, summarizes the effects of neglect on children from birth through adolescence in terms of age and physical, cognitive/behavioral, and socioemotional development.

TABLE 2B

Effects of Neglect on Children from Infancy through Adolescence

Age	Physical Development	Cognitive/Behavioral Development	Social/Emotional Development
0–3 years	Significant growth delays	Decreased vocalization	General unresponsiveness, withdrawn and isolated
	Poor muscle tone	Language and intelligence deficits	Difficulty in forming close relationships
	NOFTT	Initially passive, grow more difficult with age	More indiscriminant social relationships
	Brain abnormalities	More behavior problems	Profound attachment problems (e.g., higher frequencies of insecure/anxious, avoidant, and resistant patterns of infant/caretaker attachment)
	Smaller head circumference	More physically aggressive with mother	Unhappy facial expressions, minimal smiling, more negative and less positive affect
	Alterations in neurobiology	Persistent infantile postures	Less affectionate with mother
	Altered physical functioning	Higher levels of active exploration, which is a precursor of ADHD	Deficits in emotional regulation, more easily frustrated
			Deficits in development of empathy
Preschool	Auditory processing deficits	Lowest IQ and achievement scores	Poor development of social skills
		Pervasive developmental delays	Impaired ability to form healthy relationships with adults and peers
		Less creative in approaches to problem-solving tasks	Retreat from relationships, do not see them as self-enhancing
		Continued language deficits	Fewer overtures of affection
		Uninvolved in learning	Less initiation of play behaviors in interactions with mother
		Inattentive	Different style of social interaction with peers
		More passive	Tend to remain isolated in free play
		Poor impulse control	Unpopular with peers
		Withdrawn	Significantly fewer interactions during classroom observations
		Less flexible	Fewer prosocial behaviors
		Less effective coping behavior	
		Aggressive	

			More apathetic, withdrawn, and dependent in social interactions Feelings of being unloved and unwanted More internalizing symptoms: depression, anxiety, affective disorders Increase in self-blaming Internalized negative affect Impaired ability to trust others
School age	Not reported	Continued language and auditory processing deficits Declining functioning Poor school performance Academic delays and difficulties School problems Increase in externalizing symptoms Behavior problems More aggressive More discipline problems Lower ego resilience Higher ego underdevelopment Higher levels of perceived external control More withdrawn Less attentive Less cooperative Lower scores on measures of imitative behavior (i.e., lacks initiative)	Socially withdrawn Continues to be unpopular with peers Continuing emotional problems Continuing internalizing problems Depression
Youth/adolescence	Eating disorders Sexual problems Alcohol/substance abuse	Academic delays and difficulties Continuing IQ and language deficits Delinquent and criminal behavior	Suicidal thoughts Depression Anxiety disorder Higher global scores on a checklist of psychiatric disorders More negative affective states Increased coping difficulties

71

Adults Neglected as Children

Mental and physical illness and emotional problems appear to be related to a history of child neglect. Ney et al. (1994) found that emotional neglect is most closely correlated with psychiatric illness in adulthood. In one study a large percentage of women with chronic mental illness had suffered various forms of child maltreatment, including neglect (Muenzmaier, Meyer, Struening, & Ferber, 1993). Widom (1999) found that 30.6% of the victims of child neglect in her study suffered from lifetime posttraumatic stress disorder (PTSD). These findings indicated that childhood neglect may result in PTSD, but other factors, such as individual and lifestyle characteristics, can also affect this outcome. The results of a study by Higgins and McCabe (2000) of the relationships between different types of maltreatment in childhood and adjustment in adulthood indicated that there is a high degree of comorbidity of types of child maltreatment. They recommended care be taken is ascribing outcomes to a particular maltreatment type.

This caveat notwithstanding, research has indicated that adults neglected as children are at increased risk for lack of hope and trust, anger or depression, emotional numbness, negative attitudes, feelings of isolation and being misunderstood, and character disorders (Cohen et al., 2001; Polansky et al., 1981; Tower, 1993). Health problems for this population include substance abuse and frequent illness (Knudsen, 1992; Tower, 1993).

Social problems also plague this population. Homelessness as an adult and severe poverty have been found to be highly correlated with being neglected as a child (Knudsen, 1992; Muenzmaier et al., 1993). Aggression or delinquent behavior has also been found to be associated with childhood neglect (Tower, 1993). In one prospective study, Widom (1989) found that adults abused or neglected as children commit violent crimes at higher rates than adults not neglected as children. Again, the majority of the neglected group did not participate in criminal behavior, indicating that adult criminality *might* be caused by childhood maltreatment or might be the result of childhood maltreatment combined with other factors.

One of the most striking outcomes of a neglected childhood is a lack of competency in many life skills and personal abilities, reflecting characteristics of neglecting parents; and supporting theory regarding the intergenerational transfer of neglecting behaviors. DiLeonardi (1993) and Polansky et al. (1981) found that adults neglected as children were unprepared to be adequate parents and/or productive workers. They have problems living independently, troubles with achievement and overwhelming dependency needs (Knudsen, 1992; Polansky et al., 1981; Thomlison, 1997; Tower, 1993). Other characteristics, also reminiscent of neglectful parents, include inability to make decisions, extremely low self-esteem, inability to accept one's own accomplishments, self-defeating behavior, impaired social skills, impaired ability to play or to enjoy even simple pleasures, impulsive behavior, irresponsibility, communication problems, lowered intellectual abilities, and relationship difficulties (Knudsen, 1992; Ney et al., 1992; Tower, 1993). These findings are not inconsistent with the findings of Perry (2002a, 2002b) regarding the areas of children's brains at risk from neglectful parental behavior. Similar outcomes have been predicted by neurobiological development theory. It seems that being neglected as a child has pervasive effects on one's sense of self and one's place in the world, and leaves one at high risk for becoming a neglectful parent.

Resilient Children

However, not all children who have been inadequately parented have negative outcomes; and the effects of neglect on some children appear to be negligible. In an attempt to explain the apparent resiliency of some children, Werner and Smith (1982) developed a model of interrelations among risk, stress, sources of support, and coping in children. This model, based on data from the Kaua'i Longitudinal Study (Werner & Smith, 1982), identifies factors at birth (e.g., chronic poverty, uneducated mother, perinatal complications, developmental problems, genetic abnormalities, and parental psychopathology) that place children at risk for maladaptive adjustments as they grow and develop. As can be seen, these risk factors are also highly correlated with child neglect. Thus, as has been amply demonstrated in the forgoing sections, neglected children are at risk for negative outcomes. Indeed—in terms of resiliency—McGloin and Widom (2001) found that neglect in childhood was a significant negative predictor of resilience. The effect of risk factors in a child's life seems to be more exponential than additive (Kirby & Fraser, 1997); and neglectful families have been shown to have multiple problems.

Werner and Smith (1982) found that the likelihood of negative outcomes for vulnerable children was affected by sources of stress, sources of support, and protective factors within the children (e.g., their coping strategies). The fewer the risk factors/stressful events and the more protective factors within the children and the caregiving environment, the more likely the children were to have adaptive developmental outcomes.

To gain a greater understanding of the contributions of risk and protective factors to child well-being, Murry and Brody (1999) studied those processes in economically stressed, rural, single-parent Black families that are linked with positive developmental outcomes for their children. They found that children's risk factors (e.g., those associated with difficult temperament) had a greater impact on self-regulation than either familial or material risk factors. However, children's self-worth was associated with parental risk factors (e.g., mother's neuroticism). Parent satisfaction had the greatest effect on buffering the impact of risk factors on children's sense of self. The conclusion was that parents who felt satisfied were able to protect their children from the risk factors of growing up in poverty.

Kirby and Fraser (1997) indicated that risk is based on probabilities. Some children who are exposed to a high level of risk (i.e., neglected children) manage to overcome the odds. The presence of protective factors in their lives may account for the apparent lack of effects of neglect in children who have been inadequately parented. These children are called resilient.

Effects of Poverty on Children

One critical issue regarding the effects of neglect model is the similarity of the effects of neglect to the effects of poverty. Neglect is closely related to poverty, which also has a major influence on outcomes for children (Garbarino, 1999; Schorr, 1988). Differentiating the effects of neglect from the effects of poverty, when most neglected children are living in poverty and both similarly affect children, is difficult at best. A further discussion of this issue is found in Chapter Ten. An analysis of the forgoing models of child neglect is presented in Chapter Four. Implications for research, policy, and practice are then put forward.

What Causes Child Neglect?

AN ANALYSIS
OF CAUSAL MODELS

Chapter Three explored four basic theoretical ways of looking at child neglect, including its causes and consequences. The *parental deficiencies model*, generated by psychoanalytic theory, suggests that there are specific parent and familial attributes that account for the differences between families who neglect their children and those who do not. These characteristics, considered to be causal, are passed from parent to child, and thus perpetuate neglectful behavior across generations of families. Interventions are, therefore, aimed at the remediation of these attributes and breaking the intergenerational cycle of neglect. Demographic variables are considered neither necessary nor sufficient to explain why families maltreat their children and, while not ignored, are accorded a secondary role.

Using social psychology theory, the *social-cultural-situational environment model* asserts that deficiencies in the social, cultural, and situational environment are the primary causes of child neglect. Parental deficits are recognized as secondary in nature or are, themselves, results of the deficient environment. Interventions are both functional and structural, with the goal of improving the environments in which families live.

The *interactional model*, including theory regarding ecology and transaction, proposes that both parental and environmental characteristics and the interplay between them are essential in explaining and predicting child neglect. Characteristics can be both potentiating (harmful) or protective (beneficial) and enduring (chronic) or temporary (acute). Neglect occurs when the potentiating factors outweigh the protective factors. Interventions are, therefore, aimed at remediating potentiating factors and strengthening protective factors.

Based on child development, attachment, and neurobiological development theory, the *effects of neglect on children model* proposes that the neglectful behavior of their parents is harmful to children and results in negative outcomes. Interventions are geared to preventing this harm by remediating parental behavior and treating the effects of neglect by providing services for the child.

Tzeng and Jackson (1991) suggested seven criteria to evaluate the quality and utility of theory development including (a) formalization and coherence, (b) integration and comprehensiveness, (c) parsimoniousness, (d) falsifiability and testability, (e) applicability of empirical data, (f) fruitfulness, and (g) scientific self-regulation. Using Tzeng and Jackson's (1991) criteria, Chapter Four will analyze each of the four basic theories associated with child neglect in terms of their quality and usefulness (see Table 3). After the discussion regarding each of the four models, the current state of theory related to child neglect and its implications for future research, policy, and practice will be addressed.

ANALYSIS OF CHILD NEGLECT THEORY

Formalization and Coherence

Formalization and coherence is the extent to which the relationships in the theory are clear and its statements and variables are explicitly defined and consistently used. As indicated in Chapter Two, definitions associated with child neglect are problematic. As a result, the definition of child neglect is not clear and consistent across studies; and this poses a considerable problem for all four models. In terms of the *parental deficiencies model* familial characteristics also are not clearly defined or consistent. The processes by which the parental characteristics cause parents to neglect their children are not explicit and, thus, this model is informal and lacks coherency.

The *environmental deficiencies model* has difficulty clarifying the distinctions between ethnicity and SES (Garbarino & Ebata, 1983). However, because factors included in this model are external to the family, they may be more easily quantified and operationalized; and, therefore, may be better and more consistently defined than the familial factors of the parental deficiency model. This point notwithstanding, definitional issues regarding constructs such as social support, high-risk neighborhoods, and culture remain unresolved across studies. In a review of the literature regarding social support/social isolation as a factor in child maltreatment, Seagull

(1987) found that for neglecting families social isolation is better defined as a parental deficiency than as an environmental factor; that is, it is parental behavior that causes neighbors to distance themselves from neglectful families. Therefore, social isolation may be caused by parental inadequacies and not vice versa, as this model proposes.

Except in the case of social isolation, this model does not explain the processes by which environmental characteristics cause child neglect. It is a little more formal than the parental deficiencies model in that some of its constructs (e.g., SES) are fairly well defined and used fairly consistently throughout the empirical literature. However, the environmental deficiencies model remains descriptive in nature, is relatively informal, and lacks coherency.

In using many of the same concepts and variables of the previous two models, the *interactional model* shares their definitional and conceptual problems. However, this model is more formal, in that it introduces multiple causation to the concept of child neglect; and the nature of the interaction processes that link cause with effect are more clearly defined. Although the interactional model remains primarily correlational and descriptive, it is advanced in a more formalized manner and presents a more coherent theoretical framework.

In addition to the definitional and conceptual problems associated with previously reported models, the *effects of neglect model* is confronted with the fact that most empirical studies examine the effects of child *maltreatment* on child development, and thus effects of neglect are not separated from effects of other forms of maltreatment. Paget et al. (1993) indicated that the use of heterogeneous groups of the broad category of child maltreatment makes it difficult to extract implications for neglected children.

Definitions and concepts taken from child development, attachment, and neurobiological development theory are clearer and more consistently used owing to the longer length of time they have been operational. They have been refined over time, and their use has gained much acceptance in the research community. The relationships between variables and the processes by which effects are obtained are based on fairly well-grounded theory (i.e., child development, attachment, and neurobiological development). These formalized frameworks are employed to explain effects of neglect on children. Thus, relationships between variables are more clearly delineated in this model; and the processes by which child neglect results in various outcomes for children are more clearly defined.

However, there is a problem of confusing cause and effect (i.e., is the phenomenon under study the cause or effect of child neglect?). "Conclusive demonstration of child maltreatment sequelae requires premaltreatment knowledge of the vicitms' characteristics. Some of what are seen as effects of maltreatment may have been preexisting behavior or temperament that contributes to vulnerability to maltreatment" (Prino & Peyrot, 1993, p. 882). Knutson (1995) pointed out that health and developmental status, and characteristics of children "may reflect either antecedents or consequences of abuse" (p. 414). Therefore, causes become mistaken for effects and vice versa, and the elements of this model are not consistent.

One central difference between this model and the previous models is the nature of the factors involved. In previous models child neglect has been the outcome of the theory. In this model it is the causal factor in the theory, with the outcome being harm to the child. This model has a more formalized and consistent theoretical framework than do the previous three theories. However, the problem of confusing causes and effects remains to be examined.

Integration and Comprehensiveness

Integration and comprehensiveness refer to the breadth of a theory and the number and integration of ecological phenomena for which it seeks to account. In this regard the parental deficiencies model, the environmental deficiencies model, and the effects of neglect model are one-dimensional as they propose a single causal factor (i.e., family characteristics, environmental characteristics, or child neglect) and wish to account for a single phenomenon—child neglect or harm to children.

In regard to the *parental deficiencies model*, Wolock and Horowitz (1979) suggested that the ability to predict child maltreatment increases as environmental and social factors are added to intrapersonal factors. Polansky et al. (1981) agreed that both traits and social situations must be considered in research related to families who neglect their children. In terms of child factors as determinants of child neglect, owing to the retrospective nature of most empirical studies of child neglect, it is difficult to determine whether some child characteristics are cause or effect.

While the parental deficiencies model does not give enough weight to ecological factors in the causation of child neglect, the reverse is true for the *environmental deficiencies model*. Polansky, Ammons, et al. (1985) suggested that the character structure of the neglecting parent remains a powerful factor in the etiology of neglect; and Seagull (1987) found that "personality factors in the parents emerged strongly from this research as a major determinant of the social environment of the family" (p. 48). Polansky, Gaudin, et al. (1985) suggested it is the psychological ecology of the neglecting parent that causes the situation in which neglect occurs. Gaudin et al. (1993) found significant differences between neglecting and nonneglecting poor families, supporting what Young (1964) had stated almost thirty years previously: "Class per se cannot explain why there are families like these, it can, however define the circumstances in which they could develop" (p. 81).

Research has demonstrated that low-income control mothers were more appropriate with respect to personality and maternal perception variables than low-income neglectful mothers (Friedrich et al., 1985); however, *most families living in poverty do not neglect their children* (Gaudin et al., 1993; Halpern, 1990; Young, 1964). Many wealthy families do (Cantwell & Rosenberg, 1990). Therefore, poverty, in and of itself, is not a sufficient explanation of neglect. However, it must be remembered that, while most poor families do not neglect their children, most neglectful families are poor.

In terms of impoverished neighborhoods, rather than impoverished families, Polansky, Ammons, et al. (1985) found that neighborhoods of neglecting families and those of comparison families were similar in terms of indicators of impoverishment (i.e., socioeconomic status of neighbors, average number of children and adults in nearby households, stability of residence, availability of instrumental and affective support, and quality of life). Contrary findings are implied by Trocme et al. (1995) when they wrote, "The association of high rates of poverty, community dislocation, and high rates of child maltreatment can mean either that these stressors put families at high-risk of maltreatment, or that maltreating families are likely to congregate in these neighborhoods" (p. 584).

The mechanism by which environmental conditions cause neglect has been explored in terms of behavior and social learning theory (Garbarino, 1981; Salzinger et al., 1983). Thus, some attempts have been made to establish causal links. However, Giovannoni and Billingsley (1974) suggested that poverty may increase stress in the family beyond the parents' capacity to cope and neglect occurs, the implication being that it is the interaction between the environmental situation (poverty) and parental attribute (stress) mediated by parents' coping abilities, and not the condition of poverty, that causes the neglect of children. While it does take a deeper look at causal mechanisms involved than does the parental deficiencies model, the environmental deficiencies model is too narrow to account for the phenomenon of child neglect.

Knudsen (1992) and Rohner (1986) proposed that any single causation model of neglect is not sufficient to predict or explain this phenomenon. Belsky (1993) went even further by suggesting that there is apparently no single cause of child neglect, and neither are there *any* necessary or sufficient causes.

In terms of the *effects of neglect* on children, this model does not take into consideration environmental factors other than child neglect that might result in harm to children; and thus, it too, lacks in comprehensiveness. It is too narrow to either predict or explain the effect child neglect has on children. This model does explore empirical phenomena, including neurobiology, in order to establish causal links between parental behavior and child development outcomes. But until the problems of confusing cause with effect, and accounting for the effects of additional factors that affect child outcomes, are resolved, the findings of this model are not well integrated and must remain descriptive, not predictive in nature.

It is clear that both the parental and environment deficiencies models are too exclusive as they ignore the multicausal nature of the problem of child neglect. Additionally, many nonneglecting families have characteristics and live in environments similar to neglecting families. Thus, the level of ecological phenomena these models include is too low to account for differences between these families. Parental and environmental deficits may be necessary, but neither is sufficient to predict with any accuracy which families will or will not neglect their children. In terms of child factors, owing to the retrospective nature of most empirical studies of child neglect, it is impossible to determine whether child characteristics are cause or effect. As a result, all three of these models are too narrow and do not provide for integration of many significant factors.

The *interactional model* is more comprehensive and better integrated than the three previously discussed models. It is multidimensional and includes more phenomena in the hypotheses. In introducing interaction to the causal pathways, this model increases the examination of the etiological links between child neglect and possible causes. However, this model is still based on empirical studies that are primarily retrospective and correlational in nature. Hypotheses, therefore, are inferential and, for this reason, are without predictive or explanatory power. However, the studies examining the interactions between person and environment are more complex and use multivariate analysis techniques resulting in an increase in accounted-for differences between study subjects.

Many of these studies, nevertheless, focus on child maltreatment, not on neglect as a distinct type of child maltreatment. Thus, some studies utilizing this model are too inclusive in terms of accounting for child neglect per se. The *interactional model*, however, is more comprehensive, coherent, and integrative than previously discussed models, although it may be somewhat lacking in specificity in terms of types of child maltreatment for the purposes of predicting and explaining child neglect.

Parsimony

Parsimony, or the principle of simplicity, is the extent to which a theory can make accurate predictions from the fewest assumptions and simplest propositions. The *parental deficiencies, environmental deficiencies,* and *effects of neglect models* are relatively simple (i.e., single causal and outcome factors), apparently meeting the criterion of parsimony. The issue is: they may be too simplistic in that they do not take into account variables that might add significantly to their predictability. As it stands, familial and environmental characteristics may be used to assess risk of neglect. However, they may not be used to predict neglect or specific outcomes for children with any degree of accuracy. Additionally, even though the frameworks of developmental theory, attachment theory, and neurobiological theory are relatively formal and complex, as applied to child neglect they may be too simplistic. Parental behavior is sufficient neither to predict what is likely to be the specific outcome for a particular victim of neglect nor to explain why a particular outcome occurred as the result of inadequate parental care, although neurobiological development theory is moving in that direction.

The *interactional model* is more complex than the parental and environmental deficiencies, and the effects of neglect models. However, its constructs remain relatively simple and rectify some of the problems of previous theory. The interactional model resolves the gaps in previous theories due to the exclusion of either familial or environmental factors. The only construct that may not be necessary to the model, and, therefore, breaks the rule of parsimony, is the evolutionary theory introduced by Belsky (1993). Belsky (1993) argued that inclusion of evolutionary theory allows for prediction of child neglect under various conditions of resource deprivation. Studies, however, have indicated that neglect is associated with such resource deprivations as lack of education and employment without resorting to a biological explanation. Resource deprivation also results when family resources are stretched, which is the case in neglecting families with single mothers/absent fathers and several children.

This biological approach, claimed Belsky (1993), also could explain findings regarding handicapped children's higher risk for maltreatment (i.e., the handicapped child is a drain on resources and is less valuable reproductively, therefore subject to neglect). However, parental deficits and/or the effects of stress on the coping mechanisms of parents can explain these conditions of child neglect. Therefore, biological imperatives are not needed to explain the phenomena under study. The law of parsimony argues for dropping sociobiological and/or evolutionary theory from the interactional model of child neglect. Belsky (1993) argued that evolutionary theory is useful in drawing attention to the risks associated with rearing children under conditions of limited social and economic resources and to issues of fertility. In this manner, it complements, if doesn't add, to psychological and sociological explanations of child neglect.

Falsifiability and Testability

The criteria of falsifiability and testability relate to the extent to which a theory can be tested or its tenets shown to be false. All four models are based on empirical research that is primarily descriptive, retrospective, and correlational in nature. Proposed causal relationships are, therefore, inferences, and must remain hypothetical (i.e., they cannot be tested or demonstrated to be false) (Sweet & Resick, 1979). For example, Murphy et al. (1991) and Kelleher et al. (1994) indicated that studies showing a relationship between child maltreatment and substance abuse do not prove or disprove a *causal* relationship. Therefore, the hypothesis that substance abuse causes child neglect cannot be tested or falsified. Thus, all four models are weak in the area of possible falsifiability and testability.

Applicability of Empirical Data

The applicability of empirical data or accuracy of a theory relates to the validity, reliability, and success of the theory's predictions, explanations, and understandings. All four models are primarily descriptive based on empirical evidence that was obtained retrospectively. Thus, the variables investigated are correlates of child neglect (whether hypothesized as cause or effect) and a causal relationship between variables has not been established.

In regard to the *parental deficiencies model*, the findings regarding familial characteristics are inconsistent and at times are contradictory. This model is not able to explain why some families abuse and some neglect; or why, given similar families, some maltreat and others do not (Hillson & Kuiper, 1994). In terms of the hypothesis regarding the intergenerational nature of child neglect, most parents maltreated as children do not maltreat their children (Belsky, 1993; Widom, 1989), and many parents who were not maltreated as children do (Wolock & Horowitz, 1979).

Based on a medical/psychological paradigm, this model promised to provide a profile of the neglectful parent, which would serve as a predictor of child neglect and the basis for diagnosis and subsequent treatment (Hillson & Kuiper, 1994). The inconsistencies in the findings regarding risk characteristics suggest that researchers have not been able to establish a consistent psychological profile of the neglecting parent. Thus, the proposed neglect profile is nonexistent and cannot be used to predict which families will neglect and which families will not. Therefore, the parental deficiencies model does not appear to have either predictive or explanatory power. It does not do what it claims to do and, consequently, it also lacks functional validity. Based on the foregoing it would appear that this model does not meet the criterion for applicability and accuracy.

The *environmental deficiencies model* does not explain the mechanisms that tie environmental deficiencies to the incidence of child neglect, and thus, these mechanisms remain unknown (Krishman & Morrison, 1995; Trocme et al., 1995). This model, therefore, cannot explain why families in similar situations maltreat and others do not. In addition, there are inconsistencies across studies in terms of findings and even nonsignificant findings may be inaccurate. Belsky (1993) suggested that researchers in this field are seeking contributing rather than determining factors. Thus, even if there are no significant findings it could mean the variable under study has no direct effect, but might have an interaction or indirect effect when combined with other variables. In terms of the multideterminant nature of child neglect, this is highly likely to be the case. As it stands, environmental characteristics may not be used with any accuracy to either predict or explain child neglect. In addition, the environmental deficiencies model lacks functional validity in that it fails to predict which parents are likely to neglect their children or explain why they do.

In regard to the *interactional model,* Sweet and Resick (1979) indicated that the integrative approach probably is the best model, but it cannot be applied to the prediction of individual behavior. There are inconsistent findings across studies, and while the interactional model includes multiple dimensions it lacks explanatory power. For example, Belsky's model does not specify whether disturbances in one system or multiple systems are necessary for maltreatment to occur; and the stress-and-coping model does not explain why some highly stressed parents abuse, neglect, or do not maltreat their children.

The *effects of neglect model* has no predictive or explanatory value in terms of child neglect as it focuses on consequences, not antecedents. In addition, it has little predictive or explanatory value in terms of the specific sequelae of child neglect. As Knutson (1995) pointed out, specific neglect-outcome patterns are not apparent and some children seem to have no unfavorable outcomes. These more positive outcomes may be related to child resiliency or environmental buffers; however, this theoretical model does not explain why some children experience no apparent harm from inadequate parenting. Perry and Pollard (1997) indicated that "while the actual size of the brain of the chaotically neglected children did not appear to be different from norms, it is reasonable to hypothesize that organizational abnormalities exist" (i.e., the children must have been harmed, we just can't see it yet) (p. 5). Neuroarcheology may be heading in a direction that will eventually result in the ability to predict specific outcomes; however, that remains in the future.

In the meantime, Knudsen (1992) indicated that the general social context within which neglect takes place makes it difficult to ascribe a cause-effect relationship between specific neglecting behaviors and specific effects as, for example, there is little distinction between the impact of neglect and the impact of poverty (see Chapter Ten). Thus, the applicability and accuracy of this model is equivocal.

Fruitfulness

Fruitfulness refers to a theory's ability to stimulate further research. The value of all of the models related to child neglect lie not so much in their predictive ability, but in their ability to generate causal hypotheses from the found associations between variables under study (Turner & Avison, 1985). They also serve to remind one of the complexity (i.e., the number and variety of factors) and intractability (due possibly to the severity and compounding effects of familial and environmental characteristics) of the problem (Feldman, 1982). The *parental and environmental deficiencies models* have been quite fruitful, in that they have led to the development of the *interactional model*. This model is still in the process of development and is continuing to be refined and expanded by researchers in the field. Thus, it continues to be fruitful in generating new research.

Child development theory, including neurobiological development and attachment theory, have combined to explore the possible ways child neglect affects children. In terms of this perspective, fueling further research in the field of child maltreatment, the *effects of neglect on children model* has been and continues to be very fruitful. There is value in this theoretical approach in the kinds of issues it raises in regard to determining the relationships between parent behavior and child outcomes.

Scientific Self-Regulation

Scientific self-regulation consists of methodological issues such as the use of control groups, provision of empirical evidence to support the theory (i.e., verification), hypothesis testing, objectivity, and replicability. Research into the etiology of child neglect is fraught with methodological issues. Owing to the retrospective nature of most empirical studies, comparison groups, not control groups, are used. These comparison groups are not randomly selected, and differences between the groups could be the result of group composition rather than the effect of the factors being tested.

Most studies are based on self-selected and self-reporting sample populations that are drawn from known child neglectors or maltreaters. Thus, sampling bias is another source of error (Feldman, 1982; Saunders et al., 1993). Self-reported information was generally gathered by interview and/ or questionnaires and was not validated with observational data (Paget et al., 1993). Measurement issues of validity and reliability of measures and coding procedures also create problems in meeting the criterion of scientific self-regulation (Feldman, 1982; Seagull, 1987).

Then there are difficulties with conceptualizing and operationalizing definitions of variables, especially child neglect; controlling for the effects of extraneous, unmeasured, and unknown factors; and small sample sizes. No empirical studies have been done that include upper-middle-class and upper-class families in their sampling populations; thus, results regarding environmental aspects may be biased (Paget et al., 1993).

A methodological strength of many studies using the *environmental deficiencies model* lies in the fact that neighborhoods and communities are the focus of investigations. As a result, sample sizes are usually large, increasing statistical power for these studies. However, ethnic minorities are overrepresented among the poor with the result that a weakness of this model is the confounding of culture with poverty (Korbin & Spilsbury, 1999).

The *effects of neglect model* results in outcomes for neglected children that are confused with: (a) the antecedents of neglect, (b) the effects of poverty, and (c) the effects of the children's personal biology, irrespective of neglectful experiences. Some prospective studies have been done; however, sampling bias is an issue, as randomly selected groups have not been used in this research. The prospective studies also have the problem of confounding causes with effects (Prino & Peyrot, 1993).

Summary

The analysis of the theoretical models regarding child neglect indicates that the parental deficiencies model does not meet the following criteria for quality and utility: (a) formalization and coherence, (b) integration and comprehensiveness, (c) falsifiability and testability, (d) applicability of empirical data, and (e) scientific self-regulation. It does, however, meet the standards for parsimony and fruitfulness. The same is true for the environmental deficiencies and the effect of neglect on children models. The interactional model rates higher, and, indeed, is the best model to date. It meets the standards of formalization and coherence, integration and comprehensiveness, parsimony, and fruitfulness. It does not measure up to the criteria of applicability of empirical data and scientific self-regulation.

The state of theory building regarding child neglect is still in its infancy. Theoretical models are based on data that are generally retrospective, descriptive, and correlational, and fail to establish the causal links

TABLE 3

Analysis of Causal Models Related to Child Neglect

	Parental Deficiencies	Environmental Deficiencies	Interactional	Effects of Neglect
Formalization and Coherence	Below Standard: Is informal and lacks coherence—definitions are not consistent, is primarily descriptive (i.e., theoretical processes are not explicit), studies are retrospective and correlational	Below Standard: Is more formal than parental deficiencies model, but remains relatively informal and lacks coherence—environmental variables are more easily operationalized and quantified; has problems making a distinction between SES and ethnicity and conceptualizing social isolation; uses theory regarding social support to make processes more explicit; however, is primarily descriptive and, with the exception of social isolation, theoretical processes are not explicit; studies are retrospective and correlational	Meets Standard: More formal and coherent than previous models—shares definitional issues with previous models; however, it introduces multiple causation and the nature of the processes is more clearly defined; remains descriptive and correlational, but presents a more formal and coherent theoretical framework	Below Standard: More formalized and coherent than previous models—however, confuses cause and effect; and fails to separate the effects of neglect from either the effects of other forms of child maltreatment or other factors in the child's environment; fewer definitional issues than previous models as uses concepts from established theory; relationships between variables are more clearly defined and processes are more explicit

Integration and Comprehensiveness	Below Standard: Is too narrow and lacks integration and compre-hensiveness—one-dimensional, parental deficiencies are not sufficient to predict neglect	Below Standard: Is more integrated than parental deficiencies model, but remains relatively unintegrated and lacks comprehensiveness—is also one-dimensional and environmental deficiencies are not sufficient to predict child neglect; does try to establish causal links by using behavior and social learning theory	Meets Standard: More comprehensive and integrated—includes multiple factors; increased examination of etiological links; more complex and uses multivariate analysis techniques, which increase accounted for variance; may lack specificity regarding child neglect; studies remain retrospec-tive, descriptive, and correlational; results are inferences without predictive power	Below Standard: Is too narrow and lacks integration and comprehensiveness—one-dimensional; is better integrated as is well grounded in established theory; however, has a serious issue of confusing cause and effect; examines empirical phenom-ena, but descriptions are not yet sufficient to predict outcomes
Parsimony	Meets Standard: A relatively simple model (perhaps too simple)	Meets Standard: A relativity simple model (perhaps too simple)	Meets Standard: Constructs remain simple—a more complex model, gaps in previous models resolved, perhaps can eliminate evolution theory as it does not add to the model	Meets Standard: A relativity simple model
Falsifiability and testability	Below Standard: Cannot be falsified/tested—studies are descriptive, retrospective, and correlational; causal relationships are inferences	Below Standard: Cannot be falsified/tested—studies are descriptive, retrospective, and correlational; causal relationships are inferences	Below Standard: Cannot be falsified/tested—studies are descriptive, retrospective, and correlational; causal relationships are inferences	Below Standard: Cannot be falsified/tested—most studies are descriptive, retrospective, and correlational; causal relationships are inferences

(Continued)

TABLE 3
Continued

	Parental Deficiencies	Environmental Deficiencies	Interactional	Effects of Neglect
Applicability of Empirical Data	Below Standard: Cannot generalize findings and lacks functional validity—variables are correlations of child neglect, causal links are not established, fails to predict child neglect, findings are inconsistent and at times contradictory across studies, fails to produce the promised profile of the neglectful parent	Below Standard: Cannot generalize findings and lacks functional validity—variables are correlations of child neglect, causal links are not established, fails to predict child neglect, findings are inconsistent and at times contradictory across studies, does not explain ties between child neglect and environmental deficiencies, does not explore possible interactions	Below Standard: Cannot generalize findings—fails to make predictions regarding individual behaviors and outcomes; integrative approach; the best overall model	Below Standard: Cannot generalize findings—neuroarcheology, in the future, may contribute to the ability to make predictable outcomes; at present the applicability of the model's findings is equivocal
Fruitfulness	Meets Standard: Has generated a considerable amount of research and has contributed to the development of more complex and integrated theory	Meets Standard: Has generated a considerable amount of research and contributed to the development of more complex and integrated theory	Meets Standard: Has generated a considerable amount of research and contributed to the development of more complex and integrated theory	Meets Standard: Has generated a considerable amount of research and contributed to the development of more complex and integrated theory

Scientific Self-Regulation	Below Standard: Methodological issues include: retrospective nature of studies; use of comparison, not control groups; nonrandom samples (i.e., are generally self-selected); inconsistent measures and self-report data; small sample sizes; lack of control of extraneous variables	Below Standard: Methodological issues include: retrospective nature of studies; use of comparison, not control groups; nonrandom samples (i.e., are generally self-selected); inconsistent measures and self-report data; tendency to confound poverty and ethnicity; lack of control of extraneous variables; still, as the unit of measurement is the neighborhood, sample sizes may not be an issue for this model	Below Standard: Methodological issues include: retrospective nature of studies; use of comparison, not control groups; nonrandom samples (i.e., are generally self-selected); inconsistent measures and self-report data; small sample sizes; lack of control of extraneous variables	Below Standard: Methodological issues include: retrospective nature of most studies, although useful prospective studies have been done; use of comparison, not control groups; nonrandom samples (i.e., are generally self-selected); inconsistent measures and self-report data; small sample sizes; lack of control of extraneous variables

among variables under study. Although research has been conducted into this form of child maltreatment for at least the last thirty years, it is sparse when compared to research examining child abuse and child sexual abuse. Therefore, there is a lack of a secure empirical platform upon which policy and intervention can be based. The next section of this chapter focuses on the implications of theory regarding the etiology and outcomes of child neglect for research initiatives, policy planning, and development of effective interventions.

IMPLICATIONS OF THEORETICAL ISSUES AND ANALYSIS OF CAUSAL MODELS

The four causal models regarding child neglect discussed in Chapters Three and Four are:

1. The parental deficiencies model that postulates there are specific parent and familial characteristics that account for the differences between families who neglect their children and those who do not. These characteristics, considered to be causes of child neglect, are passed from parent to child, and thus, perpetuate neglectful behavior across the generations.

2. The deficiencies in the social-cultural-situational environment model that theorizes inadequacies in the social, cultural, and situational environment are the primary causes of child neglect.

3. Combining hypotheses from the parental and environmental deficiencies models, interactional models propose that both parental and environmental characteristics and their interactions are essential in explaining and predicting child neglect. Characteristics can be both potentiating (harmful) or protective (beneficial) and enduring (chronic) or temporary (acute). Neglect occurs when the potentiating factors outweigh the protective factors.

4. Based on child development, attachment theory, and neurobiological theory, the effects of neglect on children model speculates that the neglectful behavior of their parents causes harmful effects to children, with the existence of neglect determined largely in terms of whether there are actually harmful effects exhibited by the child.

Findings from research in the field of child neglect indicate that, in general, neglecting parents are undereducated, helpless, hopeless, withdrawn, impulsive single women who seem incompetent and unable to work toward a goal. They seem to be distant from their children, and lack knowledge and skills relevant to good parenting. Neglecting families have more children and more problems, including substance abuse, than nonneglecting families; and live in impoverished environments. While sometimes inconsistent and failing to provide a "neglect profile," the findings provide stark evidence of the multiple problems that are encountered by these families. Theorists in the field hypothesize that these problems, combined with a lack of resources, both personal and structural, to deal with them, cause parents to neglect their children.

The evidence from empirical research is also equivocal regarding the characteristics of neglected children. There is a question of whether the found characteristics are related to neglect, or are the results of other factors. If these characteristics are related to neglect, there remain the questions regarding the nature of the relationship. Are they cause or effect? Are they the direct result of neglectful behaviors or the result of the interaction of neglect with other factors? Answers are not easily available.

Implications for Research

Design. Causal models regarding child neglect have a considerable number of difficulties in design and methodology. In terms of overall research design, most studies are retrospective rather than prospective and their findings are descriptive and correlational rather than causal. Therefore, they do not address the processes by which characteristics lead to neglect (Ammerman, 1990; Belsky, 1993; Crouch & Milner, 1993; Feldman, 1982; Sweet & Resick, 1979). This makes it difficult to support or reject any of the models. Hillson and Kuiper (1994) recommend going beyond description to developing explanatory, process-oriented models that would be tested a priori in proscriptive rather than retrospective studies. Socolar et al. (1995) pointed out the lack of longitudinal studies, and suggested the need for ethical guidelines in terms of informed consent, confidentiality, and reporting laws.

Most studies look at one variable at a time and seek contributing rather than determining factors; thus they are focusing primarily on the direct effects of child neglect. If there is more than one variable, interactions among model components are not explored. Such studies take the risk of finding no direct effects, and miss the possibility of finding intervening variables and/or effects that are the results of interactions among the variables under study (Belsky, 1993; McCubbin et al., 1995). It is recommended that interactions of the model components be included in future research designs.

Focusing on group differences and the identification of deficits, most studies regarding child neglect fail to take into account that "many families living under conditions of social stress and individual limitations similar to those of maltreating families do not maltreat their children, and many maltreated children display no overt problems" (Howing, Wodarski, Kurtz, & Gaudin, 1989, p. 4). Studies often proceed without clear or consistent definitions, without a priori predictions to test theoretical relationships, and without a single theoretical model to hypothesize those relationships (Belsky, 1993; Howing, Wodarski, Kurtz, & Gaudin, 1989; Nelson et al., 1990). Thus, as Belsky states, studies regarding child neglect are "little more than empirical fishing expeditions" (p. 414).

Maltreating families are not homogeneous. Studies have shown that abuse and neglect have fundamentally different effects (Perry, 2002b; Prino & Peyrot, 1993) and, thus, need to be studied as separate variables (Crouch & Milner, 1993). Paget et al. (1993) recommended studies to compare correlates across abuse and neglect groups. Research focused on conceptualizing and measuring a wide range of maltreatment subtypes, to include etiologies and consequences of the subtypes; and differentiating between types of child maltreatment would assist in the development of explanatory models for neglect, separate from abuse; and set the stage for a separate theory of child neglect. This position argues in favor of more studies that (a) focus on neglect and the circumstances in families that affect its occurrence, (b) investigate families who are functioning well to determine differences between them and neglectful families, and (c) differentiate neglectful families from various other types of maltreating families (Friedrich et al., 1985; Martin & Walters, 1982). Manly et al. (2001) recommended collecting operationally defined information from multiple sources that describe children's maltreatment experiences during each stage of development.

One of the problems in developing a separate model for neglect is the comorbidity of types of maltreatment, especially physical abuse and neglect (Zuravin, 1991). Therefore, research to explore the nature and conditions of comorbidity and the conditions that give rise to it would be useful in the evolution of a body of theory focused on child neglect. In order to achieve these ends, when studying neglect, researchers could also assess for other types of maltreatment. Jonson-Reid et al. (in press) suggested, at the very least, other maltreatment types could be used as control variables in multivariate analysis. Within the neglect population, Crouch and Milner (1993) suggested the use of classification systems that organize subtypes of neglect in a developmentally sensitive manner. They also point to the need to study the severity of neglect and racial and gender differences.

It is clear that the development of invariant, unambiguous, and conceptually clear theories of child neglect that delineate causal connections between proposed causes and negligent behavior (i.e., go beyond description to develop explanatory, process-oriented models) is an appropriate goal of future research in this field. Hypotheses developed from these models and tested a priori in prospective studies would be useful in the development of theory, policy, and interventions.

Methodology. In addition to research design issues, there are methodological issues of definition, measurement, control, and sampling (Crouch & Milner, 1993; Howing, Wodarski, Kurtz, & Gaudin, 1989; Nelson et al., 1990; Socolar et al., 1995). As was made apparent in Chapter Two, definitions of child neglect are not consistent across studies. In addition, the failure to differentiate maltreatment by type leads to confusion and contradictory findings. Subtypes of maltreatment coexist and occur with other potentiating factors confounding the search for the separate effects of neglect (Bath & Haapala, 1992; Howing, Wodarski, Kurtz, & Gaudin, 1989). The Child Neglect Index (Trocme, 1996) and the Maltreatment Classification System (MCS) (Barnett, Manly, & Cicchetti, 1993; as reported in Stouthamer-Loeber et al., 2001) may be steps in the right direction in operationalizing definitions of neglect on the one hand and other maltreatment types and subtypes on the other. These might be especially valuable when exploring the issues of comorbidity of maltreatment types.

Measurement instruments have problems of reliability and validity, and the same measurements are not consistently used across studies. Samples are generally nonrandom, self-selected, and self-reporting via questionnaire or interview. They usually are derived from social service agencies thus limiting their heterogeneity (Crouch & Milner, 1993). Studies, thus, are liable to increased sampling error. In regard to methodology, therefore, it is proposed that (a) observational coding systems to record manifestations of reported familial and environmental characteristics; (b) reliable, valid, and consistent measures across studies; (c) control groups; (d) random sampling, including non-social service neglect subjects; and (e) consistent definitions be utilized in future research efforts.

Parental deficiencies model. In terms of specific family characteristics, Paget et al. (1993) suggested that (a) parental intellectual ability be systematically used as a variable across studies, (b) paternal and family system characteristics be studied to supplement empirical evidence regarding neglecting mothers, and (c) replication studies regarding parent/child interaction be executed, emphasizing variables (including developmental states of the child beyond infancy; that is, preschool, school age, preadolescence, and adolescence) that determine the risk status of parent/child dyads. Twentyman and Plotkin (1982) saw the need to determine the relationship between the directionality (either too high or too low) of parental expectations of the child and child neglect; and Baumrind (1994) wanted to know what the specific effect of substance abuse is on the incidence of child neglect. Research is recommended to develop explanations as to why some mothers with childhood histories of maltreatment do not neglect their children and vice versa (Weston et al., 1993). In light of focusing on bad mothering as the source of child neglect (usually because father is absent), the introduction of a feminine voice to the discourse is clearly warranted (Washburne, 1983). Gender issues have been sorely overlooked in the field of child neglect. Finally, the possibility of a biological factor in the etiology of child neglect should be considered.

Social-cultural-situational environment deficiencies model. In regard to the environmental deficiency model, given the high correlation between neglect and poverty, a fundamental question that has not been satisfactorily answered is why some at-risk families living in poverty neglect their children and others do not (Baumrind, 1994; Crittenden, 1999; Krishman & Morrison, 1995). Further research into the links between structural inadequacies of communities and child neglect would clarify the role of socioeconomic differences in a causal framework regarding child neglect (Krishman & Morrison, 1995). Knowledge about the way class affects parents' child-rearing practices, and the way the hopelessness and helplessness of the under class affect its members, the expectations they have for their children, and the investment they are willing to make in them, would inform the child neglect literature regarding the relationship between child neglect and class (Baumrind, 1994). Paget et al. (1993) suggested studies examining sociodemographic correlates of neglect in more depth; that is, (a) according to subtype; (b) across income levels; and (c) as distinct from abuse. Baumrind (1994) agreed that there is a need to study child maltreatment in the middle class to control for poverty.

In terms of social isolation/social networks, Salzinger et al. (1993) suggested a study of the effects of impoverished social networks on children and the implication these effects have for treatment interventions. Nelson et al. (1990) saw the need to explore the amount and nature of contact neglecting families have with extended family members, including whether or not the contacts were supportive. Coohey (1995) proposed (a) looking for gaps in supportive services and discovering reasons for those gaps, (b) examining the types of supports neglectful mothers value and under what circumstances they might consider entering an exchange relationship, and (c) examining the types of resources and network members that would enable neglectful mothers to gain greater control over their lives. Studies to explore the bidirectional nature of social supports are suggested by Beeman (1997). Relationships can be both positive and negative; and the nature of social ties (positive and negative) needs to be carefully examined. Mutuality and fairness in supportive relationships is another area for consideration.

Research is also suggested regarding the relationship between child neglect and culture in order to design interventions that are culturally responsive to the differences in meaning of socioeconomic situations and of child maltreatment for families and children of various ethnic backgrounds (Hampton, 1987). Such research would incorporate

> physical and social dimensions of the community environment and cultural differences in the use of supportive resources for childrearing. Certain types of resources for parenting may be more critical for one subculture relative to another, while certain types of community environments may present obstacles to the expression of those preferences. (Spearly & Lauderdale, 1983, p. 104)

Garbarino and Ebata (1993) suggested research to identify the unique risks and strengths of specific cultural and ethnic groups; and Baumrind (1994) advocated for studies looking at how culture affects parents' child-rearing practices; and the way abuse and neglect differ across ethnic groups.

Interactional model. Research regarding interactional models would focus on specifying the contributions of model variables (i.e., family and environmental characteristics) to the etiology of child neglect (Cohen & Wills, 1985; Hillson & Kuiper, 1994; Knudsen, 1992; Tymchuk & Andron, 1990). The meanings of these characteristics across gender, SES, and culture could be explored. Thus, multideterminant, interaction effects, not main effects, would be the focus of research using interactional models. To facilitate this process the various levels of interaction would be identified, operationalized, and defined (Cicchetti & Lynch, 1993). Hillson and Kuiper (1994) recommended going beyond description to developing explanatory, process-oriented models. Belsky (1993) advocated investigating differential etiologies of abuse and neglect across various subpopulations, and exploring the stability of maltreatment to inform the study regarding factors of chronicity.

In order to design interventions more appropriate to neglect, Erickson and Egeland (2002) and Jonson-Reid et al. (in press) suggested studying the current child welfare system. Information could be obtained regarding how and what services professionals are able to secure for neglectful families, especially when they do not meet the threshold for CPS intervention. Current programs could be evaluated to determine to what extent, for whom, and under what conditions a program is effective in preventing or treating child neglect (Erickson & Egeland, 2002). Research utilizing interactional models is moving in a more formalized direction and may bear fruit in terms of increasing ability to predict and explain when and why parents neglect their children, and what happens to the children when they do.

Effects of neglect on children model. In respect to outcomes for neglected children, there is a need for longitudinal studies into the long-term effects on children of specific situations (i.e., differentiate the effects of neglect from other forms of maltreatment and the effects of various subtypes of neglect). Such longitudinal studies would make it possible to take into consideration the age and developmental stages of children (Bolger & Patterson, 2001; Erickson & Egeland, 2002; McGloin & Widom, 2001; Perry et al., 2002; Rose & Meezan, 1993).

Exploring the objective and subjective effects of neglect, utilizing groups of neglect-only children and parents, would be valuable in adding to knowledge about the specific effects of neglect (Paget et al., 1993). Rutter (1979) and Manly et al. (2001) suggested focusing on the processes by which parent/child interactions develop, and on the links between childhood experience and parenting behavior (i.e., the processes by which neglect impacts childhood development). Such studies would provide an increased understanding of the developmental roots of psychopathology, which could inform the design of more effective prevention and intervention programs (Bolger & Patterson, 2001).

Neuroarcheology is a move in this direction. Using a biological model, Perry (2002b) argued for a research agenda focused on neurodevelopment and the neuroarcheology of child maltreatment. This would include volumetric studies of key areas of the brain and magnetic resonance imaging (MRI) studies to examine the functional impact of neglect (Perry & Pollard, 1997).

Studies to gain knowledge as to why children subjected to similar conditions have such dissimilar outcomes (i.e., what accounts for the seeming resiliency and/or invulnerability of some children and the vulnerability of others?) are appropriate topics for future research. To aid in expanding knowledge in this domain, research into the role of protective/buffering factors in positive outcomes for apparently neglected children would be informative (McGloin & Widom, 2001; Paget et al., 1993; Rutter, 1979; Widom, 1989).

Bonner et al. (1998) recommended studies to determine the difference between parents who neglect their children and parents whose neglect results in the death of a child. Finally, given the relationship between neglect and poverty, studies to clarify the effects of neglect as opposed to the effects of poverty would shed light on this crucial issue (Erickson & Egeland, 2002).

Summary regarding research implications. Theory regarding child neglect is still in the formative stages. At present it is relatively informal, primarily descriptive and correlational, and has little explanatory or predictive power. Although interactional models are more inclusive in terms of conditions within which child neglect occurs, the conclusion regarding causal models of child neglect is that, to date, no single causal model contains the necessary and sufficient conditions to explain or predict child neglect.

However, models have provided risk factors (a) for neglecting behavior on the part of parents and (b) for poor outcomes for children. While risk factors do not lead to reliable predictions about individuals or single cause-and-effect relationships, they do lead to accurate assessments of probabilities (Kirby & Fraser, 1997; Schorr, 1988). Thus categories of families can be identified as being at risk for neglect using risk factors as a guide to determining the categories. The same is true for children at risk for unfavorable outcomes owing to their parents' neglectful behaviors.

Much of current theory regarding child neglect has been based on research that also includes other forms of child maltreatment. Relatively few studies have focused on the etiology of child neglect, separate from other types of harm. Thus, risk factors for neglect could be established, in part, as a result of research not specific to neglect. There is need for research to focus on the development of theory related specifically to neglect, independent from other subtypes of child maltreatment. In addition, exploration of the various subtypes of neglect would add to knowledge regarding the differences between etiology, consequences, and treatment of different kinds of child neglect. Differing neglectful behaviors may require different responses.

The National Institutes for Health (NIH) (1999), in response to this relatively sparse research regarding child neglect, issued a "Request for Applications" initiating a five-year grant program to "enhance our understanding of the etiology, extent, services, treatment management, and prevention of child neglect" (NIH, 1999, p. 1). Fifteen research grants were awarded and the projects are currently underway. It is fairly early in the process for results to have been obtained; however, it is hoped that at the end of the five-year time frame (approximately 2005) new light will be shed on various aspects of child neglect. This ambitious project is certainly a step in the right direction toward building a body of knowledge specific to this issue.

Implications for Policy

Perry (2002b) recommended that policymakers become aware of the neurobiology of child neglect, in order to understand the ways in which child neglect generates damage in children. The recognition by policymakers of child neglect as a distinct and devastating type of child maltreatment, which may not respond to the traditional interventions employed with families who maltreat their children in other ways, would lead to the fostering of research specific to families who neglect their children; and could support the development and implementation of interventions that build on family strengths while remediating family problems.

> Research indicates that neglect and emotional abuse may result in as much or more harm to children than physical or sexual abuse. Yet these cumulative, long-term harms are often not addressed by the child protection system. Although the laws governing public agency responses to child maltreatment are broad, inadequate resources have produced a narrow system for protecting children from harm at the hands of their parents or caregivers. (English, 1998, p 51)

Policy initiatives to remedy this situation would include welfare reform; universal health care, including coverage for family planning services and substance abuse treatment; family support legislation that is family based and culturally competent; child welfare programs; and neighborhood revitalization initiatives, including provisions for increasing safe and adequate housing. However, in order for such policies to be fashioned, the existence of a "public will" to develop the concept of what is competent child rearing and to fund multifaceted service models at all levels is necessary.

Relative to the issue of policy development, Garbarino (1981) indicated that the *quality* of a neighborhood needs to be a concern of social planners. In planning for services, an ecological approach applied to the allocation of resources would ensure the most effective use of scarce resources (Garbarino & Crouter, 1978; Zuravin & Taylor, 1989). This approach is accomplished by using child neglect data regarding high-risk neighborhoods to target services.

> Programmatic decisions can be made concerning the appropriate allocation of scarce resources and/or the need to improve utilization of existing services. In addition, programs to encourage the development or enhancement of informal networks of mutual exchange can be targeted to specific communities and efforts can be made to integrate formal and informal sources of support. (Spearly & Lauderdale, 1983, pp. 103–104)

Baumrind (1994) indicated that a policy to change the environments of people needs to include sanctions for the widespread use of contraceptives, culturally competent parenting classes in the high schools, prenatal care and counseling for high-risk mothers, parental leave, educational and home visitor support services for all first-time mothers, well-baby medical care for all children, quality child care at reasonable cost, outreach child and family services for the homeless, treatment programs for abused and neglected children and their parents, and financial and emotional support for indigent caregivers.

Trocme et al. (1995) found that children in the United States are at substantially higher risk for neglect than children in Canada. They suggested that this difference is accounted for by Canadian social policy that, as opposed to the United States, includes (a) universal medical care, (b) increased financial assistance for children living in poverty, (c) lower crime rates, and (d) improved housing and community conditions.

Policy that focuses on promoting the creation of environments within which the well-being of children is assured is a matter of national importance (see Chapter Ten). Community support for the family is considered necessary to create nurturing neighborhoods. Structural changes are basic to resolving the issues of children living in poverty in unsafe neighborhoods. Refocusing policy on services for children, in addition to services for adults, would support remediating the outcomes of child neglect for children.

Cicchetti and Lynch (1993) emphasized the need for far-reaching policies that go beyond the community level to actually redesign ecologies within which children live. Young and Gately (1988) concluded that these policies must address structural inequities that place families at risk. Wolock and Horowitz (1979) advocated for guaranteed employment, guaranteed income, and a national health care system. They called for a realignment of public priorities to focus on family support services. Such programs are costly and not currently politically correct. As Perry et al. (2002) pointed out, less than optimal parenting is not a crime. Successful intervention standards generally are minimally acceptable, not optimal, child-rearing practices. The broad, sweeping changes called for to ensure children's well-being in our society can only be accomplished if policies provide the flexibility, resources, and philosophical orientation needed (Jonson-Reid et al., in press). *Thus, policy comes back to the will of society to support children and families.*

Summary regarding policy implications. It is key that policy to support needed research and intervention initiatives be formulated specific to child neglect. The NIH (1999) grants mentioned in the previous section are a positive indicator that those responsible for setting policy are demonstrating interest in the issue of child neglect by way of sponsoring research initiatives specific to the issue.

Such policy issues as family support, welfare reform, health care, and child welfare impact on family life and can act as potentiating or protective factors for families who are at risk for child neglect. Policy designed to ensure that protective components, supportive of children and families, are enhanced, and potentiating factors are reduced would benefit not only neglected children but also all children and their families.

Implications for Practice

In general, even though the child protection system is not as responsive to neglectful as to abusive families, research has shown that most families experience more than one kind of child maltreatment (Higgins & McCabe, 2000; Jonson-Reid et al., in press; Lujan et al., 1989; Marshall & English, 1999; Ney et al., 1992, 1994; Perry et al., 2002; Zuravin, 1991). Case acceptance and subsequent intervention generally focuses on other forms of child maltreatment, in spite of the likelihood that neglect is also taking place (Jonson-Reid et al., in press; Marshall & English, 1999; Perry et al., 2002). This is evidenced by the findings of Jonson-Reid et al. (in press) and Marshall and English (1998) that, *consistently*, child neglect is the reason families are re-referred to CPS, regardless of the reason for the initial referral. "Victims of neglect are likely to fall to the bottom of the list (of CPS priorities) and receive few services. Yet the harm these children may suffer from years of chronic neglect can be more damaging and pervasive than bruising or broken bones" (English, 1999, p. 51). Thus, many neglected children never come to the attention of responsible adults, or if they do it is later in life, long after significant damage has been done (Perry et al., 2002).

Given the harm to children caused by being reared in neglectful environments, the child welfare system needs to reassess its practice with these families. A first step would be to screen for neglect in all families at the time a complaint is received and to screen all neglect complaints for other needs (Jonson-Reid et al., in press). Marshall and English (1998) suggested prioritizing neglect cases for more intensive, up-front interventions (i.e., earlier in the CPS process), in order to prevent the buildup of long-term effects associated with chronic neglect. It is clear that early identification is a critical element of intervention with neglectful families (Perry et al., 2002).

In the design of prevention and intervention programs, theoretical models suggest factors to be taken into consideration. These factors include, but are not limited to, (a) parental characteristics and the social situation (Polansky et al., 1981), (b) ways to assist mothers in achieving a sense of control over their lives (Zuravin & Greif, 1989), and (c) the social and behavioral needs of children and their families (Lujan et al., 1989).

Parental deficits model. Within this context, specific deficient familial characteristics suggest specific remedial interventions. For parents and children with psychological, behavioral, and relationship problems such services as individual, family, and group therapy; substance abuse treatment; and interventions to strengthen parent/child attachment are appropriate (Daro, 1988; Kelleher et al., 1994; Murphy et al., 1991; Paget et al., 1993; Perry et al., 2002). Information-processing theory suggests parents may require assistance in changing the way they receive and interpret information (Crittenden, 1993).

For parents feeling overwhelmed by their circumstances, a characteristic of many neglectful families, family support services such as parent education programs, home visitor programs, support groups, and respite care might prove helpful in reducing stress and incidence of neglect (Belsky, 1993; Daro, 1988; Helfer, 1987a; Twentyman & Plotkin, 1982). As neglect is associated with larger families, Saunders et al. (1993) and Zuravin (1988) suggested family planning services be offered to all neglecting families. For families with health issues, intervention strategies to improve health care are essential (Perry et al., 2002; Saunders et al., 1993). When all else fails, interventions may include the placement of children out of the home in a hospital or foster care setting (Daro, 1988).

Environmental deficiencies model.

> Recognition of the impoverished context of child neglect points us to the need for concrete services directed at the dangers of poverty, services such as house-finding, rat control, in-home babysitter services, installation of window guard-rails, and emergency cash for the repair of boilers or plumbing, the payment of gas and electric bills, a security deposit on a new apartment, or the purchase of food, crib, playpen, etc. . . . reducing the immediate stresses of poverty may have a rapid and positive impact upon the parent's behavior . . . remediation of situational defects should take precedence over psychological treatments. (Pelton, 1978, p. 616)

Given the multidimensional nature of child neglect, intervention must also be at the neighborhood and community level. The neighborhood thus becomes the client in terms of service provision (Garbarino, 1981; Garbarino & Crouter, 1978; Garbarino & Sherman, 1980).

The provision of material supports (e.g., employment and housing) would increase the safety and security of families, reduce stress, and allow parents greater opportunities to care for their children (Pelton, 1994). In order to effect the provision of such supports, the child welfare system would need to reconstruct neglect as a social issue rather than a personal problem (Swift, 1995a). Community interventions could include (a) income support and employment programs; (b) improved housing resources; (c) neighborhood safety and revitalization; (d) public awareness programs; (e) community action programs; and (f) systemic reforms of the health, education, and welfare systems (Daro, 1988; Halpern, 1990; Perry et al., 2002; Saunders et al., 1993).

To ease the loneliness and isolation experienced by neglectful families, it would be helpful to enhance both their formal and informal support networks (Polansky, 1985; Polansky, Gaudin, et al., 1985; Salzinger et al., 1983). These kinds of services include mutual support groups that could involve neglecting and nonneglecting families, homemaker services, parent aide programs, volunteer visitors, the utilization of natural helpers, and the development of cooperative child-care programs. Zuravin and Greif (1989) suggested linking families with support networks and assessing the viability of the mother's family as a source of support.

Thompson (1994) advocated for social support that goes beyond families' immediate neighborhoods. It was suggested that extended kin; workplace networks, including unions; distant friends; and other community groups, such as churches and schools, be considered when assessing and building family support networks. Gaudin and Polansky (1986) recommended using community education, lay helpers, and volunteers to mobilize social networks. Perry et al. (2002) suggested that professionals using family strengths as assets would encourage parents to join in alliances with service providers; and, as a result, service providers could become a part of and enhance parents' support networks.

In turn, programs that encourage parents to experience the satisfaction of contributing to a mutual relationship would be helpful in empowering families to form satisfying support networks (Beeman, 1997). Such interventions could include an assessment of the functioning of parents' support systems accompanied by appropriate interventions, the development of parents' interpersonal skills, and the provision of supportive resources for families. However, as Seagull (1987) and Polansky, Ammons, et al. (1985) pointed out, focusing on enhancing social networks will produce disappointing results without enhancing parental social and child-rearing skills. What is required is a flexible mix of concrete, clinical, and supportive services in a family-like context (Halpern, 1990). Interventions to reach these goals could include (a) concrete services to increase family resources, (b) social skills building, and (c) quality day care (Halpern, 1990; Polansky, 1985; Polansky, Ammons, et al., 1985; Polansky, Gaudin, et al., 1985; Wolock & Horowitz, 1979).

Garbarino and Ebata (1983) pointed out the need for culturally responsive interventions focused on socioeconomic adequacy, values regarding children and special classes of children, beliefs about child development, and the place of the child in the family and society. Perry et al. (2002) suggested programs designed to take into account cultural beliefs that would hinder the seeking of services so that adequate programs would be provided for and sought by families without attendant stigma. In this regard, service delivery processes, also, would be designed to be culturally appropriate.

Interactional model. Interventions suggested by the interactional model are aimed at remediating potentiating factors and strengthening protective factors. Some interactional models have focused on social support (protective) and isolation (potentiating) as variables associated with child neglect. According to this model, interventions to remediate or prevent child neglect would focus on the enhancement of social support and increasing the size and supportiveness of families' social support networks (Gaudin et al., 1993; Turner & Avison, 1985). This model suggests that case work services to improve family functioning and reduce social isolation, depression, and loneliness would be effective in preventing and/or reducing incidents of child neglect (Gaudin et al., 1993). Jonson-Reid et al. (in press) and Perry et al. (2002) suggested a broad-range assessment of families with capacity-building interventions tailored to the needs of the child and the family. The findings of Murry and Brody (1999) suggested interventions to build parent satisfaction as a protective factor to increase children's well-being.

Stress-and-coping theory indicates that services aimed at strengthening parental competence, enhancing coping strategies, and reducing stress would be effective with families who neglect their children. Both cognitive and behavioral interventions (i.e., cognitive therapies and skill building) might prove useful (Hillson & Kuiper, 1994). McCubbin et al. (1995) suggested concentrating on the natural healing qualities of family life, including ethnic beliefs and values that emerge during family adaptation processes. Community-level interventions could include an increase in resources for dealing with life stressors, including access to housing, health care, and supportive services (Gaudin et al., 1993; Tymchuk & Andron, 1990).

Effects of neglect model. A child who does not exhibit obvious signs of harm, often the case with neglected children, may not be picked up by the child welfare system. Thus, very young children suffering from neglect when they are most vulnerable to devastating injury may not receive any intervention. Even if these children come to the attention of service agencies, they may not receive effective services. Little attention has been paid to direct interventions with neglected children. Most intervention strategies involve work with the parents to improve their parenting skills. However, the child may need treatment in order to overcome the effects of neglect.

For infants Perry et al. (1995) recommend interventions that provide the child structure, predictability, and nurturance. Interventions would be based on a thorough understanding of the neurobiological development of children and the neuroarcheology of child maltreatment (Perry, 2002b). Law and Conway (1992) suggest providing help with communication skills that is age-appropriate and child-oriented for young, neglected children. These interventions would include strategies to address social, cognitive, and language deficiencies. Self-esteem building and competence/skill training to enhance self-concept and sense of internal control would strengthen child protective factors (Bolger & Patterson, 2001). Age-appropriate strategies to reduce isolation might include children's play groups, day care, or extracurricular activities. Age-appropriate therapeutic interventions such as play therapy and individual counseling may help children with the particularly damaging problem of having an inadequate parent. Perry et al. (2002) recommended interventions focused on the child's resilience, coupled with a realistic assessment of the child's current and potential abilities. In extreme cases it may be necessary to hospitalize the child or place the child in foster care.

The findings of Werner and Smith (1982) suggested strategies that would reinforce supportive child and environmental factors, and reduce sources of stress. Interventions with parents, on behalf of the child, might include (a) providing empowerment parenting training, (b) teaching child management skills, (c) promoting healthy feeding routines for infants, and (d) increasing social interactions for mothers (Bousha & Twentyman, 1984). Training in child development may assist parents in having more realistic expectations of their children. In cases of NOFTT, Weston et al. (1993) found focusing on the mother/child dyad, treating the family on an outpatient basis, and using day-care services to be helpful. Owing to an infant's rapid development and vulnerability, it is important to begin interventions with families at risk for neglect as early as possible. Prenatal services would be ideal (Erickson & Egeland, 2002).

Summary regarding intervention implications. Theory suggests that families who neglect their children are impacted by factors both personal and environmental that either increase or decrease the likelihood of neglecting their children. This suggests interventions that focus on methodologies that enhance those factors that decrease the risk of neglect and remediate those factors that increase the risk. In assessing the intervention needs of families who neglect their children, Ammerman (1990) suggested (a) a multidisciplinary approach, (b) ecological assessments, (c) multiple sources of information, and (d) a focus on indirect measures of family dysfunction such as family interactions and parenting skills. Such an assessment would include both potentiating factors (family needs) and protective factors (family strengths).

Interventions with families need to be focused on skill building and family competencies, and could include training in: (a) parenting skills, (b) anger management, (c) social skills, (d) marital communication, (e) job skills, (f) home safety, (g) coping strategies, and (h) stress reduction. Where indicated, treatment for substance abuse, psychiatric disorders, and attachment disorders should be provided.

Enhancing family support and increasing family support networks by the use of extended family; home visitors; satisfying, mutual support groups of both neglecting and nonneglecting families; various community groups; respite care; and concrete services would provide or augment protective factors. Family planning and health care services are also essential. Out-of-home placement of either the child or the perpetrator may be necessary in extreme cases.

At the community level, primary and secondary prevention programs would be appropriate. Community interventions might include (a) income support and employment programs, (b) improved housing resources, (c) neighborhood safety and revitalization programs, (d) public awareness programs, (e) community action programs, and (f) nothing less than systemic reforms of the health, education, and welfare systems.

Programs responsive to cultural attitudes regarding socioeconomic adequacy, values regarding children and special classes of children, and beliefs about child development and the place of the child in the family and society are recommended. Research also suggests that service delivery processes be culturally appropriate.

Services to children could include help with skills that are age-appropriate and child oriented. These interventions could include strategies to address social, cognitive, and language deficiencies; techniques to build self-esteem and skills/competency; and methods to reduce social isolation (i.e., play groups, day care, and extracurricular activities).

As has been demonstrated, a range of interventions for parents, children, families, and communities is required in order to enhance protective factors and remediate potentiating factors of child neglect. What is vital is a flexible mix of concrete, clinical, and supportive services that are culturally competent and provided at the individual, family, and community levels. Such services would employ behavioral, cognitive, and community organization methods; and provide primary, secondary, and tertiary services.

For this to happen; however, first and foremost, the system responsible for interventions to ensure the safety of children must recognize (a) that child neglect is a serious form of child maltreatment that devastates children's potentials and (b) that child neglect is a social, as well as a personal, issue, which, in addition to individual and family services, requires a contextual response to support parents in caring for their children. Policy decisions, without a doubt, greatly impact what happens to families who neglect their children. The following chapter explores the evolution of public policy as it relates to neglectful families; discusses policy and policy decision-making processes; analyzes current child welfare policy; and explores implications of the outcomes of policy processes and decisions for future research, policy, and practice. Chapters Six and Seven will then review interventions that have been generated by those policy decisions and processes.

Chapter Five

What Impacts Children of Neglect?
PUBLIC POLICY

The focus of this chapter will be on child welfare policy, in general, and how it relates to neglected children, in particular. It will present the evolution of child welfare policy in the United States, including descriptions and results of major federal and state child welfare policy initiatives, using Hawai'i state law as an example. Policy development process will be outlined, current child welfare policy will be analyzed, and a summary including the implications of current policy for future research, policy, and practice will be offered. The history of the development of child welfare policy acts as a backdrop for understanding the ways in which interventions with families have evolved over the years. At present there is no social policy that uniquely addresses neglected children and their families (Gelles, 1999); and there are no intervention programs, other than a few, time-limited demonstration projects, that are specifically for neglectful families (see Chapters Six and Seven).

In order to see where we are going, however, we first need to know where we have been (i.e., where we are coming from). Child welfare policy, which results in the kinds of programs that are developed to intervene with families, is a reflection of societal and cultural values. Continuing value issues underlying policy regarding child welfare include (a) balancing the rights of the parents and the rights and needs of the child; (b) evaluating the harm that might befall children by leaving them with their families (i.e., family preservation) versus the harm caused by placing them in alternative settings (i.e., child protection); (c) determining whether resources are better spent on preventive or remedial programs; and (d) in light of the possibility that policies resulting in efforts to eliminate poverty may be more effective in ameliorating neglect than any other form of intervention, deciding whether to support residual or institutional initiatives (i.e., is child neglect a personal or a social problem?). Social reforms tend to be halting and incremental rather than broad and sweeping. The history of the development of child welfare policy in the United States supports this assertion.

EVOLUTION OF CHILD WELFARE POLICY IN THE UNITED STATES

English Common and Poor Laws

Prior to the late nineteenth century there was no public policy regarding children. The United States followed the tradition of English common law that dictated that children were the property of their parents (McGowan, 1990; Schene, 1998), whose right to custody was tempered only by parental duties to maintain, protect, and educate (Giovannoni & Becerra, 1979). Children, as laborers, served an economic function; and, in the tradition of English poor laws, poor parents could lose their children if they were unable to perform their parental duties. Society sanctioned and encouraged the practice of removal of children from their families for reasons of poverty (Schene, 1998). Parents were responsible for the care of their children; and the state was not responsible for the circumstances within which that care took place (Swift, 1995b). Thus, inadequate child rearing (i.e., neglect) was traditionally associated with poverty, which was a personal problem of the parents, not a social responsibility of the state; and the traditional response was removal of children from their families, not a program to prevent/ameliorate poverty (Swift, 1995b). In return for assistance, paupers forfeited their rights to their children (Giovannoni & Becerra, 1979; McGowan, 1990). Intrusion into family life was commonplace, the focus was on parents—not children; and economic factors were more important than familial bonds.

Private Child-Caring Agencies

The nineteenth century saw the development of voluntary and public institutions to provide for dependent children. In 1838 the concept of *parens patriae* regarding the custody of children was adopted in the United States. It was declared that the Bill of Rights did not apply to minors and when parents were unable to provide for their children, the community had the right to assume guardianship of them. *Parens patriae* ultimately became the fundamental legal principle establishing the right of court intrusion into family life (Giovannoni & Becerra, 1979; Swift, 1995b).

During the mid-nineteenth century the processes of industrialization, urbanization, and economic downturn resulted in many children inhabiting the streets of large cities. Charitable organizations began to focus on the problems of impoverished and neglected children (Lindsey, 1994; Nelson, 1995; Swift, 1995b). The Truancy Act, passed in 1853, gave the state the power to arrest children for, essentially, being poor (Nelson, 1995). The Children's Aid Society (CAS), established in 1853, picked up poor, urban children and sent them by the trainload out of the city to foster homes (Fraser, Nelson, & Rivard, 1997; Giovannoni & Becerra, 1979; McGowan, 1990; Nelson, 1995; Schene, 1998), thereby saving the city money it would have had to spend in supporting these children in institutions. Private funds supplemented public expenditures for child welfare services; and the economics of public child-caring services superseded consideration of parents' rights to raise their own children. While the public agencies may have had an economic agenda, CAS was motivated, also, by the desire to prevent delinquency in poor children. The purpose was to save the souls of indigent, urban children through placement in good Christian homes and institutions where they could receive an education and employment; religious and moral training; and be rescued from the temptations of city living and the "evils" of poverty (Lindsey, 1994; Nelson, 1995; Williams, 1980a). Thus, predelinquency, associated with poverty, was included as a reason to remove children from their families.

Also, during this period of time, the struggle to prohibit abuse of children in the workplace, coupled with the compulsory education movement and the growth of the notion of the state as a regulatory agency (Neubauer, 1996), gave impetus to legislation to prohibit child abuse in the home (Williams, 1980a). In 1874 the Society for the Prevention of Cruelty to Children (SPCC), which grew out of the Society for the Prevention of Cruelty to Animals (SPCA), began arranging for the removal of children from abusive families (Lindsey, 1994; McGowan, 1990; Schene, 1998; Williams, 1980a). The focus was more on punishing the parents and saving/rescuing the children than on providing for the children's or family's well-being. The primary social response to destitute, neglected, predelinquent, and abused children continued to be removal from their families.

The American Humane Association (AHA), which grew out of the SPCC (Williams, 1980a), and the Charity Organization Society (COS), both established in 1877, began working with abusive (AHA) and poor/neglectful (COS) families in their homes in order to keep families together, establishing the idea of reducing the need for out-of-home placement of children by providing services to strengthen the family (Fraser et al., 1997; Schene, 1998). Forerunners of social welfare agencies, these societies later evolved from private child-rescuing organizations into child and family service (private) and child welfare and protection (public) agencies.

Public Child-Caring Agencies: Child Welfare Services

Family support services of the 1880s, in the form of home visiting and private charity organizations, gave way to settlement houses (Daro, 1988; Kairys, 1996) and family service agencies in the early twentieth century. In addition to the principle that parents are responsible for their children, it became accepted that society had a responsibility to support parents in this function, as well as to intervene if children were destitute, abused, neglected, or predelinquent (Daro, 1988). Thus, child welfare services began with a dual nature—support for the families to keep them intact (i.e., family preservation), while investigating their adequacy with the underlying threat of removal of the children (i.e., child protection) (Pelton, 1998). Focusing on the parent/child relationship, government intervened only after a family failed in its function of caring for children, providing residual services (Lindsey, 1994). The purpose of the interventions, from the government's point of view, was to protect children. However, from the families' point of view it was seen as punishment for inadequacy (Samantrai, 1992).

The 1909 White House Conference on Children supported the principle of maintaining children in their own homes (Fraser et al., 1997; Giovannoni & Becerra, 1979; McGowan, 1990). As a result of this official devaluation of the practice of removing children from their parents for reasons of poverty alone, (a) child neglect (the form of child maltreatment most closely associated with poverty) was incorporated into laws dealing with child abuse; and (b) the first public assistance act was passed in 1911 in Illinois. Consequently, society's responsibility to provide funding to keep families intact was established as public policy at the state level. Connecticut added a fitness test to the means test to be eligible for assistance, and thus poor families were open to government inspection of their parenting practices (Giovannoni & Becerra, 1979). These state initiatives were the precursors of federal welfare and child welfare programs. State policy exerted its influence on the federal level, contributing to the growth of the welfare state.

Another result of the 1909 White House Conference on Children was the establishment of the U.S. Children's Bureau in 1912. Public responsibility for monitoring the well-being of children was taken to the federal level (McGowan, 1990). In 1919 the Children's Bureau published *Standards of Child Welfare*, for the first time setting public standards for the care of children (Giovannoni & Becerra, 1979; Lindsey, 1994).

During the first half of the twentieth century there was a gradual development of the notion that government, rather than the private sector, should be dealing with child welfare, a further expansion of the welfare state. Also, as a result of war and depression, private agency funding was decreasing; and it was thought that perhaps it was not best to have a single agency protecting both children and animals (Williams, 1980a). Owing to a growing concern regarding their police power, in the early twentieth century, SPCCs began shifting from a punitive approach toward parents to a social service model of prevention and treatment (Giovannoni & Becerra, 1979; Pelton, 1998; Williams, 1980a). The movement for more direct involvement of social workers gained momentum in the early 1900s eventually leading to the current predominance of the social work profession in the identification, investigation, and treatment of neglect situations (Giovannoni & Becerra, 1979). Parental (usually maternal) responsibility for the care of children continued to be the focus of intervention; and social workers became the experts in determining parental adequacy (Swift, 1995b). Concern for the physical abuse of children became less important and child welfare focused on dependent, predelinquent, and neglected children (Lindsey, 1994).

In 1935 the passage of the Social Security Act (SSA) Titles IV and V created policy and funding to establish government support of families. Title IV set up what became the Aid to Families with Dependent Children (AFDC) program; and Title V, later Title IV-B, created state administered funding for child welfare services. Federal policies and funding, accordingly, entered the child welfare arena and began to exert influence on state child welfare policy and practice. The force behind this policy emphasis was the profession of social work, which continued to focus on the family, rather than the child, as the unit of service (Swift, 1995b; Williams, 1980a). This approach led, in the 1950s, to the Family Centered Project in St. Paul, Minnesota, the first attempt to deal with families with multiple problems in their own homes (Kairys, 1996).

Nevertheless, from its inception in the 1930s until the late-twentieth century, when it was replaced by Temporary Assistance to Needy Families (TANF), *AFDC was the single, most effective program in keeping children in their own homes* (Brandon, 2000; McGowan, 1990; Williams, 1980a), lending support to the premise that parenting adequacy, in many cases, is closely related to material adequacy. With the advent of AFDC, child welfare focused less on resolving the issues of poor children, and more on the issues of families with neglected and predelinquent children. However, the funding provided by Title IV-B, earmarked for preventive and protective services, was generally used by the states to place children in foster care (Schene, 1998).

Child welfare services, thus, were put into practice in a residual context (i.e., intervention takes place in reaction to urgent family needs), focusing on protection rather than prevention; and the primary child welfare intervention (i.e., that supported by public policy regarding the expenditure of funds) continued to be out-of-home placement of children (Lindsey, 1994). The dual role of the child welfare social worker (i.e., investigator and helper) was maintained; and parents remained the focus of intervention (i.e., responsible and inadequate), not children or society (Lindsey, 1994; Swift, 1995a, 1995b).

The Battered-Child Syndrome

In order for policymakers to take action, a social problem must be perceived to be significant. The problem of child maltreatment was not perceived to be significant until the publication in 1962 of "The Battered Child Syndrome" in the *Journal of the American Medical Association* by Kempe et al., which focused national attention on the issue of child abuse. This article described clinical manifestations and psychiatric aspects of physical child abuse. These included clinical findings (e.g., multiple fractures in various stages of healing) and a marked discrepancy between the clinical findings and accounts of the injuries presented by the parents. The article also noted the medical profession's reluctance to accept the radiological signs as indicators of abuse. But

> to the informed physician, the bones tell a story the child is too young or too frightened to tell (Kempe et al., 1962, p. 18) . . . To summarize, the radiologic manifestations of trauma are specific, and the metaphyseal lesions in particular occur in no other disease of which we are aware. The findings permit a radiologic diagnosis even when the clinical history seems to refute the possibility of trauma. Under such circumstances, the history must be reviewed, and the child's environment carefully investigated. (p. 23)

This article brought child abuse to the attention of the public and made maltreatment a salient social problem (Newberger & Bourne, 1978). It also engendered the realization that neither social casework nor medicine alone could solve the problem of child abuse and led to the development of a multidisciplinary approach to the management, treatment, and prevention of child maltreatment (i.e., child abuse and neglect). As a result of these medical concerns, by 1970 all states had passed regulations regarding the mandatory reporting of child abuse and neglect (Cohn, 1987; Daro, 1988; Gil, 1981; Giovannoni & Becerra, 1979; Stein, 1984; Valentine et al., 1984).

One State's Reporting Law:
Child Abuse Act—Hawai'i Revised Statute Chapter 350

Typical of state reporting laws, Hawai'i's mandatory reporting law, Hawai'i Revised Statute Chapter 350 (HRS 350) entitled Child Abuse, was passed in 1967. The passage of this law codified a medical diagnosis into a legal framework (Newberger & Bourne, 1978). Under provisions of this law (a) any person may report a suspected incident of child abuse or neglect, (b) reports are kept confidential, (c) child abuse and neglect are defined, (d) mandated reporters are listed, (e) penalties for not reporting are set, (f) a system of responding to reports is outlined, (g) immunity from liability for reporting in good faith is established, and (h) admissible evidence is determined. As a result of this law, Child Protective Services (CPS) was established under the then Hawai'i Department of Housing and Human Services to receive and investigate these reports and to intervene with the families and provide services as necessary.

Public Child-Caring Agencies: Child Protective Services

One effect of state mandatory reporting laws enacted in the 1960s was an increased community awareness regarding the problem of child maltreatment; and in the next several years reports of abuse and neglect increased dramatically (Lindsey, 1994). Services were made available to a population of children whose families otherwise would not have received treatment. As a result, reporting laws saved many children; and the policy fostered cooperative case management of protective service cases (McCaffrey, 1978).

However, reporting laws, which grew out of concern for child abuse, created a situation whereby child neglect was conceptually joined with child abuse under the broader category of child maltreatment. Child welfare services began to focus more intensely on abused children. Consequently, another effect of mandatory reporting was the obscuring of the differences between two subtypes of child maltreatment (i.e., abuse and neglect); and policies regarding child neglect became less clear than for child abuse. The previous child welfare system, which focused on needy families, began to transform into a child protection system that focused on maltreating families and privileged the out-of-home placement of children. Instead of focusing on institutional and structural causes of neglect, child protection agencies channeled neglectful families into the CPS system (Gelles, 1999; Lindsey, 1994). As a result, more traditional policy themes relative to child neglect were reinforced. Parents continued to be at fault for the family situation; and the only remedies available to CPS social workers were to fix the parents or remove the children. The problems of child poverty were no longer a target of intervention (Lindsey, 1994; Pelton, 1998; Swift, 1995a); and social workers maintained their dual supportive/policing role (Waldfogel, 1998).

Reporting laws, also, created a large pool of people coming to the attention of public agencies—agencies that did not have the resources to deal with them (Lindsey, 1994; McGowan, 1990; Waldfogel, 1998). In addition to state laws that mandated the reporting of suspected child maltreatment, the ensuing media campaign regarding child abuse following the publication of "The Battered Child Syndrome" generated a tremendous response to the new laws. This response overwhelmed CPS agencies and gave rise to the need for more efficient and effective interventions to provide services for the families who came to their attention. This need brought about the passage of PL 93-247 in 1974 (Williams, 1980a).

The Child Abuse Prevention and Treatment Act of 1974: Public Law 93-247 (CAPTA)

Prior to the passage of this federal mandate, the SSA was revised in 1962 and 1967 to include social services for families. Children in their own homes would now have the same benefits as children in foster care. In 1961, AFDC foster care was added to the SSA; and, as a result, there was unlimited support for children receiving AFDC who were removed from their families. Moreover, there were no financial incentives to keep children in their own homes (McGowan, 1990; Schene, 1998). As a result, punitive responses to poor families (child removal) continued to be privileged.

Child maltreatment was a recognized social problem, state laws were being passed to mandate reporting of abuse and neglect to child protective services agencies, increasing referrals for services were being received by these agencies, and funding was being provided to support policies to protect children; yet there was little knowledge about how to treat maltreating families (Daro, 1988). Studies regarding the effectiveness of traditional casework interventions indicated that they had little impact on child and family outcomes (Lindsey, 1994). The U.S. Congress passed Public Law 93-247 (CAPTA) in 1974 to undertake to rectify this situation. CAPTA established the National Center for Child Abuse and Neglect (NCCAN) to (a) research the causes of child maltreatment, (b) research effective prevention and intervention strategies, (c) fund demonstration and training projects, (d) publish an annual research summary, (e) establish a clearing house for abuse and neglect reports, (f) provide technical assistance to public and private nonprofit agencies setting up programs, (g) establish an advisory board on child abuse and neglect, and (h) conduct an incidence study of child maltreatment (Child Abuse and Prevention Treatment Act, 1974; Cohn, 1987; Gil, 1981; Giovannoni, 1982; Giovannoni & Becerra, 1979; Stein, 1984).

Funding over 100 small grants for demonstration and training projects, this act did not provide substantial money for services. To receive grant money, state laws had to comply with federal guidelines. As a result, many state laws were revised to come into compliance with the federal mandate. The grants also accounted for the rise in such private-sector initiatives as Parents Anonymous, Parents United, and the National Committee for the Prevention of Child Abuse (NCPCA). In 1976 the NCPCA initiated a major media campaign regarding child abuse. As a result public awareness of child abuse issues, as opposed to neglect, went from 10% to 90% in the next decade (Cohn, 1987).

Not surprisingly, most of the projects established child rescue policies—focusing on child safety and using foster care for protective reasons, continuing the tradition of punitive responses in the name of child protection. Programs were not well coordinated and were expensive (Kairys, 1996). The narrower legal definition of child abuse and neglect did not include society's abuse and/or neglect of children (Gil, 1981); and, therefore, projects were primarily remedial and residual in nature. However, this was a milestone in the history of child protection because it was the first time parental abuse and neglect of children had been the focus of national mandates (Williams, 1980a).

With the focus of federal funding on child maltreatment, CPS became the dominant child welfare service and a system of child protection supplanted a system of child welfare. Schene (1998) described the core functions of child protection social workers as follows.

- Respond to reports of child abuse and neglect, identifying children who are experiencing or at risk of maltreatment.
- Assess what is happening with those children and their families—the safety of the children, the risk of continued maltreatment, the resources and needs of the parents and extended families, and their willingness and motivation to receive help.
- Assemble the resources and services needed to support the family and protect the children.
- Provide settings for alternative or substitute care for children who cannot safely remain at home.
- Evaluate progress of the case during service provision, and assess the need for continuing child protective services. (p. 36)

In addition to privileging child protective services, the statutory provisions for mandatory reporting and investigation to monitor family situations caused unprecedented, coercive intervention into family life
(McGowan, 1990; Stein, 1984). However, resources allocated to support
these policies were not adequate to deal with the complicated and difficult
problems of child neglect. As a result, professionals became reluctant to
report child neglect; laypersons' reports were often unfounded; and confirmation rates for neglect were relatively low. Neglect, formerly the focus
of the child welfare system, became secondary to abuse in the child protection system (Swift, 1995a).

As with the mandatory reporting laws enacted by the states, the federal law led to an increased number of reports (e.g., there was a sevenfold
increase in the number of reports between 1975 and 1986 [Lindsey, 1944])
without a corresponding increase in funding to provide for increased staff-
ing and service needs. For that reason, child protection may actually have
decreased rather than increased. Accordingly, questions were raised as to
whether or not child abuse laws had resulted in actions that actually increased the safety of children.

Stein (1984), in opposition to Gil (1981) (who called for inclusion of
societal neglect of children in CPS mandates), called for excluding from
mandated interventions (a) complaints from lay people, owing to their low
confirmation rates, and (b) complaints that were at variance with public
practice. For example, neglect accounted for the greatest percentage of
complaints, and 50% of all neglect complaints involved leaving children
unattended, yet society would not fund child care for low-income parents.
Therefore, neglect (i.e., lack of supervision) should not be included as a
reason for CPS involvement. The argument was—parents should not be
held responsible for that which society was not willing to provide support
(Stein, 1984).

In 1975 SSA Title XX created fiscal incentives at the federal level for
states to establish a social service system to provide services to adults and
children to promote self-support and self-sufficiency, prevent child abuse
and neglect, and prevent inappropriate institutionalization (McGowan,
1990; Schene, 1998). This act funded services for other than public assistance recipients (Giovannoni & Becerra, 1979) and increased the competi-
tion for increasingly limited federal money. Eventually, in 1981, block grants
replaced much of Title XX funding (see below), but it still accounted for
about 30% of state social service budgets (McGowan, 1990). In any event,
by this time about 75% of Title XX money was being expended on foster
care, not family support/preservation services (Schene, 1998).

Foster care remained a primary protective intervention for maltreated
children. Growing concerns regarding consequences to children of (a) sepa-

ration from their parents (due to the developing literature of attachment theory in the 1970s) and (b) foster care drift (i.e., children being left in foster care for indeterminate periods of time) led child welfare profession-als to look for ways to provide permanent homes for children by keeping their families intact (i.e., family preservation), or when all else failed, plac-ing children in permanent out-of-home arrangements (i.e., adoption) (Lindsey, 1994; McGowan, 1990).

The Adoption Assistance and Child Welfare Act of 1980: Public Law 96-272

The many studies and demonstration projects that resulted from the pas-sage of CAPTA yielded a rich base of empirical research that informed the design of laws and interventions by policymakers and practitioners (Daro, 1988; Lindsey, 1994). As a result PL 96-272, enacted in 1980, had a broader knowledge base than PL 93-247 and established government responsibil-ity for assisting families in fulfilling their child-rearing functions (Samantrai, 1992). The principles of "reasonable efforts," "least restrictive environ-ments," and "permanency planning" were introduced. Reimbursement for foster care by the federal government was subject to judicial review aimed at determining whether agencies had made reasonable efforts toward pre-venting the placement of a child or reuniting the family. In addition, chil-dren served by the public child welfare system should be cared for in the least-restrictive, most-permanent environment possible (Adoption Assis-tance and Child Welfare Act, 1980; Frankel, 1988; Lindsey, 1994; McGowan, 1990). The doctrines that actions taken should be in the child's best inter-est, that every child has a right to a permanent home, and that foster care should be employed as a last resort became explicit public policy (Blythe, Salley, & Jayaratne, 1994; Kairys, 1996; McGowan, 1990) and resulted in permanency planning for children's long-term care (Lindsey, 1994). Unlike previous legislation, this act mandated clear protections against unwarranted public intervention into family life. The SSA was amended so that AFDC foster care was replaced with the Title IV-E funded Foster Care and Adop-tion Assistance Program (Adoption Assistance and Child Welfare Act, 1980; Schene, 1998).

As a result of the passage of PL 96-272, national and state attention was focused on, among others, the issue of the use of foster care as an intervention approach. Concerns regarding children languishing in foster care (i.e., foster care drift) were addressed and incentives were given to states to keep children in their own homes whenever possible (Frankel, 1988; McGowan, 1990; Samantrai, 1992). Family preservation became the privileged child protective service. This directed public attention to the need for home-based services. Two compelling reasons may have gained programs employing intensive family preservation interventions the positive attention of state legislatures as models to be used in treating abusive and neglectful families and to prevent out-of-home placement. First, the programs had been represented as being more cost-effective than the out-of-home placement of children and, therefore, were seen as tax-saving measures. Second, employing these programs enabled states to be eligible for federal funding under the provision of the act that required states to make reasonable efforts to have children remain in their own homes and, thus, they were seen as revenue-producing programs. Expenditure decreases and revenue increases may have provided strong motivation for the widespread growth of state-funded family preservation services in the 1980s.

In relation to neglect, as indicated earlier in this chapter, a relatively small proportion of reports of child neglect were confirmed, and when neglectful families did receive services recidivism rates approximated 50% (Daro, 1988). In addition, research suggested that 70–80% of children who grew up in foster care had positive outcomes; and children in adoptive or single, long-term foster homes had better outcomes than children returned to their own homes (Barth & Berry, 1987). Findings regarding the effectiveness of family preservation services were equivocal at best (Fraser et al., 1997), especially with the neglect population (see Chapter Seven). Therefore, it could not be assumed that family preservation necessarily would lead to better outcomes for children at risk, and especially for children at risk due to neglect.

The level of commitment implied by PL 96-272, backed up with financial incentives for states, to keeping children in their own homes or reunifying them with their families, in the face of findings that reunification may risk children's well-being, required a commitment to the better support of children in their own homes. To leave children in homes that were not safe or to return children to homes that were not safe or would not be safe is neither humane nor efficient. Instead, it was suggested that CPS move to reallocate resources to provide additional services for families beyond the point of placement prevention (Barth & Berry, 1987).

However, one year after the passage of PL 96-272 the Reagan administration, in an effort to (a) minimize the role of the federal government by cutting federal spending and (b) resolve the issues of increased demands of the welfare state in the face of declining revenues (Neubauer, 1996), suspended the regulations and created block grants (mentioned above) and massive funding cuts through the Omnibus Budget Reconciliation Act (OBRA) of 1981. Interpretation and implementation of PL 96-272 were left to the discretion of the states, thus abolishing mandated services for children and eliminating many federal fiscal incentives (Howing, Wodarski, Gaudin, & Kurtz, 1989; Samantrai, 1992).

When the Reagan administration later proposed repealing this act entirely, there was a quick response from the private sector. The formation and lobbying efforts of the National Child Abuse Coalition, which included the NCPCA, National Parents Anonymous, the AHA's Children's Division, the National Association of Junior Leagues, and the National Association of Social Workers (NASW), resulted in the Federal Child Abuse Act being reauthorized in 1981 (Cohn, 1987).

The federal government did continue to sponsor conferences and training programs related to child abuse and neglect. President Reagan commissioned the National Public/Private Sector Partnership on Child Safety to address issues of child abuse and exploitation, and what the relative roles of the public and private sectors should be. However, even though caseloads kept increasing, there was not an increase in federal funding owing to the government's interest in reducing government spending by curtailing funding of social services. In response to what in effect was a reduction of federal support, the Children's Trust Fund, a privately funded trust, was established to provide monies for child abuse prevention (Cohn, 1987).

Perhaps due in part to the Reagan cutbacks, the initial reduction in foster care placements, which occurred right after the passage of PL 96-272, ceased and the number of children placed out of their homes increased in the 1980s. Some studies have indicated that out-of-home placements declined again in the early 1990s, due possibly to the increased utilization of family preservation programs (Kairys, 1996). However, Hawai'i's figures were not as encouraging. In fiscal year (FY) 1988, 1,799 children were placed out of their homes in Hawai'i. In FY 1996, 4,164 children were placed in substitute care (J. Rinehart, personal communication, December 10, 1996). Petit et al. (1999) echoed Hawai'i's figures. In 1990, 403,782 (6.3 per 1,000 children) were in out-of-home placement in the United States. In 1996, 530,496 (7.7 per 1,000 children) were in some kind of substitute care. This represents a 31.4% increase in children removed from their homes between 1990 and 1996.

One State's Child Protection Law: The Child Protective Act—HRS 587

Passed in Hawai'i in 1983, in response to PL 96-272, this law broadened the definition of harm to children to include risk of harm, in order that more children could be provided protective services, including preventive services for children at risk. This law also mandated the use of a service plan and agreement to remediate issues that placed children at harm or risk of harm. Twenty-seven safe home guidelines determined what constitutes a safe home and formed the legal justification for treatment interventions. Thus, this public policy initiative addressed intervention issues. The safe home guidelines were used to determine what the family needed to do in order to have a safe home and to develop treatment goals and objectives. These goals and objectives formed the basis for a service plan and agreement. When the objectives of the service plan were reached, the family was determined to be providing a safe home for their children and protective services would be terminated. The service plan was also used to provide justification for the assertion that reasonable efforts had been made to prevent out-of-home placement of children or to reunify children with their families (Child Protective Act, 1983).

As previously indicated, there were problems in instituting permanency planning as a universal policy objective. There remained the failure of past policies to ensure the institutional supports required to enable parents to meet their children's needs. The increased number of children in foster care, children returning to foster care after reunification, and the Reagan administration's cutbacks added to the struggle of implementing the new concepts of family support and preservation (McGowan, 1990). Serious questions were raised as to whether or not child abuse laws had resulted in programs that actually increased the safety of children. In fact, reports to CPS continued to increase, as did investigations of these reports; services to families were being cut back, in part to pay for the increased need for investigation; serious injuries to children and child fatalities were on the rise; and, as mentioned above, out-of-home placements of children were increasing (Lindsey, 1994; Pelton, 1998; Sedlak & Broadhurst, 1996).

In addition to cutbacks in funding, societal changes contributed to the failure of the CPS system to either support families or protect children (Lindsey, 1994). The traditional approach to child welfare (i.e., focusing on the parent/child relationship) had evolved during a time of relative economic security, low divorce rate, and few children born out of wedlock. Two-parent families, with mother staying home to provide the child-rearing functions, were the norm (Lindsey, 1994; Swift, 1995a). Over time, economic instability and increases in the divorce rate and out-of-wedlock pregnancies proliferated the number of families headed by poor, single women—changing the norm (Lindsey, 1994). This basic change in the structure of families in the latter part of the twentieth century called for a structural approach to resolving issues associated with society level change. Traditional child welfare interventions were not equipped to accomplish this.

The Omnibus Budget Reconciliation Act of 1993, Family Preservation and Support Services Program: PL 103-66 (FPSSP)

FPSSP was intended to promote family strength and stability by enhancing family functioning, and to protect children by providing supports for states to adopt or expand family preservation initiatives (Blythe et al., 1994). Amending SSA Title IV-B, this legislation authorized approximately $1.2 billion in federal and state matching money over a five-year period for family preservation and family support programs (Omnibus Budget Reconciliation Act, 1993). A new body of information resulting from evaluations of the kinds of reasonable efforts that were implemented to avoid placement by strengthening families contributed to the drafting of this legislation (Gershenson, 1995).

The first new federal child protection legislation since 1980, this measure was a victory for the family preservation movement. It provided states with funds to use as a new capped entitlement, which allowed them to develop a variety of child protective services to protect children and strengthen, support, and preserve troubled families, reunifying them when placement was necessary. This measure focused on providing for community development of a system of family support services to prevent the out-of-home placement of children (Schene, 1998). Family preservation was the paradigm shift of the 1990s, generating new practice methods and values and a commitment to promoting competence in families (Kairys, 1996).

One State's Response to PL 103-66: Hawai'i's Five-Year Plan

In order to receive funds authorized by PL 103-66, states had to submit a five-year plan to the federal government. Hawai'i opted to submit such a plan and implement FPSSP (Hawai'i Department of Human Services, 1995). The program was developed by nine working groups in various geographic regions of the state, and seven goals were set for FY 1996 through FY 2000. The goals of the Hawai'i program were (a) to keep children safely in their homes, (b) to increase parenting competence and/or effectiveness, (c) to facilitate communities being more supportive of families, (d) to increase child well-being, (e) to provide for safer families, (f) to improve service coordination and access to services, and (g) to increase family economic self-sufficiency (Hawai'i DHS, 1995).

As indicated by the goals of the Hawai'i proposal, FPSSP supported community involvement in developing primary prevention programs. This encouraged community needs assessments, which brought to light the invisibility of the needs of families and the necessity for a continuous and

consistent system of supports available to families. FPSSP also created a
new way to look at funding. In consideration of the limited amount of federal and state funds available for family support programs, new technologies of pooling resources, both financial and human, had to be developed
(National Resource Center for Family Centered Practice, 1998); and pub-
lic/private partnerships were encouraged.

Owing to budgetary processes state programs ran one year behind
federal appropriations. Granting budget authority for five years, while al-
locating funds on a yearly basis, allowed the federal and state governments
leeway to manipulate appropriations in terms of the political and economic
fields at the time the appropriation was made. There was a five-year commitment to FPSSP; however, the amount of support (i.e., funding available) was subject to annual review.

Responsibility and Work Opportunity Reconciliation Act of 1996: PL 104-193 (PRWORA)

"Society . . . is contributing to child neglect by neglecting the poor"
(Garbarino & Collins, 1999, p. 17). Technically welfare reform is not child
welfare legislation; however, they are inextricably intertwined. Change in
either system has an impact on children and their families, especially neglected children, owing to the close association between poverty and child
neglect (Dubowitz et al., 1993; Garbarino & Collins, 1999; Gelles, 1999;
Pelton, 1998; Sedlak & Broadhurst, 1996; Swift, 1995b). PROWRA in one
bold stroke eliminated the one program most successful in eliminating the
out-of-home placements of children, AFDC. This act created Temporary
Assistance for Needy Families (TANF), "a block grant program designed to
make dramatic reforms to the nation's welfare system by moving recipients into work and turning welfare into a program of temporary assistance"
(Temporary Assistance for Needy Families [TANF] Program, 1999). In addition to eliminating federal entitlement to income supports for dependent children, TANF imposed time limits on receipt of assistance and inplied
that work incentives would result in self-sufficiency for families (Berns &
Drake, 1998). It has been predicted that with the elimination of the AFDC
program the economic lives of poor children will worsen (Ozawa & Lum,
1996), and children will move from welfare to child welfare programs (Brandon, 2000; Christensen, 1998). Berns and Drake (1998) reported that these
predictions had not yet materialized; however, in 1998 time limits on welfare receipt had not yet been reached.

Duncan, Harris, and Boisjoly (2002) predicted that millions of families and children will soon be facing sanctions and cut offs of financial
support. Ozawa and Kim (1998) indicated that current welfare reform policy

is both inadequate and inappropriate to resolving the issue of the declining income status of children (see Chapter Ten). Brandon (2000) reported results that

> emphasize the positive role that public assistance can play in keeping children and mothers together . . . Perhaps when scholars revisit and research the old welfare system, they will note that although the old system was at odds with one set of American values—hard work, self-responsibility, and individualism—it was in agreement with another set—protecting children and maintaining the bond between a biological mother and her children. (p. 228)

These findings suggest that the values underpinning the welfare system are, at least partly, at odds with the values underpinning the child welfare system. It is not surprising, then, that the welfare reform movement does not appear to have child welfare in mind.

It has been suggested that in order for TANF to work there must be community-based initiatives to provide a full range of developmental services for families (National Resource Center for Family Centered Practice, 1998). This suggestion is reminiscent of the provisions of FPSSP and implies the idea of child welfare as a covert welfare program (i.e., that child welfare programs may be expected to include services to fill the gaps left by the welfare assistance program). More services are provided through CPS than through TANF; and it has been suggested that parents must become CPS clients in order to provide for their children (Gelles, 1999; Lindsey, 1994; Swift, 1995a, 1995b). Thus, CPS fills the vacuum left by a nonstructural approach to child poverty and becomes a de facto poverty program. All families have to do is agree to be defined as deficient in their parenting roles.

In any event, both welfare and child welfare are segments of a larger system that impacts families living in poverty. Given the high correlation between poverty and child neglect, it is reasonable to predict that changes in either structure will have an impact on the children of neglect. Just how reform in one system (i.e., the cutoff of a significant family support resource) will affect the other system (i.e., child protection, including child neglect) remains to be seen.

The Adoption and Safe Families Act of 1997: Public Law 105-89 (ASFA)

Enacted November 19, 1997, just four years after FPSSP, ASFA amended Title IV-B and IV-E of the Social Security Act, to indicate that the goals of the national child welfare system were safety, permanency, and well-being. The purpose of the act was "to promote the adoption of children in foster care" (ASFA, 1997, p. 1). Emphasis switched from "Family Preservation and Support Services (FPSSP) to promoting safe and stable families" and the Promoting Safe and Stable Families Program (PSSFP) was born. Perhaps in reaction to a perceived overzealous acceptance of family preservation principles in child welfare practice; and to the increase of children in foster care, with the resultant increase in the need for permanent homes for these children, this law established five principles that form the basis for current national child welfare policy. These five principles are as follows.

1. The safety of children is the paramount concern that must guide all child welfare service.
2. Foster care is a temporary setting and not a place for children to grow up.
3. Permanency planning efforts for children should begin as soon as a child enters foster care and should be expedited by the provision of services to families.
4. The child welfare system must focus on results and accountability.
5. Innovative approaches are needed to achieve the goals of safety, permanency and well-being. (U.S. Department of Health and Human Services, 1998, pp. 2–3)

This law maintained the principle of reasonable efforts to preserve and/or reunify families; however, now the states would not be required to make reasonable efforts if to do so would place a child in jeopardy. In addition, prompt proceedings to terminate parental rights, if the parents could not provide a safe home, were authorized and adoption was strongly encouraged. The intent was to reduce the amount of time children spend in state custody. However, Glisson et al. (2000) reported findings that suggested

> an emphasis on earlier termination and alternative permanency plans *might* shorten the time that *some* children spend in state custody (p. 275) . . . But it appears that the time children spend in custody is a much more complex and multifaceted phenomenon than these strategies suggest . . . findings raise questions about the potential of these policies for reducing time *most* children spend in state custody. (p. 276) [italics added]

States, which were still in the process of implementing programs designed under the previous law (FPSSP), now were being required to "reform the reform" and work toward safe and stable families (ASFA) (National Resource Center for Family Centered Practice, 1998). The new policy reflects old themes. Parents remain ultimately responsible for the care of their children—child maltreatment remains a personal, not a social, problem. Interventions are remedial and residual; previous levels of financial support have been reduced; and CPS workers maintain their dual role of helping/policing families. The focus of attention is parents, not children; out-of-home placement (now permanent) of children is again supported as a primary protective option; and there remains no policy that specifically addresses the children of neglect. As indicated above, these policies have generated practices that have not been particularly effective in either protecting children or preserving families (also see Chapter Seven). It becomes obvious that a re-evaluation of policy is necessary.

National Institutes of Health: Request for Applications (1999)

As noted in Chapter Four, the National Institutes of Health in 1999 issued a "Request for Applications" for fifteen research grants to "enhance our understanding of the etiology, extent, services, treatment management, and prevention of child neglect" (NIH, 1999, p. 1). These projects are currently underway. As previously stated, it is hoped that at the end of the five-year time frame (approximately 2005) new light will be shed on the various aspects of child neglect under study. This ambitious project is an indicator that policymakers are becoming interested in child neglect as an appropriate issue to explore, independent from other forms of child maltreatment. This is the first step in developing policy that specifically addresses children of neglect. An overview of how policy, in general, is developed is discussed in the following section of this chapter.

CHILD WELFARE POLICY DEVELOPMENT PROCESS

As the evolution of child welfare policy in the United States illustrates, the interplay between policy development, program development, and public and private financing is dynamic in nature. Policy affects funding, funding affects program development, and program development affects policy (Nelson, D., 1991). For example, PL 96-272 resulted in the flourishing of family support and family preservation efforts. Evaluations of the outcomes of those efforts informed the drafting of PL 103-66 (FPSSP) and PL 105-89 (ASFA).

The Public Policy Process

Briefly, the public social policy process is as follows. A social problem is recognized, defined, and determined to be significant enough to warrant the allocation of public resources to its resolution (e.g., "The Battered Child Syndrome" [Kempe et al., 1962]). A policy decision is made to search for effective solutions. Research studies and demonstration projects may be authorized and funded through legislative action (e.g., CAPTA). Policymakers then used research results and outcome/evaluation studies of projects in rendering decisions regarding future policy and program allocations (e.g., PL 96-272 in 1980, FPSSP in 1993, and ASFA in 1997). Policy issues are thus translated into research questions; and findings regarding answers to the research questions are retranslated back into policy recommendations (Gershenson, 1995; Gil, 1981; Lloyd & Sallee, 1990). Recommended policies are implemented in the form of service programs; and outcomes are evaluated resulting in new recommendations for policy and practice. Thus, program evaluation and policy analysis help make legislators and administrators aware of the effects of governmental actions on families. Policymakers are provided with the framework they need to analyze the impact on families of proposed and existing public policies (Lloyd & Sallee, 1990). As indicated above, child neglect is in the beginning stages of being discerned as a social issue, separate from child maltreatment, which demands attention; and public resources are currently being used to fund research into the problem (NIH, 1999).

There are, however, barriers to the use of empirical data in designing policy. These issues include: (a) methodological problems (i.e., small, unrepresentative samples and the absence of control groups); (b) uncertainty regarding which variables to examine; (c) the narrow range of intervention strategies to assess; (d) the combining of maltreatment groups that leads to overgeneralization of results; (e) research findings that are frequently not connected to planning or programmatic concerns; (f) various disciplines fail to communicate their findings in a useful way (Daro, 1988; Lynch, 1995); and (g) time lags between arriving at evaluation outcomes of programs and the needs of policymakers for information. Policy is, therefore, made on the basis of the best available information, no matter how limited or questionable that information may be (Gershenson, 1995).

As an example of difficulties surrounding research based policy, both the sociological and interactional models suggest that the provision of social supports is appropriate to remediate child neglect. However, the empirical evidence is not yet sufficient to support a set of public policy recommendations regarding such interventions (Thompson, 1994). Whittaker, Schinke, and Gilchrist (1986) quoted Kiesler in regard to social supports: "Current data are inadequate for even preliminary policy analy-sis and even the most consistent findings in the literature do not lend them-selves to conclusions at a level appropriate for immediate policy implementation" (p. 497).

Bases for Policy Decisions

Policymakers use multiple sources of data to assist in making policy deci-sions. Among these are program evaluations, policy analyses, cost/benefit and cost/effectiveness analyses, and nonempirical sources. These informa-tion sources are discussed below. Chapter Seven reviews reports regarding evaluations of practice strategies used with neglectful, high-risk, and mal-treating families.

Program evaluation. As indicated in the previous section, policymakers frequently base policy and budgetary decisions on the results of program evaluations (Lynch, 1995) and/or policy analyses, both forms of empirical research. Johnson and Clancy (1991) and Lynch (1995) indicated that policymakers and program administrators use program evaluations to as-sess the efficiency of an intervention program. According to Johnson and Clancy (1991), efficiency, which is the ratio of inputs to outputs, is an indi-cator of a program's effectiveness. Thus, a program is judged to be efficient (i.e., effective) if the benefits/outcomes of the program outweigh the costs/interventions.

   Publicly funded behavior-changing programs (e.g., programs to in-crease parental adequacy) are widely perceived as inefficient. To prove it-self effective a program must establish that the interventions used produced the desired outcomes. Such data must be developed through empirical re-search. Therefore, true experimental research designs are required. How-ever, as indicated above, there are barriers to using empirical data in developing policy. Lack of proven efficiency may mean a cutback of effec-tive programs or funds expended on programs that are not effective. Most programs do not use experimental designs in their program evaluations and thus most programs cannot prove their effectiveness. Yet programs continue to be funded. Johnson and Clancy (1991) pointed out that the impulse to resolve issues is the source of willingness to support unproven programs. They recommended that some reasonable adaptation of proven efficiency should be tried with publicly funded behavior-changing programs to ensure that they do change behavior before public resources are com-mitted to them.

Policy analysis. The Family Impact Seminar was created in 1976 to explore how government policy affects families. The research group was designed to provide practical policy recommendations in a short period of time by analyzing laws and regulations and interviewing key informants to determine the impact on families of proposed or current policy. By providing needed information in a timely manner, the Family Impact Seminar cuts down the time lag between research outcomes and the need for information to support policy development, and can have a definite impact on policy decisions (Lloyd & Sallee, 1990).

Values are critical in designing family policy. For example, intensive family preservation policy presents a value issue regarding the targeting of services. The policy debate revolves around the matter of targeting a narrowly defined population likely to be most at risk of child placement or reaching out to a larger population of families who could benefit from services even if placement might be averted without such intervention. In addition, IFPS have proven to be less effective with neglect families than with any other subtype of maltreatment (see Chapter Seven). Yet these services are provided for neglectful families, further complicating the issues of which families are most appropriate for this type of intervention; and/or whether the intervention could/should be modified to fit a broader range of families needing longer-term services. An analysis of social values could shed light on the debate (McGowan, 1990).

Cost/benefit analysis. The costs versus the benefits of a program are appropriate factors in the policy decision-making process (Lynch, 1995), although they should not be the only factors. Policymakers need to weigh the gains of different investment strategies (Daro, 1988). However, most program evaluations do not consider cost/benefit issues (McGowan, 1990). Daro (1988) indicated that difficulties of preparing cost/benefit analyses may account for this lack of attention. They are as follows.

1. The quantification of benefits and costs is extremely problematic for programs designed to improve the quality of life. The problem lies in the area of determining what value to assign to a life, and placing dollar values on factors such as intrusion into the family versus a child's security and safety.

2. Present gains are considered more valuable than possible future gains; thus future benefits need to be discounted. This method of cost/benefit analysis favors programs that produce immediate results. Programs serving children have fewer immediate results for society than programs serving adults; thus programs for children do not fair as well when cost/benefits are calculated.

3. Decisions need to be made regarding what costs and benefits to include in the analysis.

4. Attention needs to be paid to who bears the costs and who reaps the benefits. The assumption is that as long as the total benefits of a program exceed the total costs society as a whole benefits. However, seemingly economically beneficial social programs could leave some groups considerably disadvantaged. For example, the diversion of resources to family preservation programs takes away from foster care programs; and the income status for children declines as the economic safety net for the elderly improves (Ozawa & Kim, 1998; Ozawa & Lum, 1996).

As can be seen, quantifying outcomes becomes a value-laden process. Thus values enter the policy and budgetary processes, where programmatic tradeoffs may be necessary (Lynch, 1995; Wildavsky, 1992).

Cost/effectiveness analysis. In order to eliminate the problems of cost/benefit analysis, cost/effectiveness analysis has been suggested. The costs of different programs are fixed at a similar level, and therefore, only the benefits need to be compared. However, this method also has problems (Daro, 1988). There is no way to evaluate whether benefits outweigh costs or whether optimal expenditures for a program have been reached. Selecting the most effective program is determined, at least in part, by the definitions selected to specify benefits; thus this method also has subjective elements.

In spite of the inherent problems of analyzing the costs and benefits of human service programs, the methods have a heuristic value. While the selection of variables to use in a cost/benefit/effectiveness model is indeed value-laden and far less objective than advocates of the method suggest, the process does require the explicit examination of the factors governing the selection of a given set of factors (Daro, 1988). Policymakers can use this information in enhancing decisions regarding where to expend public resources.

Nonempirical bases for decision making. As indicated above, public funding decisions are shaped primarily by value choices, political interests, and economic constraints, not by empirical research and a rational decision-making process (Lynch, 1995; Schick, 1995; Wildavsky, 1992). Advocates for child neglect policy need to remember that program evaluations, policy analyses, and cost/effectiveness studies are not the only sources of information utilized by policymakers. When proposing policy and budget allocations, policy advocates must take the political field into consideration. Gershenson (1995) indicated that other factors that are used by policymakers to make decisions include anecdotal testimony, historical material, polling surveys, census and economic data, social data, mass media stories, petitions, and "wise-person" judgments. Ultimately intervention strategies concerning child neglect will be selected on the basis of their availability, and the political and economic feasibility of implementing them.

> Services are not provided because they benefit the recipient, but rather because they benefit the providers (the society). That is, social problems worthy of social investment are defined as such partly because they are sufficiently disturbing to society that it must try to do something about them. These social values ultimately are expressed in practical policies that dictate funding. (Giovannoni, 1982, p. 29)

Ultimately the question is: what cost is society willing to pay to make the same long-term commitment to child well-being that it is demanding of parents?

ANALYSIS OF CURRENT CHILD WELFARE POLICY

Adequate Child Welfare Policy

The literature indicates that an adequate child welfare policy would be institutional in nature and broad in scope. In terms of child neglect, reducing economic disadvantage could reduce the risk and incidence of neglect. Policy analysts have ignored the importance of the idea of child welfare services as a de facto poverty program (Courtney, 1998). Child welfare policy would incorporate what would be considered welfare assistance programs aimed at increasing the economic status of children. It would include structural, preventive, and remedial provisions to enable families to fulfill their child-rearing functions, including (a) adequate income to provide an economic safety net for families with children, (b) universal health care, (c) decent housing, (d) safe and supportive communities, (e) employment programs, (f) universal day care, (g) adequate education, (h) substance abuse programs and other remedial and/or concrete services to meet families' immediate needs, (i) skill and competency building interventions, and (j) adequate representation of class and ethnic groups in decision-making forums (Gelles, 1999; Gil, 1981; Lindsey, 1994; Nelson et al., 1990; Nelson, D., 1991; Newberger & Bourne, 1978; Wolock & Horowitz, 1984).

Interventions would include children as well as parents, and provide early intervention to prevent/ameliorate/remediate the effects of abuse and neglect (Gelles, 1999; Perry, 2002a; Perry, 2002b; Perry et al., 1995, 2002; Perry & Pollard, 1997). To make the system more user-friendly, investigative functions would be separated from intervention functions (Emery &

Laumann-Billings, 1998; Lindsey, 1994; Pelton, 1998), and social workers could take on a more assertive client/child advocacy role (Lerman, 1994; Swift, 1995a). Community-level approaches would promote parents being offered/seeking assistance before maltreatment takes place, ideally prior to the birth of the child (Lindsey, 1994). Focus on root causes of child neglect, over and above parental deficiencies (e.g., material disadvantage), would be included (Gelles, 1999; Lindsey, 1994; Pelton, 1998; Swift, 1995a).

Current Child Welfare Policy

Current child welfare policy remains residual in nature and services are primarily remedial, not preventive. CPS continues to be "a coercive apparatus, wrapped in a helping orientation" (Pelton, 1998, p. 126), parents remain responsible (i.e., at fault) for the care of their children, and poor children are still being removed from troubled families. Recent initiatives have focused on the family as the unit of intervention; however, implemented services are predominantly focused on the adults in the home (i.e., family preservation/fix the parents) or the child in foster care (i.e., child protection/remove the child) (Lloyd & Sallee, 1990; Pelton, 1998), with an emphasis on permanent out-of-home placement of children (i.e., adoption) (ASFA, 1997). The incremental development of child welfare policy has produced services that are categorical and fragmented. The provisions indicated by the literature as constituting adequate child welfare policy are not, universally, in effect; and the residual approach has failed to benefit children (Lindsey, 1994).

Current preventive and therapeutic models are not based on scientifically proven risk factors and causes. Thus, the debate for best policy is often based on opinion and incomplete data. An understanding of family support systems must be seen in the context of this causal uncertainty. Kairys (1996) quoted the U.S. Advisory Board on Child Abuse and Neglect's 1990 report:

> The most serious shortcoming of the nation's system of intervention on behalf of children is that it depends on a reporting and response process that has punitive connotations, and requires massive resources dedicated to the investigation of allegations. State and county child welfare programs have not been designed to get immediate help to families based on voluntary requests for assistance. As a result, it has become far easier to pick up the phone to report one's neighbor for abuse than it is for that neighbor to request and receive help before the abuse occurs. If the nation ultimately is to reduce the dollars and personnel needed for investigating reports, more resources must be allocated to establishing voluntary, non-punitive access to help. (p. 177)

To date, such child welfare reform has not taken place; and welfare assistance reforms have placed children, and, above all, neglected children, at greater risk. The following outcomes reflect the current state of the child welfare system—substantial increases in (a) reports to CPS, (b) serious injuries to children, (c) child fatalities, and (d) out-of-home placements of children.

In 1994 Lindsey called attention to the notion that:

> The child welfare system in modern market economies must play a vital role in promoting and ensuring the economic opportunity for all children. In this sense, public concern with the welfare of children, expressed through the child welfare system, allows these economies to tap the energies and possibilities of the most important resources for their future—and that is their children. When the child welfare system fails to protect children's economic futures, the long-term consequences for the nation are support of a large welfare class along with the increased need for "residual services" for such problems as drug and alcohol abuse, delinquency, child abuse, teenage pregnancy, and so on. (p. 227)

Two years later Sedlak and Broadhurst (1996) reported that the above-indicated increases in child maltreatment might be related to decreased economic resources among poorer families and increased numbers of children living in poverty. As Swift (1995b) pointed out, "Given the serious social and economic problems faced by many mothers accused of neglect, we might wonder if the real 'outrage to common decency' is the failure of child welfare services over the past century to confront the pressing need for change" (p. 87).

IMPLICATIONS OF CHILD WELFARE POLICY

Implications for Research

There needs to be greater specificity in policy-related research endeavors, including epidemiological, etiological, and evaluative research that focuses on child neglect (Giovannoni & Becerra, 1979). Service delivery systems need to be examined to ensure that clients needing services are getting them (Nelson et al., 1990). Risk factors for child neglect need to be identified, along with studies regarding which kind of risk situations respond to which kind of services (McGowan, 1990). Program evaluations need to include studies regarding how variations in programs affect their effectiveness, how effective such programs are in a variety of communities, and how effectiveness varies by characteristics of clients (Gelles, 1999). Research is needed to determine why programs that have been proven to be successful are underutilized (Schorr, 1988).

Program evaluations using experimental designs are recommended in demonstrating program effectiveness (Johnson & Clancy, 1991). However, Gershenson (1995) suggested that linear models seldom reflect the human dynamics of service delivery systems. Thus nonlinear models are also needed, along with qualitative methods, to institute systems-level analyses. Daro and Donnelly (2002) described the need for diversified research methods including (a) linking specific change mechanisms with specific families and situations, (b) client stories using structured interviews, (c) single-case studies, and (d) theory of change models.

Swift (1995a) suggested that the focus on mothers (i.e., interventions with families) is at the expense of gaining an understanding of and the ability to impact the social and economic context in which child neglect occurs. Thus research aimed at structural causes of child neglect (e.g., poverty) is imperative, including determining the impact of federal economic programs (i.e., welfare to work and TANF) on children and the incidence of child neglect (Black & Dubowitz, 1999; Pelton, 1994).

McGowan (1990) indicated that it is irresponsible to make a major public investment in programs without investing simultaneously in demonstration projects designed to examine the short- and long-term cost/benefits of alternative service structures and practice technologies. Black and Dubowitz (1999) suggested policy-oriented research to enable policymakers to base decisions on more than emotional appeals and best guesses.

> There are many professions, bureaucracies, advocates and opinions involved in shaping public policy about the prevention and treatment of child abuse. Unfortunately, the many factions have not been able to reach a consensus about the services needed for effective interventions. Federally funded consensus panels consisting of representatives from those professions and agencies dealing with child safety and children should be organized to dispassionately review the data currently available and make policy and research recommendations that can be developed, adequately tested, and evaluated. Until more formal inquiry takes place, programs will continue to be based on prevailing theory and economic incentives. (Kairys, 1996, p. 185)

For policy advocates, Samantrai (1992) suggested studying the implementation process of social policies to determine the factors related to success that can be manipulated by social workers more successfully in shaping future social policies and programs.

Implications for Policy

As indicated at the beginning of this chapter, there is no overriding social policy that addresses child neglect. Many of the risk factors for child neglect are structural; yet the political response to the problem is focused on individual families and/or children, not on the societal conditions that give rise to the problem (Nelson, 1995). "The greatest threat to poor children's welfare is society's neglect, not their parents' neglect" (Baumrind, 1994, p. 366). During this time of experimentation with the economic safety net for families, many children may suffer unnecessarily (Courtney, 1998; Schorr, 1997). Thus, any policy designed to impact child neglect must tackle the issue of poverty and the material deprivation of families (Collins & Garbarino, 1999; Dubowitz et al., 1993; Gelles, 1999). A significant reduction in the incidence of child neglect depends upon reforms in the quality of housing, medical care, schools, and employment opportunities available to poor families (Daro, 1988; Ozawa & Kim, 1998). There is a national need to recognize that (a) changes in social programs and welfare policies automatically affect children, (b) it is difficult to develop a policy for children that is independent from their caregivers, and (c) policies are needed to help parents *and* communities protect and nurture their children (Black & Dubowitz, 1999).

Categorical and deficit-focused interventions, which have not worked, may be inappropriate foci of policy initiatives related to child neglect (Wolock & Horowitz, 1984). Policy focused on prevention (Cohn, 1987; Emery & Laumann-Billings, 1998; Pelton, 1998; Young, 1964), supporting the eradication of social and economic inequality (Newberger & Bourne, 1978; Ozawa & Kim, 1998), and the development of new mechanisms for resource allocation and new models of service programs may be more successful. Schorr (1997) suggested (a) extending national programs of proven efficacy to all who are eligible, (b) broadening the scale of successful community programs, and (c) recognizing that it is in the national best interest to invest in first-class services for children. Daro and Donelley (2002) envision systems that encourage parents to seek and receive the support they need in caring for their children. Such systems would require society to accept the vision of shared responsibility for children's welfare.

These policies will require a resource commitment beyond that which has been available for community-based programs up to the present (Halpern, 1990); and it is unlikely that such new policies will be supported as the social and political will to address contextual issues is barely discernible (Belsky, 1993; Halpern, 1990; Nelson et al., 1990). However, the NIH (1999) funded research projects are a positive step in the right direction; and Petit et al. (1999) reported that public opinion was supportive of government expenditures for children. Seventy-three percent of those polled were in favor of increased spending on programs to help children, while 22% were opposed. In terms of then-current spending level, 49% believed it should be expanded, 37% believed it was about right, and 10% believed it should be cut back. Thus it would appear that the public is supportive of programs to assist families and children. However, this public support has not been translated into public policy. In 1988, Schorr suggested that the "fear of actually doing harm while trying to do good, together with the threat of unmanageable costs, have paralyzed national policy making" (p. xix). In 1997, Schorr suggested the following strategies for policymaking:

1. Recognize . . . attributes of highly effective programs and the environments that will support them;
2. Spread what works . . . break the hidden ceiling of scale;
3. Look for ways to overcome fundamental obstacles to change . . . don't look only for innovation;
4. Make sure that funders, managers, front-line staff and program participants agree on valued outcomes and all understand how the initiative's activities and investments are related to outcomes, so all can be able to use results to judge success;
5. Give up single, quick fixes . . . take a broader view . . . look for opportunities to impact a neighborhood or neighborhood institutions, not just opportunities to impact a circumscribed problem;
6. Forget about getting results overnight . . . be prepared to build for a future your generation may not see . . . take a longer view;
7. Recognize that intensity and critical mass may be crucial . . . create the synergy than can bring about real change and tip a neighborhood toward becoming functional;
8. Forget about choosing between bottom-up or top-down approaches . . . effective neighborhood transformation requires that community based organizations be able to draw on funding, expertise, and influence from outside; and that outsiders be able to draw on information, expertise, and wisdom that can come only from the neighborhood itself. (pp. 381–383)

A social policy addressing the issue of child neglect would ensure that families and communities would be supported in protecting and caring for their children, and is sorely needed.

Implications for Practice

Ory and Earp (1980) found an inverse relationship between utilization of institutional social services and the likelihood of child maltreatment. Supporting this finding, Howing, Wodarski, Gaudin, et al. (1989) indicated that a lack of appropriate community resources had been identified as a primary barrier to the provision of effective interventions with maltreating families.

Programs to assist both parents and communities in protecting and nurturing their children need to be developed (Black & Dubowitz, 1999). However, only when policy supports prompt and adequate services to address the roots of deficient child rearing can genuine changes be anticipated. Interventions in general, and foster care in particular, have been criticized on the grounds that they can damage children more than poor parenting. These arguments, however, deflect attention from addressing root causes of problems in families (Knudsen, 1992), including material deprivation. Ideally a coordinated response (including housing, medical care, education, and employment/job training opportunities) to the problem of poverty would create a network of services sufficient to support poor families and to allow protective service agencies to focus only on those cases that pose an immediate and serious threat to a child's well-being (Daro, 1988; Lewit, Terman, & Behrman, 1997; Pelton, 1994; Schorr, 1988). Belsky (1993) suggested targeting high-risk neighborhoods, selecting young women from those neighborhoods, and paying them incentives to stay in school and avoid pregnancy. The incentives would include guaranteed minimal income, child allowances, housing benefits, and affordable (free) high-quality child care. Schorr (1997) indicated that child welfare reform should include (a) a full array of services, both formal and informal, for biological, foster, and adoptive families; (b) services based in neighborhoods; (c) high standards and extensive training and consultation for workers in accurate case assessment and planning; (d) continuous evolution and adaptation to new circumstances; (e) a comprehensive commitment to improving child and family well-being; and (f) support from private agencies and foundations as well as federal and state governments.

Given the relative ineffectiveness of programs in dealing with the neglect population, some authors support the position that intervention focus should shift to prevention efforts (Cohn, 1987; Emery & Laumann-Billings, 1998; Lindsey, 1994; Pelton, 1998; Young, 1964). Program evaluations have consistently found that families at risk for maltreatment are more amenable to change and more likely to experience positive outcomes than those families who have already been involved in maltreatment (Daro, 1988). Cohn (1987) suggested making a long-term commitment to prevention efforts, as special initiatives and quick fixes do not work.

Emery and Laumann-Billings (1998) advocated for a supportive (not punitive) social service response to minor abuse and families under stress and a law enforcement approach for families whose children are at serious risk. Pelton (1998) proposed that CPS focus its efforts on preventive interventions with impoverished families who come to the agency voluntarily. Mandated reports would be handled by an investigative/law enforcement system; and, if necessary, out-of-home placements would be conducted by an adoptive/foster care system. In similar models, Waldfogel (1998) and Daro and Donnelly (2002) suggested community-based public-private partnerships for child protection. "This approach emphasizes targeting investigations by CPS toward only high-risk families, building collaborative community networks that can serve lower-risk families (on a voluntary basis), and providing a differentiated response to both high- and low-risk families that is tailored to each family's situation" (Waldfogel, 1998, p. 104). These approaches would separate the traditional punitive/helping role of the child protection worker into separate functional units whether within the child welfare system or utilizing the law enforcement system in addition to the child welfare system.

More options for assistance would be available for families and agencies than "fix the parents or place the child" as communities would also be targets for interventions. Family-centered programs tend to focus on parents and as a result lose sight of the child. Melton and Barry (1994) argued for adoption of policy that explicitly establishes the government's responsibility for the protection of children's well-being, and supported a focus on neighborhoods as sources of support for children and their families.

In regard to welfare, as well as child welfare, the preventive approach would require putting more energy up front in the form of family-centered assessment, rather than waiting until benefits have expired and the family is underemployed. "Unfortunately it is not too difficult to imagine a 'TANF expired' family, dismembered to multiple foster homes on a finding of severe neglect due to homelessness" (Christensen, 1998, pp. 20–21).

In order to impact policy decisions, social workers can actively work toward the election of governors and legislators who believe in government responsibility for services to families. Other strategies include eliciting support of citizens groups, utilizing the media to mobilize public opinion (Samantrai, 1990), supporting lobbying efforts on behalf of families, personally lobbying state and national legislatures, and employing other tactics and strategies suggested by the nonempirical bases of policy decisions outlined previously in this chapter.

CONCLUSIONS REGARDING CHILD WELFARE POLICY AND NEGLECT

Elimination of child neglect will require a reordering of financial priorities in the United States. "It rests on the nation's political will to devote more resources to this end rather than on any hard economic or budgetary limits and will require a long-run commitment to sustain efforts and consider new approaches" (Plotnick, 1997). This country clearly has the resources to nourish and enhance its children, yet policymakers may not see the value in doing so.

> The emphasis on temporary expediency as the implicit guideline for child abuse and neglect programs is reminiscent of a people described in Jewish legend, the Fools of Chelm, a community of smug simpletons who lacked insight into their incredible stupidity. They lived at the top of a steep mountain from which they had to traverse a narrow, winding path in order to go to the market at the foot of the mountain. In the course of their frequent journeys to the market, droves of Chelmsians were killed or maimed as they dropped off the narrow path into the deep valley below. After decades of ignoring the carnage, the survivors finally took action against the problem. They voted funds to build a hospital at the bottom of the valley to treat those unfortunates who dropped off the mountain into the valley. (Williams, 1980a, p. 62)

As Schorr (1988) stated, "Considering the wealth of our knowledge about the dangers of growing up in areas of concentrated poverty—areas now readily identified—and our knowledge about interventions that can change outcomes even for the most disadvantaged children, it becomes unconscionable not to take whatever action is needed to make these interventions available" (p. 288). Yet in the clamor of the competing claims on the dwindling federal discretionary dollar, the small voices of children are hard to hear.

Chapter Six

∞

What Impacts Children of Neglect?

PRACTICE STRATEGIES

The focus of this chapter is on prevention of neglect in the general population, prevention of neglect in families considered to be at high-risk for inadequate parenting, and remediating the already existing condition of child neglect and preventing its reoccurrence. This book proposes four approaches that guide the categorization of interventions with neglected children and their families. These strategies for practice are drawn from the causal models found in Chapter Three. The practice approaches are as follows:

1. Intrafamilial practice focuses on interventions with adults to change behaviors and/or personality or family characteristics, which can result in neglectful parenting. The parental deficiencies model, that suggests interventions aimed at remediating the deficient familial characteristics that lead to child neglect, implies these strategies. Constructed from social learning, behavioral, developmental, neurobiological, and information-processing theory, the parental deficiencies model proposes interventions to remediate the deficient familial characteristics that result in child neglect.

2. Environmental or sociological practice focuses on interventions with social structures or the environment to relieve family stress, and thus, the incidence of child neglect. These strategies are suggested by the environmental deficiencies model, which is based on social learning, social ecology, social psychology, and behavior theory. These theories imply interventions at the neighborhood, community, and/or societal levels to remediate social and environmental conditions related to neglect.

3. Psychosocial or ecological practice includes elements of the first two practice approaches, intervening at both the family and community levels to provide clinical as well as supportive services. This approach has its foundation in the interactional model, which is based on developmental, transactional, evolutionary, sociobiological, and ecological theory, that implies interventions to remediate risk factors both in the family and in the environment that are believed to place children in harm's way, and to strengthen resiliency factors both in the family and in the environment that are related to the prevention of child neglect.

4. Child-focused practice includes therapeutic and supportive interventions with children and adults to prevent or ameliorate the effects of child neglect. These strategies are informed by child development theory, attachment theory, and neurobiological development theory, which form the basis for the effects of neglect on children model that implies services for children and their families that focus on the child. Table 4 diagrams the relationships between causal models, theory, and practice.

Practice strategies are developed from intervention approaches, which are suggested by causal models that, as indicated in Chapter Three, are not well grounded in scientifically established risk factors and/or causes (Kairys, 1996). This may account for some of the unsuccessful results of programs based on these strategies. Irrespective of theoretical framework, most researchers agree that neglecting families are the most difficult families to engage and retain in services (Berry, 1991, 1992; Duggan et al., 1999; Nelson & Landsman, 1992; Smokowski & Wodarski, 1996) and present the most difficult problems to resolve in terms of severity, complexity, and multiplicity (Berry, 1992; Nelson & Landsman, 1992; Rose & Meezan, 1993). The characteristics and numbers of problems associated with the etiology and consequences of child neglect tend to be chronic, especially those associated with personality and environment. The chronicity of these factors may also account for the seeming intractability of the problem (Herrenkohl et al., 1983).

Allen, Reiter, and Landsman (1990) indicated that social workers find chronically neglecting families among the most difficult with which to work. DiLeonardi (1993) stated:

> A major difficulty in serving these families is the emotionally draining effect that the apathy of neglectful families may have on professionals, volunteers, and community paraprofessionals. The hopelessness and helplessness of these families make it extremely difficult for workers to initiate and follow through on plans that might alleviate the families' situation. (pp. 558–559)

TABLE 4
Child Neglect Theory and Practice

Theoretical Models	Parental Deficiencies	Environmental Deficiencies	Interactions	Effects of Neglect
Theoretical foundations	Social learning theory Behavior theory Psychological development theory Neurobiological development theory Information processing theory	Social learning theory Social ecology theory Social psychology theory Behavior theory	Psychological development theory Transaction theory Evolution theory Sociobiology theory Theories regarding ecology	Child development theory Attachment theory Neurobiological development theory
Practice methods	Parent education programs Skill/competency development Individual, family, and group therapy Substance abuse treatment Health care Interventions to assist parents in changing the way they process information Foster care/adoption	Material supports: income, employment, child care, housing, education, health care access Enhance formal and informal support networks: family, neighbors, home visitors, cultural activities, formal institutions/agencies	In addition to all of the previously outlined methods: Enhance coping strategies and teach stress reduction Focus on natural healing qualities of family life, including ethnic beliefs and values	Therapeutic day care/treatment Parent/child activities Father/parent surrogates Group/community activities Individual, family, and group therapy Skill/competency building Early intervention Foster care and/or adoption

Landsman et al. (1992) indicated that the difficulty in achieving positive results with this population results in a sense of futility and apathy in the social workers that is similar to that experienced by the families themselves (i.e., symptom contagion).

The possibility of a genetic or congenital predisposition for risk factors associated with neglect (e.g., depression) or a biological imperative to neglect (Belsky, 1993) also can have far-reaching implications for the design of effective interventions. Thus theoretical shortcomings, difficulties with parental motivation and participation that result in recruitment and retention issues, nature and chronicity of problems, social worker symptom contagion, and a possible biological link may account for the seeming intractability of child neglect and the relative ineffectiveness of most intervention programs.

The literature regarding practices with families who neglect their children falls roughly into two categories: (a) descriptive reports regarding program services and (b) empirical studies that provide program outcomes in addition to program descriptions. This chapter, using the framework of practice approaches, will present descriptions of various practice strategies that have been reported in the literature. Empirical findings of various practice models will be presented in Chapter Seven where implications for research, policy, and practice will be discussed.

PRACTICE STRATEGIES: DESCRIPTIVE REPORTS

There are few studies regarding programs that specifically focus on neglectful families and fewer still empirical studies. Therefore, unless otherwise noted, approaches reviewed in this chapter are focused on maltreating families in general, not neglectful families specifically; and the studies presented describe intervention programs without reporting empirical testing of their effectiveness.

Studies describing practice with maltreating families and families at risk for maltreatment indicated that interventions must be based on an assessment of individual family problems and needs. The focus is, therefore, on problem resolution for individual families, and steps necessary to reach this goal are related to the needs of a particular family, including coercive strategies if appropriate (e.g., court-ordered intervention). More than one type of maltreatment can occur in a family (Bath & Haapala, 1992; Eckenrode et al., 1993; Fischler, 1985; Howing, Wodarski, Kurtz, et al., 1989; Lujan et al., 1989; Nelson & Landsman, 1992; Ney et al., 1992, 1994; Paget et al., 1993; Watters et al., 1986; Wolock & Horowitz, 1979; Yuan & Struckman-Johnson, 1991; Zuravin, 1991) and interventions may focus on the different aspects of the family associated with each type of maltreatment.

Specific to child neglect, the literature suggests that treatment with neglectful parents would focus on provision of supportive services and the development of increased family cohesion and parental responsiveness (Howing, Wodarski, Gaudin, et al., 1989), and include fathers as well as mothers. Owing to the chronic multiproblem nature of child neglect, long-term treatment is usually necessary (Cantwell & Rosenberg, 1990; Crittenden, 1999; Daro, 1988; Dubowitz, 1999; Gaudin, 1993). Treatment goals that are (a) related to parenting behavior, (b) meaningful to and developed by the family, (c) clearly delineated in a written treatment plan, (d) realistic, and (e) prioritized so that the focus is on a few easily achievable goals at a time may be more successful in treating neglectful families as many have difficulty with change (Cantwell & Rosenberg, 1990; Crittenden, 1993; Dubowitz, 1999; Gaudin, 1993).

Intrafamilial Practice

As indicated in Chapter Three, neglectful families are particularly isolated and withdrawn. Tomlinson and Peters (1981) described necessary components of any treatment program for disengaged families that certainly could apply to neglectful families. These components include (a) reaching out to the family, (b) involving all family members, (c) involving the therapist with external family systems, and (d) intensifying treatment. In terms of specific practice with neglecting families, home visitation is a key practice component (Crittenden, 1993; Thompson, 1995).

Behavioral and psychological developmental theories, which underpin the parental deficiencies model of child neglect, imply that interventions are needed to ameliorate the deficient characteristics of maltreating/neglectful families. Thus, for parents with psychological, behavioral and relationship problems such interventions as individual, family, and group therapy (including drug therapy for mood or psychiatric disorders, and treatment for verbal inaccessibility) are prescribed (Daro, 1988; Helfer, 1987a; Polansky et al., 1974; Wells, 1981). In addition, neurobiological theory implies that parents neglected as children may have parenting deficits due to interference with their neurobiological development, especially in terms of their affective capacities. Steele (1987) indicated that:

> Providing a facilitating environment opens up new channels of growth, development, and maturation that were blocked and distorted early in life. Only by improving the parents' basic life patterns, can we significantly improve their child-caring potentials. Parents must be heard and cared for themselves before they are able to hear and care for their children. (p. 391)

Nurturing neglectful parents may enable them to be more nurturing with their children (Crittenden, 1999). Substance abuse treatment and parent/ child attachment activities are reported as additional interventions to remediate psychological, behavioral, and/or relationship issues (Cantwell & Rosenberg, 1990; Howing, Wodarski, Gaudin, et al., 1989; Kelleher et al., 1994; Murphy et al., 1991; Paget et al., 1993; Thompson, 1995).

Social learning theory suggests that parental deficiencies are due to a lack of knowledge regarding appropriate parenting techniques (Sweet & Resick, 1979). As a result, interventions to teach individuals and families new skills are utilized with neglecting families. Such interventions include parenting instruction, behavior-shaping techniques, and modeling of de- sired behavior (Daro, 1988; Howing, Wodarski, Gaudin, et al., 1989; Sweet & Resick, 1979; Thompson, 1995; Twentyman & Plotkin, 1982; Whittaker et al., 1986). Both Cantwell and Rosenberg (1990) and Crittenden (1993, 1999) indicated innovative methods might be necessary in providing par- ent education for neglecting parents. According to information processing theory, these parents tend to block out information necessary for action and may do better with assistance in accepting new information prior to any kind of parent education (Crittenden, 1999). Utilizing interactive rather than didactic teaching methods in regard to parenting skills may be more effective with these families (Cantwell & Rosenberg, 1990).

Many neglecting parents feel overwhelmed. Family support services such as home visitor programs, support groups, and respite or day care have been provided to help in reducing stress and the incidence of neglect (Belsky, 1993; Cantwell & Rosenberg, 1990; Daro, 1988; Giovannoni & Billingsley, 1974; Helfer, 1987a; Thompson, 1995). Homemakers or volun- teers to help families with money management and financial planning, stress management, and client advocacy are other services delineated in studies describing intervention strategies (Cantwell & Rosenberg, 1990; Daro, 1988; Dubowitz, 1999; Helfer, 1987a; Knudsen, 1992; Saunders et al., 1993).

For families with health issues, interventions to improve utilization of health care resources at the family level include thorough health assess- ments and public health nursing services (Cantwell & Rosenberg, 1999; Dubowitz & Black, 2002; Helfer, 1987a; Knudsen, 1992; Saunders et al., 1993; Thompson, 1995). In terms of medical neglect, recognition and build- ing on family strengths, addressing risk factors, focusing on the child's needs, mental health services, social services, demonstration of caring con- cern for the family and child, and identification of issues underlying non- compliance are recommended in preventing and/or ameliorating neglect of children's health care (Cantwell & Rosenberg, 1990; Dubowitz, 1999; Dubowitz & Black, 2002). Parent aides could provide mothers with trans- portation, organization of medical appointments, and respite from caring for a chronically ill child (Cantwell & Rosenberg, 1990). As neglect is associated with larger families, Saunders et al. (1993) and Zuravin (1988) described family planning services to be offered to all neglecting families.

Cantwell and Rosenberg (1990) describe the following interventions for specific types of neglect:

1. *Lack of appropriate supervision.* Teach caretakers how to supervise and keep their children safe; and how to make appropriate child care arrangements. A community standard regarding at what age children may be left unattended would be helpful.

2. *Educational neglect.* Determine the barriers to having the children go to school. Working with the parent at the school may be helpful. State law regarding compulsory education may have to be invoked.

3. *Prenatal and postpartum neglect.* As prenatal and postpartum neglect frequently involves substance abuse, interventions can range from enlisting voluntary compliance from the mother to an order of confinement of the mother to prevent her from endangering her unborn child.

As a secondary prevention intervention Chasnoff and Lowder (1999) recommended that all pregnant and postpartum women be assessed for substance abuse. Any woman found positive for substance abuse would then be further evaluated in terms of the risk this posed for her unborn/ newborn child. Any woman using alcohol or other substances posing a risk would be referred to substance abuse treatment. Noncompliance could result in termination of parent rights. Chapter Nine presents an in-depth look at child neglect and substance abuse.

When less intrusive interventions fail, services may include the placement of children in a hospital or foster care setting (Cantwell & Rosenberg, 1990; Daro, 1988). In the event of a fatality due to neglect, steps need to be taken to protect other children in the home. These steps could include involvement with CPS, Family Court, and/or Criminal Court to prosecute the caretaker. The level of the intervention would depend on the risk to the remaining children, the parent's capacity for judgment, and community standards of reasonable care (Bonner et al., 1999).

Some research has reported concerns about the use of individual therapy with neglectful families. Biller and Solomon (1986) indicated that there is no empirical evidence that individual psychotherapy is effective in remediating neglectful behavior. Howing, Wodarski, Gaudin, et al. (1989) were concerned that individual therapy has not been systematically evaluated and may not be appropriate for low-functioning family members or clients with urgent needs.

Crittenden (1993) provided a theoretical framework for understanding neglecting behavior on the part of parents as a problem of information processing. Some parents have difficulty in perceiving signals from their child indicating that the child is in need. These parents need to be taught to identify and attend to their children's signals of need by (a) establishing a basis for their attention and (b) addressing the parents' affective responses to their children's signals. Other parents are able to recognize that their children are sending signals; however, they misinterpret them. These parents need information regarding child development and help in understanding the benefits of meeting their children's needs. Owing to the parent's affective responses to the child, this may require a therapeutic process rather than simple parent education. Many neglectful parents are able to perceive and interpret their children's needs, but are unable to select an appropriate response. These parents need to be taught a range of parenting skills and a way to seek and obtain nonjudgmental help with parenting over the long run. Even if able to attend, understand, and select an appropriate response, many parents are unable to implement that response. They intellectually know what to do, but are not able to translate that knowledge into behavior. Home visitation may be necessary to help parents act on what they know. The home visitor may have to work with the entire family to reinforce behavioral changes.

Environmental Practice

Informed by social learning, social ecology, social psychology, and behavioral theories, the environmental deficiencies model proposes that poverty, unemployment, inadequate education, inadequate medical coverage/resources, violent crime and drug trafficking, and unsafe and inadequate housing are structural factors associated with child neglect. In theory parents' behavior is shaped by the ecologies in which the family lives. Thus, this causal model implies that child maltreatment is a community problem and intervention to prevent/remediate the problem must be at the neighborhood and community level (Barry, 1994; Garbarino, 1981; Garbarino & Crouter, 1978; Garbarino & Sherman, 1980; Giovannoni & Billingsley, 1974; Melton & Barry, 1994; Weber, 1998). Structural issues make the task of preventing and/or remediating child neglect more complex and, as difficult as it is, the environment in which neglecting families live is the target for change (Giovannoni & Billingsley, 1974). CPS alone cannot be expected to resolve these issues. A network of services implying interagency coordination and cooperation and public and private partnerships is required to prevent and ameliorate child maltreatment (Carroll & Haase, 1987; Daro, 1988; Melton & Barry, 1994; Mulroy, 1997; Weber, 1998).

Dubowitz et al. (1993) indicated that any strategy to reduce child neglect must deal with the issue of poverty. Studies have described interventions to deal with this issue as those encompassed by the welfare system, including AFDC (now Temporary Assistance to Needy Families [TANF]), Supplemental Security Income (SSI), and other income/in-kind support measures. However, as indicated in Chapter Five, it has been projected that under TANF millions of low-income families will face sanctions or have their benefits cut off as the result of time limits (Duncan et al., 2002). It has been predicted that there will probably be an increase in child neglect as a result (Garbarino & Collins, 1999; Larner, Terman, & Behrman, 1997).

Even if parents are able to secure employment, it has been found that high child poverty/high public assistance neighborhoods have a greatly reduced child care capacity (Queralt & Witte, 1998). This has important implications in terms of the push to move parents from "welfare to work." "As long as the infrastructure for full-day center care is not in place and the family child-care supply remains deficient, it will be difficult for parents of young children to obtain and retain jobs" (Queralt & Witte, 1998, p. 43); again leaving families vulnerable to child neglect either as a result of not having an income or, if parents do go to work, not having adequate child care.

Berns and Drake (1998) stated that the outcomes of welfare reform depend upon how it is implemented. Program development will require

> the ability to find the maximum degree of innovation and service development that the reform will support within the context of the administrative structure within which a given state operates. If we use our new flexibility and available resources wisely, we can promote safe and stable families. (p. 8)

Christensen (1998) agreed that welfare reform could result in increases in child maltreatment, family homelessness, and domestic violence; which increase the potential for a rise in the foster care population accompanied by further family disruption. "If TANF legislation is to be a success, family stability and child well-being must be the desired outcome. Self-sufficiency through employment is one means to this end" (Christensen, 1998, p. 23). Cantwell and Rosenberg (1990) suggested that a thorough family assessment should routinely include an evaluation of the parent's employability.

Unemployment insurance, vocational rehabilitation, and other employment programs address the issue of unemployment (Daro, 1988; Helfer, 1987a; Saunders et al., 1993). However, these systems may be unable to meet the demand for employment of millions of families if, indeed, they are removed from the welfare rolls.

The school system can aid in resolving issues related to parents' educational deprivation, including adult education and general equivalency diploma (GED) courses (Daro, 1988; Helfer, 1987a). In terms of primary prevention, effective parenting techniques could be taught in the public schools. Health care at the community level, including state public health, public health nurses, Medicaid, and state health insurance programs, can contribute to the resolution of inadequate provision of health care resources (Helfer, 1987a). Legislation to control the drug trade and law-and-order reforms are community interventions to create safe neighborhoods (Halpern, 1990; Saunders et al., 1993). Communities also can work to improve housing resources and revitalize neighborhoods, thus enhancing resources and reducing stress for families living in high-risk neighborhoods (Garbarino & Kostelny, 1994; Halpern, 1990; Saunders et al., 1993).

To ease the isolation experienced by neglectful families, programs have been designed to enhance both their formal and informal support networks (Polansky, Gaudin et al., 1985; Polansky, 1985; Salzinger et al., 1983; Zuravin & Greif, 1989). Programs that treat social isolation include mutual support groups that could include both neglecting and nonneglecting families, seeking out and linking with supportive family members, homemaker services, parent aide programs, volunteer visitors, and the development of cooperative child care programs (Giovannoni & Billingsley, 1974; Howing, Wodarski, Gaudin, et al., 1989). In terms of preventing child maltreatment, Thompson (1994) reported that social support alone is unlikely to be effective. However, the integration of social support services into already established secondary prevention programs (i.e., programs that serve high-risk families) may be useful.

In terms of primary prevention, using the media to raise public awareness regarding the risks and consequences of child neglect may be useful. As reported in Chapter Five, awareness of child abuse in the general public went from 10% to 90% as the result of a successful media campaign (Cohn, 1987). Public health campaigns have been helpful in raising awareness of the consequences of cigarette, alcohol, and drug use. Taking a public health stance and characterizing child neglect as a social issue could result in a media campaign regarding the risks and consequences of child neglect that might prove helpful in raising public consciousness of the problem; and in gaining public support for policies to provide for the development of programs to nurture and support all families.

As can be seen, accomplishing the enormous task of creating healthy environments within which children and families are nurtured requires nothing less than programs that range from raising the level of public awareness and community action to the level of systemic reforms of the health, education, welfare, and child welfare systems. Melton and Barry (1994) reported that "neighbors helping neighbors," a strategy to accomplish this task, has been developed by the U.S. Advisory Board on Child Abuse and Neglect. Based on the American traditions of volunteerism and mutual assistance, the strategy is as follows:

1) Strengthen urban, suburban, and rural neighborhoods as environments for children and families.

2) Reorient the delivery of human services so that it becomes [as] easy to provide services to prevent child maltreatment and other forms of family disintegration as it is to place a child in foster care after the fact.
3) Improve the role of government in child protection.
4) Reorient societal values that may contribute to child maltreatment.
5) Strengthen and broaden the knowledge base about child maltreatment. (pp. 8–9)

Nevertheless, as Garbarino and Ebata (1983) pointed out, whether programs are aimed at structural changes or reducing social isolation, service delivery processes must be culturally appropriate.

Psychosocial/Ecological Practice

Seagull (1987) made the point that focusing on enhancing social networks will not produce positive results without also enhancing parental social and child-rearing skills. However, intervention programs must also be constructed to address the broad etiological structure of child neglect within families (Biller & Solomon, 1986). Halpern (1990) suggested a flexible mix of concrete, clinical, and supportive services in a family-like context; and DePanfilis (1999) reported that an ecological-developmental framework is a basic principle that has been suggested by research in the field. Based on the implications of psychological development, transaction, evolution, sociobiology, and ecological theories, the interaction model of child neglect indicates psychosocial/ecological interventions that target both familial and environmental issues.

Programs that take a psychosocial/ecological approach to the prevention and treatment of child neglect tend (a) to be comprehensive; (b) to be relatively long-term; (c) to be individualized—taking (i) parental characteristics; (ii) developmental levels of children, caretakers, and the family; (iii) the type of neglect (i.e., acute or chronic); and (iv) the social situation into consideration—(d) to intervene as early in the child's life as possible; (e) to focus on strengths and needs, not problems, and match interventions to client needs, not available resources; (f) to include families (biological, foster, and adoptive) as partners in planning, implementing, and evaluating services; (g) to be culturally appropriate; (h) to be flexible; (i) to routinely assess progress and adjust treatment plans when necessary; (j) to be outreach and advocacy oriented; and (k) to require interdisciplinary and interagency cooperation (Barry, 1994; Beyer, 1997; Biller & Solomon, 1986; DePanfilis, 1999; Dubowitz & Black, 2002; Erickson & Egeland, 2002; Gaudin, 1993; Guterman, 1997; Polansky et al., 1981; Wolfe, 1993). These services, utilizing both casework and community resources, focus on parental competence, enhancing coping strategies, and reducing stress (Gaudin et al., 1993). However, as Daro (1988) and Thomlison (1997) pointed out, it is most difficult to find services for neglecting families that have been empirically demonstrated to be effective. In fact, interventions with neglecting families are successful only about 50% of the time (Daro, 1988; Erickson & Egeland, 2002; Gaudin, 1993; Williams, 1980b); and there is little empirical support for choosing one intervention over another (DePanfilis, 1999).

As can be seen, programs that take a psychosocial/ecological approach, whether public (e.g., CPS) or private (e.g., HomeBuilders), provide or arrange for a variety of interventions.

1. Concrete services that increase family resources include, but are not limited to: (a) food, (b) clothing, (c) income supports, (d) employment services, and (e) transportation (Christensen, 1998; Daro, 1988; Gaudin, 1993; Gaudin et al., 1993; Pelton, 1994; Smokowski, 1998; Tymchuk & Andron, 1990; Wolock & Horowitz, 1979).

2. Behavioral interventions such as skill-building training are designed to improve parents' social, communication, and parenting skills (Daro, 1988; Gaudin, 1993; Guterman, 1997; Hillson & Kuiper, 1994; Polansky, 1985; Polansky, Ammons, et al., 1985; Polansky, Gaudin, et al., 1985; Smokowski, 1998; Thompson, 1995; Whittaker et al., 1986).

3. Cognitive interventions are designed to promote emotional growth and learning, develop positive parenting behaviors and attachment, reduce loneliness and depression, and decrease hostile and aggressive behaviors. Such interventions include individual, group, and family therapy (Daro, 1988; Gaudin, 1993; Gaudin et al., 1993; Hillson & Kuiper, 1994; Polansky, Ammons, et al., 1985; Polansky, Gaudin, et al., 1985; Thomlison, 1997; Thompson, 1995).

4. Quality child care is an intervention designed to both relieve caregiver stress and promote healthy child development (Daro, 1988; Halpern, 1990; Thomlison, 1997; Thompson, 1995).

5. Interventions to increase the size and supportiveness of families' formal and informal social networks are conceived to assist in reducing stress and social isolation. Such interventions could include friendly visitors, parent aides, natural helpers, extended family, long-term support groups, and state extension services (Gaudin, 1993; Gaudin et al., 1993; Guterman, 1997; Helfer, 1987a; Thomlison, 1997; Thompson, 1995; Turner & Avison, 1985; Whittaker et al., 1986; Wolfe, 1993).

6. Appropriate health care needs to be provided (Daro, 1988; Dubowitz & Black, 2002; Gaudin et al., 1993; Guterman, 1997; Thompson, 1995; Tymchuk & Andron, 1990; Wolfe, 1993).

7. Interventions at the community level would include community partnerships for child protection whereby neighborhoods would become protective of children and families, thus reducing the risk of child abuse and neglect, while honoring parents' rights and responsibilities to raise their own children (Chadwick, 2001; Gaudin, 1993; Mulroy, 1997; Schene, 1998). The neighborhood-based approach allows for geographic accessibility and comprehensiveness of services; and includes local networking, coordination, decision making, and program/protocol development (Barry, 1994; Chadwick, 2001; Mulroy, 1997). However, in order for community level practice to take place, investments in improvements in high-stress, low-resource neighborhoods in such areas as safety, housing, education, municipal services, opportunities for social support and cultural expression, and economic development might be needed (Barry, 1994; Garbarino & Kostelny, 1994). Barry (1994) suggested at minimum such community interventions should include neonatal home visitation, school health clinics, a single agency providing services, and adequate health and housing resources. These objectives can be achieved by an incremental approach, keeping the long-term outcomes in focus.

Irrespective of what interventions are being provided a family, McCubbin et al. (1995) suggested concentrating on the natural healing qualities of family life, including ethnic beliefs and values that emerge during times of stress. In this respect, Fischler (1985) found that restoring social networks through provision of recreational and community activities, outreach family support services plus informal temporary foster care, and substance abuse treatment were effective forms of treatment for child abuse and neglect for urban Native-American families. For Native Americans living on reservations understanding local beliefs regarding child rearing, the use of traditional healers, short-term counseling, social services, and local support mechanisms proved useful in reducing incidents of child maltreatment.

Hartley (1987) described an example of a program with the elements of a psychosocial/ecological approach as a blueprint for practice with neglectful families. Starting with a comprehensive assessment, a plan for family treatment is formulated. Based on the assessment, family treatment may include: (a) family therapy, (b) parenting training, (c) parent/child attachment services, (d) substance abuse treatment, (e) development of community and kinship support systems, (e) parent aides, and (f) other community support services.

Therapeutic services would be provided by a confidence clinic that works with parents in accentuating competencies, correcting erroneous self-thinking, enhancing positive assertiveness and positive self-care, managing anger, setting self-goals, and planning for themselves. Local churches are encouraged to adopt a family and provide various social support and concrete services. The program includes community service networking, the components of which are connected and coordinated by a primary family treatment worker/case manager. However comprehensive and appropriate this approach to neglect appears, efforts to implement such programs are hampered by a lack of empirical evidence of their effectiveness (Whittaker et al., 1986).

Wolfe (1993) described a transitional approach to intervening with at-risk families and families who neglect their children. This prevention/intervention strategy takes into consideration how child maltreatment progresses. The initial stage, exhibited by a reduced tolerance for stress and inhibition of aggression, is based on neglectful parenting models and is generally benign. A supportive spouse, socioeconomic stability, successful life experiences, and positive social supports can buffer this risk factor. If these buffers are not forthcoming, the next stage includes poor crisis/provocation management. Compensatory factors for this stage include community programs to assist parents in coping with difficult family-related issues. The third and most rigid stage includes chronic/habitual behavior patterns of extreme behavior to avoid the stresses of parenting. There are few compensatory factors that aid in the process of behavior change at this level. Changing chronic behavior is most difficult. Families must first come to realize that the benefits of changed behavior outweigh the costs. This approach to intervention with families points to prevention strategies, which include interventions taking place as early in a child's life as possible. It may be easier to work with families before chronic, negative parent-child behavior patterns have been established; and before the damage has been done to the child.

Child-Focused Practice

There are few descriptive studies that address interventions with neglected children. The prevailing philosophy has been that the best way to help high-risk or neglected children is to prevent or stop the neglect; and thus, most intervention strategies involve work with parents to reduce stress and improve parenting skills. However, grounded in child development theory, attachment theory, and neurobiological development theory, the conclusions of the causal model regarding the effects of neglect on children indicated that there is a need for direct practice with children, irrespective of successful interventions with parents. The work of Wolfe (1993), Perry (2002a, 2002b), Perry et al. (1995, 2002), and Perry and Pollard (1997) indicated the urgency of early intervention with at-risk or neglected children.

Prenatal and postpartum parents may be more amenable to intervention; and there is less chance of damage to the child.

The findings of Egeland and Sroufe (1981), and Werner and Smith (1982) suggested that even under adverse conditions children can have positive outcomes (i.e., even if parents fail to receive services other factors in the child's life can have ameliorative effects). Their research implies, therefore, that strategies to reinforce supportive child and environmental factors and to remediate sources of stress for children can produce positive outcomes. Smokowski (1998) has suggested an ecological approach to promoting resilience in children who have been abused and/or neglected. This approach would reduce vulnerability and risk by reducing stressors and increasing resources. Protective processes would be mobilized and "resilience strings" of beneficial behaviors would be fostered.

Beyer (1997) proposed a strengths/needs-based approach to child welfare that starts with the principle that children belong with their families and need enduring relationships with adults. To accomplish this principle, children would receive comprehensive, intensive, individualized services and supports that build on their strengths and are responsive to their needs. When children cannot remain in their own homes, the out-of-home placement would be considered an extension of family life, not a replacement for it; and their needs for attachment would be addressed. The following are specific child-focused practices that have been suggested by theory to prevent or remediate the consequences of child neglect.

Child development theory implies play therapy, individual therapy, and therapeutic day care as interventions for young children (Law & Conway, 1992; Smokowski, 1998; Thomlison, 1997). Williams (1980b) and Cantwell and Rosenberg (1990) reported that group therapy is helpful for school-age and adolescent children. However, psychotherapy is not routinely provided for children. Law and Conway (1992) and Cantwell and Rosenberg (1990) reported communication deficits in children as the result of faulty parenting. They suggested age-appropriate, child-centered speech/language and communication skills programs for young, neglected children. These interventions, also based on child development theory, included strategies to address social, cognitive, and language deficiencies.

Social isolation may be a problem for neglected children, as well as for their parents (Polansky, Ammons, et al., 1985). Programs that provide children with opportunities for socialization and the promotion of social competence include children's play groups, extracurricular activities, therapeutic play schools, public schools, and day care (Cantwell & Rosenberg, 1990; Law & Conway, 1992; Smokowski, 1998; Thompson, 1994, 1995; Williams, 1980b). Neglected children have low self-esteem and poor self-concepts. Programs to build self-esteem and competence/skills training to enhance self-concept are reported by Law and Conway (1992) and Smokowski (1998).

Community infant development programs for young children and special education and social services in the schools for older children are utilized to treat children at risk for or who have developmental delays and/or school difficulties (Helfer, 1987a; Smokowski, 1998; Thomlison, 1997; Thompson, 1995; Williams 1980b).

Fatherless homes are the rule for neglecting families; therefore, father deprivation is an issue. Attachment theory suggests fostering supportive relationship between children and responsible adults. Biller and Solomon (1986) proposed Big Brothers, Boy Scouts of America, athletic teams, camps, churches, and settlement houses as programs that provide meaningful father-surrogates for both boys and girls. In addition a "Big Brother," "Big Sister," or homemaker in the home can have a "normalizing" effect on neglected children (i.e., people do go on outings, bake cookies, make beds, and do the laundry), and provide at-risk children with adult support and assistance outside the family, yet still in the community (Cantwell & Rosenberg, 1990; Thompson, 1995).

Neglect has been shown to be harmful or even lethal to children (AHA, 1983, 1988; Bonner et al., 1999; DiLeonardi, 1993; Margolin, 1990; Rieder & Cicchetti, 1989; Trocme et al., 1995; Wolock & Horowitz, 1984; Zumwalt & Hirsch, 1987). Therefore, hospitalization and/or foster care have been reported as interventions in cases of highest risk (Beyer, 1997; Cantwell & Rosenberg, 1990; Law & Conway, 1992; Smokowski, 1998).

Practices with parents that focus on children include (a) parenting training, (b) teaching child management skills, and (c) promoting healthy feeding routines for infants (Bousha & Twentyman, 1984; Cantwell & Rosenberg, 1990; Smokowski, 1998; Thomlison, 1997; Thompson, 1995). Training in child development is utilized to assist parents in having more realistic expectations of their children.

In addition to interventions with children and interventions with parents that are focused on children, attachment theory suggests child-focused interventions that include both parents and children. Smokowski (1998) indicated, "The personal attention from a caring adult is one of the most powerful protective mechanisms for early childhood development" (p. 350). Programs that address attachment issues, therefore, are of utmost importance. In order to increase positive parent/child interactions, family interventions, including parents and children, may employ home-based professionals or paraprofessionals to teach attachment behaviors using modeling, positive reinforcement, and role playing (Smokowski, 1998; Thomlison, 1997). In this manner, family bonds are strengthened at the same time parents are learning to care for, supervise, and serve as resources for their children (Beyer, 1997; Thomlison, 1997).

Moreover, parents and children may be involved in services aimed at preventing/ameliorating emotional neglect and nonorganic failure to thrive.

Emotionally neglected children can be time-consuming and need a lot of care (Cantwell & Rosenberg, 1990). Perry (2001) outlined a strategy, derived from neurobiological theory, for helping children with attachment problems due to emotional neglect that includes (a) giving a lot physical care and affection; (b) taking a nonpunitive approach to teaching positive behavior; (c) responding to the children's emotional age, not their chronological age; (d) being consistent and repetitive as these children are sensitive to change; (e) modeling and teaching appropriate social behaviors by coaching them when they play; (f) listening to them, and talking and playing with them; and (g) having realistic expectations of the children. Because their brains are more difficult to modify (Perry, 2001), emotionally neglected children need someone to pay attention to them in a tender and consistent way for many years (Cantwell & Rosenberg, 1990). If parents are unable to do so, a relative, Big Brother/Big Sister, or someone from church, a teacher, or a volunteer may be engaged to provide the needed relationship with a caring adult (Thompson, 1995). If out-of-home placement is necessary, it must be remembered that multiple foster home placements are counterindicated for these children and termination of parental right would be a consideration (Cantwell & Rosenberg, 1990).

In cases of NOFTT, Weston et al. (1993) described a program that includes focusing on the mother/child dyad, treating the family on an outpatient basis, and utilizing day care services. Cantwell and Rosenberg (1990) recommended focusing on assisting parents in developing empathy for their children, while teaching them to appropriately feed and play with their kids.

Summary of Practice Strategies

The foregoing studies have described practices with families who are at risk for or neglect their children as being comprehensive, intensive, flexible, culturally appropriate, and long-term (6–18 months), and as emphasizing enhancement of social supports, parenting skills, and provision of concrete services. Prevention and/or early intervention programs are critical to prevent/ameliorate harm to children caused by neglect. A combination of community and home-based programs that foster community partnerships and interdisciplinary and interagency cooperation may be most effective.

Individualized practice based on an assessment of family strengths and needs, which addresses risk factors and environmental, as well as family and individual issues, is recommended. Interventions would involve all family members, including fathers whenever possible, as partners in planning, implementing, and evaluating service; and be tailored to the clients' needs, not available resources. Service goals would be clear, realistic, related to behavioral changes, meaningful to the family, and prioritized (after ensuring the safety of the child) to focus on one or two easily achievable goals at a time. Service providers would demonstrate caring and concern for all family members, and act as advocates for the family.

Given the above-detailed context within which practice with high-risk and neglectful families takes place, *intrafamilial practice*—derived from social learning, behavioral, developmental, neurobiological, and information-processing theories—provides services for adults to assist in changing personality characteristics or behaviors that result or could result in child neglect. These interventions include:

1. Mental health services including individual, family, and group therapy. As indicated above, there is some concern regarding the effectiveness of individual therapy for neglectful parents. However, if an individualized assessment indicates the need for individual therapy, it could be provided.
2. Substance abuse treatment. If pregnant women refuse treatment, maternal confinement, as a last resort, has been considered in some jurisdictions.
3. Interventions to strengthen parent/child attachment.
4. Parenting instruction utilizing behavior-shaping techniques, role play, and modeling of desired behavior. Prior to instruction, parents may need assistance in learning to accept new information. Interactive teaching methods seem to be more effective than didactic presentation of material. Depending on need, teaching could be home-based and involve the whole family.
5. Teaching individuals and the family new competencies such as money management and financial planning, stress management, and social and communication skills.
6. Family support services such as home visitor programs, support groups, respite, or day care.
7. Family-planning service.
8. Interventions to improve health care would include health assessments; identifying issues regarding noncompliance; public health nursing services and parent aides to provide transportation, organize medical appointments, and provide respite.
9. Services to assist parents in ensuring that their school-age children attend school.
10. Placement of children in a hospital or foster care setting, and/or involving the CPS, the Family Court, and/or the Criminal Court systems.
11. Client outreach and advocacy.

Within the aforementioned context, *environmental practice*—developed from social learning, social ecology, social psychology, and behavior theory—focuses on manipulating social structures and environments to relieve family stress. Primary prevention strategies include raising public consciousness by means of media campaigns regarding child neglect and teaching parenting in the public schools. Structural services include: (a) the welfare system, including TANF, SSI, and food supplement programs, unemployment insurance, and other income support measures; (b) vocational rehabilitation and other employment programs; (c) the education system, including adult education and GED courses; (d) the health care system, including public health, Medicaid, and state health insurance programs; (e) law-and-order reforms, including drug enforcement; and (f) community programs to improve housing resources and revitalize neighborhoods.

Environmental interventions include programs that treat social isolation and enhance formal and informal support networks. These programs include (a) mutual support groups including neglecting and nonneglecting families, (b) the development of relationships with supportive family members, (c) homemaker services, (d) parent aide programs, (e) volunteer visitors, (f) the utilization of natural helpers, and (g) cooperative child care programs. Social support services seem to work best when integrated into already established secondary prevention programs.

Psychosocial/ecological practice, based on developmental, transactional, evolutionary, sociobiological, and ecological theory, includes both intrapsychic and sociological services, intervening at the individual, family, and community levels to provide clinical as well as supportive services. These interventions are designed to remedy the gaps in services created when focus is placed on one level of intervention as opposed to another. These interventions include:

1. Concrete services that increase family resources such as food, clothing, income supports, employment services, and transportation.
2. Behavioral interventions that increase family competencies, such as social skills training, communication skills training, and parenting skills training.
3. Cognitive interventions, including individual, group, and family counseling aimed at emotional growth and learning, developing positive parent behaviors and attachment, reducing loneliness and depression, and decreasing hostile and aggressive behaviors.
4. Quality child care.
5. Interventions to increase the size and supportiveness of families' community and kinship support systems, including formal and informal social networks, such as friendly visitors, parent aides, natural helpers, extended family, and state extension services.

6. Appropriate health care.
7. Community and neighborhood improvement and revitalization efforts to include safety, housing, health care, education, and municipal services. Community services could include neonatal home visitation; school health clinics; substance abuse treatment; opportunities for social support, cultural expression, and economic development; and a single access point for services.

Borrowing from child development, attachment, and neurobiological theory, *child-focused practice* includes therapeutic and supportive services for children and adults that prevent or ameliorate the effects of child neglect and promote children's resiliency. Aimed at reducing stressors and increasing resources, interventions focused on children include (a) play, individual, and group therapy; (b) speech/language and communication skills programs; (c) children's play groups; (d) extracurricular activities; (e) therapeutic play schools; (f) public schools; (g) day care; (h) programs to build self-esteem; (i) competency/skills training; (j) community infant development programs; (k) special education for older children; (l) Big Brothers/Big Sisters; (m) Boy and Girl Scouts; (n) athletic teams; (o) camps; (p) church programs; (q) settlement house programs; (r) homemaker services; (s) social services; and (t) hospitalization and/or foster care that would be treated as an extension of family life.

Interventions with adults that are focused on children encompass training in (a) parenting techniques, (b) child management skills, (c) healthy feeding routines, and (d) child development. Services to nurture parent or caretaker/child attachment are generally focused on the mother/child dyad and are aimed at enabling the caretaker to develop empathy for the child, and teach the caretaker to appropriately play with the child. These techniques may be taught in-home and include (a) modeling, (b) positive reinforcement, and (c) role play.

Irrespective of the practice model utilized, McCubbin et al. (1995) suggested concentrating on the natural healing qualities of family life, including ethnic beliefs and values. Garbarino and Ebata (1983) pointed out that useful services and service delivery processes would be culturally appropriate.

As indicated above, practice with families who neglect or are at risk for neglecting their children would be comprehensive, addressing issues in the environment as well as within the family. However, most interventions are focused on adults and not specifically on the neglecting population. More consideration needs to be given to assessing the needs of children and including them in service plans for the family, and to developing programs specific to neglected children and their families.

Chapter Seven

What Impacts Children of Neglect?

PRACTICE OUTCOMES

Studies have demonstrated that families involved in different types of maltreatment represent different subpopulations (Daro, 1988). Research has indicated that interventions are less successful with neglecting than with abusive parents; and suggest that differential approaches to these two problem areas need to be developed, including longer-term treatment of the neglecting family (Bath & Haapala, 1992; Berry, 1992; Daro, 1988; Helfer, 1987a; Kempe & Goldbloom, 1987; Nelson & Landsman, 1992; Rose & Meezan, 1993; Yuan & Struckman-Johnson, 1991). However, as previously stated, there have been few programs designed exclusively for neglectful families and, therefore, there has been little research that focuses on interventions intended to remediate the problem of families who neglect their children per se. Unless otherwise noted, the interventions outlined below have been designed for maltreating, not solely neglectful, parents. These studies are differentiated from those discussed in the last chapter in that they have included outcomes as a part of the research.

Overall, neglectful families tend not to do well in services and generally have the least successful outcomes regardless of the nature of the intervention (Bath & Haapala, 1992; Berry, 1991, 1992; Gaudin, 1993; Knudsen, 1992). The success of various programs working with the neglect population remains mostly undocumented (Gaudin, 1993; Knudsen, 1992). To reemphasize the point, barriers to successful outcomes for neglectful families seem to be the (a) weak theoretical base supporting interventions,

(b) parents' difficulty in engaging in treatment and following through on a service plan (i.e., recruitment and retention), (c) number and severity of the problems faced by these families, (d) chronic nature of the problems, (e) frustration and eventual sense of futility and apathy experienced by social workers involved with this population, and (f) possible biological factors. The capacity of neglecting parents to stop neglecting behavior appears to be very difficult to develop. It would appear that neglecting families are amenable to long-term support but are resistant to change (Herrenkohl et al, 1983; Wolfe, 1993).

In an interesting study, Polansky et al. (1978) asked three lay groups their expectations of the effectiveness of various interventions with neglecting families. These groups (waitresses, blue-collar workers, and college students) indicated that they believed the assignment of a social worker to monitor the situation and referral of parents to a mental health clinic would be the most effective ways of treating these families.

Intrafamilial Practice

In 1989, Howing, Wodarski, Kurtz, et al. reviewed the literature regarding practice with maltreating families. They found that successful program elements included home visits and twenty-four-hour phone availability of the social worker. Behavioral techniques that were effective included modeling, role play, relaxation techniques, systematized desensitization, cognitive restructuring, self-instruction, and stress inoculation. Interventions producing the most positive outcomes were (a) parent training groups that included information regarding child development and child behavior management, (b) stress reduction programs, and (c) anger management training. Discussion films and homework were effective teaching tools. Family therapy was found to be effective with neglectful families, and group treatment, such as Parents Anonymous (PA), as an adjunct to other services was reported to be effective in reducing maltreatment. Individual therapy was less successful than group or family therapy. Thomlison (1997) found that the level of severity of the clients' problems was the best predictor of success; and more effective interventions with parents included money management and nutrition education.

In a later review Dore and Lee (1999) looked at parenting programs for abusive and neglectful parents that addressed not only parents' child management skills, but also their emotional and cognitive needs. These programs were generally preventive in nature and were not initially interested in changing parenting behavior. Before the behavioral component of the intervention was introduced, cognitive and affective dimensions of parenting were addressed. Developing self-understanding was a significant component of this intervention. The results of the study indicated that parents who had children with specific behavior problems and parents who had the personal resources to enable them to translate the learning into behavioral changes benefited most from the parenting programs. These findings support Crittenden's (1993) information-processing framework for interventions with neglectful families.

Biller and Solomon (1986) reported research that examined a program designed to improve maternal and child attachment. This program provided counseling, recreation, housekeeping, and child care for as long as it was clinically necessary. Other than a 50% dropout rate, no empirical data regarding outcomes were given. It was believed that the high dropout rate was due to the indeterminate length of treatment and the lack of commitment on the part of the participants to stay in the program on a long-term basis.

Beyer (1997) indicated that foster care should be an extension of family life, not a substitution for it. Kinship care, which will be presented later in this chapter in regard to practice with children, has been developed to keep children within the boundaries of the extended family, hopefully to maintain the parent/child relationship to the greatest extent possible; and still ensure safety and continuity for the child. To test this basic assumption, O'Donnell (1999) studied the involvement of African-American fathers who had children placed in kinship foster arrangements. It was found that few fathers were involved in case assessments, case planning, or receipt of services. There were major gaps in information concerning fathers, including assessments of their ability to provide a home for their children; and caseworkers did not view this as an issue. If there was contact with fathers it was usually by telephone. Fathers who had children placed with paternal relatives were more likely to have involvement with planning, participation in services, and contact with the caseworker. However, in most cases family members were no more anxious to involve fathers than were the caseworkers.

In 1998, Meezan and O'Keefe evaluated the effectiveness of multifamily group therapy in child abuse and neglect by comparing families who participated in multifamily group therapy with those who were treated by traditional group therapy. The multifamily group intervention included a case management component. At the end of treatment the multifamily group families had significantly lower child abuse potential scores and significantly higher social support scores than those who receive traditional therapy. Additionally, families receiving multifamily therapy improved in a significantly larger number of areas of functioning than the traditional therapy group. Multifamily group therapy appears to be effective in reducing maltreatment potential and increasing social support. This group also had a smaller dropout rate, had a greater number of planned closings, and therapy was less expensive to deliver.

Tymchuk and Andron (1990) compared two groups of developmentally delayed, primarily neglectful mothers. One group of mothers had at least one child placed in foster care. The other group did not have a child placed out of the home. The difference between the two groups was the mothers' successful completion of parenting training and a supportive relative in the home. Thus, this study indicated that parenting training and social support are effective in keeping children of developmentally delayed, neglectful mothers in their own homes.

Paget et al. (1993), in a review of the literature regarding interventions with neglectful families, found that intervention strategies were limited in scope but promising in implications. The services provided included training in problem-solving, home cleanliness, and safety skills; and providing adequate stimulation for children. Outcomes suggested that neglectful parents are able to incorporate problem-solving training into familiar and novel child care dilemmas and generate additional effective solutions with success. Personal cleanliness of children improved, infant stimulation skills were learned, and homes with developmentally delayed mothers were made physically and nutritionally safe. "Overall, the studies suggest that neglecting mothers, including those with limited intellectual capacity, are receptive and responsive to a variety of interventions. These results also suggest that child neglect may be the result of skill or motivational deficiencies that are reasonable targets of behavioral interventions" (p. 164).

Another study evaluating parenting training focused on emotionally abusive and neglectful parents (Iwaniec, 1997). Parents who received individual, weekly sessions focusing mostly on child development, parenting attitudes, and children's needs were compared with parents who received individual counseling to prepare them for group participation followed by ten weekly sessions of group training. The group training was set up to meet parents' unmet needs and skill deficits. Iwaniec (1997) found that the individual/group training group had a significantly higher overall level of improvement. The individual/group training group improved more in self-esteem and confidence when dealing with their children and other aspects of their lives. Both groups improved in the way they related to and managed their children, and achieved significant reduction in emotionally abusive behaviors occurring often—the individual/group training group improving more than the individual training only group. There were no differences between the groups in terms of emotionally abusive behaviors occurring occasionally and almost never. In addition, those parents who received additional training in groups, and more important whose needs were addressed in the group, did much better in the long term than those who had only individual training. These findings support Crittenden (1999) and Steele (1987) in their assertions that nurturing neglectful parents results in improved nurturing of their own children.

In a study of parenting values in a low-income, African-American population, Abell et al. (1996) found that the effects of poverty were not linear with respect to the quality of parent/child interaction. Parenting styles differed and one parenting style did not fit all. Since most neglectful families are living in conditions of poverty, this finding could be relevant in designing parenting education programs. However, behavioral interventions disregard situational factors; and programs that address parenting skills and fail to address socioeconomic stressors will probably be ineffective in preventing further maltreatment. It is suggested that intrafamilial practice is too narrow in scope and would be more effective if supplemented by the provision of basic needs (Dore & Lee, 1999; Howing, Wodarski, Kurtz, et al., 1989). In any event, there have been few long-term studies of the impact of intrafamilial interventions on child outcomes; no observed changes in parent/child interactions have been reported; and there is limited empirical evidence for their long-term effectiveness (Biller & Solomon, 1986; Howing, Wodarski, Kurtz, et al., 1989; Williams 1980b).

Environmental Practice

Horowitz and Wolock (1981) studied the relationships between material deprivation, child maltreatment, and social service interventions with poor families. A review of social service case records revealed that services offered were primarily sociological in nature (e.g., help with budgeting, food shopping, and securing welfare benefits; day care; family planning; housing; and health care). There was little follow-up to determine whether families were actually utilizing services. Case records indicated that during the time of their involvement with the agency 44% of the families had at least one child placed out of the home and 73% showed either no change in behavior or a worsening of the maltreatment. Almost no records noted progress that was likely to be long-lasting.

Ory and Earp (1980), however, found that the utilization of social services counterbalanced social disorganization in families to reduce the likelihood of child maltreatment. The probability of child maltreatment went from 42.1 for families with high social disorganization and low use of social services to 7.6 for families with high social disorganization and high use of social services. High utilization combined with low social disorganization reduced the odds to 0.3.

Spearly and Lauderdale (1983) reported finding that the amount of the AFDC benefit per month, per child had an inverse relationship with child abuse (i.e., as welfare benefits increased, rates of physical abuse decreased). Interestingly, since neglect is more highly correlated with poverty than is abuse, there was no increase in rates for neglect cases in relation to the level of AFDC benefits. Also in regard to AFDC, Brandon (2000) reported that public assistance played a positive role in keeping children and mothers together; and more generous benefits lowers the risk of out-of-home placement for children.

The Patch approach moves human service practice to the neighborhood (AHA, 1997). This method reduces isolation of both service providers and clients by building on strengths at all levels, and increasing access to supports and services needed to strengthen families and address their needs. This is done through the partnering of service providers, residents, and local institutions/organizations to share decision making and responsibility in meeting family and neighborhood needs (AHA, 1997). In a review of the outcomes of Patch initiatives the AHA (1997) found that (a) the focus of social services became the neighborhood; (b) potential networks of formal and informal social supports for residents were expanded; (c) there was a greater emphasis placed on prevention efforts; (d) new ways for service providers to partner with each other and the neighborhood were developed and facilitated; (e) neighborhood residents were empowered to take a more active role in planning and providing services and supports; (f) frontline workers took on more management responsibilities; (g) residents took on more decision-making responsibilities; (h) a more responsive allocation of resources was promoted; and (i) to some extent categorical funding barriers were removed.

Tochiki (1996) reported on a pilot project to test the use of mediation in settling cases of child maltreatment brought before the Family Court. Outcomes indicted that all who participated in the program benefited to some degree. Parents left the process feeling (a) that their point of view had been heard, (b) that they had gained an understanding of the child welfare system, (c) that they could own part of the decision-making process, and (d) that they had regained some of their rights to self-determination. Seventy-two percent of mediations ended in settlement; and the court accepted almost all mediated settlements. It was concluded that mediation is an effective process for the out-of-court resolution of disputes in child abuse and neglect cases headed for trial, and for increasing communications among the parties involved in a child welfare case. This study did not report regarding the relationship between outcomes of the mediation process and outcomes for children. However, the following study may have some bearing regarding possible inferential outcomes.

In their review of the literature regarding the effectiveness of interventions with maltreating families, Howing, Wodarski, Kurtz, et al. (1989) found that interventions included providing (a) basic needs such as food, shelter, and clothing; (b) economic support; (c) medical transportation; (d) legal services; (e) respite care; and (f) formal supports such as home visitors, homemaker services, or lay therapists. What seemed to be most helpful was a cooperative relationship between families and the child welfare system. In terms of the outcomes for children of family court mediation, one might infer from this research that if parents felt attended to, gained an understanding of the child welfare system, felt in control of at least part of the decision-making process regarding their family, believed they had regained some of their rights to self-determination, and achieved better communication with the child welfare system, then there would be better outcomes for children.

This review (Howing, Wodarski, Kurtz, et al., 1989) indicated that there was no evidence of treatment gains with formal supports (i.e., lay counseling, home visitors, and homemaker services). Evidence of the importance of informal support networks in sustaining gains was limited. Thus, empirical evidence for the hypothesis that formal or informal support networks, alone, are effective interventions with neglectful parents was not forthcoming from these studies.

Psychosocial/Ecological Practice

Psychosocial/ecological approaches utilize interventions to address both intrafamilial and environmental issues. In a study of outcomes of self-regulation and self-worth in Black children living in poor, rural, single-mother-headed households, Murry and Brody (1999) found that protective factors, which buffered the impact of risk factors, were parent satisfaction, external support systems, and kin network systems. Thompson (1994) pointed out that social support alone is unlikely to be an effective preventive program. These findings support the premise that successful programs would include components to deal with intrafamilial and environmental issues. Schorr (1988) concluded that high-risk families require high-intensity, quality services. Successful programs provide intensive, comprehensive, individualized services with aggressive outreach and long-term involvement with families (Schorr, 1988, 1997). Daro and Donnelly (2002) found that positive outcomes were associated with (a) early intervention; (b) group facilitation by parents; (c) long-term service availability; (d) focus on parent strengths, decision making that has long-term effects, and child specific developmental levels; (e) a commitment to ongoing staff training and supervision; (f) parents modeling learned behavior; (g) social support; (h) recognition of cultural differences; and (i) a balance of home-based and group-based activities. These interventions may be provided by a state agency such as CPS, or private agencies generally contracted by the state to provide these services. These interventions can be classified into three types: (a) standard child welfare services, including community initiatives; (b) home-based family support/preservation services to prevent maltreatment and/or placement of a child out of the home; and (c) intensive family preservation services (IFPS) to prevent placement of children at risk for placement or to reunify children with their families after placement.

Standard child welfare services. These are services generally provided by CPS or equivalent state agencies, and/or private agencies contracted by the state to provide services not provided by the state agency. In order to receive child welfare services, a family must have been called to the attention of CPS, or its equivalent, as having either harmed or been at risk for harming their children. As outlined in Chapter Five, CPS is responsible for (a) responding to reports; (b) assessing family circumstances; (c) arranging for services (including placement if necessary) to ensure the current and continued safety of children in a stable, nurturing family situation; and (d) monitoring family progress (Schene, 1998). Usually a combination of counseling, concrete, and supportive services is provided by various service providers with the CPS worker acting as case manager. Thus, in addition to the CPS worker, families may be seeing any number of service providers. These services may or may not be in the home and are designed to assure child safety.

If it is determined that the children cannot safely be kept in the home without court intervention or must be removed from the family against the family's wishes, the family will become involved with the legal, as well as the social service system. Aimed at formulating and legalizing (court ordering) a service plan that is in the best interests of children, the legal system will include judges, attorneys for the parents and agencies involved, and court-appointed special advocates (CASA) or guardians ad litem (GAL) to represent the children's interests. In this event, families must deal not only with CPS and various service providers but also with judges, lawyers, and CASAs or GALs. In addition, they must attend court hearings in a setting that is basically adversarial—hearings that are often characterized as more punitive than helpful. The following are studies that have explored outcomes of the child welfare system.

In 2002 *Child Maltreatment 2000* (USDHHS) provided the following information regarding the current state of child welfare practice in the United States. More than 60% of child victims experienced neglect; thus children continue to experience neglect more than any other form of child maltreatment. An estimated 41.7 children out of every 1,000, or 3,000,000 children, received preventive services, which included respite care, parenting education, housing assistance, substance abuse treatment, day care, home visits, individual and family counseling, homemaker help, transportation, and crisis and domestic violence intervention.

The average time from the start of a child welfare investigation to the provision of service was 35.8 days and only 55.4% of child victims (478,000) received postinvestigation services. An additional estimated 384,000 (18.7%)

received services even though maltreatment was unsubstantiated. Postinvestigation or remedial services included individual counseling, case management, family-based services (e.g., family counseling, family support services), in-home services (e.g., family preservation), foster care, and court intervention (USDHHS, 2002).

Information concerning child fatalities indicated that 14.9% of families of victims had received family preservation services. Only 2.6% of children had been placed in foster care, returned to their families, and later died there.

Watters et al. (1986) reported results of Children's Aid Society intervention in Canada. They compared three groups of families: (a) those who abused their children, (b) those who neglected their children, and (c) those who both abused and neglected their children. They found that the families who were more likely to show reduced family functioning after agency involvement were families who were both abusing and neglecting; and the profile of these families was closer to the profile of the neglect families than to the profile of the abusive families.

Studies of the recidivism rates in child maltreatment have found that neglect is associated with the highest rates of recurrence of any type of child maltreatment (DePanfilis & Zuravin, 1998; Jonson-Reid et al., in press; Marshall & English, 1999; USDHHS, 2002). The majority of cases with recurrences of maltreatment had only one recurrence. Recurrences seemed to be clustered within a month or two after the initial report.

Reporting on the National Center For Health Services Research findings regarding eleven federally funded child abuse and neglect treatment programs Williams (1980b) indicated that overall only 40–50% of the programs' participants stopped abusing or neglecting their children. Interventions were more effective if they lasted for over six months, and combined professional and lay therapy.

Daro (1988) described the findings of the National Clinical Evaluation Study of programs sponsored by NCCAN that included four projects designed to intervene with neglecting families. Although success rates were low (46% showed no improvement at the end of the program, 70% were expected to neglect again, and 77% continued neglectful behavior during treatment), 53% showed some improvement. The length of time of intervention was positively related to the more successful outcomes. Thirteen to eighteen months appeared to be optimal for neglect cases. However, simply retaining a neglectful family in a program for that length of time was not sufficient to ensure success. Clients retained longer actually began to decline. In this event the outcome was to change treatments or permanently remove the child from the home.

Effective interventions were family counseling and the use of a broad range of community programs to provide concrete/supportive services.

Counseling focused on problem solving. Child care was taught during supervised parent/child interactions using modeling techniques and encouraging parental nurturing behavior. Child development classes were not helpful for this population; and clinical intervention, alone, was not effective owing to the multiple problems these families experienced. Therefore, it was determined that clinical intervention must be augmented by concrete/supportive services (Daro, 1988).

Nelson et al. (1990) followed chronically neglecting families receiving child welfare services for one year. At the end of that time period the families demonstrated improvement in mental health, social supports, and parenting knowledge and attitudes.

Waldfogel (1998) explored efforts at child welfare reform in Missouri, Florida, and Iowa. With some variations these new approaches to child welfare practice targeted investigations by CPS toward only high-risk families and building collaborative community networks to serve lower-risk families. Differential responses to high- and low-risk families were tailored to each family's needs. It was too soon in the process to have reliable outcomes, although Florida reported greater family satisfaction, more community partners involved in cases of maltreatment, and better safety outcomes for children in the districts that were implementing the new differential response mode.

In 1996, Pithouse and Lindsell compared families who received standard child welfare field social work service and families who were referred to a family support center. The family center included an assigned social worker who provided individual and family therapy, group work, and general advice and support; a children's toy library and supervised play facilities; and a kitchen and lounge where clients could relax and take meals with other families and staff. The families seen at the center had fewer subsequent involvements with the child welfare system than the families receiving field social work intervention.

Home-based family support and preservation programs. These home/community-based programs focus on family specific interventions with high-risk families that utilize strategies developed for maltreating families to prevent out-of-home placement (Thompson, 1995). They, therefore, are designed to prevent maltreatment in high-risk families and to keep maltreating families together by reducing stress and improving family functioning to ensure child safety (i.e., prevent a recurrence of maltreatment). Services provided by these programs may include peer support groups, education regarding parenting and/or child development, socialization, and learning experiences for young children, adolescents, and parents (McCroskey & Meezan, 1998). Families referred to these programs may or may not have been subject to a CPS investigation. However, in order to receive services, they had to be found by the referral source to be at least at risk for harming their children.

In 2001, Layzer, Goodson, Bernstein, and Price completed a national evaluation of family support programs. They concluded that there is no single effective program model in working with high-risk or maltreating parents; and in 2002 Daro and Donnelly also pointed out that any single intervention strategy has limitations. With neglecting parents Gaudin (1993) found that behavioral approaches (e.g., modeling, coaching, role playing, and mothers critiquing their own videos) have proven to be effective in building parents' child-caring and social skills. Such interventions would be structured with clearly defined, short-range goals and well-defined activities.

In a study of home-based interventions with multiproblem families, Tannen (1990) found that of families served for an average of one year, 92% remained intact. In addition, by the end of the intervention 17 of 22 chronic welfare recipients were employed or were in vocational training programs.

Nelson and Landsman (1992) summarized results from three home-based, family preservation programs serving neglectful families. Services included public assistance, protective services, information and referral services, parenting education, paraprofessional services, transportation services, and individual and family counseling. The neglect cases were open longer and had more services than the physical abuse or sex abuse cases. Over 50% of neglecting families improved in behavior, family relations, emotional climate, perceptions of their problems, and use of services and material resources. However, there was a higher rate of cases terminating in placement of children out of the home for this group than for nonneglecting families. Twenty-four percent of the neglect cases terminated in out-of-home placement. This was a rate 10% higher than for the physical abuse or sex abuse groups. Accounting for this discrepancy, Nelson and Landsman (1992) indicated that neglectful families were in worse situations at referral and were more difficult to engage in services than the other two groups. Predictors of success were parents' participation in services, stability of caretaking, paraprofessional services, the number of children at risk, and prior placements of children. Client motivation and cooperation were also key to successful outcomes.

Investigating the effect of a home-based prevention program—which included parenting training, social support, information on services available in the community, and assistance in obtaining child care, educational opportunities, job training, and government assistance—on the resiliency of poor, single, African-American, teen, first-time mothers, Mulsow and Murry (1996) found that the level of mothers' education was an important factor in the prevention of reported child abuse and neglect. The outcomes of the program indicated that it was successful in reducing the number of subsequent pregnancies, increasing child immunization rates, and producing healthier babies. Although the program had no effect on subsequent reports of abuse and neglect, it was believed this result was confounded with the fact that the participants had more involvement with professionals, and these professionals made most of the reports. It was determined that the social support provided by the home visiting program fostered positive outcomes; and that increasing parent educational levels is vital to the prevention of abuse and neglect.

The Chronic Neglect Consortium consisted of six demonstration projects funded by grants from the NCCAN. These projects were programs specifically designed to intervene with neglecting families. Some of the services offered by these programs included family empowerment; therapy; substance abuse referrals; parent aides or volunteer visitors to help with concrete services, friendships, and supportive relationships; parenting classes; GED classes; job training; crisis nurseries; parent support groups; and remedial services for children as needed. The length of service averaged eighteen months. DiLeonardi, Johnson, Spight, and McGuinness (undated) and DiLeonardi (1993), reporting overall program outcomes, noted improvement in socialization skills, household cleanliness, and child discipline. At the beginning of the programs, participants scored at 62% of a measure of minimum level of parenting adequacy. At the end of the programs mean scores were at 82% of parenting adequacy, and many families reached the minimum level. Elements related to success were individualized services, group work, paraprofessionals or volunteers working in the home, and length of time the families remained in the program (i.e., the longer in the program, the greater the gains).

In a study of families participating in one of the Chronic Neglect Consortium's projects, Allen et al. (1990) found that positive external support was created among members of the treatment group. Self-esteem improved and dependency on the social service system decreased as parents helped each other. As a result social workers were less frustrated in working with this population. Reporting on the same study, Landsman et al. (1992) found that neglecting families were assisted in making significant changes in their lives. The program enabled parents to direct their own course of service and establish their own goals for treatment. Both parents and children were involved in interactional activities and as a result parent/child relationships were improved.

Reporting on another consortium project DiLeonardi, Johnson, Spight, McGuinness, and Heinke (1992) indicated that on average project participants increased to a minimum level of adequate parenting. The staff's assessment of the project was positive, most indicating that at the end of service clients had low-moderate to no chance of neglecting their children in the future. Those clients who remained in the project the longest made the greatest gains.

Family group decision making may involve immediate family members, extended family members, service providers, representatives of community/neighborhood resources, and any other parties who might be supportive of the family involved with child welfare services. Decisions regarding a safety plan for the children are made at a family group conference, which can include any of the above-mentioned resources for the family. Reasons for the intervention and options for resolution are placed before the family, who then determines its own safety plan. Based on the assumption that children belong to their families, family group decision making is committed to the strengths found in families (Tochiki, 1996). The American Humane Association (1997) reported that family group decision making results in decreases in (a) the number of children living outside the family home, (b) the number of transracial placements of children, and (c) the number of court proceedings the family has to go through. Increases in (a) family involvement in decision making, planning, and monitoring child safety; (b) professional involvement with extended family; (c) number of children living with kin; and (d) community involvement were also noted. In addition, social, psychological, and economic (i.e., program cost savings) benefits were realized as a result of using this process.

As indicated above, home visitation is a primary intervention strategy in preventing child maltreatment (Thompson, 1995) by decreasing parental stress and assisting the parents to learn new child-rearing techniques (Gomby, Culross, & Behrman, 1999). Programs that have included CPS referrals as an outcome measure in their studies to provide evidence of the potential for home visiting to prevent child abuse and neglect are Parents as Teachers (PAT) (Gomby et al., 1999; Wagner & Clayton, 1999), Hawai'i's Healthy Start Program (HSP) (Duggan et al., 1999; Gomby et al., 1999; Thompson, 1995), Nurse Home Visiting Program (NHVP) (Eckenrode et al., 2001; Gomby et al., 1999; Olds et al., 1999; Schorr, 1988; Thompson, 1995), and Healthy Start America (HSA) (Daro & Harding, 1999; Gomby et al., 1999).

The PAT program services included parent education through home visits and group meetings, parent support groups, child assessments, and referrals for other services as needed. The Teen PAT program also included a case management component, which was comprised of (a) goals/needs assessments, (b) service planning and monitoring, (c) connections to other services, (d) advocacy, (e) transportation, and (f) other support services as needed (Wagner & Clayton, 1999). When comparing clients who participated in PAT and those who did not, PAT, overall, had small and inconsistent positive effects on parent knowledge, attitudes, and behavior. Families receiving the more intensive services fared better than families receiving less intensive services. In contrast to the comparison group, teen mothers receiving PAT and comprehensive case management services had significantly fewer opened child maltreatment cases and their children were subjects of significantly fewer child maltreatment investigations. There were no significant differences in child maltreatment rates between teens receiving PAT alone and the comparison group (Gomby et al., 1999; Wagner & Clayton, 1999).

Hawai'i's Healthy Start Program is a home visitation program designed to prevent child abuse and neglect. Trained paraprofessionals visit in the family home to promote nurturing parenting practices and healthy child development. HSP was successful in linking families with pediatric medical care, improving maternal parenting efficacy, decreasing maternal parenting stress, promoting the use of nonviolent discipline, and decreasing injuries resulting from partner violence in the home. However, in terms of referrals for child maltreatment, HSP did not make a difference when compared to control groups (Duggan et al., 1999; Gomby et al., 1999; Thompson, 1995).

Unlike HSP, which uses trained paraprofessionals, NHVP employs nurses as home visitors. The Elmira project of NHVP has produced long-term results that indicate home visiting is effective in preventing child abuse and neglect. Nurse-visited mothers were significantly less likely to abuse or neglect their children (Eckenrode et al., 2001; Gomby et al., 1999; Olds et al., 1999; Schorr, 1988; Thompson, 1995). As most of the families in the project were neglectful (Eckenrode et al., 2001), this study has implications specifically for the prevention of child neglect. The program also had a significant number of participants go back to school, not get pregnant again, join the workforce, and end their dependency on welfare assistance (Olds et al., 1999; Schorr, 1988). The benefits of this program were greatest for families at greatest risk (i.e., low-income, single women who felt they had little control over their lives), again presenting implications for families with risk factors for neglect (Olds et al., 1999).

HSA, an intensive home visitation program utilizing trained home visitors, has proved to be most successful in improving parent/child interactions and less so in preventing child maltreatment. None of three randomized trials reported a significant difference between the number of confirmed reports of maltreatment for those involved in HSA and the control groups. In some programs (nonrandomized) there were significant differences with comparison groups, with the HSA families having fewer substantiated maltreatment reports (Daro & Harding, 1999).

As indicted above, the results of evaluations of home-based family support and preservation programs are mixed with often modest positive results (Daro & Donnelly, 2002; Gomby et al., 1999; Layzer et al., 2001; McCroskey & Meezan, 1998). The National Resource Center on Family Based Services (NRCFBS) (1988) reported success in keeping children out of foster care and making positive changes in families; and Wolfe (1994) reported that family support studies tend to show that family support programs improve general maternal functioning rather than specific dimensions of personal adjustment. However, on average family support programs have no consistent meaningful effects on child safety. When focused on neglect the results are even less promising (Gaudin, 1993). Those programs that did have a significant effect on child maltreatment rates (including neglect) worked with younger families (i.e., teenage mothers and/or children under three), provided case management services, and involved clients in parent/child activities (Layzer et al., 2001). These findings are again consistent with the work of Wolfe (1993), Perry (1995, 2002a, 2002b), Perry et al. (2002), and Perry and Pollard (1997), which indicated that early intervention is vital for preventing/ameliorating the effects of child neglect.

Efforts have also been made at the community level to provide family support systems to prevent child abuse and neglect. One such venture included a family cooperative, a family nurturing program, a mentoring program, a home-health visiting program, and a home-based substance abuse program. A study of this project indicated that for such a collaboration to be successful there needs to be (a) a culture of mutual trust, (b) a sound administrative infrastructure, (c) incremental growth of the system (i.e., start small and grow in planned increments), and (d) a shared vision. The study found that an interorganizational collaboration can be used to produce a systemic neighborhood service network that meets more community needs than one agency can do alone (Mulroy, 1997).

Intensive family preservation services. Based on the HomeBuilders model, IFPS focus on the provision of comprehensive, intensive services to clients in their own homes with the goal of preventing the out-of-home placement of children and, more recently, supporting the reunification of families after placement. In the child welfare field, as separate from mental health and juvenile justice, these services are generally available only for CPS clients. The key elements of IFPS include (a) crisis intervention, (b) twenty-four-hour availability of a social worker; (c) focus on the family as the unit of service, (d) home/community-based interventions, (e) need-based services, (f) small (usually two or three families per worker) caseloads, and (g) short-term (usually four to six weeks) services. Based on a mix of ecological, systems, social learning, psychoeducational, and crisis theory, IFPS often include the provision of concrete services, supportive counseling, skill building, and advocacy (Fraser et al., 1997; Kinney, Haapala, & Booth, 1991; Whittaker & Tracy, 1990). Thus, IFPS provide crisis intervention focused on improving family functioning to ensure the safety of the children.

Schorr (1988) reported that initially 92% of families receiving HomeBuilders services avoided out-of-home placement of their children. Follow-up studies indicated that 90% of children still remained at home.

Barthel (1992) reported that IFPS had documented an average 80% success rate in keeping families together one year after the intervention had ended. In terms of reunification, a six-year follow-up study of families who received IFPS to assist in the return of children to the home after foster care placement indicated that, when compared to families who did not receive IFPS, significantly more were reunified and their cases terminated significantly more frequently owing to the stabilization of the family. However, no differences were found in referrals for child abuse and neglect (i.e., child safety) (Walton, 1998).

Pecora, Fraser, and Haapala (1991) and Fraser et al. (1997) found that the elements of IFPS that seem to be highly correlated with successful outcomes for families (i.e., prevention of out-of-home placement of children) are home visits, empowerment, crisis intervention, marital and family intervention, collateral services, client advocacy, provision of concrete services, focus on skill building, and the amount of time the social worker spends in the clients' homes. Frankel (1988), however, indicated that underorganized abusive and neglectful families are likely to be among those that do not meet the intake criteria for IFPS; and Smokowski and Wodarski (1996) indicated that family preservation services might be more appropriate for families who are experiencing transitory rather than chronic stress and crisis. Holliday and Cronin (1990) suggested that chronic neglect cases were inappropriate referrals for IFPS.

However, IFPS does accept and treat families who neglect their children; and there are studies in the context of evaluating the outcomes of IFPS that have included outcomes for neglecting families. The following studies report results for this population.

Supporting the work of Nelson et al. (1990) and Smokowski and Wodarski (1996), which indicated that there is a difference between acute and chronically neglecting families, Campbell (1997) explored the differential impact of IFPS on three patterns of neglect. This study found that IFPS can enhance parental functioning and external supports, both of which are needed by neglectful families. However, there need to be differences in the way services are organized and delivered depending on the neglect issues in the family. If the issue is one where the parents have abandoned their parenting role, IFPS may be able to temporarily counterbalance the factors that led to parental breakdown. However, if services are terminated precipitously, parents can become angry and disappointed and reject further offers of help. Thus, in addition to relieving parental stressors, successful intervention would focus on building formal and informal social supports that will continue after IFPS ceases. If the family has become neglectful owing to an acute crisis situation, IFPS would focus on (a) early identification of the crisis, (b) empowerment strategies to validate the family's emotional responses to the crisis, and (c) family strengths/competencies to provide opportunities to deal with the crisis. Self-help and mutual-aid groups may be beneficial; and chronic neglect may be prevented. Finally, if the family is neglectful owing to a chronic deficit in the family structure (e.g., isolation, disability), ways must be found to fill the leadership gap in order to ensure continuity of core family functions. IFPS can get the process going in such cases, but does not work well for those needing ongoing services (Campbell, 1997).

Wells and Biegel (1992), in a review of findings of empirical studies of IFPS, reported that IFPS prevented or delayed placement of about 50% of children who were truly at risk of placement. The results were not long-lasting and dissipated after twelve months, and both groups under study were still at risk after termination of treatment.

In a study that compared neglect families with other families receiving IFPS, Berry (1991, 1992) indicated a worsening of orderliness, cleanliness, comfort, and safety in the neglectful homes at the termination of IFPS. These cases were open longer, but received less intensive services than other study participants. The provision of concrete services increased success rates; however, these families had the least successful outcomes, with the highest placement rates of any maltreatment group.

Across studies, in terms of placement rates for families being provided IFPS, neglecting families had significantly higher (2.5 times greater) rates for out-of-home placements of children than other kinds of maltreatment, including physical and sexual abuse. When neglect was combined with abuse, placement rates were even higher (Bath & Haapala, 1992; Nelson & Landsman, 1992; Yuan & Struckman-Johnson, 1991). Neglected children who had been previously placed out of the home were at highest risk for placement of all groups (Yuan & Struckman-Johnson, 1991).

K. Nelson (1991) reported that the placement rate for neglect in five IFPS programs was 20%. Neglect, along with substance abuse and concurrent community mental health services, was the most powerful predictor of out-of-home placements for these five programs. Outcomes seemed, therefore, to be related more to family characteristics and history than to elements of the IFPS intervention.

In a review of the effectiveness of IFPS, Fraser et al. (1997) found that in child welfare cases treatment was less effective with families with multiple problems and more effective with families whose problems were limited to children's behavior. Most programs had lowered levels of success with neglecting families. Most researchers agree that neglecting families present the most difficult problems to resolve (Berry, 1992; Nelson & Landsman, 1992; Rose & Meezan, 1993). IFPS, which encompass a broad range of interventions, are less effective in keeping children in their own homes with neglecting than with abusing families. There remain, at the present time, no intervention techniques that have been proved to be significantly successful with families who neglect their children. In fact, there is no systematic evidence concerning the impact of HomeBuilders on child maltreatment in general (Thompson, 1995). Outcomes seem to be related more to family characteristics than to specific elements of interventions.

Thompson (1995) concludes that when the goal is maltreatment prevention IFPS by itself is not comprehensive or long-term enough to provide effective assistance to families. What is needed is a more comprehensive program of social support and ancillary services; and components of IFPS (e.g., intensive, home-based services by a highly trained caseworker; caseworker availability; a wide variety of services; small caseloads; and an ecological approach) may be useful components of a longer-term maltreatment prevention/intervention program.

Child-Focused Practice

Up to 85% of the programs funded by NCCAN and OCD did not provide psychological services for children. Focusing on efforts to keep families together, programs allocate resources to the treatment of parents, not children. Child-focused interventions are usually included as a part of a larger program of services that focuses on the family; and usually treatment of the child does not occur without concurrent services being offered to the parents. It is rare that a child would receive services without the family first being involved in the types of services discussed above (i.e., CPS and/or high-risk prevention programs).

Daro (1988), in reviewing program outcomes, found services to children were more successful than services to adults. These services included individual therapy, group counseling, therapeutic day care, speech and physical therapy, and medical care. For young neglected children the most effective intervention was therapeutic day care, which focused on attachment; self-concept; speech and language; and emotional, behavioral, and physical problems—all seemingly intractable issues in the population of children experiencing long-term neglect. Effective interventions for adolescents included skill building, group counseling, and emergency shelters.

Howing, Wodarski, Kurtz, et al. (1989), K. Nelson (1991), and Landsman et al. (1992) found that involving children in treatment programs increased the probability of successful outcomes for the entire family. Interventions usually included play, art, writing, and biblio therapies. Behavioral techniques to change child behavior seem to be effective, as is group treatment, especially with adolescents. Thomlison (1997) and Layzer et al. (2001) found that parent/child activities (e.g., in-home instruction to improve attachment focusing on consistent feeding and child care and infant stimulation) tend to result in positive long-term outcomes for children.

However, Howing, Wodarski, Kurtz, et al. (1989) found that the effectiveness of social skills training groups and therapeutic day care programs had not been evaluated systematically; and therapeutic day care programs required a significant outlay of resources.

Two studies have looked at outcomes for children participating in therapeutic child day care programs. Culp, Richardson, and Heide (1987) studied a day treatment program for maltreated children based on a cognitive developmental model involving a high student/teacher ratio and group treatment and special education, which took place in the classroom for six hours each day. In addition, play therapy, speech therapy, and occupational therapy on an individual basis supplemented the group intervention. The children were also provided transportation; nutritious breakfasts, lunches, and snacks; and regular nap periods. Parents received individual therapy and support group counseling. They also received parent education, volunteer parent aides, twenty-four-hour crisis hot line, emergency aid, and clothing and toy exchange services. Interventions that involved parents and children included family therapy and parent/child interaction training. Foster parents also received ongoing consultation. Intake category (i.e., maltreatment subtype) was a significant predictor of children's gains in social-emotional and cognitive development. Abused children tended to make the greatest gains. High-risk children made the smallest gains. Neglected children did not benefit in the area of cognitive development. Since the interventions designed to enhance cognitive development took place in the classroom group setting, neglected children (not unlike their parents) may need to be taught how to learn in group activities before participating in them.

In 1998, Moore, Armsden, and Gogerty completed a twelve-year follow-up study of maltreated and at-risk children who received early therapeutic child care. The treatment program was based on an ecological model in which children received daily physical care and nurturing plus medical, developmental, psychological, and educational services. Their parents received concrete services; participated in practical parenting education, the child's program, support groups, and counseling; and were referred to additional professional services as needed. The children in the comparison group received standard community services. A preliminary study indicated that 69% of the children in day treatment showed improvement on all clinical indicators. The length of time they were in treatment and the degree of their parents' participation in the program were positively related to child improvement. At the twelve-year follow-up, the families who had participated in the treatment program had significantly more positive and developmentally supportive home environments and better caregiver/child relationships than the comparison families. The children (now youths) received significantly more comments from caregivers and teachers related to their good interpersonal skills, competency, and/or good character than did the comparison children. In fact, the comparison children demonstrated significantly more behavior problems according to caregivers, were arrested at younger ages, were involved in more frequent violent delinquency, and experienced increasing school disciplinary problems.

Outcomes for the Elmira NHVP (Olds et al., 1999) indicated that nurse-visited infants born to low-income teens had 80% fewer verified cases of child maltreatment during their first two years of life than did the infants in the comparison group. These results were greatest for children whose mothers initially had little belief in their control over their own lives. This and the previous studies support the promise of early childhood intervention programs to prevent or mitigate the effects of child maltreatment.

A study of adolescents living in high-risk neighborhoods has implications for interventions to strengthen resilience in older children. Bowen and Chapman (1996) found that interventions to increase adolescents' level of social support had a buffering effect on the risk factors of poverty and neighborhood violence, and promoted more positive adaptation to their environment. Support from teachers, from neighbors, and especially from parents significantly affected the ability of adolescents to positively adapt to their high-risk environments, and played an important role in the psychological well-being of these at-risk youths.

Paget et al. (1993), in reviewing studies focused on interventions with neglecting families, found neglected preschoolers were more responsive in peer-mediated than adult-mediated social interactions. This finding supports the use of intervention strategies for enhancing social relationships between neglected children and their peers. In terms of interventions to improve speech and language skills, combining children's play with mother/child dialogue increased children's learning and improved mother/child relationships.

Studies have shown poor outcomes of nonorganic failure to thrive (NOFTT). In one study of NOFTT, 68% of children were still failing to thrive three and four years after treatment; and up to 50% showed other developmental delays. It was not specified what interventions or follow-up services were provided by these programs (Kempe & Goldbloom, 1987).

Jonson-Reid (2001) explored the relationship between family receipt of child welfare services and outcomes for children (i.e., youth involvement in the juvenile corrections system). The receipt of child welfare services for reasons of neglect (i.e., lack of supervision) of non-White children was associated with a reduction in the risk for later juvenile corrections entry. Youth involved in child welfare cases involving recidivism, substance abuse, and mental health services were most at risk for being involved with juvenile corrections.

In their analysis of family support programs, Layzer et al. (2001) found these programs resulted in small, but significant improvements in children's cognitive development and social and emotional development. However, as Biller and Solomon (1986) and Howing, Wodarski, Kurtz, et al. (1989) have noted, there has been limited empirical analysis of the effects of therapeutic interventions with children. Biller and Solomon (1986) also found that when treatment of children was concurrent with treatment of parents, there was no correlation between the child's and the parent's treatment; and program evaluation designs did not include a framework to measure intervention outcomes.

When efforts to keep the family together are unsuccessful, children may be placed in out-of-home living situations. In regard to foster care, the USDHHS (1999) reported that approximately 171,000 child victims were placed in foster care; and 49,000 who were not victims (maltreatment was unsubstantiated) were also placed out of home. About one-fifth of the victims (21.2%) placed in foster care had received family preservation services, and about 5% had previously been placed and later reunified with their families. The largest percentages of children being placed in foster care were 11–15 years old. Most states reunified children with their families in a timely manner, reunification occurring within 12 months of placement. However, there was a high correlation between early reunification and re-entries into foster care within 12 months after reunification, which raises concerns about the rush to reunify. Most states were able to limit the number of foster care settings within the first 12 months of placement; however, the number of placement moves experienced by children increased with the time spent in foster care. On average 25% of children were placed in adoptive homes within 2 years of foster care placement. The 2000 figures are as follows: 20.5% of victims and 3.5% of nonvictims were placed out of their homes (USDHHS, 2002). In all, approximately 250,000 children were removed from their families.

When children are removed from their families and placed in an adoptive or a single long-term foster care home, outcomes have been positive. Barth and Berry (1987) found that adoption of older children highly increased child well-being and satisfaction for those children, and foster care increased child well-being for those children placed in foster care over children who were returned home. Barth and Berry (1987) concluded that out-of-home placement has developmental advantages for children and is appropriate if viewed as permanent. Foster care at times presents a problem when children age out of the system, but it does not preclude lifelong attachments. Daro (1988) also found that foster care placement was not a critical variable in stopping repeated incidents of neglect by the child's parent.

Long-term, single-placement foster care is not significantly injurious to children (Barth & Berry, 1987; Smokowski & Wodarski, 1996). However, a significant number of children placed in the foster care system come to the placement already psychologically, physically, and/or emotionally injured. These children are at high risk to remain in the system for a longer period of time and possibly graduate to residential living. Unfortunately, residential treatment centers are more effective at servicing children with fewer problems than these children present (Smokowski & Wodarski, 1996).

When general licensed foster care was compared with kinship care it was found that kinship homes provided a similar level of safety, support, and supervision to children as did nonrelative homes. However, kinship foster parents were less likely to have the material necessities or skills that would assist them in an emergency owing to poverty, inadequate access to resources, and insufficient training (Berrick, 1998). Berrick (1998) indicated that some studies have suggested that the care in some kinship foster homes is inadequate. Research has indicated that the placement histories of children placed with relatives are more stable; however, relatives are more reluctant to terminate the parental rights of family members and are, therefore, more reluctant to provide an adoptive home. In addition, some kinship care can result in delayed reunification (Berrick, 1998). Yet kinship care has the potential to build on family strengths and offer children connections to their extended families. Furthermore, children placed in kinship care were more likely (a) to say that they were "happy" to "very happy," (b) to say that they "always felt loved," and (c) to rate themselves as happy in fifteen domains of life than were children living in nonrelative homes (Berrick, 1998).

Generally, few programs are designed specifically for children and specific treatment modalities are not widely disseminated. Empirical evidence on effectiveness is sparse.

Summary of Practice Outcomes

Families involved in different types of maltreatment represent different subpopulations, yet most interventions designed to treat families who maltreat their children deal with this group as a homogeneous population. That these interventions are less successful with neglecting than with abusive parents suggests that differential approaches to these two problem areas need to be developed, including longer-term treatment of the neglecting family. However, there have been few programs designed to target the neglectful family and, therefore, there has been little research that focuses on the outcomes of interventions intended to remediate the problem of families who neglect their children.

Schorr (1988) summarizes the attributes of programs successful at "breaking the cycle of disadvantage" as "comprehensive, intensive, and flexible . . . Their climate is created by skilled, committed professionals who establish respectful and trusting relationships and respond to the individual needs of those they serve" (p. 259). Research has shown that these attributes also pertain to interventions that have had some success with neglectful families. Additional programmatic qualities associated with positive outcomes included (a) home-based services; (b) early intervention; (c) concrete and supportive services; (d) a strengths/needs-based perspective including client empowerment; (e) an ecological approach; (f) attending to clients' affective as well as behavioral and cognitive needs; (g) family participation in all phases of the intervention; (h) services for children; (i) structured interventions with clearly defined, short-range goals and clearly specified activities, some of which include both parents and children; (j) long-term programs that maintain continuity of service provision; (k) consideration of cultural differences; (l) well-trained and supervised staff; (m) small case loads; (n) twenty-four-hour availability of staff; (o) comprehensive case management; and (p) aggressive outreach and advocacy.

Successful outcomes were also affected by characteristics of the clients (usually mothers) the programs served. Client characteristics that are linked with positive outcomes include (a) level of motivation, cooperation, and participation (higher), (b) level of education (higher), (c) number and severity of client issues (fewer), (d) prior out-of-home placement(s) of children (fewer to none), (e) the number of children at risk (fewer), (f) the stability of caretaking (more stable), (g) a supportive relative in the home, and (h) the age of the parents and children (younger). Research has shown neglectful parents (usually mothers) generally are apathetic; poorly educated; have multiple, severe problems; have higher rates of out-of-home placements of children; have more children; and have a history of unstable caretaking. Other than being young, these mothers do not have the characteristics that have been associated with positive outcomes. It is not surprising, then, that programs working with families who neglect their children have not been overwhelmingly successful.

Intrafamilial practices producing the most positive outcomes within the above-outlined context were (a) home- and/or agency-based parent training, individual and/or group, that included information regarding infant/child stimulation, child development and child behavior management, children's nutritional needs, and attended to parents' affective needs; (b) skills enhancement programs, including training regarding stress reduction, anger management, money management, problem solving, and home cleanliness and safety; (c) individual counseling to prepare parents to participate in group parenting and skill enchantment interventions; (d) multifamily group therapy; (e) therapeutic self-help groups such as PA; and

(f) social support such as parent aides or a supportive relative in the home. Successful techniques included role modeling, role play, relaxation techniques, systematized desensitization, cognitive restructuring, self-instruction, stress inoculation, discussion films, and homework.

However, interventions that address parenting skills and fail to affect socioeconomic stressors will probably be ineffective in preventing further maltreatment. In addition, there have been few long-term studies of the impact of these interventions; and there is limited empirical evidence of their long-term effectiveness.

The provision of concrete and social services, within the context of the attributes of successful programs and focused on reducing stressors in the environment, have been effective in reducing the probability of maltreatment of children. Such *environmental practices* include: (a) provision of basic needs such as food, shelter, and clothing; (b) economic support; (c) medical transportation; (d) legal services; (e) respite care; (f) formal social supports such as home visitors, homemaker services, or lay therapists; and (g) neighborhood strategies to reduce isolation and increase social supports. What seemed to be most helpful was a cooperative relationship between families and the child welfare system. One review indicated that there was no evidence of treatment gains with the use of formal support services and evidence of the importance of informal support networks in maintaining treatment effects was limited. Another study indicated no change in neglect rates when AFDC payments were increased or decreased.

In terms of *psychosocial/ecological practice, standard child welfare services* have been shown to be ineffective in reducing neglecting behavior in families. Interventions were more effective if they lasted over six months; and the most effective interventions were family counseling focused on problem solving and the use of a broad range of community programs to provide concrete/supportive services. Child development classes were less helpful for this population; and clinical interventions, alone, were not effective owing to the multiple problems these families experienced. To be effective it was considered necessary that clinical services be augmented by concrete/supportive services. Preliminary results indicate some promise for the effectiveness of differential responses to high- and low-risk families in increasing child safety.

Home-based interventions that had positive outcomes, in accordance with and/or in addition to those identified as attributes of successful programs, included such components as

1. Home visitation by professionals, paraprofessionals, and/or volunteers.
2. Concrete services such as public assistance, transportation, and crisis nurseries.

3. Parenting education provided individually in the home and/or in groups that included child care, and (a) was taught during supervised parent/child interactions, (b) provided developmental information specific to the clients' children, and (c) used modeling and encouragement of nurturing behaviors. (Groups facilitated by parents who had overcome circumstances similar to the group participants were especially effective.)
4. Individual, marital, family, and/or group therapy/counseling that encouraged parent participation.
5. Social support including drop-in centers where clients could gather informally with staff and other clients.
6. Individualized services planned by the clients (i.e., family empowerment by including the family in decision making).
7. Long-term services.
8. Services for children.
9. Provision of collateral interventions through information and referral services, including referrals for substance abuse treatment, mental health treatment, and educational services to increase the parents' educational level (i.e., adult education and GED classes).

One study indicated that 92% of families receiving home-based services for an average of one year remained intact. Another study reported 76% of neglecting families remained intact, which was a lower rate than for physical or sexual abuse. Parenting adequacy did improve for many neglecting families; however, although there was improvement, the families barely met or failed to meet minimum standards of care at the termination of services.

Elements of *intensive family preservation services* that seem to be highly correlated with successful outcomes for families (i.e., prevention of out-of-home placement of children) are client advocacy, crisis intervention, provision of concrete services, focus on skill building, and the amount of time the social worker spends in the client's home (i.e., intensity). One study indicated that IFPS prevented or delayed placement of about 50% of children who were truly at risk of placement. The treatment effects were not long-lasting and dissipated after twelve months; and both experimental and control groups were still at risk after termination of treatment. Neglectful families receiving IFPS have the least successful outcomes, with the highest placement rates of any maltreatment group. The efficacy of IFPS in improving child well-being and safety outcomes has not been established.

It has been suggested that IFPS may be more appropriate for families experiencing acute neglect due to a situational crisis than for families experiencing the more complex matrix of factors that contribute to chronic neglect. Perhaps IFPS can "jump start" the healing process with chronically neglectful families; however, more long-term intervention is recommended to produce lasting gains.

Given that involving children in treatment programs increased the probability of successful outcomes for families, it is puzzling that few programs are designed for children. *Child-focused practices* that produced positive results with all ages of children included individual counseling, group therapy, and appropriate medical care. Techniques included behavioral interventions to change children's behavior and cognitive/affective interventions including art, writing, and biblio therapies. As with adults, the longer the children remained in treatment programs, the better were the outcomes. Child welfare services had positive long-term effects for neglected African-American children who had come to the agency's attention owing to lack of supervision.

In addition to the above, programs that were designed specifically for young children (0–3 years old) that had positive outcomes were therapeutic day care/treatment focused on attachment and self-concept; peer social initiation; and, for neglected children, interventions to teach them how to learn in group activities. Techniques used included play, speech/language, occupational, and physical therapies. The more successful programs included activities that involved both the parents and children. These activities included integrating parents into the children's programs. For example, involving mothers in teaching the child speech/language skills and supervised play with their child improved the mother/child relationship. Additional effective activities were teaching (a) attachment behaviors, (b) consistent feeding and child-caring skills, and (c) infant stimulation techniques in the mother/child dyad.

Behavioral techniques, group treatment, and skill-building activities have been especially helpful for adolescents. Emergency shelter care is also useful when intervening with older children. When children are unable to remain at home for longer periods of time, foster care, when viewed as permanent, has proved to produce positive outcomes. Kinship foster homes and adoption also have proved to be successful.

Empirically, services to children have proved to be more successful than services to adults. However, the effectiveness of social skills training groups and therapeutic day care programs has not been evaluated systematically for this population.

In conclusion, research indicates that the attributes of programs successful in preventing/ameliorating child maltreatment and/or child neglect support the use of psychosocial/ecological practice to intervene early on with neglecting families, including direct interventions with children to foster resiliency and prevent/remediate the effects of neglect, whether that neglect is familial or societal. Unfortunately, the chronic neglect population has the poorest outcomes for all types of interventions; and there remain, at the present time, no intervention techniques that have been proved to be consistently successful with families who neglect their children. Interventions with children hold more promise for preventing/reducing the effects of neglect.

However, program evaluations are primarily short-term, descriptive, nonexperimental, or quasi-experimental designs—many not reporting outcomes related to child well-being or safety; therefore, empirical evidence regarding effectiveness in terms of preventing and/or preventing the recurrence of neglect is sparse. In fact, program evaluations that do report outcome data regarding maltreatment occurrence and/or recidivism indicated that the programs did not make a significant difference in preventing child neglect at any level (i.e., primary, secondary, or tertiary).

IMPLICATIONS OF CURRENT PRACTICE

Implications for Research

The findings of both descriptive and empirical studies regarding interventions to ameliorate child neglect indicate that even the most comprehensive, intensive services are relatively ineffective with families who neglect their children. More research is needed to discover why this is the case and what can be done about designing more effective programs. This book has suggested six possible barriers to successful practice with neglecting families. Further research is needed to test the accuracy of these assertions. Thus research is needed

1. to strengthen theoretical underpinnings of practice with neglectful families;
2. to explore successful methods of engaging families in services and retaining them long enough to make substantial gains (e.g., assisting them in learning to make and follow through on plans);
3. to discover ways to support families in dealing with the number and severity of their problems;
4. to look at the nature of chronic behavior and investigate effective methods of changing embedded behavior patterns;
5. to encourage, support, and motivate service providers working with neglectful families; and
6. to research adaptive strategies to manage potential biological issues (e.g., depression, substance abuse, history of child neglect).

The research literature suggests that maltreating families are not a homogeneous population, and differential treatment strategies need to be developed for maltreatment subpopulations, including child neglect. Systematic studies of various intervention models are needed to investigate the relative impact of the various strategies on various subtypes of neglecting families, including acute and chronic. In addition, the individual components of intervention strategies need to be studied to determine which are most effective with the neglect population. Owing to the limited effectiveness of current practices, specific knowledge regarding what works best for whom under what circumstances, including specific protective factors for specific risk situations, is of utmost importance (Daro & Donnelly, 2002; Daro & Harding, 1999; DePanfilis, 1999; DiLeonardi et al., 1992; Erickson & Egeland, 2002; Jonson-Reid, 2001; McCroskey & Meezan, 1998; Meezan & O'Keefe, 1998; NRCFBS, 1988; Smokowski, 1998).

Studies are needed to investigate the optimal length of time for a family to receive services, the optimal intensity of treatment (i.e., the amount of time the service provider spends with the family during the course of the intervention), the long-term impact of interventions, and the use of survival analysis to determine the technology of maintaining treatment gains over time (Chadwick, 2001; DePanfilis, 1999; DePanfilis & Zuravin, 1998; Jonson-Reid, 2001). Where a service is delivered (e.g., in the home) may make a difference in effectiveness, and thus research regarding the impact on neglecting families of the settings of various interventions is needed.

Studies are needed to clearly describe characteristics of neglectful families, including motivational variables, and the impact these characteristics have on treatment outcomes (DePanfilis, 1999). Knowledge of the specific effects of demographic factors, mental health issues, and substance abuse on treatment results would be valuable; and the routine use of drug assessment tools has been suggested (DiLeonardi et al., 1992; Jonson-Reid, 2001; Moore et al., 1998).

The ecological context of programs including (a) service system characteristics, (b) agency and community characteristics, (c) informal and formal support systems, and (d) the availability and placement of resources needs to be examined to determine the impact of the environment on service delivery and ultimately on the families served. In addition, knowledge about the nature of social isolation and its consequences, the social support needs of various subpopulations of child maltreatment, and the nature of the social networks of troubled families would be valuable (Thompson, 1994, 1995). Such information about the environment in which families receive services could lead to the eventual development of minimal standards for a family-supportive community and determination of the role neighborhood-based programs play in relation to income supports, housing, law enforcement, and social services (Barry, 1994; Daro & Harding, 1999; Garbarino & Kostelny, 1994; Pelton, 1994; USDHHS, 1999).

Clear and detailed descriptions of programs including (a) definitions of the type, severity, and chronicity of neglect in the client population; (b) client recruitment/selection procedures and/or eligibility requirements; (c) the flow of clients through the program and subjects through studies; (d) the change process (i.e., the intervention itself); (e) retention strategies, and (e) data collection procedures and determining how these elements are related to specific outcomes would assist in future program/study design (Daro & Donnelly, 2002; Daro & Harding, 1999; Garbarino, 1993; Gaudin, 1993; Nelson, K., 1991; Paget et al., 1993; Wells & Biegel, 1992). Additional valuable research could include (a) testing the theoretical assumptions underlying programs, including the etiology of neglect and theory of change models; (b) involving fathers, including adolescents, and other male members of households in research studies; (c) analyzing the cost/benefits of various intervention strategies; (d) monitoring the consistency of interventions (i.e., program drift); (e) focusing on breaking the cycle of intergenerational transfer of parental deficits; and (f) examining effects of neglect for all ages of children in order to provide developmentally appropriate interventions for children to remedy cognitive and social deficits (Chadwick, 2001; Daro & Donnelly, 2002; DePanfilis, 1999; Dore & Lee, 1999; Duggan et al., 1999; Fraser et al., 1997; Gaudin, 1993; O'Donnell, 1999: Olds et al., 1999; Wolfe, 1994).

Dore and Lee (1999) found more information is needed about additional populations at risk, such as adolescent mothers and fathers, stepparents, and low-income parents. In relation to low-income families, Pelton (1994) recommended looking at successful parents to see how they manage parenting; and Abell et al. (1996) suggested taking into consideration the differences in child-rearing values, parenting behaviors, and goals for their children expressed by these families. Wolfe (1993) indicated that studying the special strengths and risk factors of diverse cultures and ethnic groups could yield valuable information regarding interventions with these populations; and DiLeonardi et al. (1992) suggested exploring the influence of individuals not living in the household on family outcomes.

As stress has been identified as a risk factor in child neglect, Pelton (1994) recommended studying the relationship between child maltreatment and stress. Thompson (1995) suggested studying the stressors that lead to the exhaustion of support providers. This could lead to knowledge about the nature and prevention of symptom contagion in people working with the neglect population.

Studying the characteristics of prevention programs, such as home visitation, would provide knowledge about successful preventive intervention strategies (Thompson, 1995). Looking at parental powerlessness and empowerment strategies that go beyond the mother/child dyad to include family and community could strengthen the long-term efficacy of prevention programs (Guterman, 1997). In regard to family preservation programs, researchers could consider studying the use of family preservation services for all families not requiring immediate placement of the children (Fraser et al., 1997), and for neglecting families to compare the outcomes of FPS for acute and chronic neglecting families (Gaudin, 1993). Walton (1998) suggested looking at the reasons for success and/or failure of using family preservation services to reunify families. These findings could assist in targeting families appropriate for the use of FPS in reunification efforts.

In terms of research methodologies, rigorous, systematic process and formative program evaluations and intervention research have been recommended (Dore & Lee, 1999; Fraser et al., 1997; Howing, Wodarski, Kurtz, et al., 1989; Smokowski, 1998). Experimental (i.e., prospective studies and randomized trials) or quasi-experimental research designs using clear and consistent operational definitions and typologies of neglect; explicit models; comparison or control groups; appropriate, well-defined and consistent outcome measures; and methodologies to control for sources of error, including robust sample sizes, are essential (Daro & Donnelly, 2002; DePanfilis & Zuravin, 1998; Dore & Lee, 1999; Duggan et al., 1999; Fraser et al., 1997; Gaudin, 1993; Howing, Wodarski, Kurtz, et al., 1989; Pithouse & Lindsell, 1996; Smokowski, 1998; Wolfe, 1994). Fraser et al. (1997) called for homogenous samples of children genuinely at risk in order to more accurately attribute outcomes to interventions.

Daro and Donnelly (2002) advocated the use of diverse strategies, methods, assessment models, and standards of evidence. Qualitative research, including stories, structured interviews, focus groups, and single-case studies, expands and enriches our knowledge base, and creates more democratic and participatory research efforts (Daro & Donnelly, 2002; Garbarino & Kostelny, 1994; Smokowski, 1998).

Implications for Policy

A broadening of the focus on abusing families to include neglecting families as a separate population with differential etiology and service needs is essential. A statement made in 1990 by Nelson et al. is as true now as it was then. "Given the potential lethal consequences of neglect—and recurrent problems that make it more destructive to children over time—this problem must receive priority in systems that now deal almost exclusively with physical and sexual abuse" (p. 123).

Policy initiatives supporting research related to the development of effective interventions for neglecting families are needed. Specific recommendations support the development of policies that encourage and support the use of kinship care for children needing out-of-home placement; the consideration of differing child-rearing values, behaviors, attitudes, and aspirations regarding their children of resource poor families; and the involvement of fathers to increase resources for children (Abell et al., 1996; Berrick, 2000; O'Donnell, 1999). In addition, large-scale drug prevention and treatment initiatives and family preservation and support services at the community level could lower the incidence of child neglect (DePanfilis, 1999).

As effective programs are developed, policy to promote and finance these efforts will be crucial to service delivery. In making decisions regarding which programs to fund, policymakers must consider what interventions work best with which populations under what circumstances. This would facilitate better utilization of scarce social service resources by targeting services to clients that are best serviced by the intervention, and perhaps not supporting the universal application of programs that have experienced some success with particular populations (Olds et al., 1999).

Wolfe (1994) suggested a multiservice, public health model of ongoing support for families. Community councils could assess the seriousness of child maltreatment in their communities and keep track of trends using epidemiological skills (Chadwick, 2001). In order to establish positive environments for families, which could prevent child neglect, communities would (a) set minimal environmental standards, (b) assess the level of risk factors in the community, and (c) establish policy to direct resources to reducing the risk factors in order to meet minimal standards (Barry, 1994; Daro & Donnelly, 2002; Thomlison, 1997).

Given the relationship with neglect, the issue of child neglect cannot be approached without consideration of the issue of poverty (see Chapter Ten). Social policy to deal with issues of material disadvantage (e.g., guaranteed minimum annual income, enforcement of child support payments, universal national health and day care, increased education and employment opportunities that are meaningful and productive, low-income housing) could reduce the risk and rate of neglect (Daro & Donnelly, 2002; DePanfilis, 1999; Gaudin, 1993; Gelles, 1999; Kissman, 1991; Lindsey, 1994; Pelton, 1994).

What is required is a shared vision that the welfare of our children is inextricably tied to the national interest. To achieve family-supportive neighborhoods, policies enabling far-reaching preventive programs, which integrate institutions with issues and create an atmosphere of mutual responsibility and reciprocity between families and the society in which they live, are necessary countrywide. What is required is for policymakers to build a system that meets the needs of children and their families (Berns & Drake, 1998; Daro & Donnelly, 2002).

Implications for Practice

Innovative means of intervention with multiproblemed families are needed, as current interventions are not consistently effective. Families who neglect their children require comprehensive, intensive, and long-term treatment. Interventions must be based on assessment of individual family members, family functioning, and the context within which the family lives, including protective/buffering (strengths) and potentiating/risk (needs) factors of the family and the environment (Campbell, 1997; Erickson & Egeland, 2002; McCroskey & Meezan, 1998; Murry & Brody, 1999; Thomlison, 1997). Early intervention is stressed to prevent or lower the risk of the effects of neglect (Erickson & Egeland, 2002; Perry, 2000a, 2000b; Thomlison, 1997; Wolfe, 1994). Programs need to be flexible to allow for cultural, religious, socioeconomic, and child-rearing differences among clients; and make an effort to involve all members of the household, fathers (whether in or out of the home), and others (in or out of the home, who may be able to act as resources for the family) in planning for and ensuring the safety of the children (Abell et al., 1996; Dore & Lee, 1999; Erickson & Egeland, 2002; Guterman, 1997; NRCFBS, 1994; O'Donnell, 1999; Thomlison, 1997; Thompson, 1995; Tochiki, 1996; Wolfe, 1993). Owing to the strong connection between child neglect and the environmental and social circumstances in which neglecting families live (i.e., poverty), multiple, integrated, community-based service strategies of prevention and protection are required, including concrete supports (AHA, 1997; Campbell, 1999; NRCFBS, 1988, 1994; Pelton, 1994; Pithouse & Lindsell, 1996).

In terms of specific interventions, if parenting and child development information is provided, it must be easily understood, practical, and accessible (Wolfe, 1994). Olds et al. (1999) concluded that the use of nurse home visitors targeted at the neediest populations using clinically tested methods of changing health and behavioral risks should be included in program practices. McCroskey and Meezan (1996) recommended intensive family preservation services for families with acute problems and rehabilitative family preservation for families whose issues are more chronic and do not pose an immediate threat to the children (i.e., chronic neglect). Owing to the relationship of drug and alcohol addiction and/or mental illness with child neglect, direct service workers would need knowledge of substance abuse and mental illness issues; and available, accessible, community-wide substance abuse/mental health assessment and treatment programs are vital (Besharov, 1998; DiLeonardi et al., 1992; NRCFBS, 1994).

Thompson (1995) asserted that of all the interventions to curb child maltreatment, adequate employment, which is well-paying and affirming, for low-income families may be the most valuable social support of all. NRCFBS (1988, 1994) found that families benefited from educational and employment services; and Mulsow and Murry (1996) found that higher education, which resulted in increased employment opportunities, was the most effective prevention for reported abuse and neglect. Guterman found that interventions that empower at-risk parents and give them a sense of control over their lives are critical to successful outcomes. These findings imply that effective preventive programs at all levels would emphasize empowerment, staying in school, and getting a good job.

When children cannot remain in their own homes, kinship care/adoption would be considered (Berrick, 1998; Besharov, 1998). Greater efforts are needed in the area of finding permanent homes for children over the age of 12; and in reducing the number of placement settings experienced by children while in out-of-home care (USDHHS, 1999). Caution must be exercised in planning the reunification of children with their families owing to the high correlation between early reunification (within 12 months of placement) and return to foster care within 12 months of reunification. "Expedited reunification should not be achieved at the risk of children re-entering the system" (USDHHS, 1999b, p. 17).

Most interventions are focused primarily on adults, and not specifically on the neglect population. More consideration must be given to assessing the needs of neglected children; and to developing programs specific to neglectful families (Culp & Heide, 1987; Erickson & Egeland, 2002; Thomlison, 1997; Thompson, 1995; Wolfe, 1993). Culp and Heide (1987) found that neglected children might need to be taught how to learn from group-taught activities before being involved in them; and Thomlison (1997) indicated that services for children should focus on self-esteem and self-efficacy building activities. Services for neglecting families need to address issues of motivation and retention (DeLeonardi et al., 1992; Dore & Lee, 1999; Duggan et al., 1999).

The interventions that seem to have at least some of the characteristics of effective programs—i.e., (a) comprehensive, including case management, concrete services, social support enhancement, and parenting education; (b) strengths-based perspective, including assessment of risk and protective factors; (c) based on clients' needs, not available resources; (d) attends to clients' emotional, as well as, cognitive and behavioral needs; (e) clients included in treatment planning and implementation processes; (f) structured interventions with clearly defined, short-range achievable goals; (g) activities that include parents and children together; (h) intensive; (i) flexible; (j) culturally appropriate; (k) community and home-based; (l) preventive/early intervention; (m) caring, well-trained, and supervised staff; (n) small caseloads; (o) twenty-four-hour staff availability; (p) aggressive outreach; and (q) long-term—do not consistently result in better outcomes for families who neglect their children. As indicated earlier, there are other challenges affecting service effectiveness that need to be addressed in relationship to neglecting families. These are (a) weak theory, (b) recruitment and retention issues, (c) the number and severity of problems, (d) chronicity, (e) symptom contagion experienced by social workers, and (f) possible biological imperatives. New technologies need to be developed to work through these issues before there will be substantial improvement in programs to resolve the problem of child neglect. Clients must enter into and remain in programs in order to reap any benefits; thus these new technologies must focus specifically on recruiting and retaining clients. Such technologies might include how to attend to the affective needs of neglectful parents; how to motivate apathetic clients and staff; and how to prepare neglectful clients for intervention prior to their participation, in order to improve their abilities to learn new behaviors in new ways. Given the resistance to change exhibited by neglectful families, change theory may be relevant to learning new ways to break up and alter old patterns of behavior. Interventions might include group settings that offer nurturing and support along with child-rearing information; home visitation and crisis intervention offering problem-solving and child-rearing education, and resource provision and management; and activities to empower clients, including furthering their education and employment opportunities.

Feminist practice principles are not incompatible with recommendations regarding treatment of neglecting families. As most, if not all, targets of neglect interventions are single, female-headed households, employing a feminist practice perspective (i.e., celebrating diversity, recognizing culture, responding to vulnerable populations, encouraging participation and equality in the treatment process, focusing on the client's perspective of problems and solutions, and empowering clients [Walker, 1988]) may be useful in designing practice that is more effective with families who neglect their children. Hopefully, more effective interventions will emerge out of the process of addressing these issues.

Practice Reform

At the nexus where policy and practice meet is practice reform. New policies are needed to implement the sweeping reforms that are suggested by outcomes of current practice. The literature indicated that the child welfare system requires restructuring to provide preventive and supportive services to families to ensure the well-being of children.

As highlighted in Chapter Five, the child welfare system as it has evolved into the child protective system focuses more of its resources and energy on investigating allegations of child maltreatment than on providing services to families. The average time it takes from the initial report of child maltreatment or threat of child maltreatment to the provision of services is

36 days (USDHHS, 2002). DePanfilis and Zuravin (1998) found that a second report to CPS, if it does occur, is more likely to happen in the 30–60 days after an initial report, indicating that the time frame for initiating services may result in child protective services that do not protect children. In addition, in 2002 the U.S. Department of Health and Human Services reported that only a little more than half (55.4%) of child victims (substantiated reports) received postinvestigation services; while 18.7% of nonvictims (unsubstantiated reports) received services; possibly indicating children who needed services didn't receive them and children who didn't need services did. Lindsey (1994) indicated that there is no evidence that children are safer as a result of the child protective system.

As indicated in Chapter Five, the primary protective service provided by CPS is foster care. However, placement data (USDHHS, 1999b) indicated that children who need placement might not remain there and other children are removed from their families unnecessarily (i.e., many children reunited with their families returned to care within twelve months and 49,000 nonvictims were placed outside of the home). In 2000, 3.5% of children who were not victims of child abuse or neglect were removed from their homes (USDHHS, 2002). These data, combined with the data in Chapter Five showing that the incidence of serious maltreatment and child fatalities is on the increase, provide additional evidence that services delivered by the CPS system may be inappropriate at times, and do not ensure the safety of children.

It has been suggested that a differential intake system, which might narrow the definitions of abuse and neglect, be developed whereby only serious/high-risk families are the subject of investigation and coercive intervention. It is believed that by the time a family reaches this level of dysfunction their problems have become intractable, resistant to change, and need intensive professional services, including the law enforcement and court systems. Pelton (1998) and Lindsey (1994) suggested severing investigative functions from child welfare. Cases of severe abuse would be reported to and investigated by the police (Emery & Laumann-Billings, 1998; Lindsey, 1994; Pelton, 1998), freeing child protective resources to provide voluntary, preventive, and family support services to promote child welfare for those families at risk for or experiencing mild to moderate dysfunction (Lindsey, 1994; Pelton, 1994, 1998; Swift, 1995a).

AHA (1997) advocated for the movement of human service practice to the neighborhood. Residents and local institutions and organizations could share decision making and responsibility for meeting family and neighborhood needs. The child protective system could evolve into a network of neighborhood-based, ongoing, preventive services focused on the welfare of children that would be provided for generally impoverished lower risk families on a voluntary basis (Pelton, 1994, 1998; Schorr, 1997; Thompson,

1995; Waldfogel, 1998; Wolfe, 1993). As pointed out in Chapter Five, these approaches would separate the traditional punitive/helping role of the child protection worker into separate functional units; and more service options would be available for families and agencies, as communities would also become responsible for supporting and protecting children.

Lindsey (1994) envisioned that the child welfare system would in essence become a social welfare system, which would include securing an economic safety net for families with children that would ensure a basic level of child care. In addition, a security account (not unlike social security for the elderly) could be set up for children to provide an economic opportunity at age eighteen for young people to make the best of their adult lives. These and like reforms imply a common vision at the national level that ensuring the welfare of children is in society's best interest (Daro & Donnelly, 2002; Lindsey, 1994).

Within a reformed child welfare system, services focused on neglectful families are essential. The consciousness of society regarding the incidence and severity of consequences to the children of neglect must be raised in order to support program development to work on resolving this issue. The creation of communities that provide services that are supportive of families and focus on the well-being of children would assist in preventing child neglect in high-risk environments. When neglect has taken place and/or is chronic in nature, new technologies of providing effective interventions need to be developed.

Chapter Eight

Child Neglect and Culture

As noted in Chapter Two, neglectful families can be found in all ethnic groups. The Department of Health and Human Services reported that in 2001 an estimated 903,000 children in the United States were victims of abuse or neglect. The majority of those cases involved neglect (USDHHS, 2003). While families who neglect their children come from various cultural and religious backgrounds, all have in common the suffering of children and disruptions in family life. Families also suffer from intrusions by community or governmental services in the event of at-risk and/or severe cases.

The National Clearinghouse on Child Abuse and Neglect (2002) described child neglect as the "failure to provide for the child's basic needs" (p. 2) but posits that there are three kinds of neglect: physical, educational, and emotional.

1. Physical neglect includes refusal of or delay in, seeking health care; abandonment; expulsion from the home or refusal to allow a runaway to return home; and inadequate supervision.
2. Educational neglect includes the allowance of chronic truancy, failure to enroll a child of mandatory school age in school, and failure to attend to a special education need.
3. Emotional neglect includes such actions as marked inattention to the child's need for attention; refusal of or failure to provide needed psychological care; spouse abuse in the child's presence; and permission of drug or alcohol use by the child. (p. 2)

Medical neglect, according to the National Exchange Club Foundation (2000), is another kind of maltreatment where the parent or substitute caregiver fails for religious or other reasons to provide appropriate health

195

care to a child even though it is financially possible. Statistics cited in 2000 indicated that of the approximately 879,000 children found to be victims of maltreatment, almost two-thirds (63%) of child victims suffered neglect, including medical neglect (National Clearinghouse on Child Abuse and Neglect Information, 2002).

The National Clearinghouse on Child Abuse and Neglect also cautions that the "assessment of child neglect requires the consideration of cultural values and standards of care as well as the recognition that the failures to provide for the necessities of life may be due to poverty" (p. 2). For families of color, especially in the cases of recent immigrants and refugees migrating to the United States, being poor is both a major problem and a deterrent to adjustments and functioning. Based upon Census 2000 data, Potocky-Tripodi (2002) described the socioeconomic characteristics of native-born and foreign-born populations (Table 5). Thus, among people who are not citizens of the United States, almost one out of five is living below the poverty line.

While poverty is one factor affecting child neglect, cultural values also loom large. Cultural values usually reflect the norms and beliefs that dictate behaviors in social environments (Fong, 2003; Fong, Boyd, & Browne, 1999). Cultural values can serve as both risk and protective factors (Fong, 2003). Living in ethnic cultures that discourage expressing emotions, as in most Asian cultural traditions, continues to be challenging for those clients who need to overcome these traditional expectations and express themselves. To express emotions may be a risk factor for such clients because it violates traditional cultural norms. In traditional Asian cultures where the display of feelings is frowned upon, it is also highly probable that emotional neglect exists but remains unreported because of another cultural value: not wanting the family to "lose face." To avoid losing face or being shamed, neglect, and similar problems are kept within the family (Choi, 2001; Fong, 1994; Jung, 1998; Lee, 1992; Segal, 2002; Uba, 1994).

While the more common form of neglect is usually manifested in infants' and children's unmet physical needs for food, clothing, and shelter, emotional neglect is also evident in families of color. Nevertheless, ignorance of a culture's values can lead to mistaken assumptions of neglect. If

TABLE 5
Socioeconomic Characteristics of Native-Born and Foreign-Born Populations

Poverty status	Native-born citizen	All foreign-born	Naturalized citizen	Noncitizen
Below poverty	11.2%	16.8%	9.1%	21.3%

Note: From Potocky-Tripodi (2002), Table 1.20 (p. 32). Based on Census 2000 data.

children of traditionally emotionally reticent families from east and southeast Asia fail to receive the praise and physical expressions of affection that are typical in the West, they can be mistakenly assumed to be victims of emotional neglect. While emotional neglect and inability to express one's emotions can be a risk factor, from a traditional and culturally based child-rearing perspective it is also a protective factor not to praise the child. Some cultures fear that evil spirits will also hear the praise and come to remove or attack a male child, and thus cause him to die (Hsu, 1981; Kessen, 1975). Since the preference for males remains common in tradition-bound Asian populations, traditional cultural values and beliefs can be misconstrued when not understood for their intended purposes in their historical and cultural contexts.

Other difficulties are also associated with misconceptions and definitions of neglect among families of color. As Chapter Two explained, what constitutes neglect is partly culturally determined. While there is disagreement about the definition of neglect, there is also the argument that the definition of neglect is biased in the direction of dominant culture practices. For example, as Chapter Two noted, in the Native-American culture neglect is viewed as a political issue, which implies that there are motivations not child-centered. In the Native American culture, which is tribal and community-based, it is not uncommon for child rearing to be a large group undertaking (Brave Heart, 2001; Weaver, 2001a). Thus what seems not to be child-centered in the dominant culture is indeed child-centered in Native-American culture; and child care is delivered through tribal practice (Weaver, 2003). What was not child-centered in the Native-American culture, but more political, was to remove Native-American children from the reservations and rear them in residential boarding schools where they would lose Native-American identity (Choney, Berryhill-Paapke, & Robbins, 1995; Nagel, 2000) and experience forms of emotional neglect.

What is in the best interest of the child and what is child-centered can raise dilemmas for professionals. Some cultures see the roles of children as defined by family need. In these ethnic communities it is assumed that the eldest child should help raise younger siblings; and it is the responsibility of the older children to care for the younger, as in Asian and Pacific Islander cultures. Culturally naïve professionals may fear that the adolescent's needs are neglected since children required to care for younger siblings sometimes suffer from "hurried child syndrome," whereby they are pushed to achieve or grow up older and faster, and lose their childhood in the process. While these are valid concerns about the child's development, there is also the protective factor that young infants and children have responsible older siblings involved in their lives. Generational child rearing is legitimate in some ethnic families, but is often misunderstood and negatively viewed by representatives of the dominant culture. As indicated in

Chapter Two, some areas that seem to be at odds with the dominant culture are the amount of responsibility given to young adults and older children and the different ways cultures handle dominance and submission between the parent and the child.

This chapter will discuss cultural issues as they relate to neglect. A review of the demographics, definitions, and misconceptions will be covered; cultural factors affecting child neglect will be reviewed; the impact of poverty will be discussed; culturally competent treatments will be reviewed; and implications for research, policy, and practice will be offered. While child neglect is a problem for children and families in both majority White culture and among minority ethnic groups, this chapter will focus primarily on issues for ethnic minority children and families in the African-American, Latino/Hispanic, First Nations Peoples/Native-American, and Asian and Pacific Islander communities. There are valid concerns about the actual neglect that occurs within families of color toward their children, but it is necessary to discriminate between those that are actual offenses and those that are perceived and misconstrued. This chapter will clarify cultural misconceptions associated with neglect, review issues related to neglect within ethnic minority groups, and make recommendations concerning research, policy, and practice.

CHILDREN OF COLOR IN THE CHILD WELFARE SYSTEM

The demographics of the number of children and families of color has drawn national attention to the disproportionate number of children of color in the child welfare system. The Child Population data in 2000 (O'Hare, 2001), as cited in McRoy and Vick (forthcoming), stated that while the number of African-American children in the United States comprised 14.7% of the population under age eighteen, the number of Black children in foster care was 38%—almost two and a half times greater. Factors attributed to this phenomenon are neglect's association with poverty, institutional racism, discrimination, unemployment, illiteracy, single parenthood, teenage mothers, social isolation, and linguistic limitations (Cohen, 2000; Korbin, 1981).

However, in reviewing the literature and the research offered from National Incidence Study of Child Abuse and Neglect (NIS-3) completed in 1996, Ferrari (2002) posits a countering viewpoint. He argues, "the NIS-3 survey did not report ethnic differences in the incidence of child maltreatment, although they did acknowledge that the public has the perception that more children of color are abused and neglected" (p. 794). Public perception is supported by research studies; and Children's Defense Fund found that there are ethnic differences between African-American and Cauca-

TABLE 6
Race/Ethnicity of Children Who Died as a Result of Abuse
and Neglect, 1996

Ethnicity	Percent of All Child Deaths	Percent of Children in the United States
Caucasian	45.6%	68.4%
African American	38.8%	15.1%
Hispanic	11.0%	12.5%
American Indian/Alaska Native	1.8%	1.1%
Asian/Pacific Islander	0.9%	3.0%

Note: Reprinted by special permission of the Child Welfare League of America. Washington, DC (http://www.CWLA.ORG)

sian children who have been maltreated (Children's Defense Fund, 1985; Zuravin & Greif, 1989).

The 1999 Child Welfare League of America Stat Book on Child Abuse and Neglect reports an overrepresentation of African-American and Native-American children in child abuse and neglect-related deaths compared to the proportion of children in the general population. The overrepresentation of African-American families in the child welfare system has warranted the attention and services needed for this population.

CULTURAL DEFINITIONS AND MISPERCEPTIONS

Neglect is a phenomenon subject to varying definitions and theoretical explanations. Several theories address the neglect of children: the psychological model encompasses drug users or parents with mental illnesses, the sociological model reflects poverty and social isolation, and the interactional model targets nonorganic failure to thrive. While explanations are needed for understanding human behaviors, all populations may not fit easily into any of these theoretical boxes. For example, many families of color who are recent immigrants and refugees to the United States often fail to conform. These families may have come from affluent socioeconomic backgrounds in their countries of origin, but lacking knowledge and skills in the English language have been relegated to working several menial jobs, sometimes to the neglect of the children.

Take the case of Dr. and Mrs. Wang, immigrants from the People's Republic of China. They were a medical doctor and teacher; however, impeded by language, they seemed to be unable to support themselves and their six-year-old daughter in the United States. Neighbors cannot communicate with the Chinese parents, who seemed to hardly ever be around anyway. In China, while resources are scarce and food not always abundant, family dwellings are simple and this family might not be considered negligent of their daughter. But, unable to communicate with the parents, neighbors in the United States conclude that they are indeed neglecting their child. The neighbors report the daughter to Child Protective Services because she is not in school, looks malnourished, and hardly leaves their scarcely furnished small apartment. The family may or may not be isolated with no financial support. That fact would have to be determined by a Chinese-speaking social worker, who could also determine the context and condition of neglect, if any, in this case.

Definitions and Misperceptions

The definition of the term "physical neglect," according to Tower (2000), is as follows: "The role of the parent is to meet the child's basic human needs. These are adequate food, clothing, shelter, medical care, educational needs, supervision and protection, and moral guidance. The failure to meet these needs is considered physical neglect" (p. 202). It is argued that in some ethnic cultures the definition of meeting basic needs, supervision and protection, and moral guidance differs greatly from that of the dominant culture. As stated in Chapter Two, the definition of neglect is partly culturally determined. For example, it is a given that "the freedom a Native-American child has on the reservation comes from the parents' knowledge that the community will assume responsibility when they are not available. In the dominant American culture, letting one's child run freely and perhaps leaving him or her for long periods of time would be considered neglectful" (Tower, 2000, p. 201).

However, in some ethnic communities that value extended family and community, there is a larger responsibility bestowed upon members other than parents to supervise and participate in the rearing of children. This may be perceived by the dominant culture as parents' shirking their responsibility, but these misperceptions are based upon differences in cultural values. Saunders, Nelson, and Landsman's study on the variations in perceptions of child neglect (1993) found there were cultural differences among Latino, Caucasian, and African-American mothers in their perceptions of neglect. African-American and Latino mothers found exploitation of children, inadequate supervision of children, and raising children in unwholesome circumstances as potentially most harmful to the children, whereas Caucasian mothers indicated lack of food was most harmful. As stated in Chapter Two, there are legitimate child-rearing practices in ethnic minority groups that are considered as neglect in the dominant culture.

It is often assumed that when biological parents are not able to care for their children, neglect occurs. This may be a misconception for ethnic cultures whose values and practices in child rearing involve extended family members. In Asian and Pacific Islander cultures, where the family is the main unit of analysis and not the individual, it is common for families of several generations to live together and raise the children collectively. Children of these cultures are brought up with multiple caregivers. While the biological parents may be working difficult jobs, aunts and uncles take responsibility for the children. In Native-Hawaiian culture, it is common for children to be *hanaied* (adopted) into nonkin families who raise and rear the children. In African-American families kinship care is a means of shared responsibility in caring and rearing of the children born into single-parent homes. In Chapter Three it was mentioned that social supports were strong deterrents to child neglect. These are examples of the strong supports that ethnic cultures have, but may be misconstrued, because it is expected that biological parents are the ones primarily responsible for the physical needs and well-being of the child.

Role Expectations and Parental Needs

Another controversial issue in the definition and misperception of neglect is focused on role expectations, parental needs, and the child's rights. The expected roles and responsibilities of the oldest children will vary in different ethnic cultures. In many Asian countries that follow traditional Confucian ideals of filial piety, the rights of the children are subsumed under the needs of the parents. Self-sacrifice is expected on the part of the child for paying back and fulfilling the obligation owed to the parents as they grow old (Hsu, 1981; Takamura, 1991). What is culturally expected of the young also affects the old in some cultures.

This is not always an acceptable practice in the dominant culture. Child protective service laws have age limits as to when children need supervision by adults. As the immigrant and refugee population multiplies, there is greater dependency upon older children to care for younger siblings. How immigrant and refugee families adapt to their new environmental stressors may depend on more societal and government assistance in child care, language skills, and employment opportunities.

While there are cultural practices to respect, there is still a need to discern when actual neglect does and is occurring among the different ethnic groups. Poverty, unemployment, and substance use continue to plague some families of color; and attention is required to protect the children and keep them from harm. However, cultural considerations need more attention. They have been neglected and ignored in working with ethnic families.

CULTURAL FACTORS AFFECTING CHILD NEGLECT

Chapter Three cites four causes that various writers have offered to explain child neglect: parental deficits, sociocultural, interactional, and effects of neglect. While these causes apply to all neglecting families, cultural values as protective factors for ethnic minority families may explain why some ethnic groups will not neglect their children owing to the long-term cultural consequences.

Cultural Values as Protective Factors

Ferrari (2002) stated: "Cross cultural literature suggests that child maltreatment is less likely in cultures where children are valued for their economic utility, for perpetuating family lines and the cultural heritage, and for sources of emotional pleasure and satisfaction" (p. 795). In Asian cultures that practiced Confucianism, *filial piety* mandates that children respect the elderly and care for their aging parents. Thus children serve a functional purpose and are less likely to be neglected for fear that when they are adults the children will, in turn, neglect their elderly parents. *Filial piety* is a cultural value acting as a protective factor in most Asian cultures.

Latino and Mexican-American cultures also have cultural values such as *familialism* to serve as a protective and preventive measure. In Latino families studies have been done on the concepts of *familialism* and *machismo* and the valuing of children. These concepts were used in Ferrari's (2002) study of 150 mothers, fathers, and nontraditional students, of which one third were African American, one third were Hispanic, and one third were European American, to test the relationships between the independent [cultural] variables of abuse and neglect. The study did not find "ethnic differences in seriousness ratings of child abuse and neglect, with the exception of the category of promoting delinquency" (p. 809).

Parental Deficits: Cultural Cautions

Tower (2000) cites Polansky et al. (1981) and the research done that categorized five types of neglectful mothers: (a) apathetic-futile, (b) impulse-ridden, (c) mentally retarded, (d) reactive-depressive, and (e) psychotic. Tower concludes, "one of the problems with the current literature on neglect, even with the research to date, is that neglect has been framed from a White middle-class perspective with little room for cultural variations. For this reason much more attention should be paid by future researchers to this area" (p. 203). The characterizations of neglectful mothers need to be carefully examined in the cultural contexts of the ethnic group. Apathy and depression can easily be misconstrued as negative characteristics, which normally are presented in some Asian cultures whose cultural values of self-control and diffidence are highly regarded (True, 1990). While these appear to be negative characteristics in the dominant culture, there needs to be discernment between the cultural values as positively regarded in ethnic cultures and negatively construed in the dominant culture. To conclude that these affects and behaviors are definitively characteristics of neglectful parenting is erroneous. The context of parental affect and child-rearing patterns need to be carefully examined before a pronouncement is made.

Cultural Contexts:
Socio-Cultural-Environmental-Situational Considerations

It is important to consider the cultural contexts of families of color since there are many inter- and intragroup differences. Supported by numerous scholars and researchers (Acevedo & Morales, 2001; Colon, 2001; Galan, 2001; Negroni-Rodriguez & Morales, 2001; Ortega, Guillean, & Najera, 1996; Villa, 2001; Zuniga, 2001), Fontes (2002) points out the diversity within the Latino population. "It is impossible to describe a unitary Latino culture. The peoples of Latin America and Latinos in the United States are far too heterogeneous. Historical influences cause diverse Latino cultures to evolve constantly. Individual Latinos grow to accept and reject aspects of their culture in different ways throughout their lives. Every person who is a Latino is also an individual, differing from others on questions of individual and family history, geographic origins, migration experience, social class, religion, dreams, values, and so on" (p. 32).

Intersectionality: The Interaction of Neglect and Other Societal Issues

Neglect is greatly affected by other societal concerns such as substance abuse and domestic violence. In child welfare cases many of the children in child protective services come from families where substance abuse and domestic violence are contributing factors to neglect and abuse. The disproportionality of African-American children in the child welfare system causes one to examine the interaction between social and physical environments and the parental deficit response to these environments, which yield neglect. As stated in Chapter Three, the interactional theory of parental deficits and community deficits presents the challenge of understanding

the contributing factors concurrently rather than sequentially, usually focusing intensely on parental deficits. In culturally competent practice, the
contextual social work practice framework as well as the intersectionality
framework (Fong, 2003) is strongly advocated in working with immigrants
and refugees. This approach can be applied to the intersection of the problems areas of child welfare (i.e., substance abuse and family violence) (Fong,
McRoy, & Ortiz-Hendricks, forthcoming).

Effects of Neglect: Parents' Needs vs. Children's Safety

While physical neglect is most common, emotional and educational neglect must also be concerns (Petr, 1998). Common symptoms of neglect are
lack of supervision, poor hygiene, constant hunger, malnourishment, developmental delays, inadequate stimulation, little emphasis on school, inadequate housing, poor sanitation, unsafe conditions, and lack of attention
to medical needs.

Neglecting children is usually not intentional in cultures and family
systems where young persons are expected as adults to care for aging parents. In some Asian and Southeast Asian cultures, which observe the Confucian doctrine of respecting elders and caring for them in their old age, to
neglect the child while young would jeopardize old-age security. Yet, in the
(Confucian-based) Vietnamese culture, Filipino culture, and Samoan culture, it is reported that immigrant parents work full-time jobs, if employment is available to them; and many youth are involved in gang activities
because parents are preoccupied with economic survival (Brummett &
Winters, 2003; Chesney-Lind, 1997; Chesney-Lind & Shelden, 1998).

Despite undesired outcomes like gang involvement, parents strive to
balance their needs and their children's safety. Fontes (2002) writes,

> Latino parents want their children to be safe and protected. This may
> be particularly true of recent immigrants who are bewildered by all the
> potential dangers of their new country. They are unlikely to leave their
> children with caretakers other than family members, even when
> professionals believe a child would be better off in an established child
> care center than at home with a member of the extended family. (p. 33)

Despite parental wishes and efforts, the parents' lack of jobs, inadequate
work skills, and dearth of economic resources contribute to the tenuous
and unsafe situations of the child and the poor conditions endured by some
families.

POVERTY AND MINORITY FAMILIES

The Kids Count Data on Asian, Native American and Hispanic Children (1990), published by the Annie E. Casey Foundation, reported children living in families with both parents working full-time, which nonetheless had incomes below the poverty line.

> Nearly 7 percent of all poor children in the U.S. lived in families where parent(s) worked full-time and yet the family income was below the poverty level. Among poor Korean and poor Central-American children, one out of every ten lived in a family where parent[s] worked full-time but the family was still poor. (p. 12)

Poverty is a major factor for families of color especially those whose family members are immigrants and refugees. Census 2000 statistics reported one out of every ten persons of color to be foreign-born. In the Latin-American population, one out of every two persons is an immigrant or refugee, whereas within the Asian and Southeast Asian populations it is one out of every four persons (Zuniga, 2003). Fontes (2002) observed that the Latino population is

> one of the fastest growing ethnic populations in the United States, due to both immigration and high rates of childbearing, and already constitute more than 12 percent of the U.S. population. . . . In addition, this is a young population with relatively high rates of births to teens and single mothers. Compared to non-Hispanic Whites, Hispanic parents are typically younger, less educated, employed at lower paying jobs and financially poorer—conditions that put children at greater risk for negative social, health and developmental outcomes. (pp. 79–80)

In addition to being financially disadvantaged, families who come into the United States with an undocumented or temporary protective status may experience aggravating circumstances because of the family's tentative status, which can impact the child's well-being and lead to neglectful child-rearing practices.

While financial and economic burdens are factors that contribute to parental neglectful behaviors, other factors may be due to macrosocietal practices of colonizing. Yellow Bird (2001b), who is Sahnish and Hidatsa First Nations, explains,

> Aside from the fact that our colonizers took our children because they felt that our people's beliefs and values would contaminate our children and keep them in perpetual slavery, other reasons for removal were

poverty, abuse and neglect, alcoholism, and violence in the home. While removing our children due to these latter conditions was a noble attempt to look out for "the best interest of the child," I don't think it has yet dawned on society that the reason we had the problems in the first place was because they manufactured them. For many years, the control we had over our own lives was kept at a minimum by our colonizer. This treatment lasted for years and as it continued the rates for homicide, suicide, child abuse and neglect, poverty, family and community disintegration, violence, and alcoholism among our people increased exponentially. (p. 11)

CULTURALLY COMPETENT TREATMENTS AND INTERVENTIONS

The treatments mentioned in Chapter Six focused on four models of intervention: intrafamilial, environmental, psychosocial, and child-focused. These models of interventions need to be examined in reference to the cultural competency of the staff and cultural responsiveness of the intervention to the ethnic population. Culturally competent treatment and interventions are based upon the client's cultural values, which are viewed as strengths and integrated into treatment planning and intervention implementation. It is important not to have just Western interventions but also treatments that are indigenous and grounded in the client's values. Fong, Boyd, and Browne (1999) wrote about the biculturalization of interventions, which is the combination of Western and indigenous interventions. Their work is based upon the premise that clients have strengths that are reflective of their cultural values that need to be incorporated into intervention planning and treatment. Thus social workers must understand and identify the cultural values important to the client and determine how these values function as strengths in the clients' lives. If clients prefer indigenous interventions, social workers should use them, and also choose Western interventions whose theoretical frameworks are compatible with the clients' cultural values. For example, Family Group Conferencing is becoming a more popular treatment approach for ethnic groups whose cultures value family decision making. Using family members to help conference, choose, and support case plans in child protective service cases is not only necessary but culturally compatible with many ethnic groups.

The seriousness of the problems children face in society without the support of negligent family members also mandates that the services offered to these families when seeking help be culturally appropriate and responsive. Ortega, Guillean, and Najera (1996) conducted a study on Latinos and child welfare and found the concerns of the participants did not focus around child welfare but about "preserving the welfare of Latino children who are becoming increasingly exposed to violence, drug/alcohol abuse and crime in neighborhoods and in local schools. . . . Child welfare services were seen as impersonal, intimidating, and in direct conflict with cultural values" (pp. 1–3). Incompatibility of clients' cultural needs and agency services is no longer an acceptable way to do social work practice. Policies need to be changed and practices improved to accommodate the needs of the families of color in the child welfare system.

POLICIES RELEVANT TO PEOPLE OF COLOR

Many kinds of policies affect ethnic minorities in the United States, particularly in the area of neglect and child welfare. Ortega et al. (1996) assert that Latino children are invisible and unaccounted for in the child welfare system; and policy changes should be made in order to "set standards for accurately identifying and tracking Latino children and hold states accountable to these standards, mandate reporting on Latino children as a separate category, and establish a monitor review board at the national level, made up of Latino child welfare experts" (pp. 1–3). They made other policy recommendations in order to move the Latinos from exclusion to inclusion.

- Facilitate the inclusion of Latinos in planning, decision-making, implementation and monitoring of child welfare policies, programs, and administrative procedures and practices.
- Develop preventive programs focused on strengthening the Latino family.
- Accelerate efforts to reunify Latino children with their families or locate other permanency planning options such as adoption.
- Educate Latino families about community services and likewise, educate community service workers about Latinos.
- Require training and assistance programs to accommodate language and cultural differences.
- Enhance the participation of Latino grassroots organization at the local, state and national level. (pp. 1–4)

Families of color in the child welfare system come from backgrounds not only of African, Asian, Mexican, and Native Americans but also the complete spectrum of immigrants and refugees. Those child welfare policies relevant to immigrants and refugees merit a close examination in terms of eligibility, availability, and accessibility. The immigrant populations of Latinos and Southeast Asians are the fastest-growing foreign-born populations. The immigrant literature refers to those arriving into the United States after the Immigration and Nationality Act of 1965 (Balgopal, 2000) as new immigrants and emphasizes the different pressures for the cohorts who come to the United States at different time periods. When reference to the overrepresentation of families of color in the child welfare system is made, there needs to be some discernment whether the families are American-born or immigrants and refugees. Immigrants and refugee families of color cannot be assumed to be familiar with the norms and regulations of the child welfare system in the United States. Furthermore, immigrants and refugees experience special stresses. Zuniga (2001) cites Padilla (1999) emphasizing the stressors of immigrants and refugees as "separation issues from family, relatives, and country of origin; journeys that are often dangerous and different durations; the relocation issues related to language and cultural incongruence; and practical aspects of finding housing and employment" (p. 52).

These stressors may seem uniform among the various immigrant groups, but those individuals and family households who carry an undocumented status are further challenged to be attentive to the child's needs when under duress to survive without official assistance or acknowledgment. Zuniga (2001) warns,

> Social workers are not immune to political sentiments, and must face the reality of how they truly feel about persons who are undocumented. They will insure that unconscious or preconscious feelings of antipathy do not cloud their ability to offer a client who is undocumented the full array of options to which they have a right, according to the NASW Code of Ethics. . . . For those social workers who feel strongly that the undocumented should not use this country's resources, they must remove themselves from those agencies that serve the undocumented. Or, in a particular case, they must refer the client to a worker who does not hold this bias. Otherwise, personal political views that disallow providing undocumented clients all their options for needed resources result in unethical professional behaviors. (p. 56)

Undocumented immigrants are trying to put themselves in a position to offer a better life to their children. But the cost to individuals and family is great. Many problems develop because of discriminatory practices and policies. Children over eighteen years who are of undocumented status may not receive federal assistance because of lack of citizenship. This severely curtails the educational opportunities immigrant parents seek for their children. It also leads to tensions in family systems, which may result in neglect and abuse.

IMPLICATIONS FOR RESEARCH, POLICY, AND PRACTICE

Implications for Research and Policy

Research implications in reference to neglect and families of color need to focus on research design, sampling, instruments, measurements, and policy formulation and analysis. Cultural biases need to be closely examined by the researchers to avoid the perpetuation of misperceptions and misinterpretations.

When the sample of families of color is determined, researchers need to be reminded of the inter- and intragroup variability. Within an ethnic group much of the variability depends on the clients' status, history of immigration, political and societal values of countries of origins, and the time of cohort arrival in the United States. Immigrants and refugees who arrive from countries whose political and governmental structures and beliefs differ greatly from those of the United States may take longer to adjust to policies and expectations. Clients from socialist countries where individual welfare is substantially dependent upon the government may not understand the different welfare rules and may, for instance, assume that accusations of neglect are just the government offering support as they did in their home countries. When child protective service workers come to remove the child because of physical neglect, those migrating from poor countries may not realize that the government is aiming to take the child away, not help raise the child with financial assistance. Cultural misunderstandings such as these are costly.

In addition to sampling concerns, instruments and measurements need to be examined for cultural responsiveness and appropriateness to the population. The content analysis conducted by Behl, Crouch, May, Valente, and Conyngham (2001) discovered that cultural disparities arise from the instruments used to measure neglect. They noted that the commonly used Childhood Level of Living Scale (CLL) developed by Norman Polansky and colleagues needs to be reexamined for cultural appropriateness. Tower (2002) writes, "Native-American, Hispanic-American, and African-American families often place emphasis on childrearing practices which do not conform to the CLL scale. Certainly these cultural differences should not be enough to label them neglectful" (p. 65).

Implications for policy formulation and analysis center on factors such as discrimination, unemployment, and poverty. Policies guiding federal monies to deal with the macrolevel issues of poverty are necessary for individuals and families immigrating into the United States without adequate skills and resources. Policies that discriminate against undocumented and migrant workers also need to be reexamined.

Implications for Practice

Practice implications can be developed in three areas: (a) increased knowledge of cultural values and beliefs about issues associated with neglect; (b) improved understanding of the role of community in ameliorating neglectful conditions; and (c) examination of professionals' attitudes and behaviors toward clients with differing values.

Increase knowledge of cultural values. Professionals who work with families of neglect need to develop an understanding of the cultural values and practices of the diverse groups. These groups are growing in the United States. The attitudes and belief systems of these ethnic minority groups frame the definition of neglect. Neglect, according to Tower (2002), is an act of omission in the areas of physical, emotional, and educational care (p. 64). There needs to be caution in developing practices that address the omission of emotional care in ethnic groups that do not emphasize or validate the expression of feelings. Because of culture-bound norms, families should not be labeled negatively when value conflicts occur.

Improve understanding of the role of community. The literature on how ethnic families care for their children in their social environments is important to understand. Neglect has been discussed at the microlevel—the impact upon the individual, usually the child, and the causal factors of poverty and unemployment. The role of the ethnic community and its place in ameliorating the impact of neglect also deserves further discussion. Ethnic families usually operate under the rules and expectations of community (Acevedo & Morales, 2001; Brown & Gundersen, 2001; Chow, 2001; Daly, 2001; Furuto, San Nicholas, Lim, & Fiaui, 2001; Grant, 2001; Manning, 2001; Matsuoka, 2001; Weaver, 2001b). It is important to approach neglect as a macro/societal and community problem, not merely the ethnic parents' problem.

Examine professionals' attitudes and behaviors. Professionals also need to examine their own values and belief systems about persons with differing values and family situations. Immigrants and refugees may come to the United States under conditions neither familiar nor acceptable to the worker. The National Association of Social Workers (NASW) Code of Ethics argues for nondiscriminatory practices, which may need more and will receive more support under the recently passed NASW Cultural Competence Standards of Practice (NASW, 2001). Personal biases of social workers, if unchecked, can increase the problem rather than alleviate it.

Chapter Nine

Child Neglect and Substance Abuse

Substance abuse is a major societal concern contributing to numerous problems, including child neglect. The 1999 Report to Congress on Substance Abuse and Child Protection from the Department of Health and Human Services declared, "substance abuse is a critical factor in child welfare" (p. 4) and "neglect is the predominant type of maltreatment in families with substance abuse problems" (p. viii). Hampton (2000) cites Chasnoff (1998), who asserted that there are "more than 500,000 children in foster care and substance abuse is the dominant characteristic of child protective services caseloads." Dunn, Tarter, Mezzich, Vanyukov, Kirisci, and Kirillova (2002) maintained that

> three times as many children are reported to Child Protective Service agencies for neglect compared to sexual abuse. . . . Notably, neglect has been documented to have more severe adverse effects on developmental outcomes than child abuse. Inasmuch as the risk for child neglect is augmented by parental substance abuse disorder, children in these families are at a higher risk for psychiatric problems and psychosocial dysfunction as well as substance abuse. (p. 1064)

Glaser (2002) stated,

> It is now increasingly accepted that emotional abuse and neglect cause significant harm to the child's development and that this harm extends into adult life. Evidence for this has come from a number of follow-up and longitudinal studies that show emotional abuse and neglect in childhood are associated with a wide range of emotional, behavioral

and cognitive difficulties in later childhood, adolescence and adulthood. (p. 698)

Sheridan (1996) researched the relationships between substance abuse, family functioning, and child abuse/neglect. He observed, "Although the link between substance abuse and an increased likelihood of abuse and neglect has been relatively well established, there is a general recognition that this is not a simple cause-effect relationship, but rather a complex interplay of multiple factors best understood within the system of the family" (pp. 519–520).

Neglectful families have several kinds of situations and conditions that qualify as parents not meeting the child's basic needs. Black (2000) cites Zuravin (1991), who identifies fourteen types of neglect:

1) refusal to provide medical care,
2) delay in providing physical health care,
3) refusal to provide mental health care,
4) delay in providing mental health care,
5) supervisory neglect,
6) custody refusal,
7) custody-related neglect,
8) abandonment/desertion,
9) failure to provide a permanent home,
10) personal hygiene neglect,
11) inadequate housing standards,
12) inadequate housing sanitation,
13) nutritional neglect, and
14) educational neglect. (p. 158)

Statistics report that almost 80% of the families in child protective services have issues with drugs and alcohol (Kropenske & Howard, 1994; Winton & Mara, 2001). The Department of Health and Human Services in 1999 reported, "11 percent of U.S. children, 8.3 million, live with a parent who is alcoholic, 2.1 million live with a parent whose primary problem is with illicit drugs and 2.4 million live with a parent who abuses alcohol and illicit drugs in combination" (p. ix). Substance abuse is heavily associated with parents who have children in the child welfare system (American Humane Association, 1994; Barth, Freundlich, & Brodzinsky, 2000; Curtis & McCullogh, 1993; Dore, Doris, & Wright, 1995; Feig, 1998; Hampton, Senatore, & Gullotta, 1998; Murphy et al., 1991; Woolis, 1998).

Parental addiction to alcohol, cocaine, heroine, PCP, and other drugs has caused children to be neglected developmentally, physically, medically, emotionally, and socially (Glasser, 2002; Hildyard & Wolfe, 2002). Use of crack cocaine during pregnancy frequently causes infants to be born with severe problems and/or deformities (Chasnoff, Griffith, Freier, & Murphy, 1992; Frank, Bresnahan, & Zuckerman, 1996; Lester, LaGrasse, & Seifer, 1998; Mayes, 1992; McFadden, 1990; Richardson, Conroy, & Day, 1996). The use of alcohol resulting in the fetal alcohol syndrome has also negatively impacted the neurological and physical function of infants (Cadoret & Riggins-Caspers, 2000; Coles & Platzman, 1992; Famy, Streissguth, & Unis, 1998; Kerns, Mateer, & Streissguth, 1997; Matson & Riley, 1998; Streissguth, Barr, Hogan, & Bookstein, 1996; Streissguth, La Due & Randals, 1988; Streissguth et al., 1991; Weiner & Morse, 1994; Yates, Cadoret, & Troughton, 1998).

The literature on substance abuse and the neglect of children often tends to focus on the type of drug used (illicit, crack cocaine, alcohol, etc.), negative effects upon the child's development (neurological damage, cognitive and behavioral dysfunctioning), and the risk posed by and to the pregnant or parenting substance-abusing mother. The characteristics of the families as a whole system are frequently ignored with most of the discussion targeted on the single-parent, poor, unwed mother. The focus on the different ethnic minority families who are using substances and neglecting their children is also lacking systematic analysis and discussion. This chapter will fill these gaps and examine the characteristics of the neglectful parents; discuss women and failed motherhood; review the developmental impact upon infants and children; analyze the problem with the ethnic minorities of African Americans, Latinos, First Nations Peoples, Asians, and Pacific Islanders; critique treatment approaches and interventions; and offer implications for research, policy, and practice.

NEGLECTFUL PARENTS

Substance abuse was generally viewed by society to be a male problem (Bride, 2001; Blumenthal, 1998; Goldberg, 1995; Peterson, Gable, & Saldana, 1996) until feminist theory and the women's liberation movement questioned the male-dominated norms and addicted women began to receive attention and treatment (Bride, 2001; Kendall, 1998). Peterson, Gable, and Saldana (1996) remind us that

> Historically, research describing substance abuse and treatment of substance abuser has been oriented towards male abusers. In the past three decades, attention to the area of women's alcohol and drug use has grown, albeit sporadically. Some researchers have even referred to the recent "epidemic" of women's substance use, noting that although the public and research attention is new, the problem of women's addiction actually is not. (p. 789)

Substance abuse, however, when associated with neglect, is usually viewed with the stereotype of the urban, poor, ethnic minority, single-parent, childbearing-age woman. Swift (1995a) states that "neglect is a category known to be reserved primarily for the poor, marginalized, mother-led families" (p. 12).

While it is the woman who has the dominant role in the prenatal and postnatal care of infants, it is the entire family that is affected when drugs and alcohol enter the home environment. Dube et al. (2001) studied parental alcohol abuse and exposure to childhood abuse, neglect, and household dysfunctions, known as adverse childhood experiences, surveying 8,629 adult HMO members and found that while retrospective reporting cannot establish a causal relationship, those "children who grew up with parents abusing alcohol were far more likely to suffer multiple adverse childhood experiences during childhood" (p. 1637). Emotional and physical neglect were listed among the adverse childhood experiences.

While substance abuse and neglect are primarily associated with addictions to alcohol and drug use, the reasons for such behaviors vary in range from poverty, depression, and domestic violence to boredom and social drinking. However, Swift (1995a) also asserted that neglect can also occur with the "home alone" type of situations with abandonment and emotional neglect more likely to be associated with the myth of neglect as "a classless phenomenon" (p. 9). She asserted that "the vast majority of middle-class parents, regardless of their child-rearing practices, will never come under the scrutiny of the child welfare authorities. . . . Neglect, as a socially constructed category, is not and never has been intended to catch out ordinary people in parenting lapses, although it occasionally operates in this way" (p. 9). The Executive Summary of the Department of Health and Human Services report states,

> Parents who are alcoholic or are in need of treatment for the abuse of illicit drugs are demographically quite similar to the U.S. population as a whole. They are [as] likely to be fathers as mothers, although mothers with substance abuse problems are much more likely than fathers to be reported to child protective services. (USDHHS, 1999a, p. ix)

Chapter Two in this book mentions that the definitions of neglect focus on parent deficits, community deficits, and child deficits. In the use of substances, the parent deficit model is a plausible answer as to why parents are not meeting the needs of children. As explained in Chapter Two, parents in families are failing to act and depriving children of the necessities. Tower (2000) describes neglectful parents as those who "exhibit immaturity and inability to meet their children's needs. They find it difficult to form more than superficial relationships. They lack judgment to parent and often have had poor parenting models in their own childhoods. Neglectful parents can be difficult to treat therapeutically, as they lack insight into their own actions" (p. 205).

Characteristics of neglectful parents, according to Sattler (1998b, p. 693) are:

1. poor, lack access to resources, find accessing services needed too complex;
2. psychologically immature, often as a result of their own deficient nurturing as children;
3. characterized by apathy, impulsiveness, anomie;
4. want to be good parents but do not have personal or financial resources;
5. need goals that are positive, relevant, realistic, clearly stated and achievable;
6. have strengths that can be mobilized;
7. may need court-ordered services for children because of apathy; and
8. may need long-term psychological treatment, especially when neglect is chronic.

Feig (1998) continues the argument that

substance abuse, by definition, impairs an individual's decision-making abilities. An individual who is abusing or addicted to alcohol or other drugs is not making rational choices about the substances and the effect on his or her life. The behaviors surrounding the acquisition and the use of the drug have at least begun to crowd out other important aspects of the abuser's daily activities. When the substance abuser is a parent, it is likely that the chemical dependence has led to parenting styles that are detrimental to his or her children. (p. 62)

Kearney and colleagues (1994), in their study on parental attitudes and behaviors of drug-dependent mothers, found the women feeling a strong sense of responsibility toward their children but because of the use of crack cocaine the mothers were lacking in attention toward the children, were drained of financial resources, and were poor role models. Harden (1998) reported that "up to 20 percent of newborns are affected by prenatal substance exposure; and that 6 million children are being reared by substance using parents" (p. 18). For these mothers treatment for alcohol, heroin, and cocaine abuse depends on the availability and accessibility of treatment programs. Kelly, Blacksin, and Mason (2001) state:

Access to any substance abuse treatment was extremely limited for pregnant women until the middle 1980's. Concerns over medical liability, a dearth of staff familiar with women's health, pregnancy and child welfare issues, and the fact that many pregnant women seeking substance abuse treatment were on public assistance, resulted in the refusal of many programs to admit pregnant women. By the late 1980's as a result of the impact of the women's movement and other self-help initiatives, treatment programs began to reexamine the appropriateness of models for largely male patients and consider the special needs of women, including pregnant women. (p. 288)

While the literature tends to focus on the women, men are as likely to use substances and contribute to the neglect of children. However, because parenting responsibilities fall mostly to the mother, when she is unable to provide for the needs of the children it is perceived as her failure not the couple's.

WOMEN AND FAILED MOTHERING

Although substance abuse has been linked to neglectful behaviors of parents, the use of drugs has been a part of the American culture for over 200 years despite the recent re-emphasis on drug addiction, fetal alcohol effects, and crack babies (Kendall, 2000). The concerns for crack use in the 1900s–1920s, marijuana in the 1930s, heroin and psychedelic drugs in the 1960s, crack again in the 1980s, and alcohol in the 1990s usually are aimed toward the woman as it relates to her role as mother.

The role of mother seems to be the primary concern that society places upon the woman and any deviations often produce the criticisms of "bad mothering," as noted by Swift (1995a). Some elements of failed motherhood are, according to Swift (1995a), deficiency in the quality of the mother's love as it is manifested by not caring; neediness and emotional immaturity; omissions in caregiving, inconsistent parenting, and poverty-ridden environments for children. According to the National Clearinghouse of Child Abuse and Neglect Information (2002), "mothers acting alone were responsible for 47 percent of the neglect victims" (p. 2). The other 53% may be attributed to mothers and fathers, fathers acting alone, other relatives, or nonrelatives.

While the study of neglect continues to put the blame on women, the literature acknowledges the role of the fathers and the male contribution to neglectful behaviors. Gordon (1988) stated that "the very concept of neglect arose from the establishment of this norm of male breadwinning and female domesticity" (p. 166). The descriptions of drug-abusing mothers include:

Addicted women frequently have poor family and social support networks; have few positive relationships with other women; and often are dependent on [an] unreliable, abusive male, thereby increasing their vulnerability to sexual abuse . . . Significant psychiatric or psychological problems, such as personality disorders or mood disorders, especially depressive illnesses, are not uncommon in women who use drugs or abuse alcohol. These factors almost invariably impede parenting capabilities further and lessen the chance for a normal developmental course for the child. (Chasnoff & Lowder, 1999, p. 137)

Nair et al. (1997) found, in a study of 152 mother/infant dyads, that infants were at increased risk and the disruption of care was highest with young mothers who were depressed, used heroin, and had other children in foster care. Stressors such as histories of drug abuse, limited education, and poverty interfered with their parenting abilities and placed the infants at increased risk of receiving substitute care. Finkelstein (1994) alluded to substance-abusing women themselves as having experienced poor role models and inconsistent or neglectful parenting. When alcoholic or drug-abusing mothers in the early recovery stages try to improve their parenting abilities, they suffer great disappointments: "Many women have unrealistic expectations for themselves as parents in early sobriety and believe they must instantly become 'perfect' mothers. In addition, any physical, emotional, or learning problems in her children may increase a woman's feelings of inadequacy and guilt and lead to hopelessness, helplessness, and relapse" (Finkelstein, 1994, p. 11).

Peterson, Gable, and Saldana (1996) argued that the low self-esteem in a substance abusing mother is due to unmet needs of self. "Until the immediate needs of self are met, it would seem difficult to persuade parents to alter higher order problematic and inaccurate cognitions . . . More basically, until the needs of self are met, it would be hard for the individual to accept other roles of parent, the one who accepts responsibility to clothe, feed, and protect the child" (p. 793).

DEVELOPMENTAL IMPACT UPON INFANTS AND CHILDREN

While studies have been critical of the mothers' use of drugs and the impact on the children, the use of alcohol and drugs has historically prevailed in society but its impact reached great heights with the advent of "crack" cocaine in the mid-to-late 1980s with maternal substance abuse leading to increased admissions to neonatal intensive-care units and serious medical problems (Freundlich, 2000, p. 2). The crack "epidemic" raised the concerns about the effects of perinatal exposure to drugs to the degree that "the need to provide specialized treatment programs for pregnant and parenting women" (Moore & Finkelstein, 2001, p. 222) was self-evident. Substance abuse has impacted the parenting abilities of adults resulting in inadequate care to and development of infants and children. Children with fetal alcohol syndrome (FAS) have had severe problems, such as difficulties with coordination, heart defects, and speech and hearing impediments. According to the 1999 DHHS report on Substance Abuse and Child Protection, FAS is also the leading known cause for mental retardation in the United States. Chasnoff and Lowder (1999) also reported the problems for substance-exposed infants to include deficient growth patterns, reduced birth weight, poor and small head growth, high rates of prematurity, obstructed ability to respond to environment and primary caretaker, motor behaviors, and state control problems. Freundlich (2000) reported the research describing the impact to be in two phases: 1970–1990 and 1990–present. She reported early predictions to be pessimistic with an emphasis on

> early neurological damage among children prenatally exposed to drugs and alcohol and predictions that these children would be unable to function normally intellectually or socially. Beginning around 1993, the tone of the research shifted as longer-term studies showed dramatic variation in the outcomes for children prenatally exposed to substances. It became clear that there were many cases in which children, despite histories of prenatal substance exposure, demonstrated normal long-term development. (p. 2)

Freundlich attributed these optimistic findings to using samples that are statistically significant in size, selecting infants that are not just high risk so that there is no longer a bias toward poor outcomes, following subjects over time and observing longer-term consequences, and considering other factors that may impact outcomes for these children: "It has been pointed out that these early studies of severely affected infants, ironically, did not take into account the less extreme effects of prenatal substance exposure which affect large numbers of children" (2000, pp. 4–5).

While the research is a little more optimistic for this population of infants and children, because of the limiting abilities of the parents who are using substances, there are yet detrimental impacts upon the development and care of infants, children, and youth. Drug-exposed infants may yet experience severe developmental delays, abnormalities, and behavior dysfunction (Winton & Mara, 2001). Cigarette smoking may continue to contribute to infant mortality and low birth weight. Alcohol consumption, the cause FAS and fetal alcohol effects (FAE), causes infants to be born with low birth weight, have small head circumferences, be unable to interact with mother or caretaker, have difficulty with attachments, not be able to respond to environmental stimuli, and experience problems with state control of overstimulation (Chasnoff & Lowder, 1999).

Hildyard and Wolfe (2002) concluded:

Past as well as very recent findings converge on the conclusion that child neglect can have severe, deleterious short- and long-term effects on children's cognitive, socio-emotional, and behavioral development. Consistent with attachment and related theories, neglect occurring early in life is particularly detrimental to subsequent development. Moreover, neglect is associated with effects that are, in many areas, unique from physical abuse, especially throughout childhood and early adolescence. Relative to physically abused children, neglected children have more severe cognitive and academic deficits, social withdrawal and limited peer interactions, and internalizing (as opposed to externalizing) problems. (p. 1)

Chasnoff and Lowder (1999) warned, "It is clear [that] substance abuse during pregnancy is a marker for familial and environmental factors that place the child at risk for harm" (p. 138).

Smith and Testa (2002), however, posed the research question whether there was a relationship between identified prenatal use and the risk of subsequent maltreatment allegations with families in the child protective service system. They found that "parents whose child welfare cases opened for substance-exposed infant are more likely than parents whose cases opened for other reasons to incur subsequent maltreatment allegations" (p. 110).

ETHNIC MINORITIES AND SUBSTANCE ABUSE

The consumption of alcohol and the use of drugs exist in all ethnic cultures; but the prevalence, choice of drug or alcohol, reason for and pattern of use, and prescribed treatment vary according to the ethnic population involved. Studies detailing the exact prevalence of the various substance uses among the different ethnic populations are difficult to pinpoint. However, the USDHHS reported in 1994–1995 regarding the ethnic composition of parents with problem drug use: "nearly three-quarters (72 percent) of problem drug using mothers and 65 percent of problem drug using fathers are White, 20 percent of these mothers and 15 percent of these fathers are Black, and 10 percent of these fathers and 7.4 percent of these mothers are Hispanic" (USDHHS, 1999a, p. 36). Straussner (2001) reports that

the prevalence of alcohol and drug problems does vary among different ethnic and racial groups. Alcohol dependence is more of a problem among Native Americans and those of Mexican background, whereas other drug problems are higher among Native Americans, Blacks, and those of Mexican and Puerto Rican background when compared with the "total surveyed populations." Asians/Pacific Islanders tend to have an almost equal problem with drugs as compared with alcohol, with all substances being abused to a much lower degree than among other populations studied. . . . It is important to note that, whereas our culturally approved substance, alcohol, is a bigger problem nationwide and particularly among [the] White population in the United States than is other drug use, illegal drugs are more of a problem among Native Americans, Blacks, Cubans, and Puerto Ricans. The implications of these differences are profound both in terms of social policy and clinical practice. (pp. 9–11)

Social and environmental circumstances that lead to substance-abusing behaviors can be examined in the approach to the treatment of the problem. The social service delivery system has tended to separate the child welfare system and the alcohol and other drug (AOD) abuse treatment programs causing delays in treatments, misunderstandings in communication, and ineffectiveness in interventions. The intervention methods suggested in dealing with substance abuse may not involve indigenous treatments and informal systems of care, which are important in some ethnic minority communities. Family-based services need to be promoted with culturally sensitive approaches to home visiting.

This section will review the prevalence of substance use among African Americans, First Nations Peoples, Latinos, Asians, and Pacific Islanders. Immigrant and refugee populations will also be discussed when applicable to these ethnic groups. Recommendations for prevention and indigenous approaches to treatment will be given.

African Americans

Problems of alcohol and drug use are present in the African-American community, like other communities in America. However, there is also the concern about the disproportionate number of African-American children in the child welfare system. The *Child Population: First Data from the 2000 Census* (O'Hare, 2001) reported African-American children at 14.7% in the population of 18-year-olds and under but 38% in foster care; Hispanic or Latino children at 17.1% in the population of 18 years and under but 15% in foster care; Native-American children at 9% in the 18 years and under population and 2% in foster care; and Asian and Pacific Islanders at 3.5% of 18 years and under and 1% of the foster care population. In the 1999 report to Congress on Substance Abuse and Child Protection, the U.S. Department of Health and Human Services concluded that "substance abusing African-American women are more likely to come to the attention of Child

Protection Services agencies than are White or Hispanic women with substance abuse problems" (p. 1).

According to Williams, Limb, and Adams (2002), "African Americans have an earlier onset of alcoholism and drug problems than Whites and have a greater likelihood of interfacing with the child welfare and criminal justice system" and "African Americans report lower rates of alcohol and illicit drug use than Whites but have more health and social problems related to substance use" (p. 7). Marcenko, Spence, and Rohweder (1994) studied 225 pregnant women with and without substance abuse history to identify their psychosocial characteristics and service needs. The majority of the 225 women were African American (94%); the remaining were Hispanic (4%) and White (2%). Women with substance abuse histories, compared to those without, less often lived with their family and more frequently lived on their own or in an institutional setting. Compared to the women with non-substance abuse histories, they waited on the average a month longer to seek health care. But both groups of women, with and without substance abuse histories, delayed their prenatal care well into their second trimester. Women with substance abuse histories had significantly higher service needs for housing and health care. Social workers and other health care providers are reminded that

> the women who abuse substances were more frequently estranged from their families or that their family was less able to provide them with support because of their own problems of abuse. This indicator implies that nonfamily sources of support must be mobilized on behalf of the women. Recognizing that the friends of the women who are substance abusers may themselves be chemically dependent, the formal delivery system may need to provide the majority of support until women are able to establish new networks. (p. 21)

There are various explanations for the use of substances in the African-American community. While some of the reasons may relate to historical patterns of use dating to times when alcohol would be a form of payment for work and habit forming (Wright, 2001), the availability of alcohol and substances in the Black community, economic frustrations due to poverty and lack of employment, and racism and discrimination may be the more dominant contributors.

Latinos/Mexican Americans

While there is great diversity in this group of Latinos, Mexican Americans, Cuban Americans, and Puerto Ricans, and problems of substance abuse do exist, advocates decry the depiction of stereotypes and overrepresentation. Moreno (2001) warns, "Substance abuse varies among the Latino subgroups and very few studies have discerned over prevalence rates, drug of choice and patterns of use among Latino subgroups and less with members of growing Latino subgroups" (p. 3).

Lewis, Giovannoni, and Leake (1997) studied 1,035 infants of Latina, White, and African-American mothers to determine the placement outcome of prenatally drug-exposed children two years after they had been placed in foster care. The study concluded that "women who were homeless, did not live with the father of the children, neglected their children, had a history of sexual promiscuity, were significantly more likely to have their children remain under supervision [with the Department of Children and Family Services] whether the children had been prenatally exposed or not" (p. 88). The majority of the Latina mothers in the study were between the ages of 18 and 35 years, never married, were homeless or lived with relatives and friends, and had multiple sexual partners. Among the Latina mothers of drug-exposed infants, 68% were more likely to have their children still under custody compared to African-American mothers at 71% and White mothers at 52%. The study concludes that the epidemic of drug use by pregnant women presents challenges not only to child welfare agencies but also to policymakers because "the ultimate impact of welfare reform on this population of children remains to be seen" (p. 90).

First Nations Peoples/Native Americans

Contrary to popular belief about the prevalence of alcoholism among the Native-American population, Weaver (2001b) exhorted:

> it is unwise to assume that widespread substance abuse exists among all Native populations. Some Native groups, such as the Lakota, have been studied extensively, whereas virtually no information is available for other groups, such as the Cayuga. . . . In addition, existing literature on Native Americans has focused primarily on negative factors and social problems, which lends credibility to stereotypes. Little attention has been given to strengths or positive factors within Native cultures and communities. Native Americans who are social drinkers are never discussed in the literature, nor studied empirically. (p. 77)

The need to make distinctions among the tribal groups within the Native-American population is very important. It is also necessary to acknowledge that among some Native-American scholars and researchers First Nations Peoples is the preferred term to address this population (Weaver, 2001a; Yellow Bird, 2001a, 2001b). Weaver (2001a) and Yellow Bird (2001a, 2001b) speak of the colonization process that First Nations

Peoples endured, destroying their values and occupying their lands. Colonization lends itself to the understanding of reasons why substance use exists among some tribal nations. It explains "physiological susceptibility, cultural loss, social and historical factors."

However, there have been protests that accompany the allegations that substance abuse dominates the Native-American population. Ledesma and Starr (2000) stated,

> Unfortunately, the one area of American-Indian life that has received attention from the dominant society in the popular press and media is the high rate of alcohol abuse and the impact of FAS/FAE. While attention is needed to remediate substance abuse problems, substance abuse throughout the life course in Indian country must be examined in context. Not every Indian child is born exposed to alcohol or drugs; not every child experiments or family has been assaulted by alcohol, there are many caregivers of children who had not had or no longer have problems with substance abuse. The spotlight on Indian drinking has typically been understood as a symptom of individual pathology. Less attention has been focused upon analysis of the social and environmental circumstances that lead to substance abusing behaviors or the role of substance abuse as a functional albeit unproductive and unhealthy, coping mechanism in a hostile environment. (p. 136)

Historical and environmental factors need to be taken into account when understanding and planning for treatment of substance use among the First Nations Peoples. DeBruyn, Chino, Serna, and Fullerton-Gleason (2001) stated that while child maltreatment exists among American Indians and Alaska Natives, with child neglect associated with alcohol abuse, many contextual factors have not been scientifically tested in relation to child maltreatment. These factors are historical trauma (Brave Heart, 2001) and unresolved or disenfranchised grief, a grief not publicly mourned or supported. When developing and implementing intervention and prevention programs for Native Peoples, history and culture need to be integrated into treatments.

> American-Indian/Alaska Native intervention programs have found cultural and historical factors within therapeutic interventions that could be integrated into prevention programs. Examples include cultural identification, cultural shame, intergenerational familial and interpersonal trauma, and reluctance to put the welfare of the individual ahead of the extended family and community. Although these issues have been clinically associated with histories of child neglect, child sexual abuse, substance abuse, suicide attempts, sex offenders, and abuse experience in residential boarding schools, they have not been examined scientifically for the significance of these associations. (DeBruyn et al., 2001, p. 8)

Asians and Pacific Islanders

Asians, Southeast Asians, Asian Indians, and Pacific Islanders have different aspects of alcohol and drug use to contend with, varying in the kind of drug used and the reasons for usage. Alcohol consumption is evident in the Chinese population and Lai (2001) asserted that alcohol addiction may be substituted by narcotics and gambling. Southeast Asians tend to consume marijuana for medicinal purposes. Asian Indians may use substances due to "acculturative stress, loneliness in the U.S., freedom from cultural restrictions and taboos, and easy access and financial accessibility" (Sandhu & Malick, 2001, pp. 379–380). Pacific Islanders have few studies on alcohol and drugs; but attribute use to interactions with the environment, stress factors, school failure, poverty, unemployment, and minority status (Mokuau, 1998).

Sasao (1991), as cited in Matsuyoshi (2001, p. 402), in a study conducted in California on substance use among Asians and Pacific Islanders found "Japanese Americans reporting the highest level of lifetime alcohol use (69 percent), Koreans (49 percent), Vietnamese (43 percent), Chinese (42 percent), Filipinos (39 percent), and Chinese-Vietnamese (36 percent)." Kurumoto and Nakashima (2000) identified several factors that contribute to the Asian and Pacific Islander use of alcohol and substance use: pressure to succeed, immigration and acculturation stressors, discrimination and racism, shame, and denial.

Asian and Pacific Islanders have high-risk attributes. While children may not be physically neglected, they are at risk of being emotionally abandoned and neglected. The immigrant and refugee populations within the Asian and Pacific-Islander communities face much stress in adjusting to the United States. Lacking language skills, compounded with the unavailability and inaccessibility of jobs, causes parents to seek whatever employment is available, often to the neglect of the children. Unsupervised youth may seek gang involvement and/or drug use, leading to more culturally sensitive treatments needed for this population.

TREATMENT APPROACHES AND INTERVENTIONS

Treatment of child-neglecting families is difficult because of systemic family problems. Denial, depression, apathy, and antisocial behaviors all challenge the treatment modalities used. Leverage for treatment may be in the form of court-ordered services because of child protective service involvement. Interventions have been implemented including criminal prosecution, withholding of drivers' licenses, and termination of parental rights. Women are being held criminally liable for the harm done to their fetuses and infants, reported Chasnoff and Lowder (1999). States have different rulings on the jurisdictions over fetuses, some giving the rights to the unborn fetuses, others to the pregnant mothers. But "thirty seven states allow drug-dependent persons to be involuntarily committed for treatment" (p. 145).

A change needs to occur to redirect involuntary to voluntary commitments to obtaining and receiving treatment. Creating female-gender-specific treatment programs including maintaining connections to children, developing positive supports and relationships, and monitoring male intrusions to recovery are highly recommended in promoting voluntary treatment approaches (Chasnoff & Lowder, 1999). The USDHHS (1999a) reported many models of treatment but concluded, "It is now generally recognized that a community-wide approach to the prevention of child maltreatment is the most promising technique for reducing its incidence and prevalence. Since child maltreatment is such a multivariate phenomenon, the resources of many different professional disciplines, as well as the resources of neighborhoods and communities at large, must be enlisted in a coordinated fashion" (p. 27). The recommendation for the most effective prevention and intervention strategies are:

(1) comprehensive, integrating the contributions of social service, legal, law enforcement, health, mental health and education professionals;
(2) neighborhood-based, strengthening the neighborhood and community by encouraging and supporting local improvement efforts, including self-help programs, that make the environment more supportive of families and children;
(3) child-centered, protecting the safety and personal integrity of children and giving primary attention to their best interests; and
(4) family-focused, strengthening families, supporting and enhancing their functioning, providing intensive services when needed, and removing children when such action is appropriate. (USDHHS, 1999a, p. 28)

Service delivery models need to include approaches that deal jointly with substance abuse and child welfare. Building collaborative working relationships and assuring timely access to comprehensive substance treatment services is recommended in the 1999 Report to Congress on Substance Abuse and Child Protection by the U.S. Department of Health and Human Services. As stated earlier, the public child protective service delivery system is overwhelmed with caseloads of neglect, with substance abuse as a leading cause. Availability, accessibility, and appropriateness of substance abuse treatment programs are critical to meet the specific needs of substance-abusing women and their children.

IMPLICATIONS FOR RESEARCH, POLICY, AND PRACTICE

Implications for Research

Substance abuse addiction is considered by medical experts to be a disease and it is recommended that it be treated through the medical model. Treatment would include activities such as identification of the problem, brief interventions, assessment of substance abuse and related problems, and treatment planning (USDHHS, 1999a, p. 14). The traditional approaches are medical model, social model, and behavioral model. The medical model recognizes the addiction as a bio/psycho/social disease; the social model emphasizes the need for self-help groups for recovery, and the behavior model emphasizes supports to change behaviors (USDHHS, 199a9, pp. 14–15).

However, more research is needed to explore other frameworks besides the medical model in designing treatment programs. The feminist theory model emphasizes relationship building and empowerment strategies. The person-in-environment model emphasizes a multilevel approach. In 1999 the USDHHS reported that successful programs allowed women to come to treatment with their children, provided therapeutic child care, and provided parent training and support services. More research is needed to determine other approaches to treatment as well as policy changes.

Research is needed to design substance abuse treatment centers with female-oriented treatment, keeping (a) children, (b) positive support systems, (c) milieu therapy, and (d) the ecological approach in mind. While the person-in-environment approach would address the social and environmental concerns associated with substance abuse, an interactional model between environment and individual is important to consider as children and positive relations are incorporated into the treatment plan.

In general, there is a dearth of literature on substance abuse and child neglect; and more is needed. However, as stated throughout the book, the research on child neglect is very sparse at best. In their child maltreatment literature review over a twenty-two-year period from 1977 to 1998, Behl, Conyngham, and May (2003) found child neglect to be an understudied area and concluded that "child neglect and child emotional abuse literature needs to be developed first by theoretical works and then by quantitative studies" (p. 223). Dunn et al. (2002) posited that the reasons for the dearth of research focusing on neglect are both conceptual and theoretical: issues related to substance use disorder and psychiatric disorders are typically comorbid; research efforts are only recent; child neglect is predictive of long-term developmental outcomes; and there is more emphasis on abuse than neglect because neglect is more difficult to assess (p. 1064).

Research on substance abuse is necessary in reference to the different ethnic groups living in the United States. Korbin (2002) strongly advocated:

> Culture needs to be included in virtually all research on child maltreatment just as age, gender, and socioeconomic status are considered "must have" variables. Just as researchers, clinical and basic, must justify exclusion of important variables, culture needs to be on the radar screen in proposing future child maltreatment research . . . Culture needs to be "unpacked," that is, research needs to go beyond census or self-identification categorizations and strive to understand how it is that culture, in its ecological context, is involved in the etiology and consequences of maltreatment and how it can be used in treatment and prevention. (p. 642)

Implications for Policy and Practice

Substance abuse treatment centers are designed to treat individuals, not family systems. In many instances, substance abuse may be a generational problem and treating the individual is ineffective if the family system perpetuates the addiction. Policy changes need to be made to include, when appropriate, the extended family as supports in substance abuse treatment. Policies of agencies and programs need to target family members as systems in the change process. Substance abuse addiction, when it is perpetuated as cycles of abuse within family members, needs to be treated to include the support systems whose own using of drugs may cause relapse and result in damage to children and other family members. Residential treatment centers and outpatient services need practices and policies that will reflect the treatment of family systems including generational family members. The 1997 Adoption and Safe Families Act has shortened the treatment time to twelve months with concurrent planning designed to find permanent homes for children in the foster care system whose parents may be drug users. Kinship care is the treatment of choice but some kin may also have been former drug users. Kin and substance-abusing parents may all need postplacement services, including substance abuse relapse prevention.

In 1995 the U.S. Advisory Board on Child Abuse and Neglect recommended that substance abuse treatment was an essential element to prevent child maltreatment. Much work is still needed in this area of prevention and treatment. There also needs to be more of an emphasis on the strengths perspective approach (Saleeby, 1997) in social work practice, especially if some of the substance-abusing parents are in relapse or might come from cultural backgrounds where the ethnic community is committed to caring for families in trouble and in need. This may apply to first-time immigrants whose adjustments to the United States is stressful and drugs are a temporary coping mechanism. The strengths perspective would be particularly helpful during the time of relapse treatment and both clients and providers may have a framework that would not be as negative or pessimistic in prognosis. Culturally competent practice is important in the area of substance abuse. The literature has begun to target the separate ethnic groups by publishing the Substance Abuse and Mental Health Services Administration's *Cultural Competent Series for Ethnic/Racial Communities, Pacific Islanders, and African Americans*. There also needs to be a bio/psycho/socio/cultural model for substance abuse treatment. The cultural component is frequently omitted; but needs to be added as a permanent part of the assessing and planning of service plans. However, as found in the Hong and Hong study (1991), in working with different ethnic groups of Chinese, Hispanic, and Whites they warned,

> community standards must be taken into account . . . This is particularly problematic in approaching children of minority groups because they are likely to be members of two communities, their minority group and the larger society. The concerns of both communities must be jointly taken into consideration, especially if they do not agree. Furthermore, the present study points to the risk of combining ethnic groups into a unitary category in research and practice. As our data suggest there could be more disparities among the minorities than their individual deviations from the majority.

A strong reminder is given about the variability within and between ethnic groups. In considering culturally competent treatment services, Fong, Boyd, and Browne (1999) advocated a biculturalization of interventions where Western interventions are matched with indigenous treatments so compatibility of cultural values and the strengths approach are upheld. These areas of cultural competent practice need to be added into treatment of families with substance abuse and neglect problems.

Chapter Ten

∞

Child Neglect and Poverty

Chapter One presented evidence that child neglect seriously injures and/ or kills children at least as often as abuse. As reported earlier, 52% of children who died as a result of maltreatment between 1993 and 1995 were victims of child neglect (Lung & Daro, as reported in Bonner et al., 1999). Evidence also was presented that indicates that neglect is the most prevalent type of child maltreatment (AAPC, 1986; AHA, 1988; Emery & Laumann-Billings, 1998; Nelson & Landsman, 1992; Petit & Curtis, 1997; Petit et al., 1999; Rose & Meezan, 1993; Sedlak & Broadhurst, 1996; Smith, 1998; Stein, 1984; Trocme et al., 1995; Wolock & Horowitz, 1984). It has been asserted that there is a strong association between child neglect and poverty, indicating that, while poverty cannot be said to cause child neglect, it is the predominant risk factor (Bath & Haapala, 1992; Berry, 1992; Daro, 1988; DiLeonardi, 1993; Emery & Laumann-Billings, 1998; Garbarino & Crouter, 1978; Giovannoni & Billingsley, 1974; Hampton, 1987; Horowitz & Wolock 1981; Jones, 1987; Kelleher et al., 1994; Knudsen, 1992; Landsman et al., 1992; Martin & Walters, 1982; Nelson et al., 1990; Nelson & Landsman, 1992; Pelton, 1978, 1981; Pettigrew, 1986; Trocme et al., 1995; Wolock & Horowitz, 1979; Young, 1964). It is clear—children who grow up in poverty are at higher risk for neglect than those who do not. To the extent that poverty is the responsibility of the society in which children live, society can be said to be neglectful in not providing the resources that reduce risks for children. This chapter will explore the relationship between poverty and child neglect, and the resultant implications for research, policy, and practice.

CHILD NEGLECT AND POVERTY: THE NUMBERS

Neglected Children

In 1996, there were 968,789 substantiated cases of child maltreatment in the United States. Of these cases, 499,871 were neglect, 229,264 were physical abuse, and 119,357 were sexual abuse. The number of children under eighteen years of age living in the United States was 69,048,323 (Petit et al., 1999). In 1995 the figures were as follows: 994,586 substantiated cases; 518,348 neglect cases; 244,427 physical abuse cases; and 126,032 sexual abuse cases. The total population was 70,486,000 (Petit & Curtis, 1997). The NIS-3 reports the following findings for 1993. The total number of children who had been abused and neglected was 2,815,600. Of these 1,221,800 were abused, including sexual abuse, and 1,961,300 were neglected (Sedlak & Broadhurst, 1996). These figures again make evident the preponderance of neglect cases in the child welfare caseloads.

Poor Children

In 1995 the federal government determined that a family of three with an income below $12,156 per year was living in a condition of poverty. In 1995 and 1996, 20%, one in five of all children in the United States, lived in families that met this criterion (Federal Interagency Forum on Child and Family Statistics, 1998; Fraser, 1997; Lewit et al., 1997; Petit & Curtis, 1997). The statistics are worse for children under the age of six. One in every four preschoolers in the United States lives in poverty (Petit & Curtis, 1997). The rates are even higher for minority children, children living in single-parent households, and children whose parents did not finish high school. Approximately 15% of White children live below the poverty line as compared to 54% of African-American children and 44% of Hispanic children. In addition, minority families experience more severe and persistent poverty than do White families; they more frequently live in resource-poor neighborhoods; and their numbers are increasing proportionately, while the numbers for White children are not (Foster & Furstenberg, 1999; Luthar, 1999). Irrespective of race, for children in single-parent households, the poverty rate is 58%. It is almost 66% for children whose parents did not finish high school (Fraser, 1997).

Extreme poverty (approximately $6,000 for a family of three or $8,000 for a family of four) is the condition in which 8% of the children of the United States live (Federal Interagency Forum on Child and Family Statistics, 1998). These figures indicate that over 14,000,000 children were classified as poor in 1995 (Lewit et al., 1997), and 5,600,000 children lived in conditions of extreme poverty. The Federal Interagency Forum on Child and Family Statistics (1998) found that 3.4% of children lived in households reporting that they did not have enough to eat. These households were more likely than not to be poor. Poor households were also more likely to include the 6% of children who are at risk of hunger, the 5% of children who experience moderate hunger, and the 1% of children who suffer severe hunger. The condition of poverty for children is not improving. Petit and Curtis (1997) found that the percentage of children living in poverty rose from 14% in 1969 to 21% in 1995. In addition, Lindsey (1994) reported that the poverty children endure has become increasingly severe. As a result, the risk of neglect for these children may also be increasing.

In comparison with other segments of U.S. society, children are the poorest. They are, as a whole, poorer than working-age adults and the elderly. In 1992, the poverty rate was 1.7 times greater for children than for elderly persons (Ozawa, 1999). Poverty for the elderly has been reduced substantially, while it has increased for children. According to the U.S. Census Bureau (2002) in 1970 25% of elders (65 years of age and older), 9% of adults (18–64 years old), and 15% of children (under 18) were living in poverty. In 2001 10.1% of people 65 and over, 10.1% of people 18–64, and 16.3% of people under 18 were classified as poor. Thus, in the United States, a significant disparity currently exists between the poverty status of children and that of elderly persons (Lindsey, 1994; Ozawa, 1999; Schorr, 1988). There is also a vast disparity between the poverty status of children in the United States and that of children in other industrialized nations. The United States has the dubious honor of ranking as the number one industrialized nation in the magnitude of the discrepancy between the rich and the poor; and as number one of sixteen industrialized nations for rates of children living in poverty conditions (Garbarino & Collins, 1999; Lewit et al., 1997; Lindsey, 1994).

Neglect and Poor Children

Children raised in poverty are 9 times more likely to be neglected (Thomlison, 1997) and 56 times more likely to be educationally neglected (Sedlak & Broadhurst, 1996) than children who are not. When compared to families whose incomes are over $30,000 per year, children raised in families whose incomes are less than $15,000 are 44 times more likely to be neglected (Sedlak & Broadhurst, 1996). Studies have shown that neglectful parenting harmed approximately 39.1 children for every 1,000 children in the United States. Of these:

- 27.2 lived in families whose income was less than $15,000 per year as compared to
- 11.3 whose family income was between $15,000 and $30,000 and
- 0.6 whose family income was more than $30,000. (Petit & Curtis, 1997; Petit et al., 1999; Sedlak & Broadhurst, 1996)

If one includes those children who were neglected, but with no evident harm, the figures are even higher:

- 72.3 neglected children per 1,000 children in the United States for families below $15,000 annual income,
- 21.6 per 1000 for families with income between $15,000 and $30,000 and
- 1.6 per 1000 for families whose incomes exceeded $30,000. (Sedlak & Broadhurst, 1996)

These figures represent a significant increase in the number of children at risk for neglect when compared to previous studies. The children at greatest increase of risk are those in families whose income is below $15,000 (Sedlak & Broadhurst, 1996).

If insufficient food can be classified as child neglect, between 1977 and 1991 2–4% of all households in the United States lived in neglectful conditions (Lewit & Kerrebrock, 1997a). In view of the fact that ten times more individuals from poor families reported food insufficiency than nonpoor families, it may be assumed that most of these households had low incomes. In the United States, in the early 1990s, two to four million children under the age of twelve did not get enough to eat (Lewit & Kerrebrock, 1997a, 1997b).

As these figures and those from previously cited studies indicate, the risk of parental and community child neglect increases in conditions of poverty. The question arises as to what are the risks in terms of children's outcomes that occur in these situations. In previous chapters the effect of neglect on children has been examined. To be considered, however, are the effects of poverty.

CHILD NEGLECT AND POVERTY: THE EFFECTS

Effects of Child Neglect

As previously indicated in Chapter Three, child neglect is associated with substantial negative outcomes for children. Neglected children are at higher risk for emotional or psychological, mental health, relationship, academic, and physical health problems than nonneglected children. As adults they have more life disruptions, substance abuse issues, suicide attempts, and lack of competency in many life skills and personal capabilities. As stated in Chapter Three, being neglected appears to have a pervasive effect on one's sense of self and one's place in the world.

Effects of Poverty: Risk Factors

As with neglect, the effects of poverty are broad and pervasive. As stated by Lewit et al. (1997), "Poor children suffer a disproportional share of deprivation, hardship, and bad outcomes. The experiences of the persistently poor fit better the stereotype of an 'under-class' trapped in concentrated poverty neighborhoods, beset by high crime rates, poor schools, substance abuse, and other social pathologies" (p. 8). The risks to children that lead to later damage are present more often in families living in conditions of poverty (Schorr, 1988).

Timing and duration. As with the effects of neglect, the effects of poverty seem to depend on the age of the child when the poverty occurs and the length of time the child lives in poverty conditions. The younger the child at the time poverty is experienced, and the longer the duration of the poverty conditions in which the child lives, the more damaging and lasting are the effects (Brooks-Gunn & Duncan, 1997; Duncan, Yueng, Brooks-Gunn, & Smith, 1998; Lewit et al., 1997; Luthar, 1999; Schorr, 1988; Smith & Yueng, 1998). This close association between poverty and risk of "bad outcomes" holds for every factor of risk from premature birth (Schorr, 1988) to limited life prospects (Smith & Yueng, 1998).

Ethnicity. Minority children, especially young minority children, are particularly vulnerable to poverty (Lindsey, 1994). As indicated above, they experience poverty more frequently and in more severe and persistent forms, including significantly resource-poor neighborhoods, than do White children (Luthar, 1999). This is particularly alarming in the light of the previous statistics, which indicated that the numbers of disadvantaged African-American children living in concentrated areas of poverty is growing substantially (Foster & Furstenberg, 1999).

Inadequate housing/neighborhoods. Poverty reduces the quality of the housing and neighborhoods in which children live (Federal Interagency Forum on Child and Family Statistics, 1998; Fraser, 1997; Kirby & Fraser, 1997; Lewit et al., 1997; Murry & Brody, 1999). Factors associated with inadequate housing and neighborhoods that may influence child outcomes include:

1. more stressful life events, including housing cost burdens (Federal Interagency Forum on Child and Family Statistics, 1998);
2. environmental hazards, such as exposure to lead (Dubowitz, 1999; Lewit et al., 1997); and
3. more hostile environments that include poor neighborhoods, high crime rates, and increased social isolation (Fraser, 1997; Murry & Brody, 1999).

Inadequate child care. As indicated above, there are more preschoolers living in poverty conditions than any other segment of society. These are the very children who are most at risk for poor outcomes owing to their early exposure to conditions of poverty. Yet for children from zero to five, when the need for child care is the greatest, universally subsidized child care is not available (Lindsey, 1994). This is especially alarming in terms of welfare reform and welfare-to-work initiatives. Children's daily learning experiences change when a mother moves from welfare to work (Larner et al., 1997). High-quality child care has the potential to provide children with opportunities to make cognitive gains; however, such child care is rarely available to families living in conditions of poverty (Queralt & Witte, 1998).

Lack of additional resources. In addition to child care, poverty can limit families' access to resources that more advantaged families take for granted, such as:

1. quality transportation (Fraser, 1997);
2. food (Dubowitz, 1999; Federal Interagency Forum on Child and Family Statistics, 1998; Fraser, 1997; Kirby & Fraser; Lewit & Kerrebrock, 1997a);
3. clothing (Kirby & Fraser, 1997);
4. quality health care, owing in part to lack of health insurance (Dubowitz, 1999; Federal Interagency Forum on Child and Family Statistics, 1998; Fraser, 1997; Kirby & Fraser, 1997; Larner et al., 1997); and
5. quality education (Fraser, 1997).

In the words of Schorr (1988):

> Persistent and concentrated poverty virtually guarantee[s] the presence of a vast collection of risk factors and their continuing destructive impact over time . . . risk factors join to shorten the odds of favorable long-term outcomes . . . both the informal supports from family and friends and the institutions and services that could buffer these risks are also less likely to be there for the poorest children. Given the way helping systems operate, these are the children who will not get the kind of attention that could provide them with protection against adversity . . . the absence of good services and schooling have, for a high proportion of vulnerable

children, actually become additional risk factors . . . the services these children need are inaccessible or do not exist. The services they can obtain are often the wrong ones, too cumbersome to reach, too fragmented, or too narrow in scope . . . these children who . . . should be getting the attention of the most skilled and wise professionals . . . and the most comprehensive services . . . have to make do with . . . the worst and the least. (p. 30)

Effects of Poverty: Outcomes

Children's health. Income and poverty status are disturbingly related to children's health (Lewit et al., 1997; *New York Times*, 2000). The Federal Interagency Forum on Child and Family Statistics (1998) found significantly higher rates of activity limitation among poor children. They were also less likely to have received the standard battery of immunizations (e.g., DPT, MMR, polio, and flu) and thus were at higher risk for contracting these diseases. Poor children also have increased exposure to environmental hazards (e.g., lead and violence), which increases the risk of adverse health outcomes (Dubowitz, 1999; Dubowitz & Black, 2002). When inner-city grandmothers gather to talk about their grandchildren's "numbers," they are not discussing SAT scores. They are discussing the children's blood lead levels (N. Boyles, personal communication, June 2002).

Low-income families have significantly more moderate to severe hunger problems than more advantaged families (Dubowitz, 1999; Dubowitz & Black, 2002; Federal Interagency Forum on Child and Family Statistics, 1998; Lewit & Kerrebrock, 1997a). The effects of hunger and malnutrition can include fatigue, irritability, dizziness, frequent headaches, frequent colds and infections, and difficulty concentrating (Lewit & Kerrebrock, 1997a). As indicated earlier, two to four million children in the United States went hungry in the early 1990s. It is believed that these figures do not adequately represent the actual number of children experiencing food insufficiency and resultant malnutrition in the United States (Lewit & Kerrebrock, 1997a).

There is an important relationship between poverty and growth stunting. The stunting rate among poor children is approximately twice the expected rate (Lewit & Kerrebrock, 1997b). Children's dental health is also affected by their poverty status. Lewit and Kerrebrock (1998) found that "poor children, because they are less likely than their wealthier peers to receive dental services, are at the highest risk of suffering the pain and consequences of untreated dental disease" (p. 134).

These outcomes are exacerbated by the aforementioned diminished access to health care that is associated with poverty; and are particularly problematic for the "near poor" who do not qualify for Medicaid and lack health insurance (Dubowitz, 1999; Dubowitz & Black, 2002). In 1993, 20% of poor children lacked health insurance owing to the expansion of Medicaid and the retraction of private insurance. In an attempt to control costs, while expanding eligibility to meet the growing need, states have turned to Medicaid managed-care contracts, the effects of which on the quality of health care for the poor are not yet known (Larner et al., 1997).

Children's mental health. Children who live in poor rural areas, and are serviced by the child welfare and/or juvenile justice systems, are the children who are most at risk for mental health problems. Moreover, rural families' economic problems are most destructive for children's mental health and functioning when those problems are chronic and seemingly without solutions (Glisson et al., 2000). Bolger and Patterson (2001) found increased internalizing of problems and perceived external locus of control in children living in conditions of economic hardship. Thus these children were at risk for depression and anxiety disorders, and felt they had little impact on their environment.

Child development. Poverty and the related increase in life-stressing events, including faulty parenting, can have major adverse effects on children's cognitive and social development (Gaudin, 1999; Kirby & Fraser, 1997; Lewit et al., 1997; Murry & Brody, 1999; Smith & Yueng, 1998). Poverty-related factors such as lead poisoning and malnutrition can contribute to poor outcomes for children's cognitive development as well as their health and physical development. In addition, population-based risk factors related to poverty other than inadequate nutrition can also contribute to poor performance on tests of cognitive ability (Lewit & Kerrebrock, 1997b).

Children's school performance. There is a strong association between poverty occurring early in a child's life and high school graduation. Low income during the preschool and early school years exhibits the strongest correlation with low rates of high school completion (Brooks-Gunn & Duncan, 1997; Duncan et al., 1998; Gaudin, 1999; Lewit et al., 1997). In addition to not completing school, children's school performance suffers when they are living in conditions of poverty (Lewit et al., 1997; Murry & Brody, 1999). On February 18, 2000, the *New York Times* reported that children living in poverty were less likely to be able to count to ten, recite the alphabet, or be in good health than their more advantaged cohorts. In addition to being an effect of poverty itself, poor health plays a part in children's school performance. Healthy youngsters are more likely to come to school and pay attention.

Adverse parenting. Evidence has related poverty to child abuse and neglect (Pelton, 1994). It is through the material hardship that poverty causes that poverty is likely to have an impact on children and families. Preoccupied with the stresses and difficulties of living in conditions of material deprivation, parents, usually single women, have trouble responding to their children's needs. These same stressors and difficulties render parents, themselves, vulnerable to psychological distress, depression, and anxiety. These factors can lead to adverse parenting, which, in turn, has negative outcomes for children (Dubowitz & Black, 2002; Fraser, 1997; Kirby & Fraser, 1997; Lindsey, 1994; Luthar, 1999; Murry & Brody, 1999; Smith & Yueng, 1998). The harmful effects of poverty may therefore, in part, be transmitted to children by its harmful effects on their caretakers, usually their mothers (Dubowitz, 1999; Garbarino & Collins, 1999; Kirby & Fraser, 1997).

Single, teenage mothers are overrepresented among the poor and are at greater risk for negative parenting behaviors. They tend to be more insensitive and impatient with their infants, have less realistic expectations, and provide less responsive, less stimulating, and less affectionate environments for their children. Their children more consistently display vulnerability to negative outcomes, indicating that the age and marital status of parents can exacerbate the already high risks faced by children who live in poverty (Luthar, 1999).

The solutions to the problems of poverty, in themselves, can result in adverse parenting and negative outcomes for children. Welfare-to-work programs may force parents out of their homes; and, in the absence of child care, children are left home alone. Food budgets may have to be cut, resulting in hungry children. Child neglect, associated with these behaviors (i.e., lack of supervision, malnutrition), may result in foster care placement for children (Larner et al., 1997). The positive effects of mothers working out of the home can be undermined by low wages, repetitive jobs, poor working conditions, and inadequate child care (Zaslow & Ernig, 1997). Research has indicated that, given these circumstances, children's home experiences begin to deteriorate, becoming less stimulating and nurturing (Parcel & Menaghan, 1997).

Poverty also influences the levels of paternal involvement with children. Fathers in poor families are less emotionally and behaviorally involved in their children's lives; and the greater the persistence of poverty, the less fathers are involved. Even when fathers are involved, there are few buffering effects of fathers in poor families (Harris & Marmer, 1996). These findings regarding adverse parenting indicate that poor children are more at risk for child abuse and neglect; unsupportive, unstimulating, and chaotic home environments; poor family management practices; and severe family disruption, including placement out of the home.

Future outcomes. As indicated earlier, children raised in poverty are less likely to graduate from high school. In view of the fact that the poverty rate for families in which the parent(s) did not graduate from high school is 66% (Fraser, 1997), lack of a high school degree places these children at risk of remaining in poverty as adults. Children raised in poverty are more likely to be unemployed at age nineteen than nonpoor children (Gaudin, 1999). African-American boys raised in the inner cities have less of a chance to reach adulthood than their more advantaged peers (N. Boyles, personal communication, June 2002). As can be seen, being raised in poverty can severely limit children's life prospects (Smith & Yueng, 1998).

Effects of Child Neglect and Poverty

As the previous discussion and Table 7 indicate, the effects of poverty and child neglect are very similar.

TABLE 7
Effects of Neglect and Poverty on Children

	Neglect	Poverty
Physical development	Growth delays/stunting Auditory processing deficits Brain abnormalities Eating disorders Sexual problems Alcohol/substance abuse	Malnutrition Fatigue Lead poisoning Growth stunting Increased vulnerability to colds and infections Untreated dental disease More limited life expectancy Premature birth Poor health
Cognitive/ behavioral development	Increased behavioral problems Developmental delays Academic delays and difficulties Attention disorders Withdrawn behaviorally	Low rates of high school graduation Attention disorders Learning disabilities Poor school performance
Social/ emotional development	Mental illness Depression/suicidal ideation Anxiety disorders Internalizing problems External locus of control Withdrawn emotionally and socially Impaired relationships Poor coping skills Few friends Limited life prospects	Mental illness/affective disorders/ anxiety disorders Internalizing problems External locus of control Underemployment Inadequate parenting/abuse and neglect/severe family disruption Remaining in conditions of poverty as adults Limited life prospects

Both children of neglect and children of poverty suffer from physical, emotional, cognitive, social, and developmental issues. Both neglected children and poor children are at risk of poor outcomes in terms of their life prospects and their place in the world. In order to improve these children's prospects, knowledge about the nature of the relationship between child neglect and poverty is of utmost importance.

CHILD NEGLECT AND POVERTY: WHERE DO WE STAND?

The Relationship between Child Neglect and Poverty

Poor children are more vulnerable to child neglect than their more advantaged peers. The pervasiveness of poverty as a factor in child abuse and neglect is evidenced by the overwhelming and consistent correlation between poverty and child maltreatment found as the result of multiple studies, studies that took place at different times and employed various definitions, methodologies, forms of abuse, and levels of severity. In addition to maltreatment itself, the severity of the maltreatment is related to families' material circumstances. "There is a strong funneling effect in regard to child abuse and neglect and their severity, with the poorest children in our society being at the greatest risk" (Pelton, 1994, p. 167).

Findings have indicated that there is a more pronounced relationship between poverty and child neglect than between poverty and other forms of child maltreatment (Garbarino & Crouter, 1978; Martin & Walters, 1982; Pelton, 1994). There is no doubt that child neglect is highly correlated with poverty and that material deprivation is the one pervasive condition of families who neglect their children. This association has been noted by practically all authors in the field (Bath & Haapala, 1992; Berry, 1992; Crittenden, 1999; Daro, 1988; DiLeonardi, 1993; Dubowitz, 1999; Dubowitz, Black, Starr, & Zuravin, 1993; Gelles, 1999; Giovannoni & Billingsley, 1974; Hampton, 1987; Horowitz & Wolock 1981; Jones, 1987; Kelleher et al., 1994; Knudsen, 1992; Landsman et al., 1992; Larner et al., 1997; Nelson et al., 1990; Nelson & Landsman, 1992; Pelton, 1978, 1981, 1994; Pettigrew, 1986; Wolock & Horowitz, 1979; Young, 1964).

Indicators of poverty other than income have also been linked with child neglect. These indicators include inadequate and unsafe housing; frequent moves due to housing problems; homelessness; employment problems including unemployment, underemployment, and sporadic employment; undereducated parents; and neighborhoods that are resource-poor, unsafe, transient, promote social isolation, and experience violence, high criminal activity, and drug abuse (Benedict et al., 1992; Crittenden, 1999; Giovannoni & Billingsley, 1974; Hampton, 1987; Herrenkohl et al.,

1983; Jones, 1987; Kadushin, 1967; Krishman & Morrison, 1995; Landsman et al., 1992; Nelson et al., 1990; Nelson & Landsman, 1992; Watters et al., 1986; Wolock & Horowitz, 1979; Young, 1964).

As indicated above, the outcomes for children of both poverty and neglect are similar. The outcomes are exacerbated when poverty and neglect coexist; and there is a demonstrable difficulty in separating child neglect from the condition within which neglected children live. Therefore, it is difficult to attribute outcomes to child neglect or to poverty. On some levels, these concepts may be indistinguishable (i.e., on an economic level poverty may be equivalent to child neglect).

Entangling child neglect and poverty. As shown above, the close association of child neglect and poverty and the similarities of their outcomes for children make it difficult to determine what outcomes are the result of neglect; what outcomes are the result of poverty; what outcomes are the result of the interaction between neglect and poverty; and what outcomes are the result of other factors, such as parental deficits. Knudsen (1992) indicated that the general social context within which neglect takes place makes it difficult to ascribe a cause-effect relationship between specific neglecting behaviors and specific effects, as there is no separation of the impact of neglect from the impact of poverty. As we have seen previously the entanglement of child neglect and poverty, in addition to difficulties in attributing outcomes, makes it difficult to define child neglect and determine its causes.

Lewit et al. (1997) emphasized two points of view regarding the relationship between child neglect and poverty. One perspective holds that parents' poor character or limited physical and mental capacities lead to both poverty and problems in parenting their children. Another perspective emphasizes the adverse impact on children of material deprivation and parental stress caused by poverty.

A third viewpoint maintains that child neglect is the result of the interaction between the personal traits of the parents and the environment in which they live. This view adds confusion to the issues when designing interventions, as practitioners in the child welfare field cannot discern whether to focus on neglect or poverty (i.e., parental deficits or economic conditions) (Swift, 1995a).

Untangling child neglect and poverty.   Research makes clear the fact that most families in poverty do not neglect their children, at least to the extent that they become involved in the child welfare system (Black & Dubowitz, 1999; Garbarino & Collins, 1999; Gelles, 1999). As Black & Dubowitz (1999) pointed out, "although poverty often contributes to family dysfunction and may also directly deprive children of basic needs, poverty per se is not usually considered neglect by the child welfare system. Indeed, many state laws or regulations specifically exclude conditions that are associated with poverty, such as homelessness" (p. 265). In addition, studies have shown that there are differences between neglecting and nonneglecting mothers over and above poverty (English, 1999). The conclusion reached by many is that other factors besides poverty need to be considered.

Swift (1995a) reported that studies of child neglect conclude, "although poverty and social deprivation are important factors in neglect, the personality features of mothers are primary causal factors" (p. 89). It may be that the pressures poverty places on parents relate it to child neglect only indirectly. Thus the effects of poverty on child maltreatment may not be as strong as that of parental deficits (Crittenden, 1999; Luthar, 1999; Thomlison, 1997).

This view is supported by the fact that nonpoor parents do neglect their children, especially in terms of providing for their supervision, stimulation, emotional, and disciplinary needs (Cantwell & Rosenberg, 1990). Pelton (1978, 1981) concluded that the middle class has more leeway to be irresponsible than the lower classes owing to their higher level of affluence; that is, they can spend household money more impulsively without risk of not having food on the table. Affluent parents may hire a nanny who provides only supervision and food, not emotional connection, the parent having little interaction with the child on a day-to-day basis. At times teenagers are left to their own devices while the parents take extended trips. Abell et al. (1996) found that the effects of poverty are not linear with respect to parent/child interaction. Some families demonstrated a great deal of resiliency when confronted with an environment of poverty.

What is apparent is that the current state of the art offers little clarity regarding the relationship between poverty and child neglect. Crittenden (1999) suggested that the

> association of poverty with neglect needs to be reconsidered. First, both poverty and child neglect may be the effects of learning to process information in distorted and limiting ways. Second, the focus on poverty may prevent us from seeing the importance of emotional neglect in more affluent families. Last, the focus on the association of poverty with neglect may lead to the conclusion that global economic solutions are primary. (p. 66)

Given the pervasiveness of poverty; the poor outcomes for children in spite of adequate parenting; and the extremely high correlation with child maltreatment, especially neglect, this last point may actually be the case (i.e., global economic solutions may, indeed, be of primary importance).

Community Neglect

It is clear that the multiple risks associated with poverty conditions are harmful to children; increase their vulnerability in all areas of their lives, and the risk of neglect in particular; and produce outcomes similar to child neglect. In terms of child neglect being defined as harm to children as the result of acts of omission, it can be argued that poverty is a form of community neglect of children and their families. "In the United States de facto neglect exists for at least five million children whose families have income less than one-half the poverty line" (Lindsey, 1994, p. 168). This fact is exacerbated by the fact that declining public support for public welfare programs also decreases the authority of traditional sources of help (i.e., school, religious organizations, and community agencies) (Fraser, 1997). Parents may have a responsibility to provide a positive home environment for their children; however, the community shapes the conditions under which the parents must create these environments (Parcel & Menaghan, 1997). As Kadushin stated in 1967,

> The community itself is guilty of neglect when it fails to provide adequate housing, adequate levels of public assistance, adequate schooling, adequate health services, or adequate recreational services, or when it allows job discrimination and makes no effort to control an open display of vice, narcotic traffic, and other illegal activity. (p. 216)

It has been stated that "persistent and concentrated poverty virtually guarantees the presence of a vast collection of risk factors and their continuing destructive impact over time" (Schorr, 1988, p. 30), shortening the odds of favorable long-term outcomes for children. We have seen that both the informal supports from family and friends and the institutions and services that could buffer these risks are less likely to be there for the poorest children. By allowing children to live in conditions of poverty, the society can be said to be guilty of neglect (Garbarino & Collins, 1999; Gaudin, 1999; Korbin & Spilsbury, 1999; Lindsey, 1994; Nelson et al., 1990; Wolock & Horowitz, 1984). We are failing to provide for children when we ignore the plight of poor families. Most families who become categorized as neglecting have virtually no access to material resources (Swift, 1995a). Parents should not be held responsible for that which society is not willing to provide support (Stein, 1984).

Poverty is damaging and even killing our children. For instance, growth stunting prevalence among children living in conditions of poverty in the United States is consistently higher than in overall child populations (Lewit & Kerrebrock, 1997b); and the life expectancy of inner-city African-American boys is consistently lower. However, as reported by Swift (1995a), "work processes and procedures in child welfare . . . operate to create repeated denials of outlay of resources. Case opening cannot be warranted simply by the need for resources but only by some demonstrated fit with ideas of what constitutes a mandated child welfare problem" (p. 86).

Focus on parental deficits. The traditional view of both poverty and child neglect is that they are due to personal problems of parents, and therefore, not the responsibility of the community to resolve. Parents, usually single mothers, are expected to manage circumstances over which they have little or no control (Lindsey, 1994; Swift, 1995a). Thus children are condemned to live in poverty because the child welfare system is about the culpability of parents, not about providing resources to resolve the issues associated with poverty (Black & Dubowitz, 1999; Swift, 1995a).

The focus on parental deficits leads to solutions that have to do with strengthening parenting skills, without providing the material resources that families need to thrive. Child welfare services "are directed at changing people rather than addressing social ills" (Swift, 1995a, p. 98). This lack of focus on resolving issues of material deprivation leads to the neglect of the neglected by our society. A major restructuring of policy and programs would be necessary to provide for disadvantaged families. We clearly have not made the necessary economic commitment to effect this kind of structural change. The current political climate makes it very obvious that the policymakers do not have the will to develop such broad programs (Crittenden, 1999).

Focus on poverty. As indicated earlier, more than one in five American children lives in conditions of poverty. It is clear that child neglect and poverty are closely related, and indeed that poverty may be a form of community neglect. As daunting as the idea of tackling poverty might appear, any strategy to reduce child neglect must deal with this issue (Dubowitz et al., 1993; Lindsey, 1994; Pelton, 1994; Schorr, 1988).

Lindsey (1994) indicated, "The major barrier to progress against child poverty has been the limited view of our collective responsibility . . . If there is to be any hope of developing workable solutions to child poverty, the child welfare system must begin looking to the wider social and economic problems which families face" (p. 186). We have provided substantial support for the elderly; we must now do the same for children. Not to do so will weaken the economic base of the United States in the future (Lindsey, 1994; Ozawa, 1999).

> The decision to combat child poverty aggressively cannot turn on whether there will be some undesired side effects and unexpected outcomes, for those are inevitable in most social interventions. Instead,

it should turn on whether the redistributive gains and long-run improvements in child well-being resulting from less poverty outweigh the negatives and are more worthy than other uses of the funds. It rests on the nation's political will to devote more resources to this end rather than on any hard economic or budgetary limits and will require a long-run commitment to sustain efforts and consider new approaches. (Plotnick, 1997, p. 85)

CHILD NEGLECT AND POVERTY: PROTECTIVE FACTORS

Regardless of the argument about parental deficits versus poverty as the primary risk factor for child neglect, the children of many families living in poverty are not harmed; and many parents living in poverty are not neglectful. The factors that seem to buffer the effects of poverty and/or child neglect for families can point to interventions on both the personal and the public levels to provide better outcomes for children, irregardless of their maltreatment or economic status.

Protective Factors: Child Neglect

Maternal employment, especially employment that is well paid and enriching for the mother, results in more supportive and stimulating home environments for children and reduces the risk of child maltreatment (Mulsow & Murry, 1996; Parcel & Menaghan, 1997). Other protective factors for parents include having been competently parented themselves and having adequate social supports. Protective factors for children include competent behavior, higher intelligence, high self-esteem, having an outgoing nature, being older at the time of maltreatment, and as infants were seen as affectionate. For families as a whole, the following characteristics buffer the risks of child neglect—family cohesiveness, resilient parents, positive role modeling, the presence of siblings, marital harmony, and the availability of supportive family members. Factors in the environment that reduce the risks of neglect for families include the availability of supportive friends, teachers, and neighbors; community well-being, stability, and cohesiveness; the availability of role models; a healthy economy; and strong informal social support networks (Smokowski, 1998).

Protective Factors: Poverty

Social support, especially that extends the family resources, has been found to mitigate the effects of poverty on families (Bowen & Chapman, 1996;

Murry & Brody, 1999). As with neglect, maternal employment outside the home is related to improved economic circumstances of the family and improved outcomes for children from low-income families (Lewit et al., 1997; Zaslow & Ernig, 1997). Harris and Marmer (1996) found few buffering effects of fathers in poor families; however, they did find that greater emotional involvement of fathers in persistently poor families reduces children's delinquent behaviors. A mother's involvement proved to be beneficial in protecting children from the adverse effects of poverty and welfare receipt. Child characteristics that seem to protect children from the adverse effects of poverty include (a) intelligence, (b) an easygoing temperament, (c) assertiveness, (d) an internal locus of control, (e) high self-esteem, (f) strong interpersonal skills, and (g) personal successes (Luthar, 1999). Table 8 illustrates risk and protective factors for child neglect and poverty.

Research has indicated that being aware of protective factors is an imported aspect of offering protection to children from the effects of both poverty and neglect. It has been suggested that the relative impact of protective factors is greater than the impact of risk factors in explaining resiliency and adaptation in children and families (Bowen & Chapman, 1996; Werner & Smith, 1982). The protective factors for both child neglect and poverty, not surprisingly, are very similar, indicating that protecting children against the ill effects of poverty may also protect them from child neglect.

IMPLICATIONS OF THE RELATIONSHIP BETWEEN CHILD NEGLECT AND POVERTY

The vast majority of child neglect takes place in conditions of poverty. The evidence of the high correlation between neglect and poverty is overwhelming. Yet when one examines the research literature, current policy, and practice, the issue of poverty is sometimes mentioned and mostly ignored. This is unconscionable, given that the harm to children living in conditions of poverty can be just as devastating as that suffered by neglected children. Indeed, the children living in poverty may be neglected children—children neglected by their nation.

Implications for Research

As Swift (1995a) pointed out, as strong a theme as poverty is in relation to child neglect, the study of poverty per se is strangely missing from the research literature. Attention needs to be paid to economic and social issues,

TABLE 8
Summary of Risk and Protective Factors in Child Neglect and Poverty

	Child Neglect	Poverty
Risk factors	Poverty and material deprivation Racial discrimination Undereducation Single mothers/absent fathers Dangerous neighborhoods Inadequate child care resources Unemployment Age of child (younger), duration of neglect (longer) Substance abuse/addiction Physical and mental illness Affective and personality disorders Low self-concept and self-esteem Poor social, coping, problem-solving, child-rearing, and other life skills Prematurity and low birth weight Faulty attachments Other types of maltreatment including domestic violence Divorce/family disruption Social isolation and loneliness High stress levels Multiplicity of problems	Minority status Undereducation Single-parent households Single teenage mothers Absent fathers Inadequate housing and neighborhoods Inadequate child care resources Unemployment/unsatisfactory employment Age of child (younger), duration of poverty (longer) Inadequate transportation, food, clothing, health care Unsupportive, unstimulating, and chaotic home environments
Protective factors	Social support, including caring adults in the child's life, especially mothers and fathers Well-paid, enriching maternal employment Child's intelligence and self-esteem (both higher), temperament (more outgoing), age (older), coping strategies, competent behavior, perceived internal locus of control Adequately parented and resilient parents who are good role models Family cohesion/marital harmony Siblings Cultural practices Material adequacy Adequate child care resources Educational adequacy Adequate health care resources Relatively few sources of stress Safe and supportive neighborhoods	Supportive adults in a child's life, including mothers, fathers, teachers, and neighbors Social supports Maternal employment Child's intelligence, easygoing temperament, assertiveness, internal locus of control, high self-esteem, strong interpersonal skills, and personal successes

and to the kinds of care that children actually receive. We need to know how social policies and programs can reduce poverty for children, thus reducing their vulnerability to child neglect (Black & Dubowitz, 1999). Compelling supportive data regarding the elimination of poverty as a means of achieving child well-being in the United States are needed to force serious consideration of the sweeping structural changes that would be required (Crittenden, 1999; Swift, 1995a).

Research is needed to understand the mechanisms by which some low-income families protect their children from the effects of poverty (Black & Dubowitz, 1999), and by which some affluent families neglect their children. We have yet to learn the effects of social programs such as TANF, Food Stamps, and Medicaid on the well-being of children (Devaney, Ellwood, & Love, 1997; Larner et al., 1997; Lewit et al., 1997). The results of such research could provide the data needed to force consideration of programs to alleviate the suffering of both poor and neglected children.

Implications for Policy

Ozawa (1999) pointed out that "welfare reform reflects negative attitudes toward and a disdain for female-headed families with children . . . the hostile public stance on social policy that touches children's lives is in stark contrast to the benign public stance on social policy for elderly people" (p. 15). This negative attitude regarding poverty may contribute to the marginalization of the problem, and the lack of awareness on the part of the public of the contribution our society makes to bad outcomes for children. Before anything can be done to improve the plight of children, there must be a systemic change in these attitudes and the policies they foster (Nelson, Landsman, et al., 1994). Society needs to be made aware that by neglecting the poor it is, in part, responsible for the neglect of children (Garbarino & Collins, 1999).

As overwhelming as making these changes might appear, any strategy to reduce child neglect must come to terms with poverty (Dubowitz et al., 1993; Gelles, 1999; Pelton, 1994). However, as Crittenden (1999) points out, the United States has not made the necessary economic commitment that such a major restructuring of society would entail. As mentioned previously, the current political climate is not conducive to action on proposals regarding support for children.

Implications for Practice

Swift (1995a) asserted that the issue of neglect invariably resolves itself into one of personal problems. The definition of a problem determines the direction one takes to arrive at a solution. Continuing to utilize the same solutions to the problems of child neglect and poverty will continue to produce the same outcomes for children. Focusing on behavior change strate-
gies for parents has not proved effective in resolving either child neglect or poverty.

Framing the problem of child neglect as an economic issue may pro-
duce better results for a broad range of children, and reduce the number of child neglect cases in the child welfare caseloads. This is not to say that the elimination of poverty conditions for children will eliminate child neglect. As pointed out in Chapters Three and Four, risk factors exist within both the family and the environment. But it would at least help to make clear to what extent environmental deficits and to what extent parental deficits contribute to neglect, thus allowing for more effective intervention strategies to be developed.

What seems to be most helpful about current practice is a cooperative relationship between families and the child welfare system (Howing, Wodarski, Kurtz, et al., 1989). However, these families see the public welfare system as punitive and not helpful (Nelson, Landsman, et al., 1994). What is needed is a change in attitude toward low-income families.

Interventions aimed at resolving the risk factors of poverty and the associated risk factors for child neglect may include the following:

1. *Income supports.* Income assistance programs, such as TANF and related employment programs, can be of great support in reducing the stresses of poverty. However, it is important to consider the kinds of jobs avail-
   able and the amount of income that will be provided (Parcel & Menaghan, 1997). Time limits on assistance may create more serious problems than they were intended to resolve. Unemployed parents could lose their only source of financial support, exposing their children to neglect owing to their lack of resources. The result could be the costly, both financially and emotionally, out-of-home placement of children (Larner et al., 1997). The outcomes of welfare reform depend on how it is implemented. Innovative programs that do not take a punitive approach can be helpful. However, continuing the status quo may hurt families (Berns & Drake, 1998). In addition to public welfare in the form of temporary assistance, Lewit et al. (1997) suggested monetary supports for families with special health needs and tax credits for children up to age 18; and Lindsey (1994) suggested a social security account be set up for children to be payable

at age 18, in order to assure poor children a more promising adulthood. In today's political climate, it is doubtful such measures would be considered.

2. *Child care.* Given the current push under welfare reform to move parents from welfare to work, child care is closely related to income support and employment programs. Unfortunately, neighborhoods with high concentrations of poverty and families who receive welfare assistance also experience low child care capacity (Queralt & Witte, 1998). What is needed is an infrastructure that includes safe, quality, full-day day care centers, child care subsidies, and fully funded Head Start programs (Larner et al., 1997; Lewit et al., 1997; Queralt & Witte, 1998).

3. *Health care.* Health care coverage for children, including Medicaid, that is independent of welfare receipt and coverage through age 19 are essential to maintaining quality health care for children (Larner et al., 1997; Lewit et al., 1997). Universal health care and subsidies for low-income families who are not Medicaid eligible would provide for children who might otherwise fall through the gaps; and help equalize access to quality health care between Medicaid recipients and privately insured children (Devaney et al., 1997; Lewit et al., 1997).

4. *Nutrition programs.* Closely related to children's health is children's nutrition. In the presence of the affluence in our country, no child should go hungry. Yet, research has shown that they do. Therefore, food supplement programs are needed to meet children's nutritional needs (Brooks-Gunn & Duncan, 1997). The Food Stamps program helps to provide for children's basic needs and, therefore, should not be cut back, unless there are other programs to take its place (Larner et al., 1997; Lewit et al., 1997; Lewit & Kerrebrock, 1997b). The Special Supplemental Food Program for Women, Infants, and Children (WIC) needs to be fully funded and other nutritional programs, such as school lunches, should be modified in terms of research regarding nutrition and child hunger (Lewit et al., 1997). In spite of the considered success of the Food Stamps, WIC, and school lunch programs, child hunger and concerns regarding children's nutrition still exist (Devaney et al., 1997).

5. *Housing subsidies.* Impoverished neighborhoods have been linked with child neglect and poor child outcomes. Thus, interventions that include housing subsidies and the opportunity to move to more advantaged neighborhoods could improve outcomes for children (Devaney et al., 1997; Larner et al., 1997; Lewit et al., 1997). Also included in housing programs would be lead abatement programs to improve the cognitive outcomes for children. Maybe then when inner-city grandmothers discuss their grandchildren's "numbers" they *will* be talking about SAT scores.

In conclusion, our children are our future. We have provided for the health and income security of our elderly; now it is time to do the same for our children. We certainly have the capacity to do so. The question is: do we have the will? If we do not, it is our future that is at stake. If we do not reduce the risks to children living in poverty, we will not have the skilled workers needed to drive our market economy in the future. Instead there will be an ever-increasing welfare class (Lindsey, 1994; Ozawa, 1999). No society can survive that is not interested in ensuring the well-being of the next generation. We must care for our children now, if for no other reason than to secure our own future.

Chapter Eleven

The Children of Neglect

WHAT DO WE KNOW, WHAT DO WE DO?

This chapter will sum up and pull together the major themes of this book. Owing to the paucity of research, policy, and practice specific to child neglect, it must be understood that some, perhaps many, of these conclusions—both of research reviewed and themes here presented—are drawn from limited data. However, it is believed that at the present time the following represents the state of the art regarding the children of neglect.

THEME 1: NEGLECT IS A DISTINCT FORM OF CHILD MALTREATMENT THAT IS THE MOST DETRIMENTAL AND THE LEAST UNDERSTOOD

What Do We Know?

Neglect is unique. We know that families involved in different types of maltreatment represent distinct subpopulations, have different etiologies, and require differential treatment. We know that child neglect is a distinct form of child maltreatment with unique etiologies and consequences; and we know that effective intervention with neglectful families requires theory, policy, and practice unique to child neglect. As early as 1964, Young reported, "One of the facts that emerges clearly from this study is that neglecting and abusing parents are two different groups, different in behavior and different in potentials for the future. Although they have been grouped together legally and generally regarded as belonging together, in fact, they are different kinds of people and require different approaches" (pp. 134–135). However, forty years after Young's statement, neglect *continues* to be combined with abuse in most studies that explore related etiology and consequences, useful policies, and effective practice regarding child maltreatment. There is a scarcity of research that focuses specifically on child neglect; and, as a result, no adequate theory (including risk factors and outcomes), policy, and/or practice (outside of demonstration projects) has been developed in regard to child neglect.

Daro (1988) stated, "If practitioners and policymakers have learned only one thing over the past two decades, it should be that allowing one type of maltreatment to dominate our thinking leaves us with a response system and practice standards inappropriate for the full range of concerns represented by this serious social welfare dilemma" (p. 204). Young (1964) and Daro's (1988) statements are as true today as when they were first published. Assessment of the effectiveness of child maltreatment interventions, whether or not they were aimed specifically at remediating or preventing child neglect, has indicated poorer outcomes for neglect than for any other subtype of child maltreatment; in fact, it has been reported that positive outcomes have been found for neglectful families in only about 50% of the cases. There have been few programs designed specifically for neglectful families and even fewer for neglected children. These programs (primarily demonstration projects) also have not produced overwhelmingly successful results.

Neglect is serious. We know that neglect harms children and devastates their potential. We know that the nature of the outcomes for children depends on the age of the child when neglected, the chronicity/duration of the neglect, and the severity of the neglect. We know that child neglect is more serious than other forms of child maltreatment both in terms of numbers of children who are at risk/or harmed and in terms of the severity of the harm incurred, including loss of life. It has been proposed that neglect may be the core issue underlying all child maltreatment; and it has been found that most cases involved with child protection services contain an element of child neglect. Given the numbers of children who experience neglect and its outcomes, it is the contention of this text that more children may be at risk of greater harm than is generally believed.

However, there is a persistent myth that child neglect is not as serious as child abuse. This book makes the assertion that neglect is more serious than abuse in terms of outcomes for children, families, and society. In a Canadian study, Watters et al. (1986) found that the implied assumption that child neglect is less serious than child abuse is a false assumption.

Substantiating this finding, Rohner (1986) reported that research has shown that emotionally neglected children have the most serious consequences of all groups of maltreated children. Up to 74% of this population experienced serious injury or impairment such as attempted suicide, severe failure to thrive, and drug overdoses. In a study of institutionalized developmentally delayed children in England, Buchanan and Oliver (1980) found a confirmed relationship between the children's impairments and abuse in 3% of the cases and a possible relationship in 8% of the cases. However, for 24% of the cases neglect was considered a causal factor. Confirming all of these findings, Kadushin and Martin (1988) stated that "from the point of view of every important criteria, child neglect is a much more significant problem than sexual abuse, and somewhat more so than physical abuse" (p. 321).

Neglect also appears to have a much more substantial influence on outcomes for children than abuse. In comparing characteristics of families involved in various types and combinations of maltreatment, research has shown that the profiles for families who neglect and maltreat in other ways are closer to the neglect-only families. Thus families who were neglectful were found to be distinct from the abuse-only groups, but not from the abuse/neglect groups (Bath & Haapala, 1992; Eckenrode et al., 1993; Watters et al., 1986; Wolock & Horowitz, 1979). When sex abuse was combined with neglect, those children also were more similar to the neglect-only group than to the sex-abuse-only group (Eckenrode et al., 1993).

Groups where neglect occurred alone or in combination with other forms of maltreatment have the poorest outcomes of any other maltreatment group (Bath & Haapala, 1992; Eckenrode et al., 1993). Neglect appears to increase a child's vulnerability to abuse (Ney et al., 1992, 1994). Watters et al. (1986) found that the most serious injuries to children, more serious than abuse alone, occurred in families where abuse and neglect coexisted. Daro (1988) found that substance abuse was a barrier to positive treatment outcomes only when coexistent with child neglect. It was not a barrier to positive outcomes when related to emotional or sexual abuse. The above and previously mentioned findings indicate that both the most serious physical and psychological harm to children occur in the presence of child neglect, yet less attention is paid to child neglect than any other form of child maltreatment.

Neglect is ignored. We know that neglect is an overlooked area of child welfare practice. We know that there is a relatively modest amount of research that has specifically addressed child neglect; and that currently there is no policy and few to no ongoing programs that are developed expressly for neglectful families. The focus of research, policy, and practice of those working in the field of child maltreatment has been on abuse, to the neglect of neglected children and their families. The few studies that have focused on neglect have produced inconsistent findings. As a result, child neglect is the least understood type of child maltreatment. In addition, the lack of attention to neglect and the focus on abuse diverts attention from structural issues that are associated with neglect and remain on the periphery of child welfare practice.

What Do We Do?

Research. Focus on neglect as a distinct type of child maltreatment, and study child neglect separate from other types of maltreatment. Develop a body of theory relative to child neglect that includes the etiologies and consequences of various subtypes of neglect; and is independent from abuse and other maltreatment subtypes. Study the comorbidity of neglect with other maltreatment subtypes; and use other subtypes as control variables to separate out the causes/effects of neglect.

Develop consistent methodologies for collecting incidence data regarding child neglect. Perform more research specific to child neglect, including epidemiological and etiological studies (especially exploring structural causes), in order to increase the pool of information that informs policy and practice. Disseminate findings to increase public awareness regarding the problem of child neglect.

Policy. Formulate policy that focuses on neglect as a separate population with differential etiology and service needs. Educate policymakers to increase their awareness of neurobiology, attachment theory, child development, and the damage neglect can do. Develop policy that supports research to increase our knowledge base about neglect in order to develop more effective interventions with neglectful families; and then develop policy that supports the implementation of such programs.

It has been suggested that policy has focused on abuse and not on neglect in part due to the connections of neglect with poverty, and the need for structural reformation to effect changes (Pelton, 1978; Wolock & Horowitz, 1984). Focusing on neglect would necessitate a thorough evaluation of the need for structural changes in our society. An additional myth regarding neglect: "The myth of classlessness persists not on the basis of evidence or logic, but because it serves certain professional and political interests. These interests do not further the task of dealing with the real problems underlying abuse and neglect; adherence to the myth diverts attention from the nature of the problems and diverts resources from their solution" (Pelton, 1978, p. 616).

Practice. Focus on neglect as a distinct form of child maltreatment that requires unique intervention approaches. Train practitioners to recognize that child neglect may be more threatening and dangerous than child abuse. Develop programs focused on neglectful families and, more importantly, on neglected children. Screen all CPS intakes for child neglect; and screen all neglect intakes for additional types of maltreatment.

THEME 2: CHILD NEGLECT IS A FAILURE TO MEET CHILDREN'S BASIC NEEDS

What Do We Know?

We know that child neglect is a failure to meet children's basic needs, a failure that places them in harm's way. Whether this failure rests in the hands of their parents (parental deficits), the environments in which they live (community deficits), or a combination of both, children are at risk (child deficits) and the focus is the child. We know that children deserve to have their needs met and to be protected from harm. We also know what children need to grow and thrive, and that there is consensus on community standards of child care (i.e., there is a community standard of minimally acceptable child-rearing practice). We know that in order to best meet children's needs child neglect must be defined as both a personal and a social issue. We know that such an inclusive definition improves the quality of family life and the quality of life in general, including the children of neglect and their families. Defining neglect as a personal issue focuses on familial and child deficits and employs a residual and at times coercive approach in order to improve family life. Defining neglect as a social issue includes community deficits and structural reform to improve the quality of life in general. Defining child neglect as a failure to meet a child's needs includes familial, community, and child deficits; and calls upon both the family to care for the child and the community to care for children and their families.

What Do We Do?

Research. Develop clear and consistent definitions of neglect and subtypes of neglect across studies. Include developmental factors (i.e., age and developmental needs of children) when classifying subtypes of neglect.

Policy. Develop policy to reframe neglect as both a personal and a social issue. Create definitions of child neglect based on (a) what we know about what children need, (b) what we know about meeting those needs, and

(c) agreed-upon community standards of child-rearing practice in terms of the respective responsibility of parents and the community for meeting children's needs and protecting them from harm (i.e., what are good, supportive parents and what are good, supportive communities?). Develop a holistic continuum of developmentally appropriate care that can act as a guideline for parents, practitioners, and communities in creating ecologies that meet children's needs.

Practice. When children's needs are not met, develop differential practices at the personal and community levels providing a continuum of responses appropriate to the type of neglect involved, the age of the children, and the level of harm/risk of harm. The level of intervention could be based on the developed community standards of how to meet these needs ranging from the availability of voluntary and/or preventive services to more coercive/intrusive interventions to protect children from serious harm.

THEME 3: CHILD NEGLECT IS ASSOCIATED WITH RISK FACTORS OCCURRING WITHIN THE FAMILY AND WITHIN THE ENVIRONMENT THAT HAVE NEGATIVE OUTCOMES FOR CHILDREN

What Do We Know?

We know that interaction theory currently is the most adequate theory regarding the etiology of child neglect. Nevertheless, for the most part, it is based on studies of child maltreatment not studies of child neglect per se; and it cannot be used to predict individual behavior. We also know that the effects of neglect model cannot predict which specific children will be harmed by neglect and what the specific nature of that harm will be. Furthermore, we know that the found effects of neglect may be the effects of some other factor, such as poverty; and theory does not provide for understanding the nature of the relationship between neglect and outcomes of neglect. Interaction theory, however, does identify useful risk factors for neglect and outcomes for children.

We know that risk factors for neglectful parenting include being poor, undereducated, helpless, hopeless, withdrawn, impulsive, single, and female. Neglectful mothers seem incompetent and unable to work toward a goal. They are distant from their children and lack parenting knowledge and skills. They have more children, more problems, and live in worse neighborhoods. While these findings are based on relatively sparse and sometimes inconsistent research, and theory/research fails to provide a predictive "neglect profile," the findings do provide stark evidence of the multiple issues neglectful families can face and the lack of inner and material resources to deal with them.

We know that while theoretical models provide risk factors for neglectful behavior and poor outcomes for children, they are not reliable predictors for individual or single cause/effect relationships. They are, however, a fairly accurate assessment of probabilities, and may be used to identify categories of families at risk for neglect and categories of children at risk for bad outcomes. Nevertheless, we also know that many parents have risk factors, yet most parents do not neglect their children; and many children are at risk of neglect, yet many children have no perceived ill effects. Moreover, we know that (a) most people living in poverty do not neglect their children; (b) some mothers with a history of maltreatment neglect their children but most do not; and (c) children raised in similar conditions have dissimilar outcomes. Some families and children appear to be more resilient than others.

As indicated above, we know that both parental and environmental deficiencies are risk factors for negative outcomes for children. We also know that protective factors/buffers can increase the probability for children's resiliency and the reduction of negative outcomes. Protective factors can be both internal (e.g., the child's coping strategies) and environmental (e.g., caring adults). In addition, we know buffers that increase the resiliency of adults maltreated as children include nurturing adults in childhood, support in the present, therapy, and personal integration of maltreatment history. Thus, we know that protective factors help beat the odds favoring risk factors and create resilient children, adults, and families. We know that such policies as family support, welfare reform, health care, and child welfare impact on family life and can be protective or place families at risk.

What Do We Do?

Research. Design research to address the processes that lead to neglect (i.e., delineate connections between proposed causes of neglect and negligent behavior). Conduct prospective studies to test a priori hypotheses regarding causes and outcomes of child neglect. Use study designs that include interactions, as well as the direct effects of the model components. Employ samples that include non-social service neglect subjects and the middle and upper classes.

Study resiliency (i.e., why do some mothers with a history of child maltreatment neglect their children and others do not; why do some poor families neglect and others do not; why do children subject to similar conditions have dissimilar outcomes?). Explore the relationship between risk and protective factors, and the processes by which protective/buffering factors reduce risk.

Policy. Establish policies that enhance protective factors and reduce risk factors. Make certain that policies don't create risk factors out of protective factors. Employ an ecological/public health approach to the allocation of resources by utilizing child neglect data to target high-risk neighborhoods.

Practice. Prioritize neglect cases for up-front services as early identification and intervention are critical. Employ a multidisciplinary approach, ecological assessments, and familial and environmental interventions.

THEME 4: THERE IS LITTLE DISCERNIBLE SOCIAL OR POLITICAL WILL TO ADDRESS CONTEXTUAL ISSUES

What Do We Know?

We know that parenting adequacy is related to material adequacy and that child neglect, traditionally, has been associated with poverty. We know that persistent themes running through child welfare practice include (a) the view that neglect is a personal, not a social problem; (b) the application of a residual rather than an institutional response to child neglect; (c) the use of removal of children from their homes as a primary protective intervention; (d) the focus on parents, not children or society; (e) the dual role of child protection social workers; and, for the past thirty years (f) the focus on abuse, not neglect. We also know that the most effective intervention for keeping children in their own homes was a welfare program, not a child welfare program.

We know that during the past thirty years the nature of the "nuclear" family has changed. However, an institutional response to this structural change has not been forthcoming. Policies continue to support a residual and remedial stance, no interest in reducing child poverty has been evidenced by policymakers (i.e., welfare reform does not have children's well-being in mind) and there remains no national policy regarding child neglect. We know that the traditional approaches to child welfare have produced negative outcomes (i.e., increases in complaints, increases in serious injuries and fatalities, and increases in out-of-home placements of children). On average the child protection system has failed to preserve families or protect children.

We know that in the late 1990s, the community became a focus of intervention in order to provide a system of family supports to prevent out-of-home placement of children. The notion that the community shares responsibility with parents for children's welfare is being developed. The results of this partial shift in focus have not yet been determined.

We know that the elements of an adequate child welfare policy focused on child neglect would (a) employ a broad, institutional, community-based approach whereby both parents and society share the responsibility for the welfare of children; (b) focus on root causes of child neglect including economic disadvantage; (c) focus on children and early intervention, as well as on adults and community; (d) make available structural, preventive, and remedial services to enable families to fulfill their childrearing functions; (e) separate investigations from services, conceivably turning investigations over to law enforcement; and (f) include adequate representation of class and ethnic groups in decision-making processes. We also know that current child welfare policy (a) focuses on child abuse, (b) is residual and remedial in approach, (c) holds parents, not the conditions in which they live, responsible, (d) provides categorical and fragmented services, (d) centers on adults (family preservation or reunification—fix the parents) or on the children only after they have been removed from their families (protection—placement of children), and (e) privileges permanent out-of-home placement, including adoption.

What Do We Do?

Research. Conduct more evaluative research that includes experimental and nonlinear designs, and that uses qualitative methods to analyze systems. Study the relationship between risk factors and service delivery systems to determine which risk factors respond to what services. Fund and evaluate demonstration projects that focus on child neglect. Examine the impact of federal programs, such as TANF, on the incidence of neglect. Explore why successful programs are underutilized. In order to implement wanted/needed policies, study the implementation processes of policies that have been implemented and use findings to effect policy changes.

Policy. Recognize that it is in the national best interest to invest in first-class services for children, including those that support parents and communities in protecting and nurturing their children. Recognize that changes in policy affect children and policy for children must include their parents. Focus on preventive programs as categorical, deficit-focused programs have not worked. Eradicate social and economic inequity by reforms in income supports and housing, medical, education, and employment services. Reorder financial priorities, and develop new methods of resource allocation and new service models. Extend successful national programs to all who are eligible and broaden the scale of successful community programs.

Unfortunately, policymakers may not have the will or see the value in focusing on improving the well-being of children. The question remains, "What cost is society willing to pay to make the same long-term commitment to child well-being it is demanding of parents?"

Practice. Provide appropriate community resources to assist parents and communities in protecting and nurturing their children, and to reduce economic disadvantage. Such a system would include (a) an income safety net for children; (b) universal health care; (c) decent housing; (d) safe and supportive communities; (e) employment; (f) universal day care; (g) adequate education; (h) substance abuse treatment, mental health treatment, and other remedial services to meet immediate needs; and (i) skill and competency building to provide for the future. Advocate for needed policy changes and implementation.

In reforming child welfare systems, focus on community-based prevention efforts. Separate service and investigative functions. Protect children's well-being—focus on the child and on neighborhoods as sources of support for children and families.

THEME 5: INTERVENTIONS FOCUS PRIMARILY ON ADULTS AND NOT ON CHILDREN

What Do We Know?

We know that most services focus on "fixing parents." It would appear that a basic assumption is that the best we can do for children is to remediate their parents' deficiencies. We also know, however, that child neglect is a seemingly intractable problem and that developing the capacity to change is difficult in chronically neglectful parents. They are amenable to long-term services but are resistant to behavioral changes. In addition, fathers are rarely involved in the treatment program.

Moreover, we know that interventions with children generally produce more successful outcomes for children and the family. This is not to say children should be served instead of parents; however, interventions with children hold more promise for the prevention/remediation of the effects of child neglect. Yet, we know that few programs address the specific needs of children, and that resources are allocated to treating parents, generally mothers.

We know that there are few studies of the long-term outcomes for children of interventions with families. No observed changes in parent/child interaction have been reported for interventions with parents. In addition, family support services have not reported consistent, meaningful effects on child safety. There is no single effective program model in working with high-risk or maltreating parents; and any single intervention strategy has limitations.

We know that services that have had some success with some maltreating or high-risk families are based on a thorough and ecological assessment of family and community needs and resources (strengths). These services generally

1. include family members whether or not they are living in the home (e.g., extended family and fathers) in all phases of the intervention;
2. enhance supportive networks, concrete resources, and personal skills and competencies;
3. are home- and community-based, comprehensive, long-term, flexible, and culturally competent;
4. have goals that are related to behavior, developed by and meaningful to the family, clearly stated, realistic, and prioritized—focus on a few easily achievable goals at a time;
5. consist of early intervention, structured interventions that include some parent/child interactive activities, child-focused services, comprehensive case management, intensive treatment, home visitation (i.e., professionals, paraprofessionals, parent aides, and/or homemakers), and aggressive outreach and client advocacy; and
6. have skilled, well-trained and supervised, caring, respectful, culturally responsive staff consisting of professionals and paraprofessionals who attend to clients' affective as well as behavioral and cognitive needs (nurture the parent), have small caseloads, and are available 24/7.

We know that families are more likely to have successful outcomes if (a) they have higher levels of motivation, cooperation, and participation (i.e., utilizing social services and staying with programs long enough to experience positive gains); (b) the mother has a higher level of education; (c) they have fewer and less severe problems, and problems that relate to specific child behaviors; (d) the parents have resources that enable them to translate learning into behavioral changes; (e) the mother has higher levels of personal satisfaction; (f) they are experiencing acute rather than chronic neglect; (g) they have had fewer to no prior out-of-home placements of children and fewer children at risk; (h) they have had more stable caretaking; (i) there are supportive relatives in the home and positive external support systems including kin network systems; and (j) they are younger parents with younger children. Unfortunately we also know that chronically neglecting families rarely enjoy these protective factors.

What Do We Do?

Research. Conduct long-term studies to explore the effects of neglect, the effects of other subtypes of maltreatment, and the effects of subtypes of neglect. When looking at subtypes, take into consideration age and developmental stages of children. Focus on parent/child interaction processes developmentally, exploring the links between childhood experience and parent behavior, and the processes by which neglect impacts child development. Study neurodevelopment, neuroarcheology, and other biological aspects of child neglect. Study the current child welfare system to determine how and what services are selected/obtained for neglectful families, especially if they are not accepted for services.

Evaluate programs to discover to what extent, for whom, and under what circumstances a program is effective in preventing or treating child neglect. Discover why programs are relatively ineffective with the neglect population, and what can be done to design more effective programs. Gain specific knowledge of what works best for whom under what circumstances. Identify specific protective factors for specific risk situations. Explore the subtypes of neglect, chronic versus acute neglect, and differential approaches to each. Study the optimal length of time and intensity of programs through long-term impact studies and survival analysis of various intervention strategies and settings. Examine motivational variables and the impact of those and other characteristics (e.g., demographics, substance abuse treatment, and mental health) on treatment outcomes; and routinely use measures of substance abuse risk assessment. Consider the ecological context of programs, research the effects of social isolation, explore minimal standards for family supportive communities, and provide clear and detailed program descriptions.

Pursue the following research possibilities to address the issue of intractability. Strengthen the theoretical underpinnings of practice with neglectful families by testing the theoretical assumptions underlying programs, including the etiology of neglect and theory of change models. Explore successful methods of engaging families in services and retaining them long enough to make substantial gains (e.g., assisting them in learning to make and follow through on plans). Discover ways to support families in dealing with the number and severity of their problems. Look at the nature of chronic behavior and investigate effective methods of changing embedded behavior patterns. Study the stressors that lead to the exhaustion of support providers. Finally, research adaptive strategies to manage potential biological issues (e.g., depression, substance abuse, and history of child neglect).

Additional valuable research projects include (a) studying the nature of the relationships of children with fathers, other male members of households, immediate family, and extended family; (b) analyzing the cost/benefits of various intervention strategies; (c) monitoring the consistency of interventions (i.e., program drift); (d) focusing on breaking the cycle of intergenerational transfer of parental deficits; (e) gaining more information about additional populations at risk, such as adolescent mothers and fathers, stepparents, and low-income parents; (f) looking at successful low-income parents to see how they manage parenting taking into consideration the differences in their child-rearing values, parenting behaviors, and goals for their children; (g) studying the special strengths and risk factors of diverse cultures and ethnic groups; (h) exploring the influence of individuals not living in the household on family outcomes; (i) studying the characteristics of prevention programs; (j) looking at parental powerlessness and empowerment strategies that go beyond the mother/child dyad to include family and community; (k) studying the use of family preservation services for all families not requiring immediate placement of the children and for neglecting families to compare the outcomes of FPS for acute and chronic neglect; (l) looking at the reasons for success and/or failure of using family preservation services to reunify families; and (m) exploring the relationship between neglect and stress, parents' intellectual ability, the developmental stages of the mother/child dyad, and the directionality (high, appropriate, or low) of parental expectations.

In terms of research design and methodologies, conduct rigorous, systematic process, and formative program evaluation/intervention research utilizing experimental (i.e., prospective studies and randomized trials) or quasiexperimental designs that employ (a) clear and consistent operational definitions and typologies of neglect; (b) explicit models; (c) comparison or control groups; (d) culturally appropriate, well-defined, and consistent outcome measures; and (d) methodologies to control for sources of error, including robust sample sizes. Provide clear and detailed descriptions of the program being evaluated including (a) definitions of the type, severity, and chronicity of neglect in the client population; (b) client recruitment/selection procedures and/or eligibility requirements; (c) the flow of clients through the program and subjects through studies; (d) the change process (i.e., the intervention itself); (e) retention strategies; and (f) data collection procedures; and determine how these elements are related to specific outcomes. Use diverse strategies, methods, assessment models, and standards of evidence. Conduct qualitative research, including the use of stories, structured interviews, focus groups, and single-case studies to expand and enrich our knowledge base and create more democratic and participatory research efforts

Policy. Develop policy to focus on neglect as a separate population with differential etiology and service needs. Support research and development of effective interventions with neglectful families. Focus on treatment programs for neglected children. Establish policies regarding kinship care, father involvement, the values of resource poor families, preventive treatment, community-level family preservation, and support services, and supporting specific services for specific populations—not the wholesale implementation of programs that have shown some success with some populations.

Use a public health model to focus resource allocation by developing minimal standards for family supportive communities, assessing risk levels in a given community and directing resources to reduce these risks by developing programs to bring the community into compliance with established standards. Develop community standards of child care, especially at what age children can be left alone, and use community standards to guide service provision.

Fund multidiscipline service models at primary, secondary, and tertiary prevention levels. Create platforms for nurturing neighborhoods and services for children. Foster policies to deal with disadvantage including guaranteed education and job training, employment, income supports, national health care, and family support services. Such policies require a shared vision that child welfare is in the national best interest—a common vision that building a system that meets the needs of children and families and that ensures children's welfare is in society's common good.

Practice. Develop intervention strategies at all levels of prevention. Primary prevention strategies include widespread use of contraceptives, culturally competent parenting classes in high school, a public health type public awareness media campaign regarding child neglect, parental leave, income supports, guaranteed job training and employment, a good education system, and national health care. Many primary prevention strategies require health, education, and welfare reforms.

Secondary prevention approaches consist of prenatal care and counseling for high-risk mothers, educational and home visitor support services for all primipara mothers, well-baby care for all children, quality low-cost child care, outreach child and family services for the homeless, and emotional support for at-risk caregivers.

Tertiary prevention methods comprise treatment programs for neglected children and their parents that are innovative, long-term, comprehensive, intensive, flexible, and culturally competent. These programs (a) focus on neglectful families and neglected children; (b) are based on an assessment of individual family members, family functioning, and the context within which the family lives; (c) employ a strengths/needs-based approach; (d) take into consideration buffering and risk factors and cultural, religious, socioeconomic, and child-rearing differences; and (e) include fathers, family members in and out of the home, and sources of support in and out of the home. Interventions include (a) child-rearing education, which consists of parenting information that is easily understood, accessible, and practical; (b) skill and competency building; (c) substance abuse treatment; (d) psychiatric treatment; and (e) individual, family, and group counseling. Adapt intensive family preservation services to focus on families experiencing acute problems and adapt rehabilitative family preservation services to focus on families with more chronic issues.

Establish child-centered practice that assesses and focuses on the needs of neglected children; is developmentally appropriate; increases social, cognitive, and language skills; and decreases attachment disorders and social isolation. Early intervention is critical and thus secondary prevention programs are preferable in order to prevent the effects of child neglect. When children cannot remain at home kinship care, foster care, and adoptions that are considered to be extensions of family life and not replacements for it are viable alternatives to consider.

Craft new technologies that address barriers to successful treatment. Focus specifically on recruiting and retaining clients. Such technologies include how to attend to the affective needs of neglectful parents; how to motivate apathetic clients and staff; and how to prepare neglectful clients for intervention prior to their participation. Given the resistance to change exhibited by neglectful families, change theory is relevant to learning new ways to break up and alter old patterns of behavior.

Generate interventions that include (a) group settings providing nurturance and support along with child-rearing information; (b) home visitation and crisis intervention offering resource provision and problem-solving, child-rearing, and resource management education; and (c) activities to empower clients, including furthering their education and opportunities to secure well-paying, affirming employment. Feminist practice principles—celebrating diversity, recognizing culture, responding to vulnerable populations, encouraging participation and equality in the treatment process, focusing on the clients' perspective of problems and solutions, and empowering clients—provide a good framework to inform practice with neglectful families.

Child welfare/welfare reform. Initiate a differential intake system that separates policing functions from service functions and high-risk from low-risk families. Construct multiple, integrated, community/home-based services of prevention and protection that provide instrumental/concrete and affective supports for families. Create safe and nurturing neighborhoods to increase family mutual support networks, and provide concrete, respite care, health care, and family-planning services. Increase the economic safety net for children and consider a child social security account payable at age eighteen to increase the chances for successful transition to adulthood.

THEME 6: NEGLECT MUST BE EXAMINED
IN A CULTURAL CONTEXT

What Do We Know?

We know that child neglect, including physical and emotional neglect, occurs in all ethnic groups. We also know that ethnic minorities and children of color are overrepresented in the child welfare system, as they are in the welfare system. Neglect in these families is associated with poverty, unemployment, and substance abuse, as it is with White families. However, we know that any definition of neglect will be biased in the direction of the dominant culture; and thus neglectful child rearing is framed in a White, middle-class perspective with little flexibility for cultural variation.

We know that cultural values and practices can serve as risk and/or protective factors. All cultures value their children; and the reasons children are valued act as protective factors in that culture. In addition, the cultural community within which the family lives serves to protect children and buffer risk factors in the family. We know that that there is a difference between neglectful behaviors and misunderstood, nonneglectful cultural practices (i.e., adaptive characteristics in one culture may be misconstrued as risk factors in another). We also know that behaviors considered to be neglectful are open to cultural interpretation.

We know that immigrants, migrant workers, and undocumented workers are especially vulnerable to neglectful behavior. They have the added pressures and stressors of immigration issues, relocation issues, language barriers, and ignorance of local customs and practices in terms of child-rearing standards. In addition, their status places them at risk for being ineligible to receive services for themselves and their children; and as a result the children lack care, a situation that is beyond the control of their parents.

What Do We Do?

Research. Examine research practices to search for cultural bias in design, sampling, measurement instruments, and analysis. Develop culturally appropriate instruments that determine neglect without cultural biases. Explore the relationship between cultural practices and child neglect including (a) protective and risk factors, (b) cultural meanings of terms, (c) cultural differences that are adaptive within an ethnic group and therefore nonneglectful, and (d) practices that would be neglectful irrespective of culture.

Policy. Set culturally relevant standards for child care; and assess the care of children within different cultural groups in accordance with these standards. Focus on discrimination, unemployment, and poverty—especially in relation to immigrants who come without adequate knowledge, skills, and resources. Reexamine policies that discriminate against undocumented and migrant workers and their children.

Practice. Generate culturally competent practice (i.e., cultural values are seen as strengths). Introduce the concept of biculturalism, whereby the client's cultural child-rearing practices are integrated with that of the dominant culture. Educate professionals regarding legitimate cultural differences in child-rearing practices by (a) increasing their knowledge base regarding cultural values and beliefs concerning issues associated with neglect, (b) improving their understanding of the role of the ethnic community in ameliorating neglectful conditions, and (c) examining their own attitudes and behaviors toward clients with differing values. Advocate for policy that would provide for children, regardless of the immigration status of their parents.

THEME 7: SUBSTANCE ABUSE CONTRIBUTES TO CHILD NEGLECT

What Do We Know?

We know that chemical dependency impairs decision-making abilities and as a result produces parenting styles that are detrimental to children. We know that neglect is the predominant maltreatment subtype in families with substance abuse issues, and that addiction is associated with all subtypes of neglect.

We know that addiction to drugs and alcohol, which results in neglect, is related to material disadvantage, depression, domestic violence, boredom, and social drinking. We know that substance abuse and neglect are both associated with single mothers living in poverty. We know that the demographics of the chemical dependency population are similar to the demographics of the population of the United States in general. However, for the most part, the chemically dependent persons who end up in the child welfare system are poor, single women. The responsibility for child rearing and the blame for "bad" parenting are placed on mothers not on fathers, who also may be addicts/alcoholics. We also know that parents who come to child welfare services with drug-exposed infants have higher recidivism rates than those who are receiving services for other reasons.

We know that substance abuse is a family disease (i.e., it involves family members other than the addict/alcoholic); and we know that addiction is also a bio-psycho-social disease that affects everyone involved with the addicted person. Family and ethnic culture affects the choice of drug, reason and pattern of use, and the types of interventions that are successful for that family. Treatments developed by and for the dominant culture may not be culturally appropriate for all ethnic groups and be less effective as a result.

We know that addicts/alcoholics in recovery have unrealistic expectations of their parenting abilities and become disappointed when they do not meet their own expectations. They also feel guilty about perceived or real consequences to their children resulting from their addiction. These reactions and feelings lead to increased feelings of hopelessness and helplessness, and increase the risk of relapse.

We know that the outcomes of substance abuse in pregnancy are inconsistent. In some cases there is no apparent long-term harm to prenatally exposed children. However, we also know that prenatal exposure to drugs, alcohol, nicotine, and other substances results in birth defects, neurological and physical dysfunction, cognitive and behavioral dysfunction, developmental delays, medical problems, fetal alcohol syndrome, fetal alcohol effect, low birth weight, and higher infant mortality rates.

We know that the system that provides interventions for neglectful families (i.e., the child protection system) is separate from the system that provides interventions for addicts/alcoholics (i.e., the health care system). This can result in delays, misunderstandings, and ineffectiveness in treatment.

What Do We Do?

Research. Investigate the nature of the relationship between substance abuse and child neglect. Examine the role of the extended family as support for and/or barriers to recovery. Research the effectiveness of targeting the family system for change on recovery outcomes. Study the design of effective residential treatment programs that serve women only. Explore the effects of positive support systems, milieu therapy, and an ecological approach on recovery efforts.

Policy. Establish policy to support research and demonstration projects that target the family system for change. Support culturally and gender appropriate substance abuse treatment as an essential element of maltreatment prevention and intervention programs. Create an integrated system that meets the needs of families involved in both the child protection and substance abuse treatment systems.

Practice. Utilize an ecological perspective. Employ a medical-psychosocial-cultural model using medical, social (e.g., self-help groups), and behavioral approaches that meet the chemically dependent person's affective needs. Place more emphasis on strengths-based methodologies, especially in relationship to relapse issues. Target the family system to include intergenerational support networks. Make use of person-in-environment and interactional strategies; and include children and positive relationships in the treatment plan.

Provide available, accessible, and ethnically and gender-appropriate substance abuse programs. Design interventions that are culturally competent and that include bicultural components. Develop treatment programs for women that employ milieu therapy, maintain communication with children, develop positive support systems, and monitor male intrusion. In the event of removal of the child from the home, given that addiction is a family disease, kinship care families, especially, will require postplacement services including relapse prevention if appropriate.

Employ the leverage of the court system, including driver's license suspension, criminal prosecution, out-of-home placement, and termination of parental rights, to gain compliance from chemically dependent parents when treatment approaches fail. Some states take jurisdiction over unborn children; and mothers may be involuntarily incarcerated to prevent the exposure of the fetus to harmful substances.

THEME 8: POVERTY CONTRIBUTES TO CHILD NEGLECT

What Do We Know?

We know that children who grow up in poverty are at higher risk for neglect than those who do not. We know that the risk factors for and effects of poverty are similar to those associated with neglect. We know that, like neglect, the effects of poverty are dependent on the age of the child when first exposed, the severity of the poverty, and the duration of the child's exposure. Moreover, we know that the severity of the maltreatment is related to the severity of the poverty; and outcomes for children are exacerbated when poverty and neglect are both present.

We know that the similarities between risk factors and outcomes for poverty and neglect result in conceptual confusion regarding determining etiologies of neglect and poverty, attributing poor outcomes to either neglect or poverty, and defining child neglect. We know that the intersection of poverty, parental deficits, and child neglect divides into three points of view: (a) parental deficits result in living in poverty and/or child neglect; (b) poverty results in parental deficits and/or child neglect; and (c) the interaction of poverty and parental deficits results in child neglect. Furthermore, we know that practitioners focus on improving parents, not improving circumstances. However, we also know that most poor families do not neglect their children and not all neglected children live in poverty. In addition, some poor families are resilient and able to protect their children from the effects of poverty (i.e., not all children raised in poverty have poor outcomes). Thus we know that poverty alone is not sufficient to account for child neglect.

We know that the United States does not take care of its children as well as other industrialized nations. Children are the poorest segment of United States society; and the rate of children living in poverty in the United States is the highest of sixteen industrialized nations. We know that our society pays little attention to the relationship between neglect and poverty. Poverty and child neglect are both dealt with as personal problems, not as social issues, and therefore are not society's responsibility.

We know that the United States has a limited view of the collective responsibility to reduce risk factors for children. We also know that any strategy to reduce child neglect requires a strategy to reduce material disadvantage. Protecting children from the risks of poverty will protect many from the risks of child neglect; however, a major restructuring of policy and programs is required to provide for disadvantaged families. The United States has not made the economic commitment needed for structural change. Given the risks and outcomes of both child neglect and poverty, allowing children to live in poverty is a form of child neglect and child neglect is also a form of poverty.

> Nearly every child who thinks he doesn't count is a child needing love. And a child who is convinced she can't do anything right is a child living in poverty. Knowing we are adequate and worthy is fundamental to sane living. It is our birthright to know ourselves as glorious, innocent creations. Deprivation of that birthright is poverty in its most serious form. (Larsen & Hegarty, 1987, March 24).

What Do We Do?

Research. Study poverty and its effects on children and families. Explore the kinds of care children actually receive. Collect data to determine whether increases in material advantage result in increases in child well-being. Examine the effects of TANF, Food Stamps, WIC, and Medicare on the well-being of children. Explore how low-income families protect their children from the effects of poverty; and how high-income families neglect their children. Research the relationship between class and neglect. Conduct research to differentiate the effects of neglect from the effects of poverty. Study the effects of structural inadequacies of communities and impoverished social networks on children and on the rates of child neglect in those communities.

Policy. Establish policy whereby society provides for material advantage and child welfare workers work with families around issues that contribute to neglect other than poverty. Increase awareness that by neglecting the poor we are neglecting our children at a societal level. Institute a systemic change of attitudes and policies regarding poor families to foster coming to terms with poverty. Establish a common vision that taking care of our children ensures our own future.

Practice. Develop a coordinated response to poverty that would create a network of services to support poor families and allow protective service agencies to focus on cases that pose an immediate threat to children's welfare. In the alternative, reframe child neglect as an economic issue and increase the chances of better outcomes for children by expanding the child welfare system's mandate to include a focus on child well-being and provision of income supports, child care, health care, nutrition programs, and housing based on need instead of parental behavior. Treating child neglect as a personal problem and focusing on changing parental behavior has failed. If we continue to do more of the same, we cannot expect better results. At the very least, focusing on improving family economies, whether by reforming the social welfare and/or child welfare systems, would reveal what issues are related to poverty and what issues are related to child neglect; and better interventions could be designed to deal with both of those issues.

WHERE DO WE GO FROM HERE?

Before looking forward we need to look back to see where we started. In the introduction to this book the authors asserted that

> child neglect is an overlooked area of child welfare practice. The consequences of neglect to children are at least as serious as the consequences of abuse. Nevertheless, the focus of those working in the field of child maltreatment has been on abuse, to the neglect of neglected children and their families. The strong association between neglect and poverty and the lack of societal will to address issues associated with poverty create difficulties in terms of effective policy and practice in regard to families who neglect their children. It is as if "no one cares,"

neither the parents of neglected children, nor the society in which they live. It is time to refocus on the issues of child neglect in families, both to assist in healing these families and as a vehicle for implementing structural changes that will benefit all families.

This book has examined research, social policy, and interventions with respect to neglectful families. Eight themes have emerged as a result of this review: (a) neglect is a distinct form of child maltreatment that is the most detrimental and the least understood, (b) child neglect is a failure to meet children's basic needs, (c) child neglect is associated with risk factors occurring within the family and within the environment that have negative outcomes for children, (d) there is little discernible social or political will to address contextual issues, (e) interventions focus primarily on adults and not on children, (f) neglect must be examined in a cultural context, (g) substance abuse contributes to child neglect, and (h) poverty contributes to child neglect. These themes and their implications for research, policy, and practice, which have been the subject under discussion in this chapter, can form the basis for a future agenda in the domain of child neglect. As indicated at the beginning of this chapter, research specific to child neglect is relatively sparse; and findings at times have been inconsistent and inconclusive. The conclusions of this text are drawn from the best data available at the time of its writing; however, there are gaps in our knowledge regarding the issue of child neglect.

In addition to those areas needing further consideration mentioned earlier in this chapter; the following fields of inquiry, which have not as yet been pursued, would enhance our knowledge regarding child neglect, its etiology, and its outcomes. Research is lacking regarding child neglect and its relationship with (a) families experiencing domestic violence, (b) parents with HIV/AIDS, (c) incarcerated parents, (d) parents involved in a high-conflict divorce, and (e) families experiencing homelessness. More research is needed to delineate typologies of neglect to determine the necessity for differential treatment modalities.

It has been reported that programs have been successful with the neglect population about 50% of the time. Further study into the differences between the families and programs that worked and families and programs that did not work might shed some light on the design of future programs directed at the neglect population.

The intersectionality of one domain in another is another area of research that can be applied to the study of child neglect. Exploring the intersections of child neglect, substance abuse, culture, being female, and being poor could yield rich knowledge about the interrelationships of these issues. In the past, support for research specific to child neglect has not been overwhelming. The recent NIH grants are a step in the right direction.

The idea that child neglect is a poor relation of child abuse must be deconstructed. Through public awareness and advocacy, it is hoped that future research, policy, and program agendas will pay attention to this issue, which affects so many children's healthy growth and development. When brought to the forefront of public awareness, child neglect may then be reconstructed as the pivotal form of child maltreatment that will enable a focus of attention on needed structural changes that will benefit not only neglectful families, but all families.

The unwillingness to deal with poverty hampers efforts to gain lasting solutions to the issue of child neglect. No one seems to care. Parents are not caring for kids and society is not caring for families. The results are poor outcomes for children. "What is required is a major redefinition of the problem as our failure to meet the physical, social and emotional needs of a large proportion of our children" (Wolock & Horowitz, 1984, p. 538). It is clear that child neglect is worthy of public attention both from the standpoint of its seriousness and as a vehicle for focusing on the need for structural changes to support family life. "As we discover what really helps to build strong families we prevent harm not only to the children of those families but also to the children of subsequent generations" (Erickson & Egeland, 2002, p. 16). It is time to show the children of neglect that someone cares.

Bibliography

Abell, E., Clawson, M., Washington, W. N., Bost, K. K., & Vaughn, B. E. (1996). Parenting values, attitudes, behaviors, and goals of African-American mothers from a low-income population in relation to social and societal contexts. *Journal of Family Issues, 17,* 593–613.

Aber, J. L., & Allen, J. P. (1987). Effects of maltreatment on young children's socioemotional development: An attachment theory perspective. *Developmental Psychology, 23,* 406–414.

Acevedo, G., & Morales, J. (2001). Assessment with Latino/Hispanic Communities and Organizations. In R. Fong & S. Furuto. (Eds.), *Culturally competent practice: Skills, interventions, and evaluations.* (pp. 147–162). Boston, MA: Allyn & Bacon.

Adoption Assistance and Child Welfare Act of 1980. 94 Stat. 500. Public Law 96-272. 26 U.S.C.A @ 50B 422 @@ 602. (1995).

Adoption and Safe Families Act of 1997. Public Law 105-89. Title IV-B and IV-E, Section 453 and Section 1130(a) of the Social Security Act.

Alderette, O., & deGraffenried, D. R. (1986). Nonorganic failure-to-thrive syndrome and the family system. *Social Work, 31,* 207–211.

Allen, M., Reiter, J., & Landsman, M. (1990). The self-sufficiency project: New motivation for neglectful families. In W. Deutelbaum, D. Haapala, J. Hutchinson, J. Lloyd, & C. Sudia (Eds.), *Empowering families: Papers from the third annual conference on family-based services* (pp. 33–42). Riverdale, IL: National Association for Family-Based Services.

Alter, C. F. (1985). Decision-making factors in cases of child neglect. *Child Welfare, 64,* 99–111.

American Association for Protecting Children. (1986). *Highlights of official child neglect and abuse reporting: 1984.* Denver, CO: Author.

American Humane Association. (1983). *Highlights of official child abuse and neglect reporting: 1981.* Denver, CO: Author.

American Humane Association. (1988). *Highlights of official child abuse and neglect reporting: 1986.* Denver, CO: Author.

American Humane Association. (1994). *Substance abuse and child maltreatment.* Englewood, CO: Author.

American Humane Association. (1997). *Innovations for children's services for the 21ˢᵗ century: Family group decision making and patch.* Englewood, CO: Author.

Ammerman, R. T. (1990). Etiological models of child maltreatment: A behavioral perspective. *Behavior Modification, 14,* 230–254.

Annie E. Casey Foundation. (1990). *Kids count data on Asian, Native American, and Hispanic children.* Baltimore, MD: Author.

Aragona, J. A., & Eyeberg, S. M. (1981). Neglected children: Mothers' report of child behavior problems and observed verbal behavior. *Child Development, 52,* 596–601.

Ards, S., & Harrell, A. (1993). Reporting of child maltreatment: A secondary analysis of the national incidence surveys. *Child Abuse and Neglect, 17,* 337–344.

Azar, S. T., Robinson, D. R. Hekimian, E., & Twentyman, C. T. (1984). Unrealistic expectations and problem-solving ability in maltreating and comparison mothers. *Journal of Consulting and Clinical Psychology, 54,* 687–691.

Baharudin, R., & Luster, T. (1998). Factors related to the quality of the home environment and children's achievement. *Journal of Family Issues, 19,* 375–403.

Balgopal, P. (2000). *Social work practice with immigrants and refugees.* New York: Columbia University Press.

Barry, F. D. (1994). A neighborhood-based approach: What is it? In G. B. Melton & F. D. Barry (Eds.), *Protecting children from abuse and neglect: Foundations for a new national strategy* (pp. 14–39). New York: The Guilford Press.

Barth, R. P., & Berry, M. (1987). Outcomes of child welfare services under permanency planning. *Social Services Review, 71,* 90.

Barth, R. P., Freundlich, M., & Brodzinsky, D. (Eds.). (2000). *Adoption and prenatal alcohol and drug exposure: Research, policy and practice.* Washington, DC: Child Welfare League of America.

Barthel, J. (1992). *For children's sake: The promise of family preservation.* New York: Edna McConnell Clark Foundation.

Bath, H. I., & Haapala, D. A. (1992). Intensive family preservation services with abuse and neglected children: An examination of group differences. *Child Abuse and Neglect, 17,* 213–225.

Baumrind, D. (1994). The social context of child maltreatment. *Family Relations,* 360–368.

Beeman, S. K. (1997). Reconceptualizing social support and its relationship to child neglect. *Social Service Review, 71,* 421–440.

Behl, L., Crouch, J., May, P., Valente, A., & Conyngham, H. (2001). Ethnicity in child maltreatment research: A content analysis. *Child Maltreatment, 6*(2), 143–147.

Belsky, J. (1993). Etiology of child maltreatment: A developmental-ecological analysis. *Psychological Bulletin, 114,* 413–434.

Benedict, M. I., Wulff, L. M., & White, R. B. (1992). Current parental stress in maltreating and nonmaltreating families of children with multiple disabilities. *Child Abuse and Neglect, 16,* 155–163.

Berns, D., & Drake, B. (1998). Promoting safe and stable families through welfare reform. *The Prevention Report, 2,* 4–8.

Berrick, J. C. (1998). When children cannot remain home: Foster family care and kinship care. *The Future of Children, 8,* 72–87.

Berry, M. (1991). Keeping families together: An evaluation of an intensive family preservation program (Doctoral dissertation, University of California, Berkeley, 1990). *Dissertation Abstracts International, 51,* 4275-A.

Berry, M. (1992). An evaluation of family preservation services: Fitting agency services to family needs. *Social Work, 37,* 314–321.

Besharov, D. J. (1978). The psychosocial ecology of child abuse and neglect. In M. L. Lauderdale, R. N. Anderson, & S. E. Cramer (Eds.), *Child abuse and neglect: Issues of innovation and implementation: Vol. 1. Proceedings of the second national conference on child abuse and neglect* (pp. 37–51). (DHEW Publication No. OHDS 78-30147). Washington, DC: U.S. Department of Health, Education, and Welfare.

Besharov, D. J. (1996). The children of crack: A status report. *Public Welfare, 54,* 32–39.

Besharov, D. J. (1998). Four commentaries: How we can better protect children from abuse and neglect. Commentary 1. *The Future of Children, 8,* 120–123.

Beyer, M. (1997). Strengths/needs based child welfare practice. *The Prevention Report, 1,* 4–7.

Biller, H. B., & Solomon, R. S. (1986). *Child maltreatment and paternal deprivation: A manifesto for research, prevention, and treatment.* Lexington, MA: Lexington Books.

Black, M. (2000). Long-term psychological management of neglect. In R. Reece (Ed.), *Treatment of child abuse: Common ground for mental health, medical, and legal practitioners* (pp. 192–210). Baltimore, MD: Johns Hopkins University.

Black, M. M., & Dubowitz, H. (1999). Child neglect: Research recommendations and future directions. In H. Dubowitz (Ed.). *Neglected children: Research, practice, and policy* (pp. 261–277). Thousand Oaks, CA: Sage Publications, Inc.

Block, R. W. (2002). Child Fatalities. In J. E. B. Myers, L. Berliner, J. Brier, C. T. Hendrix, J. Carole, & T. A. Reid (Eds.), *The APSAC handbook on child maltreatment* (2nd ed.) (pp. 293–301). Thousand Oaks, CA: Sage Publications, Inc.

Blythe, B. J., Salley, M. P., & Jayaratne, S. (1994). A review of intensive family preservation services research. *Social Work Research, 18,* 213–224.

Bolger, K. E., & Patterson, C. J. (2001). Pathways from child maltreatment of internalizing problems: Perceptions of control as mediators and moderators. *Development and Psychopathology, 13,* 913–940

Bonner, B. L., Crow, S. M., & Logue, M. B. (1999). Fatal child neglect. In H. Dubowitz (Ed.), *Neglected children: Research, practice, and policy* (pp. 156–173). Thousand Oaks, CA: Sage Publications, Inc.

Bousha, D. M., & Twentyman, C. T. (1984). Mother-child interactional style in abuse, neglect, and control groups: Naturalistic observations in the home. *Journal of Abnormal Psychology, 93,* 106–114.

Bowen, G. L., & Chapman, M. V. (1996). Poverty, neighborhood danger, social support, and the individual adaptation among at-risk youth in urban areas. *Journal of Family Issues, 17,* 641–666.

Brandon, P. (2002). Did the AFDC program succeed in keeping mothers and young children living together? *Social Service Review, 74,* 214–230.

Brave Heart, M. (2001). Culturally and historically congruent clinical social work: Asessment with native clients. In R. Fong & S. Furuto (Eds.), *Culturally competent practice: Skills, interventions, and evaluations.* (pp. 163–177). Boston, MA: Allyn & Bacon.

Bride, B. E. (2001). Single gender treatment of substance abuse: Effect on treatment retention and completion. *Social Work Research, 25,* 223–232.

Brodzinsky, D. (2000). In R. P. Barth, M. Freundlich, & D. Brodzinsky (Eds.), *Adoption & prenatal alcohol and drug exposure: Research, policy and practice* (pp. 83–113). Washington, DC: Child Welfare League of America.

Bronfenbrenner, U. (1979). *The ecology of human development.* Cambridge, MA: Harvard University Press.

Brooks-Gunn, J., & Duncan, G. J. (1997). The effects of poverty on children. *The Future of Children, 7,* 55–71.

Brown, E., & Gunderson, B. (2001). Organization and community intervention with American Indian Tribal Communities. In R. Fong & S. Furuto (Eds.), *Culturally competent practice: Skills, interventions, and evaluations* (pp. 299–312). Boston, MA: Allyn & Bacon.

Brown, S. E. (1984). Social class, child maltreatment, and delinquent behavior. *Criminology, 22,* 259–278.

Brummett, P., & Winters, L. (2003). Gang affiliation and self-esteem: The effects of mixed heritage identity. In L. Winters & H. DeBose (Eds.), *New faces in a changing America: Multiracial identity in the 21st century* (pp. 335–354). Thousand Oaks, CA: Sage.

Buchanan, A., & Oliver, J. E. (1980). Abuse and neglect as a cause of mental retardation: A study of 140 children admitted to subnormality hospital in Wiltshire. In B. J. Williams & J. Money (Eds.), *Traumatic abuse and neglect of children at home* (pp. 311–323). Baltimore, MD: The Johns Hopkins University Press.

Burgess, R., & Conger, R. (1978). Family interactions in abusive, neglectful, and normal families. *Child Development, 49,* 1163–1173.

Cadoret, R. J., & Riggins-Caspers, K. (2000). Fetal alcohol exposure and adult psychopathology: Evidence from an adoption study. In R. P. Barth, M. Freundlich, & D. Brodzinsky (Eds.), *Adoption and prenatal alcohol and drug exposure: Research, policy and practice* (pp. 83–113). Washington, DC: Child Welfare League of America.

Campbell, L. (1997). Child neglect and intensive-family-preservation practice. *Families in Society: The Journal of Contemporary Human Services,* 280–290.

Cantwell, H. B., & Rosenberg, D. A. (1990, October). *Child neglect.* Paper presented at a national Council of Juvenile and Family Court Judges continuing judicial education project, Honolulu, HI.

Carroll, C. A., & Haase, C. C. (1987). The function of protective services in child abuse and neglect. In R. E. Helfer & R. S. Kempe (Eds.), *The battered child* (pp. 137–151). Chicago: University of Chicago Press.

Casey, A. (1990). *Kids Count Special Report.* Baltimore, MD: Author.

Casey, A. (2000). *Kids Count Special Report. Children at risk: State trends 1990–2000.* Baltimore, MD: Author.

Chadwick, D. (2001). Community organization of services to deal with and end child abuse. In J. E. B. Myers, L. Berliner, J. Brier, C. T. Hendrix, C. Jenny, & T. A. Reid (Eds.), *The APSAC handbook on child maltreatment* (2nd ed.) (pp. 509–523). Thousand Oaks, CA: Sage Publications, Inc.

Chaffin, M., Kelleher, K., & Hollenberg, J. (1996). Onset of physical abuse and neglect: Psychiatric, substance abuse, and social risk factors from prospective community data. *Child Abuse & Neglect, 20*(3) 191–203.

Chasnoff, I. (1998). Silent violence: Is prevention a moral obligation? *Pediatrics, 102*,45–149.

Chasnoff, I. J. (1989). Drug use in women: Establishing a standard of care. *Annals of the New York Academy of Science, 562*, 208–210.

Chasnoff, I. J., Griffith, D. R., Freier, C., & Murray, J. (1992). Cocaine/poly-drug use in pregnancy. *Pediatrics, 89*, 284–289.

Chasnoff, I. J., & Lowder, L. A. (1999). Prenatal alcohol and drug use and risk for child maltreatment: A timely approach to intervention. In H. Dubowitz (Ed.), *Neglected children: Research, practice, and policy* (pp. 132–155). Thousand Oaks, CA: Sage Publications, Inc.

Chesney-Lind, M. (1997). *The female offender: Girls, women, and crime.* Thousand Oaks, CA: Sage.

Chesney-Lind, M., & Shelden, R. (1998). *Girls, delinquency, and juvenile justice* (2nd ed.). Belmont, CA: West/Wadsworth/ITP.

Child Abuse Act. Hawai'i Revised Statutes Chapter 350, Vol. 7, Title 20, Social Services (1993).

Child Abuse Prevention and Treatment Act, 1974. United States Code Annotated. Title 42, The Public Health and Welfare (pp. 199–205).

Child Protective Act. Hawai'i Revised Statutes Chapter 587, Vol. 12, Title 31, Family (1993).

Child Welfare League of America (1999). *Child abuse and neglect: A look at the states. 1999 CWLA stat book.* Washington, DC: Author.

Child Welfare League of America. (April 17, 2002a). Child abuse and neglect fatalities by maltreatment type, 1998. CWLA National Data Analysis System. http://ndas.cwla.org/Report.asp?PageMode=1&ReportID=18&UID= {9BB7E80B-EAB8

Child Welfare League of America. (April 17, 2002b). Percentage of substantiated/ indicated allegations, by maltreatment type, 1999. CWLA National Data Analysis System. http://ndas.cwla.org/Report.asp?PageMode=0&ReportID=351

Children's Defense Fund. (1985). *The state of America's children. Year 1985.* Washington, DC:Author.

Children's Defense Fund. (2000). *The state of America's children. Year 2000.* Washington, DC: Author.

Choi , N. (Ed.). (2001). *Psychosocial aspects of the Asian-American experience: Diversity within diversity.* New York: Haworth Press.

Choney, S., Berryhill-Paapke, E., & Robbins, R. (1995). The acculturation of American Indians: Developing frameworks for research and practice. In J. Ponterotto, J. Casas, L. Suzuki, & C. Alexander (Eds.), *Handbook of multicultural counseling* (pp. 73–92). Thousand Oaks, CA: Sage.

Chow, J. (2001). Assessment of Asian American/Pacific Islander Organizations and Communties. In R. Fong & S. Furuto (Eds.), *Culturally competent practice: Skills, Interventions, and Evaluations* (pp. 211–224). Boston, MA: Allyn & Bacon.

Christensen, B. (1998). Family centered TANF reform: Implications for staff development. *The Preservation Report, 1,* 20–23.

Christensen, M. J., Brayden, R. M., Dietrich, M. S., McLaughlin, F. J. Sherrod, K. B., & Altemeier, W. A. (1994). The prospective assessment of self-concept in neglectful and physically abusive low-income mothers. *Child Abuse and Neglect, 18,* 224–232.

Cicchetti, D., & Lynch, M. (1993). Toward an ecological/transactional model of community violence and child maltreatment: Consequences for children's development. *Psychiatry, 50,* 96–118.

Cohen, P., Brown, J., & Smailes, E. (2001). Child abuse and neglect and the development of mental disorders in the general population. *Development and Psychopathology, 13,* 981–999.

Cohen, S., & Wills, T. A. (1985). Stress, social support, and the buffering hypothesis. *Psychological Bulletin, 98,* 310–357.

Cohn, A. H. (1987). Our national priorities for prevention. In R. E. Helfer & R. S. Kempe (Eds.), *The battered child* (pp. 444–455). Chicago: The University of Chicago Press.

Coles, C., & Platzman, K. (1993). Behavioral development in children prenatally exposed to drugs and alcohol. *International Journal of Addictions, 28,* 1393–1433.

Colon, E. (2001). Program evaluation in health and human service agencies serving Latino communities. In R. Fong & S. Furuto (Eds.), Culturally competent practice: Skills, interventions, and evaluations (pp. 384–395). Boston, MA: Allyn & Bacon.

Coohey, C. (1995). Neglectful mothers, their mothers, and partners: The significance of mutual aid. *Child Abuse and Neglect, 19,* 885–895.

Coohey, C. (1996). Child maltreatment; testing the social isolation hypothesis. *Child Abuse and Neglect, 20,* 241–254.

Courtney, M. E. (1998). The costs of child protection in the context of welfare reform. *The Future of Children, 8,* 88–103.

Craft, J. L., & Staudt, M. M. (1991). Reporting and founding of child neglect in urban and rural communities. *Child Welfare, 70,* 359–370.

Crittenden, P. M. (1993). An information-processing perspective on the behavior of neglectful parents. *Criminal Justice and Behavior, 20,* 27–48.

Crittenden, P. M. (1999). Child neglect: Causes and contributors. In H. Dobowitz (Ed.), *Neglected children: Research, practice, and policy* (pp. 47–68). Thousand Oaks, CA: Sage Publications, Inc.

Crouch, J. L., & Milner, J. S. (1993). Effects of child neglect on children. *Criminal Justice and Behavior, 20,* 49–65.

Culp, R. E., Richardson, M. T., & Heide, J. S. (1987). The differential developmental progress of maltreated children in day treatment. *Social Work, 32,* 497–499.

Curtis, P., & McCullogh, C. (1993). The impact of alcohol and other drugs on the child welfare system. *Child Welfare, 71,* 533–542.

Daly, A. (2001). A heuristic perspective of strengths in the African American community. In R. Fong & S. Furuto, (Eds). *Culturally competent practice: Skills, interventions, and evaluations* (pp. 241–254). Boston, MA: Allyn & Bacon.

Daro, D. (1988). *Confronting child abuse: Research for effective program design.* New York: Free Press.

Daro, D. A., & Donnelly, A. C. (2002). Child abuse prevention: Accomplishments and challenges. In J. E. B. Meyers, L. Berliner, J. Briere, C. T. Hendrix, C. Jenny, & T. A. Reid (Eds.), *The APSAC handbook on child maltreatment* (2nd ed.) (pp. 431–448). Thousand Oaks, CA: Sage Publications, Inc.

Daro, D. A., & Harding, K. A. (1999). Healthy families America: Using research to enhance practice. *The Future of Children, 9*, 152–176.

Dean, A. L., Malik, M. M., Richards, W., & Stringer, S. A. (1986). Effects of parental maltreatment on children's conceptions of interpersonal relationships. *Developmental Psychology, 22*, 617–626.

DeBruyn, L., Chino, M., Serna, P., & Fullerton-Gleason, L. (2001). Child maltreatment in American Indian and Alaska Native communities: Integrating culture, history, and public health for intervention and prevention. *Child Maltreatment, 6*(2), 89–103.

DePanfilis, D. (1999). Intervening with families when children are neglected. In H. Dubowitz (Ed.), *Neglected children: Research, practice, and policy* (pp. 211–231). Thousand Oaks, CA: Sage Publications, Inc.

DePanfilis, D., & Zuravin, S. J. (1998). Rates, patterns, and frequency of child maltreatment recurrences among families known to CPS. *Child Maltreatment, 3*, 27–42.

Devaney, B. S., Ellwood, M. R., & Love, J. M. (1997). Programs that mitigate the effects of poverty on children. *The Future of Children, 7*, 88–112.

DiLalla, D. L., & Crittenden, P. M. (1990). Dimensions of maltreated children's home behavior: A factor analytic approach. *Infant Behavior and Development, 13*, 439–460.

DiLeonardi, J. W. (1993). Families in poverty and chronic neglect of children. *Families in Society, 74*, 557–562.

DiLeonardi, J. W., Johnson, P. M., Spight, M. S., & McGuinness, T. J. (undated). *Evaluation of the chronic neglect consortium: Final report.* Chicago: Author.

DiLeonardi, J. W., Johnson, P. M., Spight, M. S., McGuinness, T. J., & Heinke, W. E. (1992). *Treating chronic child neglect: Report on a demonstration.* Chicago: Children's Home and Aid Society.

Doerner, W. G. (1987). Child maltreatment seriousness and juvenile delinquency. *Youth and Society, 19*, 197–224.

Dore, M., Doris, J., & Wright, P. (1995). Identifying substance abuse in maltreating families: A child welfare challenge. *Child Abuse & Neglect, 19*(5), 531–543.

Dore, M., & Lee, J. M. (1999). The role of parent training with abusive and neglectful parents. *Family Relations, 48*, 313–335.

Doueck, H. J., Ishisaka, A. H., & Greenaway, K. S. (1988). The role of normative development in adolescent abuse and neglect. *Family Relations, 37*, 135–139.

Dube, S., Anda, R, Felitti, V., Croft, J, ,Edwards, V., & Giles, W. (2001). Growing up with parental alcohol abuse: Exposure to childhood abuse, neglect, and household dysfunction. *Child Abuse & Neglect, 25*, 1627–1640.

Dubowitz, H. (1999a). Neglect of children's health care. In H. Dobowitz (Ed.), *Neglected children: Research, practice, and policy* (pp. 109–131). Thousand Oaks, CA: Sage Publications, Inc.

Dubowitz, H. (Ed.). (1999b). *Neglected children: Research, practice, and policy*. Thousand Oaks, CA: Sage.

Dubowitz, H., & Black, M. M. (2002). Neglect of children's health. In J. E. B. Myers, L. Berliner, J. Briere, C. T. Hendrix, C. Jenny, & T. A. Reid (Eds.), *The APSAC handbook on child maltreatment* (2nd ed.) (pp. 269–292). Thousand Oaks, CA: Sage Publications, Inc.

Dubowitz, H., Black, M. M., Starr, R. H., & Zuravin, S. J. (1993). A conceptual definition of child neglect. *Criminal Justice and Behavior, 20,* 8–26.

Dubowitz, H., Klockner, A., Starr, R. H., & Black, M. M. (1998). Community and professional definitions of child neglect. *Child Maltreatment, 3,* 235–243.

Duggan, A. K., McFarlane, E. C., Windham, A. M., Rohde, C. A., Salkever, D. S., Fuddy, L., Rosenberg, L. A., Buchbinder, S. B., & Sia, C. C. J. (1999). Evaluation of Hawai'i's healthy start program. *The Future of Children, 9,* 66–89.

Duncan, G. J., Harris, K. M., & Boisjoly, J. (2002). Time limits and welfare reform: New estimates of the number and characteristics of affected families. *Social Service Review, 74,* 55–75.

Duncan, G. J., Yeung, W. J., Brooks-Gunn, J., & Smith, J. R. (1998). How much does childhood poverty affect the life chances of children? *American Sociological Review, 63,* 406–423.

Dunn, M., Tarter, R., Mezzich, A., Vanyukov, M., Kirisci, L., & Kirillova, G. (2002). Origins and consequences of child neglect in substance abuse families. *Clinical Psychological Review, 22,* 1063–1090.

Eckenrode, J., Laird, M., & Doris, J. (1993). School performance and disciplinary problems among abused and neglected children. *Developmental Psychology, 29,* 53–62.

Eckenrode, J., Zielinski, D., Smith, E., Marcynyszyn, L., Henderson, C. R., Kitzman, H., Cole, R., Power, P., & Olds, D. L. (2001). Child maltreatment and the early onset of problem behaviors: Can a program of nurse home visiting break the link? *Development and Psychopathology, 13,* 873–890.

Egeland, B., & Sroufe, L. A. (1981). Attachment and early maltreatment. *Child Development, 52,* 44–52.

Egeland, B., Sroufe, L. A., & Erickson, M. (1983). The developmental consequences of different patterns of maltreatment. *Child Abuse and Neglect, 7,* 459–469.

Egeland, B., & Vaughn B. (1981). Failure of "bond formation" as a cause of abuse, neglect, and maltreatment. *American Journal of Orthopsychiatry, 51,* 78–84.

Emery, R. B., & Laumann-Billings, L. (1998). An overview of the nature, causes, and consequences of abusive family relationships: Toward differentiating maltreatment and violence. *American Psychologist, 53,* 121–135.

English, D. J. (1999). Evaluation and risk assessment of child neglect in public child protection services. In H. Dobowitz (Ed.), *Neglected children: Research, practice, and policy* (pp. 191–210). Thousand Oaks, CA: Sage Publications, Inc.

Erickson, M. F., & Egeland, B. (2002). Child neglect. In J. E. B. Myers, L. Berliner, J. Brier, C. T. Hendrix, C. Jenny, & T. A. Reid (Eds.), *The APSAC handbook on child maltreatment* (2nd ed.) (pp. 3–20). Thousand Oaks, CA: Sage Publications, Inc.

Famy, C., Streissguth, A., & Unis, A. (1998). Mental illness in adults with fetal alcohol syndrome or fetal alcohol effects. *American Journal of Psychiatry, 155,* 552–554.

Federal Interagency Forum on Child and Family Statistics. (1998). *America's children: Key national indicators of well-being.* Washington, DC: U.S. Government Printing Office.

Feig, L. (1998). Understanding the problem: The gap between substance abuse programs and child welfare services. In R. Hampton, V. Senatore, & T. Gullotta (Eds.), *Substance abuse, family violence and child welfare* (pp. 62–95). Thousand Oaks, CA: Sage Publications, Inc.

Feldman, K. W., Monastersky, C., & Feldman, G. K. (1993). When is childhood drowning neglect? *Child Abuse and Neglect, 17,* 329–336.

Feldman, R. A. (1982). Damaged parents and child neglect: An essay review. *Social Work Research and Abstracts, 18,* 3–8.

Ferrari, A. (2002). The impact of culture upon childrearing practices and definitions of maltreatment. *Child Abuse and Neglect, 26,* 793–813.

Finkelstein, N. (1994). Treatment issues for alcohol and drug dependent pregnant and parenting women. *Health and Social Work, 19*(1), 7–15.

Fischler, R. S. (1985). Child abuse and neglect in American Indian communities. *Child Abuse and Neglect, 9,* 95–106.

Fong, R. (1994). Family preservation: Making it work for Asians. *Child Welfare, 53*(4), 331–341.

Fong, R. (2003). Cultural competence practice with Asian Americans. In D. Lum, *Culturally competent practice: A framework for understanding diverse groups and justice issues* (pp. 261–281). Pacific Grove, CA: Brooks/Cole.

Fong, R., Boyd, T., & Browne, C. (1999). The Gandhi technique: A biculturalization approach for empowering Asian and Pacific Islander families. *Journal of Multicultural Social Work, 7,* 95–110.

Fong, R., McRoy, R., & Ortiz-Hendricks, C. (forthcoming). Intersecting child welfare, substance abuse , and family violence: Culturally competent approaches. Washington, D.C.: Council on Social Work Education.

Fontes, L. (2002). Child discipline and physical abuse in immigrant Latino families: Reducing violence and misunderstandings. *Journal of Counseling & Development, 80*(Winter), 31–40.

Foster, E. M., & Furstenberg, F. F. (1999). The most disadvantaged children: Trends over time. *Social Service Review, 73,* 560–578.

Frank, D. A., Bresnahan, K., & Zuckerman, B. S. (1996). Maternal cocaine use: Impact on child health and development. *Pediatrics, 26,* 49–76.

Frankel, H. (1988). Family-centered, home-based services in child protection: A review of the research. *Social Service Review, 62,* 137–157.

Fraser, M. W. (1997). The ecology of childhood: A multisystems perspective. In M. W. Fraser (Ed.), *Risk and resilience in childhood* (pp. 1–9). Washington, DC: NASW Press.

Fraser, M. W., Nelson, K. E., & Rivard, J. C. (1997). Effectiveness of family preservations services. *Social Work Research, 21,* 138–141.

Freundlich, M. (2000). The impact of prenatal substance exposure: Research findings and their implications for adoption. In R. Barth, M. Freundlich, & D. Brodzinsky (Eds.), *Adoption and prenatal alcohol and drug exposure* (pp. 1–21). Washington, DC: Child Welfare League of America.

Friedrich, W. M., Tyler, J. D., & Clark, J. A. (1985). Personality and psychophysiological variables in abusive, neglectful, and low-income control mothers. *Journal of Nervous and Mental Disease, 173,* 449–460.

Furuto, S., San Nicholas, R., Kim, G., & Fiaui, L. (2001). Interventions with Kanaka Maoli, Chamorro, and Samoan Communities. In R. Fong & S. Furuto (Eds.), *Culturally competent practice: Skills, interventions, and evaluations* (pp. 327–342). Boston, MA: Allyn & Bacon.

Galan, F. (2001). Intervention with Mexican American families. In R. Fong & S. Furuto (Eds.), *Culturally competent practice: Skills, interventions, and evaluations* (pp. 255–268). Boston: Allyn & Bacon.

Garbarino, J. (1981). An ecological approach to child maltreatment. In L. H. Pelton (Ed.), *The social context of child abuse and neglect* (pp. 228–267). New York: Human Sciences Press.

Garbarino, J., & Collins, C. C. (1999). Child neglect: The family with a hole in the middle. In H. Dubowitz (Ed.), *Neglected children: Research, practice, and policy* (pp. 1–23). Thousand Oaks, CA: Sage Publications, Inc.

Garbarino, J., & Crouter, A. (1978). Defining the community context for parent-child relations: The correlates of child maltreatment. *Child Development, 49,* 604–616.

Garbarino, J., & Ebata, A. (1983). The significance of ethnic and cultural differences in child maltreatment. *Journal of Marriage and the Family, 45,* 773–783.

Garbarino, J., & Kostelny, K. (1994). Neighborhood-based programs. In G. B. Melton & F. D. Barry (Eds.), *Protecting children from abuse and neglect: Foundations for a new national strategy* (pp. 304–352). New York: Guilford Press.

Garbarino, J., & Sherman, D. (1980). High-risk neighborhoods and high-risk families: The human ecology of child maltreatment. *Child Development, 51,* 188–198.

Gaudin, J. M. (1993). Effective interventions with neglectful families. *Criminal Justice and Behavior, 20,* 66–89.

Gaudin, J. M. (1999). Child neglect: Short-term and long-term outcomes. In H. Dubowitz, (Ed.), *Neglected children: Research, practice, and policy* (pp. 89–108). Thousand Oaks, CA: Sage Publications, Inc.

Gaudin, J. M., & Polansky, N. A. (1986). Social distancing of the neglectful family: Sex, race, and social class influences. *Children and Youth Services Review, 8,* 1–12.

Gaudin, J.M., Polansky, N. A., Kilpatrick, A. C., & Shilton, P. (1993). Loneliness, depression, stress, and social supports in neglectful families. *American Journal of Orthopsychiatry, 63,* 597–605.

Gelles, R. J. (1999). Policy issues in child neglect. In H. Dubowitz (Ed.), *Neglected children: Research, practice, and policy* (pp. 278–298). Thousand Oaks, CA: Sage Publications, Inc.

Gershenson, C. (1995). Social policy and evaluation: An evolving symbiosis. In P. J. Pecora, M. W. Fraser, K. Nelson, J. McCroskey, & W. Meezan (Eds.), *Evaluating family-based services* (pp. 261–275). New York: Aldine de Gruyter.

Gil, D. G. (1981). The United States versus child abuse. In L. H. Pelton (Ed.), *The social context of child abuse and neglect* (pp. 291–324). New York: Human Sciences Press.

Giovannoni, J. M. (1982). Prevention of child abuse and neglect: Research and policy issues. *Social Work Research and Abstracts, 18,* 23–31.

Giovannoni, J. M., & Becerra, R. M. (1979). *Defining child abuse.* New York: Free Press.

Giovannoni, J. M., & Billingsley, A. (1974). Child neglect among the poor: A study of parental adequacy in families of three ethnic groups. In J. E. Leavitt (Ed.), *The battered child: Selected readings* (pp. 170–177). Fresno, CA: General Learning Corporation.

Glaser, D. (2002). Emotional abuse and neglect (psychological maltreatment): A conceptual framework. *Child abuse and neglect, 26,* 697–714.

Glisson, C., Bailey, J. W., & Post, J. A. (2000). Predicting the time children spend in state custody. *Social Service Review, 74,* 251–280.

Gomby, D. S., Culross, P. L., & Behrman, R. E. (1999). Home visiting: Recent program evaluations—analysis and recommendations. *The Future of Children, 9,* 4–26.

Gordon, L. (1988). *Heroes in their own lives.* New York: Penguin.

Grant, D. (2001). Evaluation skills with African American organizations and communities. In R. Fong & S. Furuto (Eds.), *Culturally competent practice: Skills, interventions, and evaluations* (pp. 355–369). Boston, MA: Allyn & Bacon.

Gray, E., & Cosgrove, J. (1985). Ethnocentric perception of childrearing practices in protective services. *Child Abuse and Neglect, 9,* 389–396.

Guterman, N. B. (1997). Early prevention of physical child abuse and neglect: Existing evidence and future directions. *Child Maltreatment, 2,* 12–35.

Halpern, R. (1990). Poverty and early childhood parenting: Toward a framework for intervention. *American Journal of Orthopsychiatry, 60,* 6–18.

Hampton, R. (2000). Child welfare, substance abuse, and domestic violence. Keynote speech given at a cultural competence conference sponsored by CSWE, Casey Family Programs, and The University of Texas at Austin. Austin, TX: The University of Texas at Austin.

Hampton, R. L. (1987). Race, class and child maltreatment. *Journal of Comparative Family Studies, 18,* 113–126.

Hampton, R. L., Senatore, V., & Gullotta, T. P. (Eds.). (1998). *Substance abuse, family violence and child welfare: Bridging perspectives.* Thousand Oaks, CA: Sage Publications, Inc.

Hansen, D. J., Pallotta, G. M., Tishelman, A. C., Conaway, L., & MacMillan, V. M. (1989). Parental problem-solving skills and child behavior problems: A comparison of physically abusive, neglectful, clinic and community families. *Journal of Family Violence, 4,* 353–368.

Harden, B. (1998). Building bridges for children: Addressing the consequences of exposure to drugs and to the child welfare system. In R. Hampton, V. Senatore, & T. Gullotta (Eds.), *Substance abuse, family violence and child welfare* (pp. 18–61). Thousand Oaks, CA: Sage Publications, Inc.

Harris, K. M., & Marmer, J. K. (1996). Poverty, paternal involvement, and adolescent well-being. *Journal of Family Issues, 17,* 614–640.

Hartley, R. (1987). *A program blueprint for neglectful families.* Unpublished manuscript.

Hawai'i Department of Human Services (1995). *Family preservation and family support five year plan, Title IV-b, sub-part 2.* Honolulu: Author

Helfer, R. E. (1987a). The litany of the smoldering neglect of children. In R. E. Helfer & R. S. Kempe (Eds.), *The battered child* (pp. 301–311). Chicago: The University of Chicago Press.

Helfer, R. E. (1987b). The developmental basis of child abuse and neglect: An epidemiological approach. In R. E. Helfer & R. S. Kempe (Eds.), *The battered child* (pp. 60–70). Chicago: The University of Chicago Press.

Herrenkohl, R. C., Herrenkohl, E. C., & Egolf, B. (1983). Circumstances surrounding the occurrence of child maltreatment. *Journal of Consulting and Clinical Psychology, 51,* 424–431.

Higgins, D. J., & McCabe, M. T. (2000). Relationships between different types of maltreatment during childhood and adjustment in adulthood. *Child Maltreatment, 5,* 262–272.

Hildyard, K., & Wolfe, D. (2002). Child neglect: Developmental issues and outcomes. *Child Abuse & Neglect, 26*(6–7), 679–695.

Hillson, J. M. C., & Kuiper, N. A. (1994). A stress and coping model of child maltreatment. *Clinical Psychology Review, 14,* 261–285.

Holliday, M., & Cronin, R. (1990). Families first: A significant step toward family preservation. *Families in Society,* 303–306.

Homma-True, R. (1997). Asian American women. In E. Lee (Ed.), *Working with Asian Americans: A guide for clinicians* (pp. 420–428). New York: Guilford Press.

Hong, G. K., & Hong, L. K. (1991). Comparative perspectives on child abuse and neglect: Chinese versus Hispanics and Whites. *Child Welfare, 70,* 463–475.

Horowitz, B., & Wolock, I. (1981). Material deprivation, child maltreatment, and agency interventions among poor families. In L. H. Pelton (Ed.), *The social context of child abuse and neglect* (pp. 137–184). New York: Human Sciences Press.

Howing, P. T., Wodarski, J. S., Gaudin, J. M., & Kurtz, D. (1989). Effective interventions to ameliorate the incidence of child maltreatment: The empirical base. *Social Work, 34,* 330–339.

Howing, P. T., Wodarski, J. S., Kurtz, D., & Gaudin, J. M. (1989). Child maltreatment research. *Social Work Research and Abstracts, 25,* 3–7.

Hsu, F. (1981). *Americans and Chinese: Passage to differences* (3rd ed.). Honolulu: University of Hawaii Press.

Hutchison, E. D. (1990). Child maltreatment: Can it be defined? *Social Service Review, 64,* 60–78.

Iwaniec, D. (1997). Evaluating parent training for emotionally abusive and neglectful parents: Comparing individual versus individual and group intervention. *Research on Social Work Practice, 7,* 329–349.

Jackson, A. P. (1998). The role of social support in parenting for low-income, single, black mothers. *Social Service Review, 72,* 365–378.

Johnson, C. F. (1993). Physicians and medical neglect: Variables that affect reporting. *Child Abuse and Neglect, 17,* 605–612.

Johnson, W., & Clancy, T. (1991). Efficiency in behavior-changing programs: The case of in-home child abuse prevention. In R. Pruger (Ed.), *Efficiency and the social services* (pp 105–118). New York: Haworth Press, Inc.

Jones, M. A. (1987). *Parental lack of supervision: Nature and consequence of a major child neglect problem.* Washington, DC: Child Welfare League of America.

Jonson-Reid, M. (2001). Exploring the relationship between child welfare interventions and juvenile corrections involvement. *American Journal of Orthopsychiatry, 72,* 599–576.

Jonson-Reid, M., Drake, B., Chung, S., & Way, I. (in press) Cross-type recidivism among child maltreatment victims and perpetrators. *Child Abuse and Neglect.* Available online July 25, 2003 http://www.elsevier.com/locate/chiabunect

Jung, M. (1998). *Chinese American family therapy: A new model for clinicians.* San Francisco: Jossey-Bass.

Kadushin, A. (1967). *Child welfare services.* New York: Macmillan.

Kadushin, A. (1978). Neglect—is it neglected too often? In M. L. Lauderdale, R. M. Anderson, & S. E. Cramer (Eds.). *Child abuse and neglect: Issues on innovation and implementation: Vol. 1. Proceedings of the second national conference on child abuse and neglect* (pp. 217–220). (DHEW Publication No. OHDS 78-30147). Washington, DC: U.S. Department of Health, Education, and Welfare.

Kadushin, A., & Martin, J. A. (1988). *Child welfare services* (4th ed.). New York: Macmillan.

Kairys, S. (1996). Family support in cases of child abuse and neglect. In G. H. S. Singer, L. E. Powers, & A. L. Olson (Eds.), *Redefining family support: Innovations in public-private partnerships* (pp. 171–188). Baltimore, MD: Paul H. Brooks Publishing Company.

Kandall, S. R. (2000). Societal attitudes toward drug-using women and their children: Past and present. In R. P. Barth, M. Freundlich, & D. Brodzinsky (Eds.), *Adoption & prenatal alcohol and drug exposure: Research, policy and practice* (pp. 199–225). Washington, DC: Child Welfare League of America.

Kaufman, J. (1991). Depressive disorders in maltreated children. *Journal of the American Academy of Child and Adolescent Psychiatry, 30,* 257–265.

Kelleher, K., Chaffin, M., Hollenberg, J., & Fischer, E. (1994). Alcohol and drug disorders among physically abusive and neglectful parents in a community-based sample. *American Journal of Public Health, 84,* 1586–1590.

Kelly, P., Blacksin, B., & Mason, E. (2001) Factors affecting substance abuse treatment completion for women. *Issues in Mental Health Nursing, 22,* 287–304.

Kempe, H., Silverman, F., Steele, B., Droegemeuller, W., & Silver, H. (1962). The battered child syndrome. *Journal of the American Medical Association, 181,* 17–24.

Kempe, R., & Goldbloom, R. B. (1987). Malnutrition and growth retardation ("failure to thrive") in the context of child abuse and neglect. In R. E. Helfer & R. S. Kempe (Eds.), *The battered child* (pp. 312–335). Chicago: The University of Chicago Press.

Kendall-Tackett, K. A., & Eckenrode, J. (1996). The effects of neglect on academic achievement and disciplinary problems: A developmental perspective. *Child Abuse and Neglect, 20,* 161–169.

Kerns, K., Don, A., Mateer, C. A., & Streissguth, A. P. (1997). Cognitive deficits in non-retarded adults with fetal alcohol syndrome. *Journal of Learning Disabilities, 30,* 685–693.

Kessen, W. (Ed.) (1975). *Childhood in China.* New Haven, CT: Yale University Press.

Kinney, J., Haapala, D., & Booth, C. (1991). *Keeping families together: The HomeBuilders model.* New York: Aldine de Gruyter.

Kirby, L. D., & Fraser, M. W. (1997). Risk and resilience in childhood. In M. W. Fraser (Ed.), *Risk and resilience in childhood* (pp. 10–33). Washington, DC: NASW Press.

Kissman, K. (1991). Feminist-based social work with single-parent families. *Families in Society, 71*(9), 23–28.

Knudsen, D. D. (1992). *Child maltreatment: Emerging perspectives.* Dix Hills, NY: General Hall, Inc.

Knutson, J. F. (1995). Psychological characteristics of maltreated children: Putative risk factors and consequences. *Annual Review of Psychology, 46,* 401–431.

Korbin, J. E. (1981). *Child abuse and neglect: Cross cultural perspectives.* Berkeley, CA: University of California Press.

Korbin, J. E. (1987). Child abuse and child neglect: The cultural context. In R. E. Helfer & R. S. Kempe (Eds.), *The battered child* (pp. 23–41). Chicago: University of Chicago Press.

Korbin, J. E. (2000). Culture and child maltreatment: Cultural competence and beyond. *Child Abuse and Neglect, 26,* 37–644.

Korbin, J. E. (2002). Culture and child maltreatment: Cultural competence and beyond. *Child Abuse and Neglect, 26,* 637–644.

Korbin, J. E., & Spilsbury, J. C. (1999). Cultural competence and child neglect. In H. Dubowitz (Ed.), *Neglected children: Research, practice, and policy* (pp. 69–88). Thousand Oaks, CA: Sage Publications, Inc.

Krishman, V., & Morrison, K. B. (1995). An ecological model of child maltreatment in a Canadian province. *Child Abuse and Neglect, 19,* 101–113.

Kropenske, V., & Howard, J. (1994). *Protecting children in substance-abusing families.* Washington, DC: U.S. Department of Health and Human Services.

Kuramoto, F., & Nakashima, J. (2000). Developing an ATOD Prevention campaign for Asian and Pacific Islanders: Some considerations. *Journal of Public Health Management Practice, 6*(3), 57–64.

Lai, T. M. (2001). Ethnocultural background and substance abuse treatment of Chinese Americans. In S. L. A. Straussner (Ed.), *Ethnocultural factors in substance abuse treatment* (pp. 345–367). New York: Guilford Press.

Lamphear, V. S. (1985), The impact of maltreatment on children's psychosocial adjustment: A review of the research. *Child Abuse and Neglect, 9,* 251–263.

Landsman, M. J., Nelson, K., Allen, M., & Tyler, M. (1992). The self-sufficiency project: The national resource center on family based services. *The Prevention Report,* 10–14.

Larner, M. B., Terman, D. L., & Behrman, R. E. (1997). Welfare to work: Analysis and recommendations. *The Future of Children, 7,* 4–19.

Larsen, E., & Hegarty, C. L. (1987). *Days of healing, days of joy.* Center City, MN: Hazelden.

Law, J., & Conway, J. (1992) Effect of abuse and neglect on the development of children's speech and language. *Developmental Medicine and Child Neurology, 34,* 943–948.

Layzer, J. I., Goodson, B. D., Bernstein, L., & Price, C. (2001). *National evaluation of family support programs: Final report: Vol. a: The meta-analysis.* Cambridge, MA: ABT Associates, Inc.

Lee, E. (1992). *Working with Asian Americans: A guide for clinicians.* New York: Guilford Press.

Ledesma, R., & Starr, P. (2000). Child welfare and the American Indian community. In Neil Cohen and contributors. *Child welfare: A multicultural focus* (2nd ed.). (pp. 117–142). Boston, MA: Allyn & Bacon.

Leiter, J., Myers, K. A., & Zingraff, M. T. (1994). Substantiated and unsubstantiated cases of child maltreatment: Do their consequences differ? *Social Work Research, 18,* 67–82.

Lerman, P. (1994). Child protection and out-of-home care: Systems reform and regulating placement. In G. B. Melton & F. D. Barry (Eds.), *Protecting children from abuse and neglect: Foundations for a new national strategy* (pp. 353–437). New York: Guilford Press.

Lester, B. M., LaGrasse, L. L., & Seifer, R. (1998). Cocaine exposure and children: The meaning of subtle effects. *Science, 282,* 633–634.

Lewis, M., Giovannoni, J., & Leake, B. (1997). Two-year placement of children removed at birth from drug-using and non-drug-using mothers in Los Angeles. *Social Work Research, 21,* 81–91.

Lewit, E. M., & Kerrebrock, N. (1997a). Childhood hunger. *The Future of Children, 7,* 28–137.

Lewit, E. M., & Kerrebrock, N. (1997b). Population-based growth stunting. *The Future of Children, 7,* 149–156.

Lewit, E. M., & Kerrebrock, N. (1998). Child indicators: Dental health. *The Future of Children, 8,* 133–142.

Lewit, E. M., Terman, D. L., & Behrman, R. E. (1997). Children and poverty: Analysis and recommendations. *The Future of Children, 7,* 4–24.

Lindsey, D. (1994). *The welfare of children.* New York: Oxford University Press.

Lloyd, J. C., & Sallee, A. L. (1990). Family policy analysis and preserving families. In W. Deutelbaum, D. Haapala, J. Hutchinson, J. Lloyd, & C. Sudia (Eds.), *Empowering families: Papers from the third annual conference on family-based services* (pp. 131–138). Riverdale, IL: National Association for Family-Based Services.

Lujan, C., DeBruyn, L. M., May, P. A., & Bird, M. E. (1989). Profile of abused and neglected American Indian children in the southwest. *Child Abuse and Neglect, 13,* 449–461.

Luthar, S. S. (1999). *Poverty and children's adjustment.* Thousand Oaks, CA: Sage Publications, Inc. (Vol. 41, Developmental Clinical Psychology and Psychiatry Series, Series ed.: Alan E. Kazdin).

Lynch, T. (1995). *Public budgeting in America* (4th ed.). Englewood Cliffs, NJ: Prentice-Hall.

Manly, J. T., Kim, J. E., Rogosch, F. A., & Cicchetti, D. (2001). Dimensions of child maltreatment and children's adjustment: Contributions of developmental timing and subtype. *Development and Psychopathology, 13,* 759–782.

Manning, M. (2001). Culturally competent assessment of African American communities and organizations. In R. Fong & S. Furuto (Eds), *Culturally competent practice: Skills, interventions, and evaluations* (pp. 119–131). Boston, MA: Allyn & Bacon.

Marcenko, M., Spence, M., & Rohweder, C. (1994). Psychosocial characteristics of pregnant women with and without a history of substance use. *Health and Social Work, 19,* 17–22.

Margolin, L. (1990). Fatal child neglect. *Child Welfare, 69,* 309–319.

Marshall, D. B., & English, D. J. (1999). Survival analysis of risk factors for recidivism in child abuse and neglect. *Child Maltreatment, 4,* 287–296.

Martin, M. J., & Walters, J. (1982). Familial correlates of selected types of child abuse and neglect. *Journal of Marriage and the Family, 44,* 267–276.

Matsuoka, J. (2001). Evaluation and assessment in Hawaiian and Pacific Communities. In R. Fong & S. Furuto (Eds), *Culturally competent practice: Skills, interventions, and evaluations* (pp. 438–453). Boston, MA: Allyn & Bacon.

Matsuyoshi, J. (2001). Substance abuse interventions for Japanese and Japanese American clients. In S. L. A. Straussner (Ed.), *Ethnocultural factors in substance abuse treatment* (pp. 393–417). New York: Guilford Press.

Mattson, S. N., & Riley, E. P. (1998). A review of the neurobehavioral deficits in children with fetal alcohol syndrome or prenatal exposure to alcohol. *Alcoholism: Clinical and Experimental Research, 22,* 279–294.

Mayes, L. C. (1992). Prenatal cocaine exposure and young children's development. *Annals of the American Academy of Pediatrics, 521,* 11–27.

McCaffrey, M. (1978). Realistic expectations for children and families: Maximization of educational resources. In L. Lauderdale, R. Anderson, & S. E. Cramer (Eds.), *Child abuse and neglect: Issues of innovation and implementation: Vol. 2. Proceedings of the second national conference on child abuse and neglect* (pp. 13–18). (DHEW Publication No. OHDS 78-30148). Washington, DC: U.S. Department of Health, Education, and Welfare.

McCroskey, J., & Meezan, W. (1998). Family-centered services: Approaches and effectiveness. *The Future of Children, 8,* 54–71.

McCubbin, H. I., McCubbin, M. A., Thompson, A. I., & Thompson, E. A. (1995). Resiliency in ethnic families: A conceptual model for predicting family adjustment and adaptation. In H. I. McCubbin, E. A. Thompson, A. I. Thompson, & J. Fromer (Eds.), *Resiliency in ethnic minority families: Native and immigrant American families* (Vol. 1, pp. 3–48). Madison, WI: University of Wisconsin System.

McFadden, R. (1990, June 19). Tragic ending to the adoption of a crack baby. *New York Times,* p. B1.

McGloin, J. M., & Widom, C. S. (2001). Resilience among abused and neglected children grown up. *Development and Psychopathology, 13,* 1021–1038.

McGowan, B. (1990). Family-based services and public policy: context and implications. In J. Whittaker, J. Kinney, E. Tracy, & C. Booth (Eds.), *Reaching high-risk families: Intensive family preservation in human services* (pp. 65–87). New York: Aldine de Gruyter.

McRoy, R., & Vick, J. (forthcoming). Intersecting child welfare, substance abuse, and domestic violence. In R. Fong, R. McRoy, & C. Ortiz Hendricks (Eds.), *Intersecting child welfare, substance abuse, and family violence.* Washington, DC: Council on Social Work Education.

Medrano, M., Zule, W., Hatch, J., & Desmond, D. (1999). Prevalence of childhood trauma in a community sample of substance-abusing women. *American Journal of Drug and Alcohol Abuse, 25*(3), 449–462.

Meezan, W., & O'Keefe, M. (1998). Evaluating the effectiveness of multifamily group therapy in child abuse and neglect. *Research on Social Work Practice, 8,* 330–353.

Meier, E. G. (1964). Child neglect. In N. E. Cohen, (Ed.), *Social work and social problems* (pp. 153–200). New York: National Association of Social Workers.

Melton, G. B., & Barry, F. D. (1994). Neighbors helping neighbors: The vision of the U. S. Advisory Board on Child Abuse and Neglect. In G. B. Melton & F. D. Barry (Eds.), *Protecting children from abuse and neglect: Foundation for a new national strategy* (pp. 1–13). New York: Guilford Press.

Milner, J., & Robertson, K. R. (1990). Comparison of physical child abusers, intrafamilial sexual child abusers, and child neglecters. *Journal of Interpersonal Violence, 5,* 37–48.

Mokuau, N. (1998). Reality and vision: A cultural perspective in addressing alcohol and drug abuse among Pacific Islanders. In N. Mokuaui (Ed.), *Responding to Pacific Islanders: Culturally competent perspectives for substance abuse prevention* (pp. 25–48).

Money, J., & Needleman, A. (1980). Impaired mother-infant pair bonding in the syndrome of abuse dwarfism: Possible prenatal, perinatal, and neonatal antecedents. In G. J. Williams & J. Money (Eds.), *Traumatic abuse and neglect of children at home* (pp. 228–239). Baltimore: Johns Hopkins University Press.

Moore, E., Armsden, G., & Gogerty, P. L. (1998). A twelve-year follow-up study of maltreated and at-risk children who received early therapeutic childcare. *Child Maltreatment, 3,* 3–16.

Moore, J., & Finkelstein, N. (2001). Parenting services for families affected by substance abuse. *Child Welfare, 53*(2), 221–238.

Moreno, C. (2001). Latino families and issues of substance abuse and family violence. Austin, TX: Task Force Meeting. Cultural Competence in Child Welfare Practice. Paper presented at The University of Texas at Austin, February 9 & 10. Unpublished manuscript.

Muenzenmaier, K., Meyer, T., Struening, E., & Ferber, J. (1993). Child abuse and neglect among women outpatients with chronic mental illness. *Hospital and Community Psychiatry, 44,* 666–670.

Mulroy, E. A. (1997). Building a neighborhood network: Interorganization collaboration to prevent child abuse and neglect. *Social Work, 42,* 255–264.

Mulsow, M. H., & Murry, V. M. (1996). Parenting on edge: Economically stressed, single, African American adolescent mothers. *Journal of Family Issues, 17,* 704–721.

Murphy, J. M., Jellinek, M., Quinn, D., Smith, G., Poitrast, F. G., & Goshki, M. (1991). Substance abuse and serious child mistreatment: Prevalence, risk, and outcome in a court sample. *Child Abuse and Neglect, 15,* 191–211.

Murry, V. M., & Brody, G. H. (1999). Self-regulation and self worth of black children reared in economically stressed, rural, single mother-headed families: The contribution of risk and protective factors. *Journal of Family Issues, 20,* 458–484.

Nagel, J. (2000). The politics of ethnic authenticity: Building Native American identities and communities. In P. Kivisto & G. Rundblad, G. (Eds.), *Multiculturalism in the United States: Contemporary issues, contemporary voices* (pp. 113–124). Thousand Oaks, CA: Pine Forge Press.

Nair, P., Black, M., Schuler, M., Keane, V., Snow, L., Rigney, B., & Magder, L. (1997) Risk factors for disruption in primary caregiving among infants of substance abusing women. *Child Abuse & Neglect, 21*(11), 1039–1051.

National Association of Social Workers. (2001). *NASW Standards for cultural competence in social work practice.* Washington, DC: Author.

National Clearinghouse on Child Abuse and Neglect Information. (2002). Summary of key findings from calendar year 2000. Washington, DC: Children's Bureau. Administration on children, youth, and families.

National Exchange Club Foundation. (2000). *Neglect.* Toledo, OH: Author.

National Institutes of Health. (1999). Research on child neglect. RFA: OD-99-006. http://grants2.nih.gov/grants/guide/rfa-files/RFA-OD-99-006.html

National Resource Center on Family Based Services. (1988). *Factors contributing to success and failure in family based child welfare services: Final report.* Iowa City, IA: Author.

National Resource Center on Family Based Services. (1994). *Family functioning of neglectful families.* Iowa City, IA: Author.

National Resource Center for Family Centered Practice. (1998). Of practice improvement and reforming reforms. *Prevention Report, 2,* 1–3.

Negroni-Rodriguez, L., & Morales, J. (2001). Individual and family assessment skills with Latino/Hispanic Americans. In R. Fong & S. Furuto (Eds.), *Culturally competent practice: Skills, interventions, and evaluations* (pp. 132–146). Boston, MA: Allyn & Bacon.

Nelson, D. (1991). The public policy implications of family preservation. In K. Wells & D. E. Biegel (Eds.), *Family preservation services: Research and evaluation* (pp. 207–222). Newbury Park, CA: Sage Publications, Inc.

Nelson, K. (1991). Populations and outcomes in five family preservation programs. In K. Wells & D. E. Biegel (Eds.), *Family preservation services: Research and evaluation* (pp. 72–91). Newbury Park, CA: Sage Publications, Inc.

Nelson, K. (1995). The child welfare response to youth violence and homelessness in the nineteenth century. *Child Welfare, 74,* 56–70.

Nelson, K., & Landsman, M. J. (1992). *Alternative models of family preservation: Family-based services in context.* Springfield, IL: Charles C Thomas.

Nelson, K., Landsman, M. J., Cross, T., Tyler, M., & Twohig, A. (1994). *Family functioning of neglectful families: Final report: Vol. 1. Findings.* Iowa City, IA: National Resource Center on Family Based Services.

Nelson, K., Saunders, E., & Landsman, M. J. (1990). *Chronic neglect in perspective: A study of chronically neglecting families in a large metropolitan county.* Oakdale, IA: National Resource Center on Family Based Services.

Neubauer, D. (1996). The five stages of the liberal state. *Locke's Pendulum: Health Care in a Postmodern World* (pp. 1–15). Unpublished manuscript, University of Hawai'i.

Newberger, E. H., & Bourne, R. (1978). The medicalization and legalization of child abuse. *The American Journal of Orthopsychiatry, 48,* 593–607.

New York Times. (2000, February 18).

Ney, P. G., Fung, T., & Wickett, A. R. (1992). Causes of child abuse and neglect. *Canadian Journal of Psychiatry, 37,* 401–405.

Ney, P. G., Fung, T., & Wickett, A. R. (1994). The worst combinations of child abuse and neglect. *Child Abuse and Neglect, 18,* 705–714.

O'Donnell, J. M. (1999). Involvement of African American fathers in kinship foster care services. *Social Work, 44,* 428–440.

O'Hare, W. (2001). *Child population: First data from the 2000 census.* Baltimore, MD: Annie E. Casey Foundation and Population Reference Bureau.

Ohlsson, A. (1979). Non-organic failure to thrive. *Child Abuse and Neglect, 3,* 449–459.

Olds, D. L., Henderson, C. R., Kitzman, H. J., Eckenrode, J. J., Cole, R. E., & Tatelbaum, R. C. (1999). Prenatal and infancy home visitation by nurses: Recent findings. *The Future of Children, 9,* 44–65.

Olsen, L., Allen, D., & Azzi-Lessing, L. (1996) Assessing risk in families affected by substance abuse. *Child Abuse & Neglect, 20*(9), 833–842.

Omnibus Budget Reconciliation Act of 1993, Family Preservation and Support Services Program, Public Law 103-66 (August 10, 1993). *U. S. statutes at large, 107, 312.*

Ortega, R., Guillean, C., & Najera, L. (1996). *Latinos and child welfare.* Ann Arbor, MI: University of Michigan, School of Social Work. National Latino Child Welfare Advocacy Group.

Ory, M. G., & Earp, J. L. (1980). Child maltreatment: An analysis of familial and institutional predictors. *Journal of Family Issues, 1,* 339–356.

Ozawa, M. N. (1999). The economic well-being of elderly people and children in a changing society. *Social Work, 44,* 9–19.

Ozawa, M. N., & Kim, R. Y. (1998). Declining economic fortunes of children in comparison to adults and elderly people. *Social Work Research, 22,* 14–30.

Ozawa, M. N., & Lum, Y. (1996). How safe is the safety net for poor children? *Social Work Research, 20,* 238–254.

Padilla, Y. (1999). Immigration policy: Issues for social work practice. In P. Ewalt, E. Freeman, A. Fortune, D. Poole, & S. Witkin (Eds.), *Multicultural issues in social work: Practice and research* (pp. 589–604). Washington, DC: NASW.

Paget, K. D., Philp, J. D., & Abramczyk, L. S. (1993). Recent developments in child neglect. In T. H. Ollendick & R. J. Prinz (Eds.), *Advances in clinical child psychology: Vol. 15.* New York: Plenum Press.

Parcel, T. L., & Menaghan, E.G. (1997). Effects of low-wage employment on family well-being. *The Future of Children, 7,* 116–121.

Pecora, P. J., Fraser, M. W., & Haapala, D. A. (1991). Client outcomes and issues for program design. In K. Wells & D. E. Biegel (Eds.)., *Family preservation services: Research and evaluation* (pp. 3–32). Newbury Park, CA: Sage Publications, Inc.

Pelton, L. H. (1978). Child abuse and neglect: The myth of classlessness. *American Journal of Orthopsychiatry, 48,* 608–-617.

Pelton, L. H. (1981). Child abuse and neglect and protective intervention in Mercer County, New Jersey. In L. H. Pelton (Ed.), *The social context of child abuse and neglect* (pp. 90–136). New York: Human Sciences Press.

Pelton, L. H. (1994). The role of material factors in child abuse and neglect. In G. B. Melton & F. D. Barry (Eds.), *Protecting children from abuse and neglect: Foundations for a new national strategy* (pp. 131–181). New York: Guilford Press.

Pelton, L. H. (1998). Four commentaries: How we can better protect children from abuse and neglect. Commentary 3. *The Future of Children, 8,* 126–129.

Perry, B. D. (2001). Bonding and attachment in maltreated children: Consequences of emotional neglect in childhood. Booklet in B. Perry (Ed.), Caregiver Education Series. Houston, TX: The Child Trauma Academy.

Perry, B. D. (2002a). Childhood experience and the expression of genetic potential: What childhood neglect tells us about nature and nurture. *Brain and Mind, 3,* 79–100.

Perry, B. D. (2002b). The neuroarcheology of childhood maltreatment: The neurodevelopmental costs of adverse childhood events. In B. Geffner (Ed.), *The cost of child maltreatment: Who pays? We all do.* New York: Haworth Press. http://www.childtrauma.org/ctamaterials/Neuroarcheology.asp

Perry, B. D., Colwell, K., & Schick, S. (2002). Child neglect. In D. Levinson (Ed.). *Encyclopedia of crime and punishment* (Vol. 1, pp 192–196). Thousand Oaks, CA: Sage Publications, Inc.

Perry, B. D., & Pollard, D. (1997). Altered brain development following global neglect in early childhood. *Society for Neuroscience: Proceedings from Annual Meeting,* New Orleans.

Perry, B. D., Pollard, R. A., Blakely, T. L., Baker, W. L., & Vigilante, D. (1995). Childhood trauma, the neurobiology of adaptation, and "use-dependent" development of the brain: How "states" become "traits." *Infant Mental Health Journal, 16,* 271–291.

Peterson, L., Gable, S., & Saldana, L. (1996) Treatment of maternal addiction to prevent child abuse and neglect. *Addictive Behaviors, 21*(6), 789–801.

Petit, M. R., & Curtis, P. A. (1997). *Child abuse and neglect: A look at the states. 1997 CWLA stat book.* Washington, DC: Child Welfare League of America Press.

Petit, M. R., Curtis, P. A., Woodruff, K., Arnold, L. Feagans, L., & Ang, J. (1999). *Child abuse and neglect: A look at the states. 1999 CWLA stat book.* Washington, DC: Child Welfare League of America Press.

Petr, C. (1998). *Social work with children and their families.* New York: Oxford University Press.

Pettigrew, J. (1986). Child neglect in rural Punjabi families. *Journal of Comparative Family Studies, 17,* 63–85.

Pithouse, A., & Lindsell, S. (1996). Child protection services: Comparison of a referred family centre and a field social work service in South Wales. *Research on Social Work Practice, 6,* 473–491.

Plotnick, R. D. (1997). Child poverty can be reduced. *The Future of Children, 7,* 72–87.

Polansky, N. A. (1985). Determinants of loneliness among neglectful and other low-income mothers. *Journal of Social Service Research, 8,* 1–15.

Polansky, N. A., Ammons, P. W., & Gaudin, J. M. (1985). Loneliness and isolation in child neglect. *Social Casework, 66,* 18–47.

Polansky, N. A., Ammons, P. W., & Weathersby, B. A. (1983). Is there an American standard of childcare? *Social Work, 23,* 341–346.

Polansky, N. A., Borgman, R. D., DeSaix, C., & Sharlin, S. (1974). Verbal accessibility in the treatment of child neglect. In J. E. Leavitt (Ed.), *The battered child: Selected readings* (pp. 66–75). Fresno, CA: General Learning Corporation.

Polansky, N. A., Chalmers, M. A., Buttenwieser, E. W., & Williams, D. P. (1979). The absent father in child neglect. *Social Service Review, 53,* 163–174.

Polansky, N. A., Chalmers, M. A., Williams, D. P., & Buttonwieser, E. W. (1981). *Damaged parents: An anatomy of child neglect.* Chicago: University of Chicago Press.

Polansky, N. A., DeSaix, C., & Sharlin, S. (1972). *Child neglect: Understanding and reaching the parents.* New York: Child Welfare League of America.

Polansky, N. A., Doroff, C., Kramer, E., Hess, D. S., & Pollane, L. (1978). Public opinion and intervention in child neglect. *Social Work Research and Abstracts,* 11–15.

Polansky, N. A., & Gaudin, J. M. (1983). Social distancing of the neglectful family. *Social Service Review, 57,* 196–208.

Polansky, N. A., Gaudin, J. M., Ammons, P. W., & Davis, K. B. (1985). The psychological ecology of the neglectful mother. *Child Abuse and Neglect, 9,* 265–275.

Polansky, N. A., & Williams, D. P. (1978). Class orientations to child neglect. *Social Work, 23,* 397–401.

Potocky-Tripodi, M. (2002). *Best practices for social work with refugees and immigrants.* New York: Columbia University Press.

Prino, C. T., & Perot, M. (1994). The effect of child physical abuse and neglect on aggressive, withdrawn and prosocial behavior. *Child Abuse and Neglect, 10,* 871–884.

Puig, M. (2001). Organizations and community intervention skills with Hispanic Americans. In R. Fong & S. Furuto (Eds.), *Culturally competent practice: Skills, interventions, and evaluations* (pp. 269–284). Boston, MA: Allyn & Bacon.

Queralt, M., & Witte, A. D. (1998). Influences on neighborhood supply of childcare in Massachusetts. *Social Service Review, 72,* 17–46.

Reidy, T. J. (1980). The aggressive characteristics of abused and neglected children. In G. J. Williams & J. Money (Eds.), *Traumatic abuse and neglect of children at home* (pp. 262–269). Baltimore, MD: Johns Hopkins University Press.

Reidy, T. J., Anderegg, T. R., Tracy, R. J., & Cotler, S. (1980). Abused and neglected children: The cognitive, social and behavioral correlations. In G. J. Williams & J. Money (Eds.), *Traumatic abuse and neglect of children at home* (pp. 284–289). Baltimore, MD: Johns Hopkins University Press.

Reyome, N. D. (1993). A comparison of the school performance of sexually abused, neglected and non-maltreated children. *Child Study Journal, 23,* 17–38.

Richardson, G., Conroy, M., & Day, N. (1996). Prenatal cocaine exposure on the development of school age children. *Neurotoxicology and Teratology, 19,* 627–634.

Rieder, C., & Cicchetti, D. (1989). Organizational perspective on cognitive control functioning and cognitive-affective balance in maltreated children. *Developmental Psychology, 25,* 382–393.

Rohner, R. P. (1986). *The warmth dimension: Foundations of parental acceptance-rejection theory.* Newbury Park, CA: Sage Publications, Inc.

Rosco, B. (1990). Defining child maltreatment: Ratings of parental behaviors. *Adolescence, 25,* 517–528.

Rose, S. J. (1990). Child neglect: A definitional perspective (Doctoral dissertation, University of Illinois at Chicago, 1989). *Dissertation Abstracts International, 51,* 296-A.

Rose, S. J., & Meezan, W. (1993). Defining child neglect: Evolution, influences, and issues. *Social Service Review, 67,* 279–293.

Rutter, M. (1979). Maternal deprivation, 1972–1978: New findings, new concepts, new approaches. *Child Development, 50,* 283–305.

Rycraft, J. R. (1990). Redefining abuse and neglect: A narrower focus could affect children at risk. *Public Welfare, 48,* 14–21.

Saleeby, D. (1997). *The strengths perspective in social work practice* (2nd ed.). White Plains, NY: Longman.

Salzinger, S., Kaplan, S., & Artemyeff, C. (1983). Mothers' personal social networks and child maltreatment. *Journal of Abnormal Psychology, 92,* 68–76.

Samantrai, K. (1992). To prevent unnecessary separation of children and families: Public Law 96-272—policy and practice. *Social Work, 37,* 295–354.

Sandhu, D., & Malik, R. (2001). Ethnocultural background and substance abuse treatment of Asian Indian Americans. In S. Straussner (Ed.), *Ethnocultural factors in substance abuse treatment* (pp. 368–392). New York: Guilford Press.

Sattler, J. (1998a). *Clinical and forensic interviewing of children and families: Guidelines for mental health, education, pediatric, and child maltreatment fields.* San Diego, CA: Jerome Sattler Publisher.

Sattler, J. (1998b). Background considerations in child maltreatment: Part 1. In J. Sattler (Ed.), *Clinical and forensic interviewing of children and families* (pp. 666–718). San Diego, CA: Jerome Sattler Publisher.

Saunders, E. J., Nelson, K., & Landsman, M. J. (1993). Racial inequality and child neglect: Findings in a metropolitan area. *Child Welfare, 72,* 341–354.

Scannapieco, M., & Conneli, K. (2001). Consequences of child neglect, children 0 to 3 years of age. *APSAC Advisor, 13,* 20–23.

Schene, P. A. (1998). Past, present and future role of child protective services. *The Future of Children, 8,* 23–38.

Schick, A. (1995). *The federal budget: Politics, policy, process.* Washington, DC: The Brookings Institute.

Schorr, L. (1988). *Within our reach: Breaking the cycle of disadvantage.* New York: Doubleday.

Schorr, L. (1997). *Common purpose: Strengthening families and neighborhoods to rebuild America.* New York: Doubleday.

Seagull, E. A. W. (1987). Social support and child maltreatment: A review of the evidence. *Child Abuse and Neglect, 11,* 41–52.

Sedlak, A. J., & Broadhurst, D. D. (1996). *Third national incidence study of child abuse and neglect: Final report.* Washington, DC: U.S. Department of Health and Human Services.

Segal, U. (2002). *A framework for immigration: Asians in the United States.* New York: Columbia University Press.

Sheridan, M. (1995). A proposed intergenerationjal model of substance abuse, family functioning, and abuse/neglect. *Child Abuse & Neglect, 19*(5), 519–530.

Smith, B., & Testa, M. (2002). The risk of subsequent maltreatment allegations in families with substance-exposed infants. *Child Abuse & Neglect, 26*(1), 97–114.

Smith, M. G. (1998). *The etiology of child neglect: A structural model.* (Doctoral dissertation, University of Hawaii, 1998).

Smith, P. K., & Yeung, W. J. (1998). Childhood welfare receipt and the implications of welfare reform. *Social Service Review, 72,* 1–16.

Smokowski, P. R. (1998). Prevention and intervention strategies for promoting reliance in disadvantaged children. *Social Service Review, 72,* 337–362.

Smokowski, P. R., & Wodarski, J. W. (1996). The effectiveness of child welfare services for poor, neglected children: A review of the empirical evidence. *Research on Social Work Practice, 6,* 504–523.

Socolar, R. S., Runyan, D. K., & Amaya-Jackson, L. (1995). Methodological and ethical issues related to studying child maltreatment. *Journal of Family Issues, 16,* 565–586.

Spearly, J. L., & Lauderdale, M. (1983). Community characteristics and ethnicity in the prediction of child maltreatment rates. *Child Abuse and Neglect, 7,* 91–105.

Steele, B. (1987). Reflections of the therapy of those who maltreat children. In R. E. Helfer & R. S. Kempe (Eds.), *The battered child* (pp. 382–391). Chicago: University of Chicago Press.

Stein, T. J. (1984). The child abuse prevention and treatment act. *Social Service Review, 58,* 302–314.

Steinberg, L. D., Catalano, R., & Dooley, D. (1981). Economic antecedents of child abuse and neglect. *Child Development, 52,* 975–985.

Stouthamer-Loeber, M., Loeber, R., Homish, D. L., & Wei, E. (2001). Maltreatment of boys and the development of disruptive and delinquent behavior. *Development and Psychopathology, 13,* 941–955.

Straussner, S. L. A. (2001). (Ed.). *Ethnocultural factors in substance abuse treatment.* New York: Guilford Press.

Streissguth, A. P., Aase, J. M., Clarren, S. K., LaDue, R.A., Randels, S. P., & Smith, D. F. (1991). Fetal alcohol syndrome in adolescents and adults. *Journal of the American Medical Association, 265,* 1961–1967.

Streissguth, A. P., Barr, H. M., Hogan, J., & Bookstein, F. L. (1996). *Understanding the occurrence of secondary disabilities in clients with fetal alcohol syndrome and fetal alcohol effects.* Seattle, WA: University of Washington Publication Services.

Streissguth, A. P., LaDue, R., & Randels, S. (1988). *A manual on adolescents and adults with fetal alcohol syndrome with special reference to American Indians.* Seattle, WA: U.S. Department of Health and Human Services.

Sweet, J. J., & Resick, P. A. (1979). The maltreatment of children: A review of theories and research. *Journal of Social Issues, 35,* 40–59.

Swift, K. J. (1995a). *Manufacturing "bad mothers": A critical perspective on child neglect.* Toronto: University of Toronto Press.

Swift, K. J. (1995b). An outrage to common decency: Historical perspectives on child neglect. *Child Welfare, 74,* 71–91.

Takamura, J. (1991). Asian and Pacific elderly. In N. Mokuau. (Ed.), *Handbook of social services for Asian and Pacific Islanders* (pp. 185–202). New York: Greenwood Press.

Tannen, M. (1990). The case for long-term intervention in the provision of home-based services. In W. Deutelbaum, D. Haapala, J. Hutchinson, J. Lloyd, & C.

Sudia (Eds.), *Empowering families: Papers from the third annual conference on family-based services* (pp. 45–50). Riverdale, IL: National Association for Family-Based Services.

Temporary Assistance to Needy Families Program (1999). Summary *Final Rule.* http://www.acf.dhhs.gov/programs/ofa/exsumcl.htm (11/25/2002)

Thomlison, B. (1997). Risk and protective factors in child maltreatment. In M. W. Fraser (Ed.), *Risk and resilience in childhood: An ecological perspective* (pp. 50–72). Washington, DC: NASW Press.

Thompson, M., & Kingree, J. (1998) The frequency and impact of violent trauma among pregnant substance abusers. *Addictive Behaviors, 23*(2), 257–262.

Thompson, R. A. (1994). Social support and the prevention of child maltreatment. In G. B. Melton & F. D. Barry (Eds.), *Protecting children from abuse and neglect: Foundations for a new national strategy* (pp. 40–130). New York: Guilford Press.

Thompson, R. A. (1995). *Preventing child maltreatment through social support: A critical analysis.* Thousand Oaks, CA: Sage Publications, Inc.

Thornberry, T. P., Ireland, T. O., & Smith, C. A. (2001). The importance of timing: The varying impact of childhood and adolescent maltreatment on multiple problem outcomes. *Development and Psychopathology, 13,* 957–979.

Tochiki, L. A. (1996). *The effectiveness of mediation in child abuse and neglect cases in family court.* Unpublished paper.

Tomlinson, R., & Peters, P. (1981). An alternative to placing children: Intensive and extensive therapy with "disengaged" families. *Child Welfare, 60,* 95–103.

Tower, C. C. (1993). *Understanding child abuse and neglect.* Boston, MA: Allyn & Bacon.

Tower, C. C. (2000). Child abuse and neglect. In Neil Cohen and contributors. *Child welfare: A multicultural focus* (pp. 193–226). Boston, MA: Allyn & Bacon Press.

Tower, C. C. (2002). *Understanding child abuse and neglect* (5th ed,). Boston, MA: Allyn & Bacon.

Trocme, N. (1996). Development and preliminary evaluation of the Ontario child neglect index. *Child Maltreatment, 1,* 145–155.

Trocme, N., McPhee, D., & Tam, K. K. (1995). Child abuse and neglect in Ontario: Incidence and characteristics. *Child Welfare, 74,* 563–586.

True, R. (1990). Psychotherapeutic issues with Asian American women. *Sex roles, 22*(7,8), 477–486.

Turner, R. J., & Avison, W. R. (1985). Assessing risk factors for problem parenting: The significance of social support. *Journal of Marriage and the Family, 47,* 881–892.

Twentyman, C. T., & Plotkin, R. C. (1982). Unrealistic expectations of parents who maltreat their children: An educational deficit that pertains to child development. *Journal of Clinical Psychology, 38,* 497–503.

Tymchuk, A. J., & Andron, L. (1990). Mothers with mental retardation who do or do not abuse or neglect their children. *Child Abuse and Neglect, 14,* 313–323.

Tzeng, C. S., & Jackson, J. W. (1991). Common methodological framework for theory construction and evaluation in the social and behavioral sciences. *Genetic, Social and General Psychology Monographs, 117,* 51–76.

Uba, L. (1994). *Asian Americans: Personality patterns, identity, and mental health.* New York: Guilford Press.

U.S. Census Bureau. (2002). Current population survey, 1960–2002 annual demographic supplements. http://www.census.gov/hhes/poverty01/povage01cht.gif

U.S. Department of Health and Human Services. (1992). *Maternal drug abuse and drug exposed children: Understanding the problem.* (DHHS Publication No. [ADM] 92-149). Washington, DC: U.S. Government Printing Office.

U.S. Department of Health and Human Services. (1996). *Child maltreatment 1994: Reports from the states to the national center on child abuse and neglect.* Washington, DC: U.S. Government Printing Office.

U.S. Department of Health and Human Services. (1998). *Program instructions: Adoption and safe families act of 1997: PL 105-89.* Washington, DC: U.S. Government Printing Office.

U.S. Department of Health and Human Services. (1999a). *Building perspectives and building common ground: A report to Congress on substance abuse and child protection.* Washington, DC: U.S. Government Printing Office.

U.S. Department of Health and Human Services. (1999b). *Safety, permanency, well-being: Child welfare outcomes annual report.* Washington, DC: U.S. Government Printing Office. http://www.acf.dhhs.gov/programs/cb/publications/cwo99/

U.S. Department of Health and Human Services. (2002). *Child maltreatment 2000.* Washington, DC: U.S. Government Printing Office. http://www.acf.dhhs.gov/programs/cb/publidations/cm00/

U.S. Department of Health and Human Services. (2003). *Child Maltreatment 2001.* Washington, D.C.: Author.

Valentine, D. P., Acuff, D. S., Freeman, M. L., & Andreas, T. (1984). Defining child maltreatment: A multidisciplinary overview. *Child Welfare, 63,* 497–509.

Villa, R. (2001). Social work evaluation with Mexican Americans. In R. Fong & S. Furuto (Eds.), *Culturally competent practice: Skills, interventions, and evaluations* (pp. 370–383). Boston, MA: Allyn & Bacon.

Wagner, M. M., & Clayton, S. L. (1999). Parents as teachers program: Results from two demonstrations. *The Future of Children, 9,* 91–115.

Waldfogel, J. (1998). Rethinking the paradigm for child protection. *The Future of Children, 8,* 104–119.

Walker, A. J., Kees Martin, S. S., & Thompson, L. (1988). Feminist programs for families. *Family Relations, 37,* 17–22.

Walker, E., Downey, G., & Bergman, A. (1989). The effects of parental psychopathology and maltreatment on child behavior: A test of the diathesis-stress model. *Child Development, 60,* 15–25.

Washburne, C. K. (1983). A feminist analysis of child abuse and neglect. In D. Finkelhor, R. J. Gelles, G. T. Hotaling, & M. A. Straus (Eds.), *The dark side of families: Current family violence research* (pp. 289–292). Beverly Hills, CA: Sage Publications, Inc.

Watters, J., White, G., Parry, R., Caplan, R., & Bates, R. (1986). A comparison of child abuse and child neglect. *Canadian Journal of Behavioral Science, 18,* 449–459.

Weaver, H. (2001a). Organization and community assessment with First Nations Peoples. In R. Fong & S. Furuto (Eds.), *Culturally competent practice: Skills, interventions, and evaluations* (pp. 178–195). Boston, MA: Allyn & Bacon.

Weaver, H. (2001b). Native Americans and substance abuse. In S. Straussner (Ed.), *Ethnocultural factors in substance abuse* (pp. 77–96). New York: The Guilford Press.

Weaver, H. (2003). Cultural competence with First Nations Peoples. In D. Lum, *Culturally competent practice: A framework for understanding diverse groups and justice issues* (pp. 197–216). Pacific Grove, CA: Brooks/Cole.

Weber, M. W. (1998). Four commentaries: How we can better protect children from abuse and neglect. Commentary 4. *The Future of Children, 8,* 129–132.

Wells, K., & Biegel, D. (1991). Conclusion. In K. Wells & D. Biegel (Eds.), *Family preservation services: Research and evaluation* (pp. 241–250). Newbury Park, CA: Sage Publications, Inc.

Wells, K., & Biegel, D. (1992). Intensive family preservation services research: Current status and future agenda. *Social Work Research and Abstracts, 28,* 21–27.

Werner, E. E., & Smith, R. S. (1982). *Vulnerable but invincible: A longitudinal study of resilient children and youth.* New York: McGraw-Hill Book Company.

Weston, J. A., Colloton, M., Halsey, S., Covington, S., Gilbert, J., Sorrentino-Kelly, L., & Renoud, S. (1993). A legacy of violence in nonorganic failure to thrive. *Child Abuse and Neglect, 17,* 709–714.

White, R. B., & Cornely, D. A. (1981). Navajo child abuse and neglect study: A comparison group examination of abuse and neglect of Navajo children. *Child Abuse and Neglect, 5,* 9–17.

Whittaker, J. K., Schinke, S. P., & Gilchrist, L. D. (1986). The ecological paradigm in child, youth, and family services: Implications for policy and practice. *Social Services Review, 60,* 483–503.

Whittaker, J. K., & Tracy, E. (1990). Family preservation services and education for social work practice: Stimulus and response. In J. Whittaker, J. Kinney, E. Tracy, & C. Booth (Eds.), *Reaching high-risk families: Intensive family preservation in human services* (pp. 1–11). New York: Aldine de Gruyter.

Widom, C. S. (1989). Child abuse, neglect, and adult behavior: Research design and findings on criminality, violence and child abuse. *American Journal of Orthopsychiatry, 59,* 355–367.

Widom, C. S. (1999). Posttraumatic stress disorder in abused and neglected children grown up. *American Journal of Psychiatry, 156,* 1223–1229.

Wildavsky, A. (1992). *The new politics of the budgetary process* (2nd ed.). New York: HarperCollins Publishers Inc.

Williams, G. J. (1980a). Cruelty and kindness to children: Documentary of a century, 1874–1974. In G. J. Williams & J. Money (Eds.), *Traumatic abuse and neglect of children at home* (pp. 68–88). Baltimore, MD: Johns Hopkins University Press.

Williams, G. J. (1980b). Management and treatment of parental abuse and neglect of children: An overview. In G. J. Williams & J. Money (Eds.), *Traumatic abuse and neglect of children at home* (pp. 483–497). Baltimore, MD: The Johns Hopkins University Press.

Williams, J. H., Limb, G., & Adams, P. (forthcoming). Exploring the connections. In R. Fong, R. McRoy, & C. Ortiz-Hendricks. (Eds.), *Intersecting Child Welfare, Substance Abuse, and Family Violence*. Washington, DC: Council on Social Work Education.

Winton, M., & Mara, B. (2001). *Child abuse and neglect*. Boston, MA: Allyn and Bacon.

Wolfe, D. A. (1993). Prevention of child neglect: Emerging issues. *Criminal Justice and Behavior, 20,* 90–111

Wolfe, D. A. (1994). The role of intervention and treatment services in the prevention of child abuse and neglect. In G. B. Melton & F. D. Barry (Eds.), *Protecting children from abuse and neglect: Foundations for a new national strategy* (pp. 224–303). New York: Guilford Press.

Wolock, I., & Horowitz, B. (1979). Child maltreatment and material deprivation among AFDC-recipient families. *Social Service Review, 53,* 175–194.

Wolock, I., & Horowitz, B. (1984). Child maltreatment as a social problem: The neglect of neglect. *American Journal of Orthopsychiatry, 54,* 530–543.

Wolock, I., & Magura, S. (1996). Parental substance abuse as a predictor of child maltreatment re-reports. *Child Abuse & Neglect, 20*(12), 1183–1193.

Woolis, D. (1998). Family works: Substance abuse treatment and welfare. *Public Welfare* (Winter), 24–31.

Wright, E. M. (2001) Substance abuse in African American communities. In S. Straussner (Ed.), *Ethnocultural factors in substance abuse* (pp. 31–51). New York: Guilford Press.

Yellow Bird, M. (2001a). Substance abuse and family violence affecting First Nations Peoples: The continuing effects of European American colonialism. Austin, TX: Task Force Meeting. Cultural Competence in Child Welfare Practice. Paper presented at The University of Texas at Austin, February 9 & 10. Unpublished manuscript.

Yellow Bird, M. (2001b). Critical values and First Nations Peoples. In R. Fong & S. Furuto (Eds.), *Culturally competent practice: Skills, interventions, and evaluations* (pp. 61–74). Boston, MA: Allyn & Bacon.

Yellow Bird, M. (forthcoming). The continuing effects of American colonialism. In R. Fong, R. McRoy, & C. Ortiz-Hendricks (Eds.), *Intersecting Child Welfare, Substance Abuse, and Family Violence*. Washington, DC: Council on Social Work Education.

Young, G., & Gately, T. (1988). Neighborhood impoverishment and child maltreatment: An analysis from the ecological perspective. *Journal of Family Issues, 9,* 240–254.

Young, L. (1964). *Wednesday's children: A study of child neglect and abuse*. New York: McGraw-Hill.

Yuan, Y. T., & Struckman-Johnson, D. L. (1991). Placement outcomes for neglected children with prior placements in family preservations programs. In K. Wells & D. E. Biegel (Eds.), *Family preservation services: Research and evaluation* (pp. 92–177). Newbury Park, CA: Sage Publications, Inc.

Zaslow, M. J., & Ernig, C. A. (1997). When low-income mothers go to work: Implications for children. *The Future of Children, 7,* 110–115.

Zumwalt, R. E., & Hirsch, C. S. (1987). Pathology of fatal child abuse and neglect.

In R. E. Helfer & R. S. Kempe (Eds.), *The battered child* (pp. 247–285). Chicago: University of Chicago Press.

Zuniga, M. (2001). Latinos cultural competence and ethics. In R. Fong & S. Furuto (Eds.), *Cultural competent practice: Skills, interventions, and evaluations* (pp. 47–60). Boston, MA: Allyn & Bacon.

Zuniga, M. (2003). Cultural competence with Latino Americans. In D. Lum, *Culturally competent practice: A framework for understanding diverse groups and justice issues* (pp. 238–260). Pacific Grove, CA: Brooks/Cole.

Zuravin, S. J. (1987). Unplanned pregnancies, family planning problems, and child maltreatment. *Family Relations, 36,* 135–139.

Zuravin, S. J. (1988). Fertility patterns: Their relationship to child physical abuse and child neglect. *Journal of Marriage and the Family, 50,* 983–993.

Zuravin, S. J. (1991). Unplanned childbearing and family size: Their relationship to child neglect and abuse. *Family Planning Perspectives, 25,* 155–161.

Zuravin, S. J. (1999). Child neglect: A review of definitions and measurements research. In H. Dubowitz (Ed.), *Neglected children: Research, practice, and policy* (pp. 24–46). Thousand Oaks, CA: Sage Publications, Inc.

Zuravin, S. J., & Greif, G. L. (1989). Normative and child-maltreating AFDC mothers. *Social Casework, 70,* 76–84.

Zuravin, S. J., & Taylor, R. (1989). The ecology of child maltreatment: Identifying and characterizing high-risk neighborhoods. *Child Welfare, 66,* 497–506.

Index